Bilingual Classics

双语经典

玩偶之家
易卜生戏剧选

〔挪威〕亨利克·易卜生 著
方华文 译

译林出版社

目 录

译者序 1

玩偶之家 001
人民公敌 109
群　鬼 241

译者序

亨利克·易卜生（一八二八——九〇六）出生于挪威东南部一个滨海小城里，父亲经营木材生意，家境富裕。大约在他八岁时，父亲破产，家境开始变得窘迫。易卜生仅接受了几年小学教育便辍学了。一八四四年，未满十六岁的易卜生独自来到小城格利姆斯达，在一家药店里当学徒。他自幼喜欢文学，在当学徒的几年里，他白天干杂活儿，晚上遨游于文学世界，阅读了许多西欧古典文学作品，并在文坛小试牛刀。一八五〇年，易卜生自费出版了剧本《凯替赖恩》。同年，他报考奥斯陆大学，未被录取，却担任了该校学生报刊的编辑，并参加工人运动。一八五〇年十月，他被挪威一家民族剧院聘为编剧，写出了《圣约翰之夜》、《勇士坟》和《厄斯特罗斯的英格夫人》等剧本。一八五七年，他担任首都一座大剧院的艺术指导；一八五八年发表《海尔格伦的海盗》，一举成名。此后，易卜生的每一部作品都引起戏剧界的关注，并引发热议。一八六二年他发表《爱的喜剧》，结果遭到山崩海啸般的攻击。此后，剧院不演他的戏，报刊不登他的文章。

一八六四年，易卜生离开了挪威，在海外侨居了二十多年。一八九一年，易卜生回国定居，结束了长达二十七年的漂泊生活。一九〇〇年，他患中风病，一九〇六年与世长辞。挪威政府为他举行了隆重的国葬。

易卜生为欧洲戏剧的复兴和发展做出了历史性的贡献。十九世纪下半期的欧洲剧坛，情节剧流行，作品的思想境界与艺术水平都不高。易卜生的剧作以其深刻的思想性和高度的艺术性，把现实主义和象征主义引入戏剧领域，从而使欧洲剧坛焕发出新的活力，使戏剧与同一时期的小说、诗歌并驾齐驱，步入新的发展时期。人们因此称他为"现代戏剧之父"。

易卜生创作达四十余年，大致可分为三个时期。早期创作属于浪漫主义文学流派，主要创作了一系列浪漫主义英雄历史剧，其中比较著名的有《觊觎王位的人》等。这类作品多采用挪威民间传说和历史故事，通过对古代英雄及民族历史的歌颂，激发人民爱国主义的情感，为挪威当时的民族独立运动呐喊。中期创作是易卜生创作旺盛、成就卓著的鼎盛时期。他身居国外，摈弃了带有离奇夸张色彩的古代英雄传说题材，转向描写日常生活，对资本主义社会予以真实的描绘和无情的揭露，实现了由浪漫主义到现实主义的转轨。这一时期，代表易卜生最高艺术成就的是《玩偶之家》《人民公敌》和《群鬼》等"社会问题剧"。这些作品涉及资本主义社会中政治、宗教、道德、家庭、妇女、教育、法律等诸多社会问题，笔锋犀利，贯穿着一种强烈的社会批判意识，属于世界戏剧史的重大成就。这些戏剧在挪威及欧洲许多国家上演，反响强烈，为他赢得了巨大声誉。一八八四年创作《野鸭》至一九〇六年逝世为晚期创作时期。此时的易卜生健康状况恶化，再加之受到欧洲悲观主义思潮的影响，他的精神变得颓废，作品思想性减弱。

本书收用了易卜生的三部代表剧作《玩偶之家》、《人民公敌》和《群鬼》。《玩偶之家》的女主人公娜拉是她丈夫海默的"小鸟儿"。海默过去患过重病，娜拉出于真诚的爱情，瞒着他，假借她父亲的签字，举债救活了他。该剧一开始，海默即将担任银行经理，一副春风得意的样子。他打算辞退一个男职员，并应娜拉的请求把这个职位让给她的女友。但这个男职员正是娜拉的债主，他以要揭发娜拉的假签字进行威胁，要求娜拉为他保住银行的职位。娜拉不忍牵连步步高升的丈夫，准备自杀，自己承担全部责任。海默知道娜拉借债后骤然翻脸，呵斥娜拉断送了他的前程。正在这时，债主受到娜拉女友的感化，退回了有假签字的字据。海默转怒为喜，又将娜拉称为"小鸟儿"，口口声声说自己是多么爱娜拉。娜拉至此恍然大悟，发现她只不过是丈夫的玩物，于是毅然决然地离开了这个"玩偶之家"。

《玩偶之家》其实反映的是"个性解放"和"妇女解放"的深层次问题。一九〇七年该剧传入我国后，产生了持久的深远影响。鲁迅从社会经济学的角度分析，认为《玩偶之家》归根结底反映的是"财权"问题。一九二三年十二月二十六日，鲁迅到北京女子高等师范学校参加文艺会，发表了题为《娜拉走后怎样》的著名演讲。他说道:"钱这个字很难听,或者要被高尚的君子们所非笑,但我总觉得人们的议论是不但昨天和今天,即使饭前和饭后,也往往有些差别。凡承认饭需钱买,而以说钱为卑鄙者,倘能按一按他的胃,那里面怕总还有鱼肉没有消化完,须得饿他一天之后,再来听他发议论。所以为娜拉计,钱,——高雅的说罢,就是经济,是最要紧的了。自由固不是钱所能买到的,但能够为钱而卖掉。人类有一个大缺点,就是常常要饥饿。为补救这缺点起见,为准备不做傀儡起见,在目下的社会里,经济权就见得最要紧了。第一,在家应该先获得男女平均的分配;第二,在社会应该获得男女相等的势力……"胡适模仿《玩偶之家》写了一出《终身大事》,剧中的"田女士"是中国妇女的形象,有着中国妇女的痛苦和委屈,这部剧为中国新戏剧的发展树立了榜样。五四时期涌现出了许多中国式的《玩偶之家》,于是中国的"娜拉"纷纷出走,如《新人的生活》中的曾玉英,《弃妇》中的吴芷芳,《打出幽灵塔》中的郑少梅等。

《人民公敌》通过一个小城镇发生的事件,揭露了政府当局、资本家以及利益相关者唯利是图的心理和行径。剧中主人公斯托克曼医生在当地的温泉浴场发现了传染病菌,建议改建供水设施,以免给来疗养的人造成危害。可是,改建工程耗资巨大,影响到了资本家和当地民众的利益,于是遭到了强烈抵制。医生拒不让步,准备在市民会议上说出真相,捍卫正义,谁知却被定性为"人民公敌"。随后,他被开除了公职,身为教师的女儿被解雇,家里的窗户玻璃被暴徒砸碎，全家被赶走……

易卜生以事关健康的病菌危害问题为题材，尖锐地揭露了资产阶级唯利是图、丧心病狂的本性，也揭露了资产阶级民主的虚伪性质。易卜生用疗养区比喻他所处的社会——这个社会打着疗养胜地的幌子，实际上是在散布害人的病菌。斯托克曼医生是小资产阶级知识分子。他感到官僚和资产阶级掌握着实权，成为社会上所谓的"多数派"，是自由和真理的最大敌人。但他不懂得，他们是虚假的多数，真正的"多数"是人民大众。他把人民也包括在虚假的多数中，一起加以抨击，最后得出结论：只有像他那样既无同盟又无依靠的"世界上最强大的人就是最孤独的人"，才能管理世界。这段台词产生了很大影响，但易卜生却不能说明，为什么这种最孤独的人才是世界上最强大的人。斯托克曼医生的形象总是带着一厢情愿的精神胜利法的气味。尽管如此，这部作品仍不失为不朽之作，是真理向黑暗势力宣战的一面旗帜，曾在五四时期对我国的戏剧创作产生过深远的影响，也在鲁迅的心中引起了强烈的共鸣，因为鲁迅本人就是一个敢于挺身而出的"真理斗士"（在他的许多作品中都有"人民公敌"这类艺术形象）。

《群鬼》中的女主人公阿尔文夫人海伦跟《玩偶之家》里的娜拉一样，也有着可悲的命运。海伦年轻时听从了母亲和两个姑姑的建议，嫁给了国王侍从阿尔文上尉。婚后不久，她就发现自己的丈夫是个荒淫无耻的花花公子，不仅在外边拈花惹草，还勾搭上了他们家的漂亮女佣乔安娜。海伦忍无可忍，去向好友曼得斯牧师求援，可后者为了自己的名誉、地位而拒绝帮助她,要她忍辱负重,守着坏丈夫过日子。后来,海伦生下了儿子奥斯瓦德,而乔安娜却怀了阿尔文上尉的孩子。他们给了乔安娜一笔钱,赶走了她。乔安娜拿着这笔钱嫁给了木匠恩格斯特兰德,不久便生下了女儿莱吉娜。莱吉娜长大后,海伦把她接到家里,虽聘为女佣,但待之甚厚。海伦不愿让儿子奥斯瓦德受到其父恶习的影响,就将他送往巴黎学习绘画艺术。后来,阿尔文病死。为了保持体面,海伦一直写信告诉儿子,说他父亲是个道德高尚的人。她还拿出大量的钱财开办孤儿院,为阿尔文脸上贴金。奥斯瓦德回家探亲,爱上了美丽的莱吉娜。后来,他发现自己从娘胎里感染了来自阿尔文的梅毒(花柳病),又通过母亲海伦的讲述发现,莱吉娜原来是他同父异母的妹妹。这时的奥斯瓦德万念俱灰,只求一死……

剧中女主人公阿尔文夫人只是千千万万不幸女性中的一个,在"社会道德"的束缚下度日如年,生不如死,没有任何美好的憧憬,成为旧礼教的牺牲品。黑暗,对她们来说,到处都是黑暗!于无声处听惊雷——《群鬼》无异于一声惊雷,惊醒了麻木不仁的人们……于是就有了妇女解放运动,而且一浪高过一浪。《群鬼》问世后,西欧各国的新剧院都以它作为开业演出的剧目。从一八八九年开始,柏林的自由剧院、巴黎的自由剧院、伦敦的独立剧院先后上演此剧,促进了西欧的戏剧革新运动。

经过许多个日日夜夜的"鏖战",易卜生的这部戏剧选终于翻译完了。其实,书中的语言并不深奥,并不难懂,难就难在要细心琢磨和翻译出戏剧主人公台词中所包含的"真情实意"：是"柔情"？是"愤怒"？是泣血的文字？是匕首一般锋利的语言？还是如花似锦的"友谊"？毕竟，易卜生塑造的艺术形象是鲜活的，是极具感染力的，演员的表演必须"声情并茂"，这也是翻译戏剧作品的一大难点。所以，我在翻译时，就假想自己是剧中人，身为"海默"时就"虚情假意"，扮演"斯托克曼医生"时便"义愤填膺"。虽然有些劳累，有些心潮澎湃，但效果还不错，该"掷地有声"或"悱恻缠绵"的都尽量做到了，希望读者能产生认同感……

方华文

作于苏州大学

二〇一八年八月二十七日

玩偶之家

人物表

托瓦尔德·海默

娜拉,海默妻

兰克医生

林德夫人

尼尔斯·克罗格斯塔德

海默夫妇的三个孩子

安妮,孩子们的保姆

女佣

脚夫

(故事发生在海默家中)

第一幕

布景：一个房间，布置得舒适、雅致，但并不奢华。房间后面，右边有一扇门通到门厅，左边有一扇门通到海默的书房。两扇门中间有一架钢琴。左墙中央有一扇门，再往前一点儿有一扇窗。靠窗有一张圆桌、几把扶手椅和一个小沙发。右墙那儿，稍靠后一些又有一扇门，在同一边靠近脚灯的地方有一个火炉、两把扶手椅和一把摇椅，而火炉和侧门中间有一张小桌子。墙上挂着几幅版画，一个橱柜上摆着瓷器和几件小古玩，一个小书橱里放满了精装书。地上铺着地毯。炉子里生着火。正是冬天。

门厅里有铃声响起，紧接着就听见有人将门打开了。只见娜拉哼着歌，兴高采烈地走了进来，身上穿着户外服装，怀里抱着几包东西。她把东西放在右边的桌子上。她进来时没关大门，可以看见外边有个脚夫正在把手里的一棵圣诞树和一只篮子递给开门的女用人。

娜拉：海伦，你把圣诞树藏好，别叫孩子们看见，等到晚上点亮时再说。（取出钱包，问脚夫）多少钱？

脚夫：六便士。

娜拉：给你一个先令①，不用找零了。（脚夫道过谢之后就走了。娜拉随手关上了门。她一边摘下帽子、脱掉外套，一边快活地笑着。她从衣袋里掏出一袋蛋白杏仁饼干，吃了一两块。随后，她蹑手蹑脚地走到丈夫的书房门口听动静。）他在呢，在里面呢。（她又哼起了歌，走到右边的桌子前。）

海默：（从他的书房里传出来）我的小百灵鸟又在歌唱啦？

娜拉：（忙着打开买来的那几包东西）是呀，你的小鸟在歌唱！

海默：我的小松鼠是不是在淘气呀？

娜拉：是呀！

海默：小松鼠什么时候回来的？

娜拉：刚回来。（把那袋蛋白杏仁饼干塞进衣袋，擦了擦嘴）托瓦尔德，快出来瞧瞧我买的东西。

海默：我正忙着呢。（过了一会儿，他手里拿着笔，开门朝外望了望。）你买东西啦？什么，买这么多！我的小败家子儿又糟蹋钱啦？

娜拉：是我买的。不过，托瓦尔德，现在咱们花钱可以松点儿了。这是咱们头一回不必勒紧裤带过圣诞节。

---

① 英国旧币制。1先令=12便士。

海默：你应该知道，现在还是不能大手大脚的。

娜拉：哦，托瓦尔德，现在是可以稍微多花一点儿的，难道不是吗？只要多花一丁点儿就可以！你就要涨薪了，能挣很多很多的钱。

海默：不错，从一月一日起是要涨薪，可是要将薪水拿到手，还得等整整三个月呢。

娜拉：没关系，咱们可以先借些钱嘛。

海默：娜拉！（走到她面前，开玩笑地捏着她的耳朵说道）你真是个不懂事的孩子！要是今天我借五十英镑，圣诞节一个星期就被你挥霍一空，万一新年前夜那天房上掉下一块瓦片把我砸死了——

娜拉：（用手捂住他的嘴）嘘！别说这么不吉利的话！

海默：要是我真的遇到不测，那该怎么办？

娜拉：假如真的发生那样的事，我想我也不会关心欠不欠债的。

海默：你会的。那些债主难道会善罢甘休吗？

娜拉：债主？谁还管什么债主不债主！我压根儿就不认识他们。

海默：真是妇人之见！说正经的，娜拉，你应该知道我的主张，那就是绝不借钱，绝不欠债！一个家庭要是靠借钱举债过日子，就无自由和幸福可言。截至目前，你我二人同舟共济，走的是一条正确的道路，目前还得继续努力一段时间，沿着这条路走下去。

娜拉：（走到火炉边）好吧，就听你的吧，托瓦尔德。

海默：（跟了过去）喂，喂，我的小百灵鸟可别这么耷拉着翅膀。怎么啦？我的小松鼠生气啦？（掏出钱包来）娜拉，你猜这里头是什么？

娜拉：（急忙转过身来）是钱！

海默：给你！（给了她几张钞票）过圣诞节，家里需要花不少钱，你以为我不知道？

娜拉：（开始数钱）十先令……一英镑……两英镑！谢谢你，谢谢你，托瓦尔德！这些钱能花很长时间呢。

海默：但愿如此。

娜拉：是的，是的，是能花很长时间。你快过来，瞧瞧我买的这些东西。你都不知道有多便宜！你瞧，这是给伊瓦尔买的一套新衣服和一把玩具剑；这是给鲍勃的一匹玩具马和一个喇叭；这个洋娃娃和洋娃娃的小床是给埃米的——这两件玩具都很粗糙，但话又说回来，埃米玩儿不了多久就会把它们弄坏的。另外还有几块衣料和几块手帕是送给女用人的。真应该买点儿好东西送给安妮她老人家。

海默：这个包里是什么？

娜拉：（大声叫了起来）别动！别动！今天晚上才能让你看。

海默：好吧，好吧。告诉我，你这个喜欢乱花钱的小家伙，你想给自己买点什么呢？

娜拉：我自己？我自己什么都不需要。

海默：你当然需要啦。老老实实告诉我，你到底想要什么。

娜拉：不需要，我真的想不出自己需要什么——托瓦尔德，除非——

海默：除非什么？

娜拉：（摆弄着丈夫的衣扣，眼睛不看他）要是你真想送给我东西的话，你可以——你可以——

海默：可以什么？快说呀！

娜拉：（脱口而出）你可以给我点儿钱，托瓦尔德。不需要很多，只要你手头富余的数目就够——以后哪天，我可以用这钱买东西。

海默：可是，娜拉——

娜拉：求求你啦，亲爱的托瓦尔德！求求你啦！我将用漂亮的镀金纸把这钱包起来，挂在圣诞树上。你不觉得那样很好玩儿吗？

海默：那些喜欢糟蹋钱的小人儿叫什么来着？

娜拉：我知道，叫败家子儿呗。托瓦尔德，你先把钱给我。这样，我就有时间考虑自己最想要的是什么了。这是一种非常理智的办法，对不对？

海默：（笑了笑）的确如此——要是你真的把我给你的钱节省下来，给自己买点儿东西的话。你要是将所有的钱都花在家用上，以及买不需要的东西，留下的窟窿还得我补。

娜拉：可是，托瓦尔德——

海默：你可不能抵赖，我亲爱的小娜拉。（他伸出一只胳膊搂住了她的腰。）这个小败家子儿十分可爱，就是太能花钱了。谁能相信，一个小小的人儿竟能耗费这么多钱！

娜拉：亏你说出这种话！我可是能省的都省了。

海默：（大笑）一点儿不错，你已经尽力了，可是省来省去也没省下什么。

娜拉：(幸福地暗自一笑)托瓦尔德，你不知道咱家的那几只小百灵鸟和小松鼠有多费钱。

海默：你真是个古怪的小精灵，跟你老爹一模一样。你总是想着法子从我这儿套钱，可是钱一到手就从指头缝里漏走了。你自己恐怕都不知道钱到哪儿去了。你天生就是这样，谁也没办法。这是骨子里就有的——说真的，娜拉，这种性格是可以遗传的。

娜拉：啊，爸爸有许多优良品质呢，但愿我都能继承下来。

海默：我可爱的小百灵鸟，你现在这样就挺好，我可不想你有什么别的优良品质。不过，不知道当说不当说——我觉得——我觉得你今天看上去有点儿——心神不宁。

娜拉：是吗？

海默：是的。你看着我的眼睛。

娜拉：(抬头瞧着他)怎么啦？

海默：(伸出一个手指头冲她点了点)你这个爱吃甜食的小姐今天进城是不是又坏了规矩？

娜拉：此话怎讲？

海默：去过糖果店了吧？

娜拉：没有，托瓦尔德，我向你保证——

海默：没吃点儿甜食吗？

娜拉：没有，当然没有。

海默：甚至连蛋白杏仁饼干也没吃上一两块？

娜拉：没有，托瓦尔德，我向你保证，真的——

海默:好啦,好啦,我只不过跟你开个玩笑嘛。

娜拉:(朝右边桌子走去)违背你意愿的事情我可不做。

海默:是的,对此我深信不疑。再说,你答应过我的——(走到她跟前)宝贝,你可要把圣诞礼物藏好喽,今天晚上给圣诞树点上灯,它们可就藏不住啦。

娜拉:你没忘了邀请兰克医生吧?

海默:我忘了。不过,也没这个必要。他理应跟咱们共进晚餐。今天上午等他来时,我邀请他来就是了。我还买了点儿好酒呢。娜拉,你不知道我是多么盼望今天晚上赶快到来!

娜拉:我也一样!孩子们该多高兴呀,托瓦尔德!

海默:一个人有了稳固的地位和丰厚的收入,那种感觉真好。想一想都叫人高兴,对不对?

娜拉:是的,那种感觉真是太好了!

海默:你还记得去年过圣诞节的情形吗?节前有整整三个星期的时间,你每天晚上都把自己关在房间里忙活,一忙就忙到后半夜,又是准备圣诞树上的饰品,又是张罗别的什么好玩意儿,想给我们一个惊喜。那是我过的最无聊的三个星期!

娜拉:我并不觉得无聊。

海默:(笑了笑)娜拉,可是后来的结果并不尽如人意。

娜拉:啊,你旧事重提,又在取笑我啦。都是那只猫闯的祸,把所有的东西都撕了个稀巴烂,你叫我有什么办法?

海默:你当然是没办法喽,可怜的小姑娘。你想尽了办法让大家高兴,这才是最重要的。不过,现在好啦,苦日子总算熬到头啦。

娜拉:是啊,真是苦尽甘来呀。

海默:现在我不用一个人无聊地闷坐了,而你可爱的眼睛和漂亮的小手也不用吃苦了——

娜拉:(拍着手)是啊,托瓦尔德,我再也不用吃那份苦啦!听了你的一席话,别提我有多高兴了!(挽起了他的胳膊)容我说一说我的想法,看怎样安排今后的小日子,托瓦尔德。一过完圣诞节——(大厅的门铃响了。)哦,有人按铃!(她把屋子稍微整理了一下。)一定是有客来了。真讨厌!

海默:如果是找我的,记住就说我不在家。

女佣:(在门口)夫人,有位女客要见你,是个不认识的人。

娜拉:请她进来。

女佣:(转向海默)先生,兰克医生也来了。

海默:他到我书房去了吗?

女佣:是的,先生。

〔海默到书房去了。女佣把林德夫人请进来之后,把大门关上了。林德夫人穿着旅行服装。〕

林德夫人:(声音沮丧、胆怯)娜拉,你好吗?

娜拉:(犹疑不定)你好——

林德夫人:你恐怕认不出我了。

娜拉:是啊,记不清——是呀,是了——不错——(突然惊呼)天呀!是克里斯蒂娜!真的是你吗?

林德夫人:不错,是我。

娜拉:我的好克里斯蒂娜!想不到我连你都认不出来了!我怎么能——(声音变得温柔)你的变化可真大,克里斯蒂娜!

林德夫人:是啊,变化的确很大。九年还是十年没见了——

娜拉:自打上次一别,真的过了这么久吗?看来是有的。可以说,这八年里我一直过着幸福的日子,真是弹指一挥间呀。你这次进城,冬天还走这么远的路——实在叫人敬佩。

林德夫人:我是搭今天的早班轮船来的。

娜拉:当然,过圣诞节嘛,就应该过得高兴一些。真是太好啦!咱们就在一起欢度节日吧!把你的外套脱下来吧。但愿你不会嫌这儿冷。(帮她脱外套)咱们坐到炉子旁边舒舒服服地烤烤火。来,你坐这把扶手椅吧,我坐摇椅。(抓住林德夫人的两只手)现在看看,你又像从前的样子了。一开始没认出你来——你的气色有点儿不如从前了,克里斯蒂娜,好像还比以前瘦了些。

林德夫人:还比从前老多了,娜拉。

娜拉:也许是老了点儿,但老得也不算太多,只是老了一点点。(突然,她刹住话头,换上了沉重的语气。)瞧我这人真粗心,只顾乱说了。亲爱的克里斯蒂娜,你可要原谅我呀。

林德夫人:此话怎讲,娜拉?

娜拉:(声音低柔)可怜的克里斯蒂娜!我忘了你守寡了。

林德夫人:是啊,我丈夫三年前去世了。

娜拉:是的,我知道,我在报上看到了。说实在的,克里斯蒂娜,我一直想写信安慰安慰你,可一拖再拖,老有事情干扰我。

林德夫人:我很理解,亲爱的。

娜拉:这都怪我不对,克里斯蒂娜。可怜的人儿啊,你一定受了不少罪。他什么都没给你留下?

林德夫人:是的。

娜拉:你们没孩子?

林德夫人:是的。

娜拉:什么都没有留下?

林德夫人:甚至连让人感到伤心和痛苦的回忆也没有留下。

娜拉:(难以置信地望着她)克里斯蒂娜,这怎么可能呢?

林德夫人:(凄楚地笑笑,用手理了理头发)有时真会发生这种事,娜拉。

娜拉:你一个人孤孤单单的,日子一定过得非常艰难。我有三个可爱的孩子,他们都跟保姆出去了,不能叫过来给你瞧瞧。现在,还是讲讲你的情况吧。

林德夫人:不,不,我想听你讲讲你的情况。

娜拉:不,你先说。今天我可不能光顾着自己,只想关心关心你。不过,有件事我必须告诉你。我们刚刚交了好运，特别好的运气，你知道吗？

林德夫人：不知道。什么好运？

娜拉：你想想吧，我丈夫当上了银行的经理！

林德夫人：你丈夫当经理了？这可是天大的好运！

娜拉：是啊，真是喜从天降！干律师这一行收入不稳定，不愿接不干不净案子的律师更是如此——当然，托瓦尔德就是这种人，绝不干违心的事，我和他看法完全一致。可想而知，我们现在该有多高兴！他元旦到银行履职，那时工资高，还有许多大红包。将来，我们的日子就会跟从前截然不同了，想怎么花钱就怎么花钱——我感到十分轻松，非常幸福，克里斯蒂娜！钱囊充盈，无忧无虑地过日子，那种感觉真好，你说是不是？

林德夫人：是的。需要的东西应有尽有，的确令人高兴。

娜拉：不仅需要的东西应有尽有，钱也多得不得了——一堆一堆的钱。

林德夫人：（笑了笑）娜拉啊，娜拉，不知你现在是否学乖了些？咱们上学那会儿，你可是花钱如流水啊。

娜拉：（哈哈一笑）不错，托瓦尔德也是这么说我的。（伸出手指冲着林德夫人点了点）但是"娜拉，娜拉"可不像你们所想的那么不懂事。再说，我们家的情况也不允许我乱花钱。我俩都得工作养家。

林德夫人：你也得工作？

娜拉：是的，做点杂活儿呗，无非就是缝缝补补、编织刺绣什么的。（说到这儿，她的声音变低了。）另外再干点别的杂活儿。我们结婚的时候，托瓦尔德辞掉了公职，这你可知道？当时，他在那里晋升的指望不大，不得不想办法多挣点儿钱。他拼死拼活地挣钱，结婚头一年体力就严重透支了。要知道，为了挣钱他什么都干，起早贪黑，最后实在撑不住，就一病不起了。医生建议他到南方疗养。

林德夫人：所以你们到意大利住了整整一年，是不是？

娜拉：是的。实不相瞒，当时离开家到意大利去并不是件容易的事。那时伊瓦尔刚出生，可是，自然喽，去还是必须去的。那次南行是一趟奇妙之旅，保住了托瓦尔德的性命。不过，钱也花得不少，克里斯蒂娜。

林德夫人：我想也是的。

娜拉：那一趟花了大约有二百五十英镑。那可是一大笔钱，你说是不是？

林德夫人：是的。遇到那样的紧急状况，幸亏你们手头有钱。

娜拉：实不相瞒，那笔钱是从我爸爸那里弄来的。

林德夫人：噢，我明白了。他老人家也就是在那个时候去世的，对不对？

娜拉：是的。你想想吧，我当时无法脱身去伺候他老人家，因为我每天都在盼着小伊瓦尔出生，而且我还要照料身患重病的托瓦尔德，结果连我那亲爱、善良的父亲最后一面也没能见上，克里斯蒂娜。那是婚后最叫我伤心的一段时间。

林德夫人：我知道你是很爱你父亲的。后来，你们就到意大利去了？

娜拉：是的。我们手头有了钱，医生又催得紧，于是我们一个月以后就走了。

林德夫人：回来的时候你丈夫完全复原了吗？

娜拉：完全复原了。

林德夫人：可是——那位医生？

娜拉：哪位医生？

林德夫人：我记得你家女佣说，跟我同时来的那人是位医生。

娜拉：是的，那是兰克医生。不过，他不是来看病的。他是我们家最好的朋友，没有一天不来看我们。从那以后，托瓦尔德连个小病都没有害过。几个孩子的身体全都结实、健康，我自己也很好。（跳起来拍了拍手）克里斯蒂娜呀，克里斯蒂娜，活着并快乐地过日子是多么幸福啊！你瞧我真糟糕，只顾喋喋不休地讲自家的事了。（在靠近林德夫人的一张矮凳上坐下，两只胳膊搭在林德夫人的膝上）你可别生我的气。实话告诉我，你真的不爱你丈夫吗？那你当初为什么要嫁给他？

林德夫人：当初家母还在，病在床上不能动。我还有两个弟弟要抚养，所以那时候我觉得不应该拒绝他的求婚。

娜拉：是啊，也许不应该吧。那个时候他是不是很有钱？

林德夫人：我想还是挺富有的吧。不过，他的生意不稳定。他死后，生意也就随之完蛋了，一分钱也没留下。

娜拉：后来呢？

林德夫人：后来我就千方百计地挣钱，能干什么就干什么——先是开了个小铺,接着办了个规模很小的学校,反正什么都干。这三年就像一个漫长的工作日,没有片刻的休息时间。现在总算熬到头了,娜拉——我那可怜的妈妈去世了,再也不需要我照料了;两个弟弟也有事情做了,可以自己打拼了。

娜拉:你现在一定感到很轻松。

林德夫人:其实并没觉得轻松,只觉得有一种说不出的空虚。没人再需要我了。(心神不定地站起身来)正因如此,我们那闭塞的小地方我再也待不下去了,只希望能在这儿找点事做,让自己忙忙碌碌的,免得胡思乱想。假如我有幸能找到一份固定的工作——一份办公室之类的工作——

娜拉:克里斯蒂娜,那种工作辛苦得要命。你看上去已经累坏了,最好到海边哪个地方去休养一阵子。

林德夫人:(走到窗口)娜拉,我可没有父亲留给我钱,让我到那儿享清福呀。

娜拉:(站起来)哦,你别生气啊。

林德夫人:(走近她)亲爱的,我应该求你别生气才对。我这种人日子过得太不顺心,说出话来就带刺。我虽然少了牵挂,然而还得活下去,还得为了生存而奋斗。一个人为了生存而挣扎,就会变得自私。刚才你说你们交了好运——你恐怕难以相信——我感到很高兴,与其说是为你们感到高兴,还不如说是为我自己感到高兴。

娜拉:这话是什么意思?噢,我明白了。你想托瓦尔德或许能为你找份工作干。

林德夫人:不错,我正是这么想的。

娜拉:他一定会帮忙的,克里斯蒂娜。此事交给我好啦。我会非常婉转地向他提出来的——我会先想办法让他高兴,然后再提出来。如果能帮上你的忙,你都不知道那会叫我有多高兴。

林德夫人:娜拉,你心肠真好,这么热心帮助我!你没有品尝过生活的艰辛还如此乐于助人,就更是难得了。

娜拉:你在说我?我没有品尝过生活的艰辛?

林德夫人:(笑了笑)亲爱的,你的艰辛就是料理一下家务什么的!你可真是个孩子,娜拉。

娜拉:(把头一扬,在屋子里走来走去)你别摆出老前辈的架子!

林德夫人:是吗?

娜拉:你跟他们一样,都觉得我能力差,干不了正经事——

林德夫人:哪里的话,哪里的话——

娜拉:你们都认为我没受过苦,没经历过磨难。

林德夫人:亲爱的娜拉,你刚才说的那些事就是磨难。

娜拉:哼,那都是芝麻大的小事。(降低声音)真正的大事我还没告诉你呢。

林德夫人:真正的大事?这话怎么讲?

娜拉:克里斯蒂娜,我知道你瞧不起我,但这是不应该的。你为了你的母亲长年累月辛苦地工作,你是不是为此感到十分自豪?

林德夫人:说真的,我没有看不起任何人。不过,想一想自己能为妈妈送终,让她老人家心无挂碍地离开人世,我倒的确感到自豪和高兴。

娜拉:想一想自己为弟弟所做的事情,你是不是也感到很自豪?

林德夫人:我觉得应该感到自豪。

娜拉:我想也是的。不过,现在听我说说吧,我也做了一件值得自豪和高兴的事情。

林德夫人:对此我毫不怀疑。不过,你指的是什么事情?

娜拉:小声点!别叫托瓦尔德听见!克里斯蒂娜,这件事,除了你,我谁都不告诉。

林德夫人:究竟是什么事?

娜拉:你过来。(把林德夫人拉到沙发上,叫她坐在自己旁边)克里斯蒂娜,我要告诉你的是,我也做过一件值得自豪和高兴的事——我挽救了托瓦尔德的生命。

林德夫人:挽救?怎么挽救的?

娜拉:我刚才不是说我们到意大利去了嘛。要是不去,托瓦尔德就永远不会恢复健康——

林德夫人:是呀,是靠你爸爸提供的资金呀。

娜拉:(笑了笑)不错,托瓦尔德和其他人都这么想。可是——

林德夫人:可是什么?

娜拉:其实家父一分钱都没给我们。钱是我弄来的。

林德夫人:你?那么一大笔钱都是你弄来的?

娜拉:对,二百五十英镑!你觉得怎么样?

林德夫人：可是，娜拉，你怎么能弄到那么多钱？难道是你买彩票中了奖不成？

娜拉：（一副鄙视的表情）买彩票？那算什么本事！

林德夫人：那你是从哪儿弄来的钱？

娜拉：（哼着歌，脸上露出一副神神秘秘的笑容）啧啧！啊哈！

林德夫人：反正不可能是你借来的。

娜拉：不可能？为什么不可能？

林德夫人：没有丈夫的同意，妻子是不能借钱的。

娜拉：（把头一扬）哦？要是妻子会想办法——是一个有头脑、有智慧的人——

林德夫人：我一头雾水，实在不明白，娜拉。

娜拉：你没必要明白。我没说钱是借来的。除了借，我还有别的办法。（身子往后一仰，靠在沙发上）也许是我的一个追求者给我的。按说，我还是有几分魅力的——

林德夫人：你净说疯话。

娜拉：我知道你心里充满了好奇，克里斯蒂娜。

林德夫人：听我说，亲爱的娜拉，你是不是有点儿太鲁莽了？

娜拉：（坐直了身子）挽救丈夫的生命能说是鲁莽吗？

林德夫人：我觉得在丈夫不知道的情况下行事就是太鲁莽。

娜拉：可是，当时的情形是，很有必要不让他知道！上帝啊，难道你不明白吗？他当时的病情很危险，但这不能让他知道。医生告诉了我实情，说他危在旦夕，只有到南方住一阵子才能保住他的性命。你以为我开始的时候没有试过别的方法吗？起初，我告诉他自己想到国外旅游，就像其他年轻的妻子一样，于是便又是流眼泪又是央求他。我让他为我的身体想一想，应该对我好一点儿，满足我的心愿才对。我甚至还暗示他借钱。他一听差点儿发脾气，克里斯蒂娜。他怪我不懂事，还说他做丈夫的决不能让我由着性子胡来——我记得他当时就是这么说我的。那时候，我心一横，认为重中之重是挽救他的生命——于是我就想出了一个摆脱困境的办法。

林德夫人：难道你丈夫一直被蒙在鼓里，没听你爸爸说那笔钱不是他给的吗？

娜拉：没有，一直没有。家父就是在那个时候去世的。我本打算把这件事告诉家父，叫他不要跟人说。可是他病得很厉害——唉，所以就用不着告诉他了。

林德夫人：你也一直没把实情告诉你丈夫？

娜拉：当然没有！你怎么会这么想？他这种人认死理——绝不向别人借钱！再说，托瓦尔德是个绝不仰人鼻息、要强的男子汉，要是让他知道自己依赖妻子的帮助才活了下来，那得让他多难受、多羞愧啊！那会破坏我们之间的关系，我们美满、幸福的家庭将会变样。

林德夫人：你打算永远瞒着他？

娜拉：（若有所思，半笑半不笑地）嗯——也许有一天会告诉他。等到多年之后，我不像现在这么漂亮的时候再说吧。别笑我！我的意思是等到托瓦尔德不像现在这么爱我的时候再说——那时候，无论我跳舞、化妆还是背诵，都会令他感到厌倦。手里有所储备毕竟是件好事。（打住了话头）瞧我净说废话！永远也不会有那么一天的。这就是我的天大的秘密，你觉得怎么样，克里斯蒂娜？你还觉得我什么事都干不了？实不相瞒，这件事耗费了我不少心血。按时履约对我来说可不是件容易的事。不妨告诉你吧，在商业中，贷款方面有按季度付息的，还有一种叫分期付款，两种形式都叫人难以应付。我必须这儿省一点儿，那儿省一点儿，要知道，那是能省就省。我无法从家用里面省多少钱，因为每一笔账托瓦尔德都记得很清楚。我又不能让孩子们穿得寒碜，觉得有必要把他给孩子们的钱都花在孩子们身上。啊，我可爱的小宝贝们！

林德夫人：所以，你就只好从自己的日常开销里省钱喽，可怜的娜拉？

娜拉：当然了。再说，一人做事得一人当嘛。托瓦尔德给我钱让我买新衣服什么的，我顶多能花一半，总是挑最简单、最便宜的买。幸亏我穿戴什么都好看，托瓦尔德从来没怀疑过。可是，克里斯蒂娜，我心里时常很难过，因为穿好衣服毕竟是件让人高兴的事，你说对不对？

林德夫人：一点儿不错。

娜拉：除了这些，我还用别的法子去弄钱。去年冬天运气好，我争取到了好些抄写的工作，每天晚上躲在屋子里一直抄到后半夜。我经常累得要死，可是能坐在家里抄抄写写挣钱，就是再累也高兴，觉得自己就像个顶天立地的男子汉。

林德夫人：你的债究竟还清了多少？

娜拉：具体多少我说不上来。要知道，这样的账务要弄清，是非常困难的。我只知道只要是能弄到钱，哪怕只弄到一便士，我也用于还贷了。我常常有走投无路、不知所措的感觉。（凄楚地一笑）有时候我就坐在那儿胡思乱想，想着有个阔绰的老头儿爱上了我……

林德夫人：什么！那人是谁？

娜拉：小声点儿！——他死的时候留下了一份遗嘱，拆开一看，里面用大号字体写着："我的所有财产都以现金形式立即交给可爱的娜拉·海默夫人。"

林德夫人：亲爱的娜拉，那人到底是谁呀？

娜拉：天呀，你怎么听不明白呢？那个阔绰的老头儿根本就不存在——那是我实在想不出生财之道时，坐在那儿遐想，臆想出来的。不过，现在好啦，对我而言，有没有那个讨厌的老头儿都无所谓了——对于他和他的遗嘱我全不放在心上了，因为我无还贷之忧了。（跳起来）天呀，想一想真叫人高兴，克里斯蒂娜！现在总算能无忧无虑、心无挂碍地过日子了，可以跟孩子们蹦蹦跳跳地玩耍，可以把家布置得漂漂亮亮，托瓦尔德喜欢什么就买什么！想一想吧，春暖花开的时候就要到了，就能看到蓝天白云啦！也许，我们还可以来一次短途旅行——也许，我又可以见到大海啦！啊，那该是多么美妙、幸福的生活呀！（大厅那儿传来了门铃声。）

林德夫人：（站起来）外头有人按铃。也许，我该走啦。

娜拉：不，别走。没人会上这儿来。那一定是找托瓦尔德的。

女佣：（站在大厅门口）打搅了，夫人，有位男士要见海默先生，而海默先生在和那位医生谈话——

娜拉：是谁？

克罗格斯塔德：（来到了门口）海默夫人，是我。（林德夫人吃了一惊，浑身一抖，急忙将脸扭向了窗口。）

娜拉：（趋前一步，态度不自然，声音低沉）是你？有何贵干？找我丈夫有什么事？

克罗格斯塔德：可以说是——银行方面的事吧。我在银行是一个小职员，听说你丈夫就要当银行的经理了。

娜拉：所以说——

克罗格斯塔德：我来没别的意思，纯粹是公事，海默夫人。

娜拉：那么请你到书房去找他吧。（娜拉冷淡地冲他躬了躬身子，把通向大厅的房门随手关上，回到火炉旁，给炉子里添了些柴火。）

林德夫人：娜拉——刚才那人是谁？

娜拉：他叫克罗格斯塔德，是个律师。

林德夫人：这么说起来真是他。

娜拉：你认识他吗？

林德夫人：从前认识——那是好多年前的事了。那时候他在我们镇上的一个律师事务所里做事。

娜拉：不错，他在那儿做过事。

林德夫人：他的样子可变多了！

娜拉：婚姻十分不幸嘛。

林德夫人：现在他是不是单身？

娜拉：是的，带着几个孩子过日子。好啦，火旺起来了。（关上炉门，把摇椅往旁边推了推）

林德夫人：听说他身兼数职，干着好几份工作。

娜拉：真的吗？也许吧，这我可是一无所知。咱们就不要光想工作不工作的，怪烦人的。

兰克医生：（从海默的书房里走出来，关门之前对海默说）不了，老伙计，我就不打搅你啦。我去跟你妻子说一会儿话。（随手拉上书房的门，一眼看见了林德夫人）哦，对不起，我怕是在这儿也打搅你们。

娜拉：不打搅，一点儿也不打搅。（给他们做介绍）这是兰克医生，这是林德夫人。

兰克：我在这里可是久闻林德夫人的大名了。我来的时候好像在楼梯那儿碰见你了，林德夫人，是不是？

林德夫人：是的，我爬楼梯爬得慢，一爬楼梯就发怵。

兰克：是吗？是不是身体有点弱的缘故？

林德夫人：不是，是因为工作太累了。

兰克：仅此而已？这么说，我猜你大概是来城里放松休息的？

林德夫人：我是来找工作的。

兰克：这是医治劳累过度的灵丹妙药吗？

林德夫人：人总得活下去呀，兰克医生。

兰克：不错，看来大家都是这么想的。

娜拉：是吗，兰克医生？你也想活下去？

兰克：当然喽。不管我感觉多么凄惨，哪怕是苦熬岁月，我也渴望多活几天。我的病人无一不是如此。那些道德败坏的人亦是如此——此时此刻正在跟海默说话的那个人，就是害了道德上的病，而且病得很严重……

林德夫人：（低声悲哀地）唉！

娜拉：你在说谁呀？

兰克：一个名叫克罗格斯塔德的律师，一个你根本不知道有多坏的人。他患的是道德品质败坏症，海默夫人，但是就连这样一个不配活着的人也贪恋人生，认为好死不如歹活。

娜拉：是吗？他找托瓦尔德说什么？

兰克：具体要说什么我不清楚，只听说是为银行的什么事。

娜拉：我以前不知道这位——他叫什么来着——这位叫克罗格斯塔德的人跟银行有什么联系。

兰克：噢，他和银行是有些联系的。（把脸转向林德夫人）不知道你们那儿有没有这样一些人，他们热衷于东闻闻、西嗅嗅，四处寻找道德品质败坏的人，一旦找到，就把这个人放到有利可图的位置上，对他盯紧不放。对于道德品质良好的人，他们则不闻不问。

林德夫人：我觉得既然患了道德病，就需要有人关怀关怀嘛。

兰克：（耸耸肩膀）有道理。于是，整个社会就变成了一个大病房，里面有许多需要关怀的病人。

〔娜拉正在想心事，忽然笑出了声，拍了拍手。〕

兰克：你笑什么？你知道这个社会的真实面目吗？

娜拉：我才不管什么社会不社会呢！我刚才笑的是一

件完全不同的事情,一件非常有趣的事情。兰克医生,我问你,银行里的那些职员是不是现在都归托瓦尔德管了?

兰克:你觉得非常有趣的事就是这个?

娜拉:(一边笑一边哼歌)我觉得非常有趣!(在屋里走来走去)想一想真了不起,我们——托瓦尔德竟有如此大的权力,能管理那么多的人。(从衣袋里掏出那包蛋白杏仁饼干)兰克医生,你要不要吃块蛋白杏仁饼干?

兰克:什么?蛋白杏仁饼干?我记得你们家不准吃蛋白杏仁饼干。

娜拉:不错。但这是克里斯蒂娜送给我的。

林德夫人:什么?!我送的?

娜拉:噢,别害怕。你又不知道托瓦尔德不准吃甜饼干。实不相瞒,他是怕我吃坏了牙齿。嗨,别管它,吃一回没关系!你说是不是,兰克医生?你来一块!(把一块饼干送到他嘴里)你也吃一块,克里斯蒂娜。我也要吃一块,只吃一小块——顶多吃两块。(来回走动)我感到幸福极啦!现在我只有一个心愿没完成了。

兰克:哦,什么心愿?

娜拉:我很想说出来,说给托瓦尔德听。

兰克:为什么不现在说呢?

娜拉:不行,我不敢说,怕说出来吓你们一跳。

林德夫人:吓我们一跳?

兰克:哦,你不愿说就别说了。但如果你愿意说,我们洗耳恭听。到底是什么事情想说给托瓦尔德听呢?

娜拉:我只是想说——算啦,该死的!

兰克：你是不是疯了？

林德夫人：娜拉，亲爱的！

兰克：你就对他说吧，他过来了！

娜拉：（把饼干袋藏起来）嘘！嘘！嘘！

〔海默从书房里走出来，外套搭在胳膊上，帽子拿在手里。〕

娜拉：托瓦尔德，亲爱的，你把他打发走了吗？

海默：是的，他刚走。

娜拉：让我给你介绍一下——这是克里斯蒂娜，刚进城。

海默：克里斯蒂娜？对不起，我好像不认识——

娜拉：就是林德夫人，亲爱的，是克里斯蒂娜·林德。

海默：噢，对，是我妻子的老同学吧？

林德夫人：是的，我们从小就认识。

娜拉：你想想，她这么老远跑来就是想见见你。

海默：此话怎讲？

林德夫人：其实也没什么，只是——

娜拉：克里斯蒂娜擅长簿记，一心想在一个有见识的人手下找点儿事情做，以便使自我更完善——

海默：这个想法非常好，林德夫人。

娜拉：她听说你当了银行经理——这个消息已经见报了——于是她就赶快跑了来。托瓦尔德，我相信你一定能为克里斯蒂娜找到事情做。看在我的分儿上，求求你了！

海默：哦，这并非完全不可能。你现在是单身吧，林德夫人？

林德夫人：是的。

海默：有一些簿记经验？

林德夫人：是的，很有经验。

海默：好！我有很大把握能为你找到事情做——

娜拉：（拍手）我说什么来着！我说什么来着！

海默：林德夫人，你很幸运，来得正是时候。

林德夫人：我该怎么谢你才好？

海默：用不着谢。（穿上外套）对不起，今天就失陪了——

兰克：等一等，我跟你一块儿走。（走到大厅把自己的皮外套拿进来，在火上烤烤）

娜拉：别耽搁太久，亲爱的托瓦尔德。

海默：大概一个小时吧，不会再多。

娜拉：你也要走，克里斯蒂娜？

林德夫人：（穿外套）是的，我得找个住的地方。

海默：哦，那好，咱们可以一起走。

娜拉：（帮她穿外套）可惜我们没有空房间，怕是不能留你住——

林德夫人：请别往心里去！再见，亲爱的娜拉，十分感谢。

娜拉：回头见。今晚你一定得来。兰克医生，你也得来。你说什么？身体好点儿就来？噢，身体肯定会好的！把扣子系紧点。（他们一边说话一边往门口走。楼梯上传来了孩子们的说话声。）

娜拉：是他们，他们回来了！（她跑过去开门。保姆带着孩子们走了进来。)进来!进来!(弯腰吻孩子们)噢,我的小宝贝!你看看他们,克里斯蒂娜!他们可爱不可爱?

兰克:咱们别站在风口说话。

海默:走吧,林德夫人,这股冷风只有当妈妈的受得了!

〔兰克、海默、林德夫人下楼去了。保姆带着孩子们进屋,娜拉把门关好。〕

娜拉:瞧你们水灵灵的,气色多好,脸蛋红扑扑的,就像熟透了的苹果和玫瑰花!(孩子们你一言我一语地跟她说起了话。)你们玩得高兴吧?太好了!什么?你用雪橇拉埃米和鲍勃?一个人拉两个人?真是好样的!伊瓦尔,你是一个聪明机智的孩子。安妮,让我抱一会儿她吧。我的小宝贝!(从保姆手里接过幼儿,在房间里跳起了舞)好,好,妈妈也会跟鲍勃跳舞的。什么?刚才你们玩滚雪球啦?真希望我也能跟你们一起玩!不用了,不用了,我给他们脱外套吧,安妮。让我给他脱吧,这会叫我很高兴的。你看上去冻坏了,快回自己的房间暖和暖和吧。炉子上有热咖啡。

〔保姆走进左边的房间。娜拉给孩子们脱衣服,把脱下来的衣服随手往旁边一扔。孩子们争先恐后地跟她说话。〕

娜拉:真的吗?一只大狗追你们?没咬着你们吧?别害怕,狗狗是不咬可爱的乖孩子的。伊瓦尔,你别看那些包裹。你问里面是什么?嗬,我敢说你一定很想知道。不,不——里面是很恶心的东西！来，咱们玩游戏吧。玩什么游戏？玩捉迷藏怎么样？鲍勃先藏。你们要我先藏？好吧，我先藏吧。（她和孩子们又笑又叫，在房间里跑出跑进。末了，娜拉藏在桌子底下，孩子们从外头跑进来到处乱找，可是找不着她。后来，她憋不住，笑出了声，孩子们听见后便冲过去掀开桌布，发现了她。一阵哈哈大笑的声音响起。她从桌子底下钻出来，装作吓唬他们的样子，结果又引起一阵大笑。这时，大厅外有人敲门，而他们却没听见。房门被推开一半，克罗格斯塔德露出脸来。他在门外等了一会儿，娜拉和孩子们还在玩耍。）

克罗格斯塔德：对不起，海默夫人。

娜拉：（低低叫了一声，转过身来，半跪在地上）啊，是你！有何贵干？

克罗格斯塔德：对不起，外头的门半开着，一定是有人出去时忘了关。

娜拉：（站起来）我丈夫刚刚出去了，克罗格斯塔德先生。

克罗格斯塔德：我知道。

娜拉：那么你来干什么？

克罗格斯塔德：我来找你说句话。

娜拉：找我说话？（柔声细语地告诉孩子们）你们去找保姆吧。什么？别担心，这个陌生人是不会伤害妈妈的。等他走了，咱们再玩儿吧。（把孩子们送到左边屋子里，随手带上门）你要找我说话？

克罗格斯塔德：是的，是要找你说话。

娜拉：今天吗？还没到一号呢。

克罗格斯塔德：不错，今天是圣诞节前夕。你们家今年能不能过好圣诞节，就取决于你了。

娜拉：这话是什么意思？今天我是绝对不可能——

克罗格斯塔德：此事以后再谈。现在要说的是另外一件事。你有空吗？

娜拉：有——有空是有空——只不过——

克罗格斯塔德：好。刚才我在奥尔森餐厅吃饭，看见你丈夫在街上走过去——

娜拉：怎么啦？

克罗格斯塔德：他和一位女士在一起走。

娜拉：那又怎么样？

克罗格斯塔德：恕我冒昧，那位女士是不是林德夫人？

娜拉：是的。

克罗格斯塔德：她是不是刚进城？

娜拉：是的，今天刚进城。

克罗格斯塔德：她是你的好友，对不对？

娜拉：是的。可是我不明白——

克罗格斯塔德：很久以前我就认识她。

娜拉：这我知道。

克罗格斯塔德：是吗？看来你什么都知道了，恐怕如此。那我就不绕圈子，索性直说了。林德夫人是不是将在银行里做事？

娜拉：克罗格斯塔德先生，你有什么资格过问这个？你只不过是我丈夫的一名下属！不过你既然要打听，我就告诉你吧。林德夫人的确将在银行里做事。实不相瞒,克罗格斯塔德先生,她的差事是我为她求来的。

克罗格斯塔德:这么说,我都猜对了。

娜拉:(走来走去)有的时候,一个人恐怕还是可以施加一点儿影响的。别以为女人就成不了事——一个人处于从属地位时,克罗格斯塔德先生,就要特别小心,千万别得罪那——那——

克罗格斯塔德:别得罪那个有影响力的人?

娜拉:一点儿不错。

克罗格斯塔德:(换了一副口气)海默夫人,你能不能行行好,利用你的影响力为我做点儿事?

娜拉:什么事?你是什么意思?

克罗格斯塔德:你能不能发发善心,帮我保住我在银行的小职位?

娜拉:你这话是什么意思?谁要抢你的位置?

克罗格斯塔德:噢,没必要装糊涂。我很清楚你的朋友躲着不愿见我,也很清楚我会因为谁而被撵走。

娜拉:我向你保证——

克罗格斯塔德:也许你真不知道。不过,还是打开窗户说亮话吧。现在,我想建议你施加一下你的影响,阻止这件事的发生。

娜拉:可是,克罗格斯塔德先生,我没有什么影响力呀。

克罗格斯塔德:没有?我记得刚才你还说——

娜拉:我自然没想到你会当真,竟把我当成个了不起的人!你怎么会以为我真的有什么影响力能左右我的丈夫?

克罗格斯塔德：上学时我就了解你的丈夫，并不觉得他比别的丈夫更加难以支配。

娜拉：要是你说话时对我丈夫不尊敬，我就赶你出去。

克罗格斯塔德：你的胆子可真不小，海默夫人。

娜拉：我再也不怕你了。一到元旦，我很快就能把那件事解决，一了百了。

克罗格斯塔德：（控制住情绪）海默夫人，你听我说。如果有必要，我会拼死一搏，哪怕豁出命也要保住我在银行的小职位。

娜拉：看来的确如此。

克罗格斯塔德：我并不专为那薪水——其实，薪水对我而言是最不要紧的。另外还有别的原因——我索性直说好啦。我想，你恐怕跟所有其他的人一样，对我的情况都知道——多年前我曾经有过一些过失。

娜拉：我好像听人说起过。

克罗格斯塔德：那件事虽然没有诉诸公堂，但自那以后，似乎所有的门都对我关上了。后来，我就干了那种营生，这你是知道的。我总得找点儿事情做。平心而论，你可不要认为我是心肠最黑的。现在，我必须洗手不干了。我的儿子们在一天天长大，为了他们，我也必须痛改前非，在这个镇上重新赢得人们的尊重。我在银行的这个职位就是我往上爬迈出的第一步，而你丈夫现在却要把我一脚再踢入泥潭。

娜拉：你必须相信我，克罗格斯塔德先生，此事我爱莫能助，实在帮不上你。

克罗格斯塔德:那是因为你没这个心。不过,我自有办法迫使你出手相助。

娜拉:你不是要把我向你借钱的事告诉我丈夫吧?

克罗格斯塔德:哼,要是我真告诉他会怎样呢?

娜拉:那你就太不地道了。(啜泣几声)想到我的秘密,原本是件令人高兴和自豪的事,却要以这种肮脏、卑劣的方式被告知,并且还是从你的口中说出来的!那会让我非常不舒服的。

克罗格斯塔德:仅仅是不舒服吗?

娜拉:(一气之下)好吧,你尽管告诉他好了。最后吃亏的还是你自己——我丈夫将会认清你的嘴脸,到时候你别想保住你的职位。

克罗格斯塔德:我刚才问你是不是仅仅害怕家里会闹别扭?

娜拉:要是我丈夫知道了此事,他当然会把我欠你的钱马上都还清。从此之后,咱们就井水不犯河水,各走各的路。

克罗格斯塔德:(走近一步)恕我直言,海默大大,你不是记性太坏,就是不懂做生意的规矩。我不得不提醒你,里面有些细节需要注意。

娜拉:你这话是什么意思?

克罗格斯塔德:你丈夫害病的时候,你来找我,说想借二百五十英镑。

娜拉:我当时不知道还能向谁求助。

克罗格斯塔德:我答应为你借到那笔钱——

娜拉：是的，你做到了。

克罗格斯塔德：我答应为你借到那笔钱，是有条件的。你当时所有的心思都在你丈夫的病上，急着拿到钱让他出国疗养，似乎没注意咱们的条件。此时提醒你，是怕有什么差池。我答应借给你钱的时候，特地写了一张借据。

娜拉：不错，我签了字。

克罗格斯塔德：你是签了字。不过，在你的签名底下有几行字，注明要你父亲做保人，需要他签字。

娜拉：需要他签字？他签了呀。

克罗格斯塔德：借据上的日期是空着的。也就是说，你父亲签字时应该填上日期。你还记得吗？

娜拉：记得，我想我记得。

克罗格斯塔德：当时，我把借据交给你，要你从邮局寄给你父亲。对不对？

娜拉：对。

克罗格斯塔德：自然，你立刻就寄了，因为没过五六天你就把借据交给了我，上面有你父亲的签名。随后，我便将那笔钱给了你。

娜拉：不错。难道后来我没有按时还钱吗？

克罗格斯塔德：是的，日子一点儿没错。不过——咱们还是言归正传吧——当时的情况对你而言十分危急，对不对，海默夫人？

娜拉：的确如此。

克罗格斯塔德：你父亲病情危重，对不对？

娜拉：他已经命悬一线。

克罗格斯塔德：不久他就去世了吧？

娜拉：是的。

克罗格斯塔德：请你告诉我，海默夫人，你能记得起他究竟是哪一天病逝的吗？我是说他病逝于哪一月哪一日？

娜拉：我爸爸病逝于九月二十九日。

克罗格斯塔德：一点儿都不错。我还亲自去查过呢。既然如此，那么这里面有一个问题（从衣袋里掏出一张纸），叫人解释不通。

娜拉：什么问题？我不知道——

克罗格斯塔德：海默夫人，问题在于，你父亲是在他病逝三天之后才在借据上签的名。

娜拉：你这话是什么意思？我不明白——

克罗格斯塔德：你父亲病逝于九月二十九日。可是你看，他签名的日期竟是十月二日。这难道不是个问题吗？（娜拉没有作声。）你能解释一下吗？还有一点也很蹊跷："十月二日"以及年份那几个字不是你父亲的亲笔，而是别人代写的，我认识那笔迹。哦，这一点当然是可以解释得通的——你父亲签名时忘了填日期，也许那个人并不知道他已经离开了人世，就胡乱填了一个日期进去。这也没什么大不了的，只要签名是真的就行。我想，签名该是真的吧，海默夫人？借据上的签名是你父亲本人的吗？

娜拉：（沉吟片刻，把头往后一仰，狠狠地瞧着克罗格斯塔德）不是，不是他本人的签名，是我代我爸爸签的。

克罗格斯塔德：知道吗，你说这话是有危险的。

娜拉：有什么危险？欠你的钱很快就会还清的。

克罗格斯塔德：恕我多嘴，你当初为什么没把借据寄给你父亲？

娜拉：那是不可能的，因为我爸爸的病情已非常危重。我如果让他签字，就得告诉他为什么要借那笔钱。他病得那么厉害，我无法告诉他，说我丈夫的生命也处于危险之中，所以不能把借据寄给他。

克罗格斯塔德：既然如此，那你就应该取消你们出国疗养的计划。

娜拉：不行，那是行不通的。到国外疗养能够挽救我丈夫的生命，这一计划是绝对不能取消的。

克罗格斯塔德：难道你就从来没想过你这是在骗我吗？

娜拉：我当时顾不了那么多了，一点儿都没想到这是在骗你。我无法容忍你的做法——因为你明明知道我丈夫病情危重，借钱给我时却千方百计刁难我，心肠太狠了。

克罗格斯塔德：海默夫人，显而易见，你还没意识到自己错在何处。实不相瞒，我自己也走错过一步，结果身败名裂。我之错跟你之过性质是一样的，轻重无差异。

娜拉：跟你一样？莫非你想让我相信，当你的妻子生命遇到危险时，你曾经挺身而出，冒险相救？

克罗格斯塔德：法律是不考虑动机的。

娜拉：那就一定是极其愚蠢的法律。

克罗格斯塔德：不管愚蠢不愚蠢，如果我向法庭出示这张借据，你就会受到法律的惩罚。

娜拉：我不信。难道法律就不允许做女儿的考虑到自己的父亲生命垂危，不愿让他老人家为她操心和忧虑吗？难道法律就不允许妻子挽救丈夫的性命吗？我不大懂法律，但我坚信法律条文中一定有这些内容，允许照顾到人的亲情。你身为律师，难道不知道有这样的法律吗？那你就是一个非常差劲的律师，克罗格斯塔德先生。

克罗格斯塔德：也许吧。不过，至于你我之间的这种交易，至于这方面的法律，你以为我不懂吗？咱们就骑驴看唱本，走着瞧吧。你爱怎样就怎样吧。但请恕我直言，我一旦再次丢掉饭碗，死也要拉你做垫背的。(他鞠了一躬，从门厅走了出去。)

娜拉：(略作思忖，随后将头一扬)胡言乱语！还想拿这话吓唬我！我可不像他想的那么傻。(开始忙着收拾孩子们的东西)可是万一——？不会的，那是绝对不可能的！我是为了我丈夫才那样做的。

孩子们：(在左边房间的门口)妈妈，那个陌生人出大门走了。

娜拉：是的，亲爱的，这我知道。你们对谁都别说这个陌生人来过！听见了吗？连爸爸都别告诉。

孩子们：好的，妈妈。你还能陪我们玩儿一会儿吗？

娜拉：不行，不行——现在不行。

孩子们：可是妈妈，你刚才答应过的呀。

娜拉：不错，但我现在抽不出身。你们玩儿去吧，我有许多事情要做呢。玩儿去吧，我的可爱的小宝贝们。(轻轻把孩子们推进里屋去，把门关上，转身坐在沙发上，拿起针线活儿缝了几针,但很快就停了下来)不会的!(丢下手里的针线活儿,站起身来,走到门口喊道)海伦!把圣诞树搬进来。(走到左边桌子前,拉开一个抽屉,手又停了下来)不会的,不会的!那是绝对不可能的!

女佣:(搬来了圣诞树)夫人,搁在哪儿?

娜拉:搁这儿,放在屋子中央吧。

女佣:还要别的东西不要?

娜拉:不要了,谢谢你。东西都齐了,不要什么了。

〔女佣走出了房间。〕

娜拉:(开始装饰圣诞树)这儿得插支蜡烛——那儿得挂几朵花。那个人真可恶,净胡说八道!我没有做错什么。圣诞树到时候一定会大放异彩!托瓦尔德,只要你高兴,我一定会想尽办法,让我干什么都行!我愿意为你唱歌,为你跳舞——(海默腋下夹着几份文件走了进来。)啊!这么快就回来了?

海默:是的。刚才有人来过吗?

娜拉:来这儿?没有。

海默:这就怪了。我看见克罗格斯塔德从咱家出去了。

娜拉:是吗?噢,对了,我忘了,克罗格斯塔德来这儿待了一小会儿。

海默:娜拉,从你脸上的表情看得出,他是来求你为他说好话的。

娜拉:是的。

海默:他还叫你假装说是你自己的意思,并且叫你别把他到这儿来的事情告诉我,是不是?

娜拉：是的，托瓦尔德，但——

海默：娜拉，娜拉，想不到你居然还要为他求情！还跟那种人说话，答应为他出力！想不到你居然对我撒谎！

娜拉：撒谎？

海默：你不是说没人来过吗？（伸出手指头冲她点了点）我的小鸟儿以后再不准撒谎了！唱歌的鸟儿要唱得清清楚楚，不要瞎唱。（用胳膊搂住她的腰）你说对不对？是的，我坚信不疑。（放开了她）这个咱们就不说了。（在火炉前面坐下）这儿真暖和，真舒服！（翻看文件）

娜拉：（忙着装饰圣诞树，过了一会儿说道）托瓦尔德！

海默：怎么啦？

娜拉：后天要到斯坦斯堡家参加化装舞会，我好期待呀！

海默：我倒期待着要看看你会给大家带来什么样的惊喜呢。

娜拉：想一想，我真怕自己会冒傻气。

海默：此话怎讲？

娜拉：因为我想不出什么好节目，所想到的节目似乎都很愚蠢，都很无聊。

海默：我的小娜拉终于江郎才尽啦？

娜拉：（站在海默椅子后面，两只胳膊搭在椅背上）托瓦尔德，你是不是很忙？

海默：唔——

娜拉：那都是些什么文件？

海默：是银行方面的。

娜拉：你已经履职了？

海默：我得到了前任经理的同意，在人事和工作方面要做一些必要的调整。我要趁着圣诞假期进行部署，新年走马上任前做到一切准备充分。

娜拉：难怪可怜的克罗格斯塔德急着——

海默：哼！

娜拉：（仍然倚在他的椅背上，抚摸着他的头发）托瓦尔德，要不是你这么忙，我倒想向你求个大人情。

海默：什么人情？你说吧。

娜拉：若论品味，谁都赶不上你。我多么想参加化装舞会时打扮得漂漂亮亮的啊！托瓦尔德，你能不能帮我出出主意，替我做个决定，告诉我应该穿什么样的服装？

海默：啊哈！原来我倔强的小姑娘也会有求于人，求人帮她救急呀。

娜拉：是的，托瓦尔德，你不出手相助，我都有点儿抓瞎了。

海默：很好，让我仔细想一想，咱们总可以想出好点子的。

娜拉：谢谢你！（重新走到圣诞树旁，忙活了一小会儿）这些红花看上去真漂亮！我想问一句，这个克罗格斯塔德犯过的错误是不是真的很严重？

海默：他伪造了别人的签名。你知道这意味着什么吗？

娜拉：他也许是迫不得已才那样做的吧？

海默：也许吧。也许就像许多人那样鲁莽行事。我也不是那种狠心肠的人，一见别人犯了点儿错，就把人家看得一文不值。

娜拉：你当然不是那种人，托瓦尔德，对不对？

海默：有过错不怕，只要能悔过自新、甘心受罚就可以。

娜拉：受罚？

海默：可是，克罗格斯塔德不甘心受罚，而是玩弄阴谋诡计逃脱惩罚，结果陷入了无可救药的泥潭。

娜拉：你觉得能不能——

海默：你想，一个人干了那种亏心事就不能不成天撒谎，成为一个伪君子，戴上一副假面具面对亲朋好友，甚至在自己的妻子儿女面前也是如此。最可怕的是，这种人会对他们的孩子产生恶劣的影响，娜拉。

娜拉：怎么影响？

海默：这种充满谎言的环境会影响和毒害整个家庭。在这样的人家，孩子们呼吸到的空气里都弥漫着罪恶的细菌。

娜拉：（靠近他）真的吗？

海默：我的宝贝，我当了多少年律师，对这类现象已司空见惯。凡是自小就不走正路的人，其根源都在于有一个不诚实的母亲。

娜拉：你为什么只归咎于——母亲呢？

海默：当然，父亲的影响也一样，不过一般来说，都是受了母亲的影响。这一点，凡是做律师的都知道。这个克罗格斯塔德谎话连篇，当面一套背后一套，一直在毒害他自己的孩子，所以我说他道德品质败坏，一点儿德行都没有了。（双手伸向她）因此，我的宝贝小娜拉得答应我，不要再为他求情了。伸出你的手,咱们拉个钩。来呀,来呀,你怎么啦?把你的手伸出来!拉钩上吊,一百年不许变。说实在的,我是不可能跟他在一起共事的——和这样的人接触,我感到浑身不舒服。

娜拉:(把手抽回去,走到了圣诞树的另一侧)这儿好热啊,我有许多事要做呢。

海默:(站起来,收拾文件)好,我也要在晚饭前看几个文件,并且还要想一想你穿什么衣服好。我还可以想一想,把什么东西用金纸包起来,挂在圣诞树上。(伸手拍拍她的头)我可爱的小百灵鸟!(他走进书房,关上了门。)

娜拉:(过了一会儿,自言自语)不会的,不会是真的。那是绝对不可能的,绝对不可能!

〔保姆打开了左边房间的门。〕

保姆:孩子们闹着要跟妈妈一起玩儿呢。

娜拉:不行,不行,别让他们上我这儿来!安妮,你陪他们玩吧。

保姆:好吧,夫人。(把门关上)

娜拉:(吓得脸色苍白)我会带坏我的孩子?毒害我的家庭?(顿了顿,把头一扬)这不是真的!不可能是真的!

第二幕

布景同第一幕。墙角的钢琴旁边立着那棵圣诞树,树上的挂件都已被人取走,乱蓬蓬的树枝上只剩下燃尽的蜡烛头。娜拉的外套和帽子扔在沙发上。她心烦意乱地独自在屋里走来走去。她走到沙发前停下脚步,将外套拿起来。

娜拉:(又把外套丢下)外头有人来了!(走到房门跟前听动静)不是的,没人来。今天是圣诞节,当然不会有客人来的——明天也不会有的。不过,也许——(打开门,朝外看了看)信箱里没有信。里头是空的,什么都没有。(走向前去)真是胡说八道!他说那话肯定不是认真的。那样的事情不可能发生,绝对不可能——我可是有三个孩子呢。

〔保姆拿着一只大硬纸盒从左边走进来。〕

保姆:放化装舞会衣服的盒子终于找到了。

娜拉:谢谢你,把盒子搁在桌上吧。

保姆:(按照吩咐做了)这衣服恐怕得好好收拾一下子。

娜拉：真恨不得把它撕成碎片。

保姆：哪里的话！收拾起来也不难，只要有点儿耐心就行了。

娜拉：好吧，那我就去找林德夫人帮一下忙吧。

保姆：怎么，又要出门？这么冷的天气还出门？你会冻坏的，夫人，会冻出病来的。

娜拉：也许还有比这更糟的情况呢。孩子们怎么样？

保姆：小不点们在玩他们的圣诞节礼物呢。不过——

娜拉：他们是不是缠着要找我？

保姆：您想，他们已经习惯了跟妈妈一起玩儿。

娜拉：是啊。不过，安妮，我以后恐怕不能像从前那样经常陪他们了。

保姆：好吧，好在孩子们什么事都容易习惯。

娜拉：你是这么想的？你说，如果他们的妈妈离家出走，他们是不是就会忘掉她？

保姆：天呀！离家出走？

娜拉：安妮，实不相瞒，我经常感到纳闷儿，不明白你怎么舍得把自己的孩子交给陌生人照料。

保姆：如果我想给小娜拉当保姆，就必须那样做。

娜拉：不错。可你怎么能舍得那份情？

保姆：有这么好的工作机会，我怎么舍不得？一个陷入困境的可怜女孩能有这么好的工作机会，自然能忍痛割爱。再说，那个可恶的家伙是一点儿忙也不肯帮我的。

娜拉：怕就怕你女儿已经把你忘了。

保姆：没忘，其实没忘。她订婚和结婚时都写信告诉我来着。

娜拉：（张开双臂搂住她的脖子）亲爱的安妮，我小时候你待我就像一个慈母一样。

保姆：可怜的小娜拉除了我，就没有母亲了。

娜拉：要是我的孩子没有母亲，我知道你一定会——瞧我在胡说些什么！（打开衣服盒子）你去陪孩子们吧。现在我必须——明天要让你看看我会打扮得多么漂亮。

保姆：我敢肯定，化装舞会上没有人会比你更漂亮的。（走进左边房间）

娜拉：（从盒子里拿出衣服，但很快又推开了）要是我敢走出这个门就好了。要是没有客人来就好了。要是能肯定家里不会掀起轩然大波就好了。胡说！不会有人来的。只要我不胡思乱想就行了。还是让我把手笼刷一刷吧。这副手套真漂亮！不要胡思乱想！不要胡思乱想！一，二，三，四，五，六——（叫了起来）啊，有人来了！（向门口走去，但中途又犹豫不决地停了下来）

〔林德夫人在大厅里脱下外套，摘掉帽子，然后走了进来。〕

娜拉：哦，克里斯蒂娜，原来是你。外头没有别的人了吧？你来得正好！

林德夫人：听说你去找我了。

娜拉：是的，我从你那儿路过来着。其实，是有件事想请你帮忙。咱们坐在沙发上谈。是这样的——明晚我们楼上斯坦斯堡家要举办化装舞会，托瓦尔德要我打扮成那不勒斯①的渔女，跳一种我在卡普里岛②所学的塔兰泰拉舞③。

林德夫人：了解，你打算扮演那个角色。

娜拉：嗯，这是托瓦尔德的意思，你瞧，这就是服装，是托瓦尔德在岛上为我定做的，现在却皱皱巴巴的，不知道——

林德夫人：很容易就能让它恢复原状。只需把这几个开了口的地方缝上几针就可以了。你有针线吗？很好，需要的就是这个。

娜拉：真是麻烦你了。

林德夫人：（飞针走线）这么说，明天你要打扮起来了，娜拉。这样吧，到时候我来一下，看看你打扮得多漂亮。噢，对啦，昨天晚上真令人高兴，我都忘记谢你了。

娜拉：（站起来，穿过戏台）噢，我觉得昨天跟往常相比，并不是个叫人愉快的日子。你要是早来几天就好了，克里斯蒂娜。当然，托瓦尔德善于把家里布置得又精致又漂亮。

林德夫人：我觉得你也善于布置家，要不然你就不像你父亲了。我问你，兰克医生昨天情绪低落，他是不是平时也是那个样子？

娜拉：平时不是的，只有昨天表现得特别明显。实不相瞒，这个可怜人患上了一种非常危险的疾病，叫作脊髓

---

① 意大利南部第一大城市。
② 位于那不勒斯湾南部的一座岛屿。
③ 广泛流传于意大利南部的一种民间舞蹈。

痨①。他父亲是个可怕的人，各种胡作非为，所以他自小就有病，知道了吧？

林德夫人：（放下手里的针线活儿）啊，我亲爱的娜拉，这种事你是怎么知道的？

娜拉：（来回走动）一个女人有了三个孩子，时而会有一些懂点儿医学常识的、结了婚的女客来访，聊天时就会谈谈这个谈谈那个。

林德夫人：（继续飞针走线，又做了一会儿针线活儿）兰克医生是不是每天都来？

娜拉：他没有一天不来。他是托瓦尔德最亲密的朋友，也是我的好朋友，简直就像是我们家的人。

林德夫人：请对我说实话——他是不是一个十分真诚的人？我的意思是，他是不是有点儿喜欢奉承人？

娜拉：根本不是。你怎么会这么想？

林德夫人：昨天你给我们介绍的时候，他说在这里久闻我的大名了。可是后来我看你丈夫一点儿都不认识我。兰克医生怎么会——

娜拉：他不是瞎说，克里斯蒂娜。托瓦尔德非常爱我，他说他恨不得将我独占。刚结婚的时候，我只要一提亲朋好友，他就好像有点儿嫉妒，所以我自然也就不提了。不过，我倒是经常跟兰克说一说我的亲朋好友，因为他喜欢听嘛。

林德夫人：听我说，娜拉。你在许多方面表现得还像

---

① 脊髓痨是一种实质性梅毒，病变主要是脊髓后根及脊髓后索发生变性所致，脑神经亦易受侵犯。

个小孩子，而我在很多方面比你老练，经验要丰富一些。恕我直言，你应该和兰克医生结束这种事情了。

娜拉：结束什么事情？

林德夫人：结束两件事。记得昨天你说了些荒唐话，说一个爱慕你的阔佬要给你留下一笔钱什么的——

娜拉：可惜那个爱慕者纯粹是子虚乌有！你提这些干什么？

林德夫人：兰克医生是不是个有钱人？

娜拉：是的，他很有钱。

林德夫人：没有娶妻生子？

娜拉：是的。可是——

林德夫人：他天天上这儿来？

娜拉：不错，我刚才说过了。

林德夫人：一个有教养的人做事怎么能如此不得体？

娜拉：你的话我听不懂，让人一头雾水。

林德夫人：你别装糊涂，娜拉。你以为我猜不出那二百五十英镑是谁借给你的吗？

娜拉：你疯了吧？怎么会说这种话？他是我们家的老朋友，天天都来，要是真像你说的，还不难堪死啦！

林德夫人：这么说，借给你钱的人不是他？

娜拉：不是，当然不是了。我可从没想过向他借钱。再说，那时他也没钱，他有钱是后来的事。

林德夫人：我觉得你幸亏不是向他借的钱，亲爱的娜拉。

娜拉：向兰克医生借钱，这种念头我可从来没有过。

不过，我坚信，假如我开口向他借——

林德夫人：你肯定是不会开这个口的。

娜拉：是的，肯定不会。我觉得也没这个必要。不过，我敢肯定的是，如果我告诉兰克医生——

林德夫人：背着你丈夫？

娜拉：另外有件事我也得了结，那也是背着我丈夫的。我必须来个一了百了。

林德夫人：是的，我昨天就跟你说过了，可是——

娜拉：（走来走去）处理这种事，男人会比女人更有办法。

林德夫人：是的，自己的丈夫更有办法。

娜拉：无稽之谈！（停住了脚步）只要把债还清，就可以把借据收回来了，对不对？

林德夫人：是的，那是自然。

娜拉：那时就可以把那张肮脏、可恶的纸撕成碎片儿，付之一炬啦！

林德夫人：（眼睛盯着她，放下针线，慢慢地站起来）娜拉，你一定有事瞒着我。

娜拉：你看我像有事瞒着你吗？

林德夫人：昨天上午我走后一定出了什么事。娜拉，究竟是什么事？

娜拉：（向她身边走过去）克里斯蒂娜！（侧耳细听）嘘！托瓦尔德回来了。你先上孩子们屋里坐坐好不好？托瓦尔德不爱看人缝衣服。叫安妮帮你。

林德夫人：（拿了几件东西）好吧。可是回头你得把那件事告诉我,不然我不走。(她进了左边的房间,而海默从大厅那儿走了过来。)

娜拉:(上前迎接丈夫)我等你好半天了,托瓦尔德。

海默:裁缝刚才来过?

娜拉:不是裁缝,是克里斯蒂娜。她来帮我整理一下化装舞会的衣服。到时候你会看到我靓丽登场。

海默:我给你出的主意好不好?

娜拉:好极了!我按照你的意愿行事,你不觉得我也很好吗?

海默:觉得你很好?按照丈夫的意愿行事,就觉得你很好?得啦,得啦,你这个小无赖,我相信你不是那个意思。我就不打搅你了——你肯定急着想试衣服呢。

娜拉:你要去工作啦?

海默:是的。(给她看一捆文件)你瞧。我刚才到银行去了一趟。(转身要到书房去)

娜拉:托瓦尔德!

海默:什么事?

娜拉:要是你的小松鼠求你点儿事——

海默:什么事?

娜拉:你肯不肯帮她?

海默:我得先知道究竟是什么事。

娜拉:要是你肯答应她,满足她的请求,你的小松鼠就会蹦蹦跳跳地在你面前耍她会的所有把戏,愿意为你做任何事情。

海默:有话你就直说吧。

娜拉：要是你肯答应她，你的云雀就会为你放声歌唱，让歌声到处回响。

海默：哦，我的云雀已经在为我歌唱了。

娜拉：我会为你扮演下凡的仙女，在月光下为你跳舞，托瓦尔德。

海默：娜拉，你求我的事该不会是上午提过的那件吧？

娜拉：（走近些）是的，托瓦尔德。我恳切地请求你——

海默：你还真敢再提那件事？

娜拉：是的，亲爱的，你必须答应我，必须让克罗格斯塔德保住他在银行里的职位。

海默：我亲爱的娜拉，我为林德夫人安排的正是那个位置。

娜拉：不错，你能帮我这个忙真是太好了。不过，你能不能辞掉别的哪个职员，而非克罗格斯塔德？

海默：你简直倔强得让人不可思议！难道就因为你答应过他为他求情，我就得——

娜拉：不是因为这些，托瓦尔德，而是因为你。这家伙为几家最为粗俗下流的报纸撰稿——这可是你亲口对我说的。他可以给你造成数也数不清的伤害。我怕他怕得要命——

海默：噢，我明白了。你一定是想起从前的事，所以才感到害怕。

娜拉：这话是什么意思？

海默：你一定是想起了你父亲的事情呗。

娜拉：是呀，是呀，那还用说。你不妨回忆一下那些恶毒的家伙是怎样兴风作浪、无中生有地造谣惑众，在报纸上贬低爸爸的。我觉得要不是派你去调查此事，要不是你处理得妥当，帮了他一把，那些家伙一定会得逞，导致他老人家被开除的。

海默：我的小娜拉，你父亲跟我完全不一样。作为公职人员，你父亲的名声并非不容置疑，而我却没有瑕疵——但愿在我任职期间永远如此。

娜拉：谁知道那些人会做出什么坏事来。咱们的日子过得这么好，有一个舒适、幸福、安宁的家，你和我以及孩子们都无忧无虑的，托瓦尔德，可别惹出事来！因此，我恳切地请求你——

海默：正因为你帮他说好话，我就更不能留着他。银行里已经都知道我要辞掉克罗格斯塔德。如果让人知道新上任的经理听了妻子的求情就改变主意——

娜拉：就算是吧，那又怎样？

海默：要是让你这个任性的小姑娘如愿以偿的话，当然会有不良影响！你以为我会在全体员工面前沦为笑柄，让别人认为我是根墙头草，容易受各种外界影响吗？我可以告诉你，用不了多久我就会尝到恶果的。另外还有一个原因——只要我是银行的经理，就不能留他。

娜拉：为什么？

海默：如果有必要的话，他品行上的缺点我倒可以不计较——

娜拉：是吗？你真的不计较？

海默：听说他的业务能力很不错。不过，我年轻的时候就和他在一起了，非常了解他。当初都怪我交友过于轻率，后来证明这段友谊对我来说是个沉重的负担。我不妨坦率地告诉你，我们曾经一度还是铁哥们呢。可是这家伙太嚣张，在外人面前对我肆无忌惮。他非但不收敛，还觉得自己有资格对我用熟稔的语气说话，一张嘴就是"我说、海默、老伙计"什么的。实话告诉你，他那样子真让人无法忍受，会让我在银行当经理如坐针毡。

娜拉：托瓦尔德，我真不敢相信你还这么计较。

海默：是吗？为什么就不能计较？

娜拉：那样看问题，就未免太心胸狭窄了。

海默：你说什么？心胸狭窄？你认为我心胸狭窄？

娜拉：不是的，恰恰相反，亲爱的——只是在这件事上心胸狭窄——

海默：反正都一样。你说我心胸狭窄，那么就当我心胸狭窄吧！很好——我索性来个快刀斩乱麻。（走到大厅门口叫了一声）海伦！

娜拉：你要干什么？

海默：（在文件堆里搜寻）我要了结这件事。（海伦走进来。）来，把这封信立刻拿到楼下，找个人马上送走。信上有地址，这是钱。

女佣：好的，先生。（拿着信走出去）

海默：（将文件整理到一起）这下好啦，任性的小小姐。

娜拉：（提心吊胆）托瓦尔德，那是什么信？

海默：是辞退克罗格斯塔德的信。

娜拉：快叫她回来，托瓦尔德！现在还来得及。快，托瓦尔德，快叫她回来！为了我，为了你自己，为了孩子们！听见没有，托瓦尔德？快叫她回来！你不知道那封信会给咱们惹出多么大的祸来。

海默：来不及了。

娜拉：是啊，来不及了。

海默：亲爱的娜拉，你如此担惊受怕是可以谅解的，但话又说回来，这对我而言是一种侮辱。你以为我会害怕一个写文章造谣生事的人打击报复，这难道不是一种侮辱吗？不过我可以原谅你，因为这充分证明你在深深爱着我。（把她抱在怀里）我亲爱的娜拉，此事只有这样处理才是正确的。不管天塌地陷你都不用担心，我有足够的勇气和力量来应对。等着瞧吧，我是个顶天立地的男子汉，所有的灾难都由我一人承担。

娜拉：（吓得声音颤抖）这话是什么意思？

海默：我是说所有的灾难都由我一人承担。

娜拉：（定下心来）你大可不必那样。

海默：那好吧，那就咱们俩承担吧，娜拉，夫妻俩共渡难关。本应如此。（安慰地抚摸她）现在你该满意了吧？好啦！好啦！瞧你的眼睛，就像吓坏了的小鸽子一样！世上本无事，庸人自扰之哟。去吧，去练习跳你的塔兰泰拉舞，敲你的手鼓吧。我到书房里去把门关上，是什么声音也听不见的，你爱怎么敲就怎么敲吧。（走到门口又转身）兰克来的话，让他到书房找我。（向娜拉点点头，带着文件走进书房，随手关上了门）

娜拉：（慌得六神无主，如脚下生根一般站着不动，嘴里念念叨叨）他是干得出来的，一定会的，一定会不顾一切地兴风作浪！不行，不能让那样的事情发生！绝对不能，绝对不能！无论如何也不能让那样的事情发生！唉，要是有人帮忙摆脱眼前的困境就好啦。（大门的门铃响了）是兰克医生！怎么都可以，就是不能让那样的事情发生！（她双手捂脸，定了定神，走过去开门。兰克医生正在外头挂他的皮外套。二人说话间，天色渐渐黑了下来。）

娜拉：你好，兰克医生。我听见门铃响就知道是你。你先别上托瓦尔德那儿去，他可能在忙着处理事情。

兰克：你有时间吗？

娜拉：（把他让进屋，然后关上了门）有呀，你知道，对于你，我总是有时间的。

兰克：谢谢。那我可要尽我所能，好好享受一下这样的时光了。

娜拉：这话是什么意思？怎么尽你所能？

兰克：啊，你听了害怕啦？

娜拉：我觉得你说话的语气有点儿怪。是不是要出什么事？

兰克：没什么，我早就知道会有这一天的，只是万万没料到它会来得这么快。

娜拉：（一把抓住他的胳膊）你发现什么了？兰克医生，你得告诉我。

兰克：（在火炉旁边坐下）我完了，没法子救了。

娜拉：（松了口气）你是在说你的事？

兰克：不是我的事，又是谁的事？欺骗自己一点儿用都不顶。在我所有的病人里，我是最不幸的。近来，我一直在给自己盘点，看自己还能活多久。结果是破产！也许过不了一个月，我就会到坟墓里跟蛆虫做伴了。

娜拉：怎么能说这么丑恶的话！

兰克：这件事本身就丑恶嘛。最为糟糕的是，我还得经历许多丑恶的折磨，才会最终走到那一步。只要再做一次检查，我就可以弄清楚可怕的大崩溃何时降临了。我得告诉你一点：海默优雅的天性使他对于任何丑陋的现象都会有一种无法遏制的厌恶感。我可不愿让他来病房看我。

娜拉：噢，可是，兰克医生——

兰克：绝不能让他去看我！无论如何也不能！我会拴上门，他来了也不许他进去。我一旦确定自己的末日快来临的时候，就把我的名片寄给你，上面画一个黑色的十字。那时你就知道我的人生走到了尽头。

娜拉：今天你可是净说荒唐话。我刚才还盼望你心情能好一点儿呢。

兰克：死到临头了，心情还能好？别人造的孽，却要我受罚！公理何在？每一家每一户，不管是这方面还是那方面，恐怕都有这样一笔无情的冤枉账。

娜拉：(捂住耳朵) 胡说！请你说点儿开心的话吧。

兰克：哈，说起来真可笑。我父亲年轻时贪图享乐，却让我可怜无辜的脊椎跟着倒霉。

娜拉：(坐在左边桌子前) 你说他贪图享乐是不是指的偏食，过分喜欢吃芦笋和鹅肝酱饼？

兰克：是的，还有松露。

娜拉：不错，还有松露。另外还有牡蛎吧，是不是？

兰克：不用说，自然有牡蛎。

娜拉：肯定还有大量的葡萄酒、香槟酒！这些东西固然美味，但不幸的是危害人的骨头。

兰克：最为不幸的是，它们伤害了并没有饱过这方面口福的人，伤害的是他们的骨头。

娜拉：是的，这正是最叫人难过的一点。

兰克：（凝神看着她）唉！

娜拉：（过了一会儿）刚才你为什么笑？

兰克：我没笑，是你在笑。

娜拉：不对，是你笑了，兰克医生。

兰克：（站起来）你比我想象的还要坏。

娜拉：我今天有点儿冒傻气。

兰克：看起来的确如此。

娜拉：（两手搭在他的肩膀上）最最亲爱的兰克医生，决不允许死神把你从我和托瓦尔德身边夺走。

兰克：这固然是一种损失，但你们很容易就能恢复过来。人一死，很快就会被忘掉的。

娜拉：（担心地瞧着他）你真这样想吗？

兰克：人只要结交新的朋友，就会——

娜拉：谁结交新朋友呀？

兰克：我死之后，你和海默就会结交新朋友。恐怕你已经在做准备了。那位林德夫人昨晚来干什么？

娜拉：天呀！你不会在妒忌可怜的克里斯蒂娜吧？

兰克：我就是在嫉妒她。她将会接替我在这儿的位置。

我一死，这个女人就会——

娜拉：嘘！说话声音别太大，她就在隔壁房间。

兰克：她今天又来了？瞧，我说对了吧？

娜拉：她是来给我整理衣服的。哎呀，你的嫉妒心可真是没有道理！（坐到沙发上）理智点儿，兰克医生！明天你来看我跳舞，我将呈献美丽的舞姿，你就全当是为了你——当然也是为了托瓦尔德。（从盒子里取出几样东西）兰克医生，坐到这儿来，我拿点儿东西给你瞧。

兰克：（坐下）什么东西？

娜拉：你瞧！

兰克：是丝袜。

娜拉：肉色的。漂亮不漂亮？这儿现在光线不好，但明天——不，不，不！你光看我的脚就行了。噢，也罢，你也可以看我的腿。

兰克：噢！

娜拉：你怎么看上去挺挑剔的？难道你觉得这袜子我穿上不合适？

兰克：对此我不好发表意见。

娜拉：（瞧了他几眼）不害臊！（用丝袜在他的耳朵上轻轻打了一下）这是对你的惩罚。（把袜子重新卷起来）

兰克：还有什么别的新鲜玩意儿给我瞧？

娜拉：不给你瞧了，因为你不老实。（她一边哼歌一边翻东西。）

兰克：（沉默了一会儿）我坐在此处和你说着知心话，不禁在想：当初我要是无缘来你们家，日子真不知会过成什么样呢。

娜拉：（笑了笑）我相信你在我们家一定感到很自在喽。

兰克：（声音更低了，眼睛直视前方）现在却要离开这一切了——

娜拉：胡说，你不会离开的。

兰克：（还是那声调）连表示感谢的一点儿纪念品都不能留下来，甚至连稍纵即逝的遗憾也来不及留下——只留下一个空位子，以后不管谁来，都可以补上这个空缺。

娜拉：如果我问你要——？算啦，不说也罢！

兰克：问我要什么？

娜拉：要一样纪念我们友谊的——

兰克：说下去！

娜拉：我的意思是，要你帮我一个大忙——

兰克：那会让我感到非常快乐的。你真的愿意给我一个这样的机会？

娜拉：啊，你还不知道是怎么回事呢。

兰克：不知道——那你就告诉我好啦。

娜拉：我实在说不出口，兰克医生。这样的事情简直匪夷所思——既要让你出主意、帮忙，还要你——

兰克：让我帮的忙越大，就越好。我猜不透你说的是什么。有话请直说。难道你信不过我吗？

娜拉：我最信任的就是你了。我知道你是我最真诚、最知心的朋友，所以要把心里的话讲给你听。好吧，兰克医生，有件事需要你帮忙加以阻止。你知道托瓦尔德爱我，爱得是那么诚挚，那么深沉，为了我，他会毫不犹豫地献出生命。

兰克:(弯身凑近她)娜拉,你以为世界上只有他一个人愿意——

娜拉:(有点儿吃惊)愿意——?

兰克:愿意为你献出生命。

娜拉:(忧伤地)你怎么能说这话?

兰克:我早就决定在死之前说出心里的话了,而现在这么好的机会以后绝不会再有了。现在你都知道了,娜拉。你还应该知道,你完全可以信任我。

娜拉:(轻轻地、不慌不忙地站起来)请让我过去。

兰克:(闪开一点儿让她过去,但仍坐在原处)娜拉!

娜拉:(在厅门那儿)海伦,把灯拿进来。(走到火炉边)亲爱的兰克医生,你说那种话真是太可怕了。

兰克:难道我就不能像其他人一样爱你吗?这算得上可怕吗?

娜拉:不是的,不是那意思。其实你没必要——

兰克:这是什么意思?莫非你早就知道——?(女佣把灯拿进来,放在桌子上,又走了出去。)娜拉——海默夫人——请告诉我,你是不是早就知道?

娜拉:噢,至于知道不知道,我怎么能说得清呢。我实在无从告知。不过,想一想你也太没有分寸了,兰克医生。你我不是一直相处得很得当嘛。

兰克:不管怎么样吧,你现在知道我完全听命于你,供你支配了。有何吩咐,但说无妨。

娜拉:(瞧着他)但说无妨?

兰克：告诉我吧，就算我求你了。

娜拉：现在我无论如何也不能说了。

兰克：求你了，求你了。你不该以这种方式惩罚我。请允许我为你效力吧，只要是男人做得到的事，我赴汤蹈火在所不辞。

娜拉：现在，我不能让你为我效力了。再说，我其实也不需要别人的帮助。你会发现，所有的一切都是我凭空瞎想出来的。情况的确如此——就是这么回事！（在摇椅上坐下，含笑瞧着他）兰克医生，你是个知趣的人！现在屋子里点了灯，你自己害臊不害臊？

兰克：一点儿也不害臊。不过也许我该走了——永远不再来了。

娜拉：不，那可不行。以后你应该跟我们照常来往。你知道托瓦尔德没有你不行。

兰克：不错，可是你呢？

娜拉：噢，你每次来这儿，我都高兴得不得了。

兰克：正是这一点让我在言语上有了不得当之处。你真是一个叫人猜不透的谜！我常常觉得你喜欢跟我在一起，就和喜欢跟海默在一起一样。

娜拉：不错——喜欢和你们在一起固然不错，然而有些人是你的挚爱，而另一些人你宁愿和他们成为同伴。

兰克：是的，这话有道理。

娜拉：小的时候，我的挚爱当然是爸爸。不过，我总觉得，偷偷溜去女佣的房间有极大的乐趣，因为她们绝不会对我进行说教，而是彼此谈论一些有趣的事情。

兰克：我明白了——现在我取代了她们的位置。

娜拉：（跳起来，向他走了过去）啊，亲爱的好兰克医生，我不是这意思。不过，你要知道，跟托瓦尔德在一块儿，有点像跟爸爸在一块儿——

〔女佣从大厅那儿走了进来。〕

女佣：对不起，夫人。（附耳低语，交给她一张名片）

娜拉：（冲名片瞟了一眼）哦！（把名片揣在衣袋里）

兰克：出什么事了？

娜拉：没什么，没什么。只是有点儿——我的新衣服有点儿问题——

兰克：你的新衣服！不是在那儿吗？

娜拉：噢，不是那件，是另外一件，是我定做的。千万别告诉托瓦尔德。

兰克：啊哈！原来是个大秘密哟。

娜拉：当然喽。你去找他吧，他在里屋。我这儿有事，别让他出来。

兰克：放心吧，我不会让他跑掉的。（走进海默的书房）

娜拉：（转向女佣）他在厨房里等着吗？

女佣：是的，他是从后楼梯上来的。

娜拉：你没跟他说家里没人吗？

女佣：我说了，可是不管用。

娜拉：他不肯走？

女佣：是的，夫人，他说不见你一面就绝不走。

娜拉：噢，那就让他进来吧，不过一定要悄悄地。海伦，此事万万不可告诉任何人。不能让我丈夫知道。

女佣：好的，夫人，我明白。（走出去）

娜拉：可怕的事情终于要发生了，我要拦也是拦不住的！不行，不行，不行，不能让它发生，决不能！（她锁上海默书房的门。女佣打开大厅的那扇门，让克罗格斯塔德进来，然后又将门关上。克罗格斯塔德身穿皮衣，头戴皮帽，脚蹬高筒靴。）

娜拉：（迎上去）说话声音小一点儿，我丈夫在家呢。

克罗格斯塔德：没问题。

娜拉：你来干什么？

克罗格斯塔德：想听你解释解释。

娜拉：有话快说！解释什么？

克罗格斯塔德：你恐怕知道我已经被辞掉了。

娜拉：我实在没法子阻拦，克罗格斯塔德先生。我为你磨破了嘴皮子，可再怎么说也不顶用。

克罗格斯塔德：难道你丈夫就这么不把你放在心上？他明知道你在我手心里攥着，竟然还敢——

娜拉：你怎么能料想他知道这种情况？

克罗格斯塔德：我这并非料想，而是断定亲爱的托瓦尔德·海默根本不可能有那么大的勇气——

娜拉：克罗格斯塔德先生，请你对我丈夫尊重些。

克罗格斯塔德：当然，他理应受到尊重。不过，鉴于你小心翼翼地隐瞒真相，恕我冒昧地假设，你今天一定比昨天头脑清楚了些，明白了你到底做过什么事。

娜拉：我心里比你说的还明白。

克罗格斯塔德：是啊，我可是个坏心眼儿的律师哟。

娜拉：你究竟来干什么？

克罗格斯塔德：只不过来看望看望你嘛，海默夫人。我一整天都在为你操心呢。要知道，甚至连我这样一个人，一个唯利是图的放债人，一个下流的撰稿人，一个——怎么说呢，总之就是像我这样的人——也是有一点儿人们常说的同情心的。

娜拉：那就想一想我年幼的孩子们，显示一下你的同情心吧。

克罗格斯塔德：你和你丈夫替我的孩子想过吗？不过，这也没关系。我来这儿只是想告诉你，不必将问题看得太严重。首先，我是不会起诉你的。

娜拉：这是自然的，对此我坚信不疑。

克罗格斯塔德：这件事可以心平气和地解决，没理由闹得满城风雨。就让它成为咱们三个人之间的秘密吧。

娜拉：绝对不能让我丈夫知道。

克罗格斯塔德：你怎么能阻止得了呢？难道你能把欠下的余款全都还清吗？

娜拉：一时还还不清。

克罗格斯塔德：或者也许你有一些筹集资金的权宜之计，很快就可以将钱凑齐？

娜拉：办法倒是有，但我不打算用。

克罗格斯塔德：即便你有办法，现在也派不上用场了。你就是有大把的钞票，我也不会把借条还给你的。

娜拉：你留着做什么用？

克罗格斯塔德：我只想留着它而已——抓在我手里。

哪怕是一丁点儿的蛛丝马迹，也不让与此事无关的人知道。这样，万一你被逼无奈，准备孤注一掷的时候——

娜拉：我曾经有过这样的念头。

克罗格斯塔德：假如你万念俱灰，打算离家出走——

娜拉：我曾经有过这样的念头。

克罗格斯塔德：或者，你甚至会有更可怕的想法——

娜拉：你是怎么知道的？

克罗格斯塔德：劝你打消这种念头。

娜拉：你是怎么知道我心里有那种念头的？

克罗格斯塔德：遇到难过的坎儿，大多数人一开始都会有这种念头。我也有过，但我缺乏那种勇气。

娜拉：（声音微弱）我也缺乏。

克罗格斯塔德：（松了口气）是吗？这很好——你也缺乏那种勇气？

娜拉：是的，我没那种勇气，我没有。

克罗格斯塔德：再说，那也是顶顶愚蠢的。家里的暴风雨过后，一旦雨过天晴——我口袋里装着一封写给你丈夫的信。

娜拉：把一切都告诉他？

克罗格斯塔德：我已经尽我所能地措辞委婉了。

娜拉：（急迫地）千万不能把信给他！赶紧撕掉它！我会找到办法筹钱的。

克罗格斯塔德：对不起，海默夫人，记得我刚说过——

娜拉：我不是指我欠你的钱。告诉我，你打算问我丈夫要多少钱，我会弄到的。

克罗格斯塔德：我一分钱都不打算问你丈夫要。

娜拉：那你想要什么？

克罗格斯塔德：告诉你吧。我想恢复我的职位，海默夫人。我想出人头地，你的丈夫必须帮助我才行。在过去的一年半里，我可是连一件不体面的事情也没做过，一直在艰难的逆境中苦苦挣扎。我原本心满意足，打算靠自己的努力步步高升，谁知现在却被撵出了门。如今，我可不仅仅满足于恢复工作了。实不相瞒，我还想高升呢。我想回到银行里去，还想有一个比较高的职位。你丈夫必须成全我——

娜拉：他决不会答应的！

克罗格斯塔德：他会答应的。我了解他，他不敢不答应。只要我回到银行跟他同舟共济，你就等着瞧吧！不出一年，我就会成为那位经理大人的左膀右臂。那时候，管理银行的将会是尼尔斯·克罗格斯塔德，而非托瓦尔德·海默。

娜拉：永远都不会有那一天的！

克罗格斯塔德：你的意思是你会——

娜拉：现在我有勇气了，有足够的勇气了。

克罗格斯塔德：哦，这话可吓不倒我。像你这么个娇生惯养、温文尔雅的女人——

娜拉：你瞧着吧！你瞧着吧！

克罗格斯塔德：是不是沉到冰底下？葬身于冰冷、漆黑的水里？当春天冰雪消融时浮到水面上来，头发都掉光了，面容可怕得叫人无法辨认——

娜拉：你吓不倒我。

克罗格斯塔德：你也吓不倒我。谁也不会干这种傻事的，海默夫人。再说，你就是干了，又有什么用？我照样会将你丈夫完全控制在手中。

娜拉：还会吗？当我不在的时候——

克罗格斯塔德：你的荣与辱掌握在我手中，难道你忘了吗？（娜拉哑口无言，呆呆看着他。）好啦，我已经给你敲过警钟了。你可别做傻事。海默看了我的信，我将静候佳音。别忘了，是你丈夫逼我走这一步棋的。对于他，我是永远也不会原谅的。再见吧，海默夫人。（他穿过大厅出去了。）

娜拉：（赶紧跑到厅门那儿，把门拉开一点儿，仔细听了听）他走了，没把信扔在信箱里。嘘，这怎么可能！（把门慢慢拉开）这是怎么回事？他还站在门外，没有下楼去。莫非他犹豫了？他会不会——？（听见一封信扔进了信箱，接着传来了克罗格斯塔德下楼的脚步声。他下楼后，脚步声也跟着消失了。娜拉低低叫了一声，穿过房间跑到沙发旁的桌子跟前，停留了一会儿。）

娜拉：信扔进信箱了！（蹑手蹑脚地走到大厅门口）信在里头了！托瓦尔德，托瓦尔德，这下子咱们完了！

〔林德夫人拿着衣服从左边的房间走进来。〕

林德夫人：衣服收拾完了，看不到有要补的地方了。你要试一试吗？

娜拉：（声音低哑）克里斯蒂娜，你过来一下。

林德夫人：（把衣服扔在沙发上）你这是怎么啦，看上去失魂落魄的！

娜拉：你过来，看看信箱里有没有一封信？那里，看——从玻璃窗朝信箱里看！

林德夫人：是的，我看见了。

娜拉：那封信是克罗格斯塔德写的。

林德夫人：娜拉，借钱给你的就是克罗格斯塔德吧？

娜拉：是的，现在托瓦尔德就要知道所有的一切了。

林德夫人：相信我，娜拉，这对你俩是再好不过的了。

娜拉：有些情况你不知道。签名是我伪造的。

林德夫人：天呀！

娜拉：我告诉你这些，克里斯蒂娜，只是想让你做证。

林德夫人：做证？你这是什么意思？要我证明——？

娜拉：万一我精神失常——这事很容易发生——

林德夫人：娜拉！

娜拉：万一我出了什么事——比如说被迫离开这里——

林德夫人：娜拉，娜拉，你简直是疯了！

娜拉：万一出现了那样的情况，就会有人企图让托瓦尔德承担所有的责任和罪名，这你清楚——

林德夫人：是的，是的，可是你怎么能想到——？

娜拉：那时候你必须出来做证，证明那不是真的，克里斯蒂娜。我的精神一点儿也没失常，意识非常清楚。我可以告诉你，那件事任何人都不知道，是我一个人做出来的。你一定要记住这一点！

林德夫人：我一定会记住的。可是，我不明白你究竟要干什么。

娜拉：你怎么会明白呢？我要完成一项惊人之举。

林德夫人：一项惊人之举？

娜拉：是的，一项惊人之举！不过，后果是非常可怕的，克里斯蒂娜，能不那样做，就绝不那样做。

林德夫人：我马上去见克罗格斯塔德。

娜拉：你别去，你去会吃亏的。

林德夫人：曾经有一个时期，他对我是有求必应的。

娜拉：是吗？

林德夫人：他住在什么地方？

娜拉：我怎么知道？噢，对啦，（在自己衣袋里摸索）这是他的名片。可是那封信，那封信！

海默：（在书房里敲门）娜拉！

娜拉：（吓得叫起来）哎，什么事？你叫我干什么？

海默：别害怕！我们不是要进去，而是门被你锁上了。你是不是正在试衣服？

娜拉：是的，是的。这衣服穿在身上很漂亮，托瓦尔德。

林德夫人：（看过名片）我知道了，他就住在这条街的街拐角。

娜拉：不错，可是现在你去也不顶用。没指望了，因为那封信已经放进了信箱里。

林德夫人：信箱钥匙在你丈夫手里吗？

娜拉：是的，一直都是他拿着呢。

林德夫人：一定得叫克罗格斯塔德把信原封不动地要回去，让他想个理由。

娜拉：可是，托瓦尔德通常都是这个时间——

林德夫人:你必须拖住他,让他在这段时间不能去开信箱。我一定尽快赶回来。(她急急忙忙从厅门走了出去。)

娜拉:(走到海默书房门前,将门打开,朝里面看了看)托瓦尔德!

海默:(在里屋)怎么?现在我可以走进自己的屋子了吧?来吧,兰克医生,咱们去瞧瞧——(在门口停下来)这是怎么回事?

娜拉:什么事,亲爱的?

海默:兰克叫我准备好,看一场精彩的表演呢。

兰克:(在门口)我原以为是这样,但显然是我弄错了。

娜拉:是的。不到明天,谁都别想看到我穿上新衣表演。

海默:亲爱的娜拉,你看上去累坏了。是不是练习得太辛苦了?

娜拉:不是,我还没开始练习呢。

海默:可是你一定得——

娜拉:是的,我会的,托瓦尔德。不过,没有你帮忙,我恐怕根本无法进行下去;我把所有的一切都忘掉了。

海默:没关系,咱们练习练习,很快就会熟悉的。

娜拉:是的,那就靠你帮助了,托瓦尔德。你可一定要帮我!我心里紧张得不得了——那么多人看——今天晚上你就把所有的时间都贡献给我吧,别的什么都不要做,甚至连你写字的笔碰都不要碰。你能答应吗,亲爱的托瓦尔德?

海默:我答应你。今天晚上我完全听你差遣,你这个可怜的小家伙。噢,对啦,我得先去——(向厅门走去)

娜拉:你去干什么?

海默:我去看看有信没有。

娜拉:别去!你别去,托瓦尔德!

海默:为什么?

娜拉:请你别去,托瓦尔德,信箱是空的。

海默:噢,我还是去看看吧。(转身向信箱那儿走去。娜拉弹起了钢琴,弹奏起塔兰泰拉舞曲的开头几节。海默在门口站住。)啊哈!

娜拉:现在不跟你在一起练一练,明天我就无法登台表演了。

海默:(走近她)你真的很害怕吗,亲爱的?

娜拉:是的,怕得要命。现在必须马上练起来,晚饭前还能练上一遍。你坐下来弹钢琴为我伴奏,亲爱的托瓦尔德,一边弹一边指导和纠正我。

海默:乐于效劳,悉听尊便。(在钢琴前坐下)

娜拉:(从盒子里拿出一面手鼓和一条长长的杂色披肩,手忙脚乱地把披肩裹在身上,一步跳到戏台中央,高声叫道)来吧,你弹吧!我要跳舞了!

〔海默弹琴,娜拉跳舞。兰克站在钢琴旁边、海默后面观看。〕

海默:(一边弹琴)慢一点儿!慢一点儿!

娜拉:我慢不下来!

海默:动作不要太猛,娜拉。

娜拉:动作就得这样。

海默:(停止弹琴)不行,不行,你的舞步根本就不对。

娜拉：（一边摇手鼓一边大笑）刚才我不是跟你说过吗！

兰克：让我给她伴奏吧。

海默：（站起来）好吧，你来弹。我腾出手好为她纠错。

〔兰克坐下弹琴。娜拉开始跳舞，越跳越疯狂。海默站在火炉旁边随时指点她，她好像没听见一样，头发松开来，披散在肩膀上，而她理也不理，照样跳个不停。林德夫人走进来。〕

林德夫人：（木雕石塑般呆立在门口）啊！

娜拉：（不停地跳）克里斯蒂娜，真好玩儿！

海默：我亲爱的娜拉，你这样跳舞，就好像到了生死关头一样。

娜拉：本来就是嘛。

海默：别弹了，兰克。这简直就是发疯。别弹了，我叫你别弹了！（兰克停止弹奏，娜拉的舞蹈也戛然而止。海默向她走过去。）我真不敢相信，你竟然把我教给你的全忘了。

娜拉：（扔下手鼓）瞧，你也看到了。

海默：你真得从头学。

娜拉：是啊，我真得从头学。你要教，就把我教到底。你可要答应我，托瓦尔德！

海默：我答应你。

娜拉：今明两天，你什么都不要想，什么都不要做，只陪我练舞，一封信都不许看，甚至连打开信箱都不许。

海默：啊，你心里还在怕那个家伙——

娜拉：不错，我的确在怕。

海默：娜拉，从你的表情我可以看出来，信箱里有他寄来的一封信。

娜拉：不知道，也许有吧。但你现在不许看，别让任何可怕的事情打搅咱们练习，一切都等到化装舞会结束之后再说。

兰克：（低声嘱咐海默）你应该听她的。

海默：（把她搂在怀里）听从宝贝的安排。但明晚你跳过舞之后——

娜拉：那时候你爱干什么就干什么。（女佣出现在右边的门道里。）

女佣：晚饭已端上桌了，夫人。

娜拉：海伦，我们要喝点儿香槟酒。

女佣：好的，夫人。（朝外走）

海默：哇！是不是要开宴会呀？

娜拉：是的，是香槟宴，一直开到深夜。（叫喊）海伦，准备一些蛋白杏仁饼干——多准备点儿，就这一回！

海默：静一静，静一静，你可不要太激动，太紧张。乖乖做我的小云雀吧，就像你以前一样。

娜拉：会的，亲爱的，我会镇定下来的。你去吃饭吧。你也去，兰克医生。克里斯蒂娜，你帮我把头发拢上去。

兰克：（一边走出去一边低声问海默）会不会出什么事？她是不是——

海默：不会的，我的老伙计。正如我方才所说，只不过是有点儿孩子气的紧张罢了。（他们走进了右边的房间。）

娜拉:怎么样?

林德夫人:他出城去了。

娜拉:刚才我看你脸上的表情就知道了。

林德夫人:他明天晚上就回来。我给他留了个字条。

娜拉:起先就不该叫你插手——是福挡不住,是祸也躲不过。再说,等着奇迹发生也很令人期待。

林德夫人:你在等什么奇迹发生?

娜拉:噢,说了你也不懂。你到餐厅里去吧。我一会儿过去。(林德夫人到餐厅去了。娜拉站了一会儿,仿佛在稳定情绪。随后,她看了看表。)现在是五点,到午夜还有七个小时,而到明天的午夜就要再加上二十四个小时。那时候,我的塔兰泰拉舞就跳完了。二十四加七?还可以活三十一个小时。

海默:(出现在右边的门口)我的小云雀在哪儿?

娜拉:(张开双臂跑过去)我在这儿!

第三幕

布景同前。桌子被放在了戏台中央,旁边有几把椅子。桌上点着灯。通往大厅的门敞开着。楼上传来了袅袅的舞曲声。林德夫人坐在桌子旁边,百无聊赖地翻看着一本书。她想看书,但好像无法定下神来,时不时竖起耳朵听门外的动静。

林德夫人:(看看表)怎么还没来!都快没有时间了。万一他不来——(又听了听动静)啊,他来啦!(走进大厅,蹑手蹑脚地打开外边的门。楼梯上有轻微的脚步声。她低声说)进来,这儿没别人。

克罗格斯塔德:(在门口)我回家看见了你留下的字条。这是怎么回事?

林德夫人:我一定得跟你谈一谈。

克罗格斯塔德:当真?难道非得在这儿谈不成?

林德夫人:在我住的地方谈是不可能的——那儿只有一个入口,毫无隐私可言。你进来,这儿只有咱们两个人,女佣已经睡了,海默夫妻在楼上开舞会呢。

克罗格斯塔德:(走进屋子)海默夫妻真的今晚还跳舞?

林德夫人:是的。为什么不可以?

克罗格斯塔德:当然可以,当然可以。

林德夫人:尼尔斯,现在咱们好好谈一谈吧。

克罗格斯塔德:咱俩有什么可谈的呢?

林德夫人:可谈的东西多着呢。

克罗格斯塔德:我可不这么想。

林德夫人:不错,那是因为你从来就没有真正了解过我。

克罗格斯塔德:有什么可了解的?这种显而易见的事情再平常不过了——一个没良心的女人见异思迁,把自己的情人甩了呗。

林德夫人:你真的认为我是个水性杨花、没良心的人?你以为我那样做心里好受吗?

克罗格斯塔德:有什么不好受的?

林德夫人:尼尔斯,你真的把我当成那号儿人啦?

克罗格斯塔德:要是你心里不好受,你为什么写给我那么一封信?

林德夫人:我那是迫不得已。既然我要跟你分手,就必须快刀斩乱麻,斩断你对我的情丝。

克罗格斯塔德:(绞着双手)原来是这么回事。原来是——原来跟我分手只是为了钱!

林德夫人:你别忘了我那时有个无依无靠的母亲,还有两个小弟弟。尼尔斯,我们一家老小实在没法子等下去,因为你自己那时的状况似乎也不好。

克罗格斯塔德：也许吧。可是，你也不该为了攀高枝就把我一脚蹬开。

林德夫人：我的确不知道自己该不该。我不知有多少次问自己：那样做应该不应该？

克罗格斯塔德：（态度缓和了一点儿）自从我失去了你，就觉得好像脚底下落了空。你看我现在的光景，好像是个从翻了的船上落水的人，死死抓住一块破船板想活下去。

林德夫人：救星也许快来了。

克罗格斯塔德：救星其实已经来了，可谁知你却跑来，挡了我的生路。

林德夫人：我不是故意的，尼尔斯。直到今天我才知道，我到银行里上班就是顶你的缺。

克罗格斯塔德：你既然这么说，我就信你吧。可是，现在你已经知道了，那么你愿意把工作还给我吗？

林德夫人：不愿意，因为那对你一点儿好处都没有。

克罗格斯塔德：唉，什么好处不好处，要是我，就不管那一套。

林德夫人：我学会了做事要谨慎——这是生活和艰难、苦涩的现实教会我的。

克罗格斯塔德：生活教会我的则是不要相信别人的甜言蜜语。

林德夫人：那么，生活教给你的是非常理智的一课。不过，你应该相信事实吧。

克罗格斯塔德：此话怎讲？

林德夫人：你说你好像是个从翻了的船上落水的人，死死抓住一块破船板想活下去。

克罗格斯塔德：我完全有理由这么说。

林德夫人：噢，我也好像是个从翻了的船上落水的女人，死死抓住一块破船板想活下去——此时的我不需要为任何人伤心，也不需要为任何人牵肠挂肚。

克罗格斯塔德：那是你自己做出的选择。

林德夫人：那时，我还有别的选择吗？

克罗格斯塔德：那么现在呢？

林德夫人：尼尔斯，现在咱们两个落水的人可以合力求生，你看怎么样？

克罗格斯塔德：你说什么？

林德夫人：两个人合力求生总比一个人苦苦挣扎胜算大一些。

克罗格斯塔德：克里斯蒂娜！

林德夫人：你以为是什么原因使得我来到了城里？

克罗格斯塔德：你是说你还想着我？

林德夫人：我一定得工作，不然活着没意思。现在回想起来，我一生都在工作——工作是我最大的乐趣，也是唯一的乐趣。而现在，我成了孤零零一个人，觉得生活异常空虚，觉得自己被这个世界所抛弃。一个人只为自己工作，是一点儿乐趣都没有的。尼尔斯，给我一个人，给我一个理由，让我工作起来有劲头吧！

克罗格斯塔德：我不信你的话——这只不过是女人家一时激动、意气用事才说出的豪言壮语。

林德夫人：你看到我有意气用事的迹象吗？

克罗格斯塔德：难道你真愿意这么做？请问：我的历史你是不是全都了解？

林德夫人：是的。

克罗格斯塔德：你了解人们对我的看法吗？

林德夫人：我觉得，你的意思是说若非我当初离开你，现在你一定会是另外一番景象。

克罗格斯塔德：那是一定的。

林德夫人：现在补救还来得及吗？

克罗格斯塔德：克里斯蒂娜，你说这话是认真的吗？是认真的，我敢肯定你是认真的，从你脸上看得出来。那么，你真的有勇气——

林德夫人：我想当母亲，而你的孩子需要一个母亲。咱们俩也彼此需要。尼尔斯，我坚信你的为人是好的，愿意和你同舟共济。

克罗格斯塔德：（抓紧她的手）谢谢你，谢谢你，克里斯蒂娜！现在，我要想办法证明我自己，让世人对我刮目相看。哦，我忘了——

林德夫人：（竖耳静听）嘘！塔兰泰拉舞开始了！你快走吧，快走！

克罗格斯塔德：为什么？这是怎么回事？

林德夫人：你听见楼上的音乐了吧？这个舞曲一结束，他们可能就回来了。

克罗格斯塔德：好的，好的，我这就走。可是，走也没有用。你当然不知道我是用什么手段对付海默夫妻的。

林德夫人:我知道,我全知道。

克罗格斯塔德:既然知道,你还有胆量——

林德夫人:我非常清楚一个人在走投无路的情况下,会做出什么事来。

克罗格斯塔德:解铃还须系铃人!

林德夫人:你恐怕解不了这个铃——你的信现在就在信箱里。

克罗格斯塔德:你确定?

林德夫人:十分确定,不过——

克罗格斯塔德:(仔细瞧她)难道这就是你的目的——不惜一切代价拯救你的朋友?老实告诉我,是不是这么回事?

林德夫人:尼尔斯,一个女人为了别人出卖过自己一次,她是不会出卖第二次的。

克罗格斯塔德:我打算把那封信要回来。

林德夫人:不行,不行。

克罗格斯塔德:我必须这样做。我要在这儿等海默回来,要求他把信还给我,就说信里写的只是关于辞退我的事,现在不想让他看了。

林德夫人:不,尼尔斯,你可千万别把信要回来。

克罗格斯塔德:老实告诉我,你要我来这儿见你,不就是为了这件事吗?

林德夫人:最初,我感到害怕,心里确实有这个打算。可是,现在一天已经过去了,而就在这一天里,我在这户人家目睹了一些匪夷所思的现象,所以必须让海默了解真相,必须把这个令人不愉快的秘密揭露出来,让他们夫妻之间达成彻底的谅解——藏藏掖掖、遮遮掩掩的话,是不可能彻底谅解对方的。

克罗格斯塔德:很好,要是你愿意担负起这个责任,那就这么做吧。不过有一件事我能做,我这就去做。

林德夫人:(竖起耳朵细听)你快走!快走!舞会散了,咱们再耽搁下去就坏了。

克罗格斯塔德:我在街上等你。

林德夫人:好,我回家时一定要你送我呢。

克罗格斯塔德:真是喜从天降!我从来没像今天一样觉得自己这么幸运过!(从大门走了出去,该房间和大厅之间的门敞开着)

林德夫人:(整理房间,把自己的衣帽准备好)多大的变化啊!多大的变化!现在我的工作有了目标,我的生活有了意义——我要给一个家庭带去温暖!我要脚踏实地地为之奋斗。但愿他们快回来吧!(竖起耳朵细听)啊,他们来啦!我得先穿戴好。(拿起自己的衣帽。外边传来了海默和娜拉说话的声音。钥匙一转,娜拉几乎是被海默硬拉了进来。娜拉穿着意大利服装,裹着一条黑色大披肩。海默身穿晚礼服,外面套着一件附带假面具的黑舞衣,敞着怀没扣好。)

娜拉:(在门口朝后退,想从海默手里挣脱)不,不,不!我不进去!我还要上楼去跳舞。我不愿意这么早回家。

海默:可是,亲爱的娜拉——

娜拉:求求你啦,亲爱的托瓦尔德,求求你啦,求求你啦!咱们再跳一个小时就回来。

海默:一分钟都不行,我的宝贝娜拉。你知道这是咱们事先说好的。快进来,站在这儿你会着凉的。(不顾娜拉的反对,轻轻一把将她拽了进来)

林德夫人:晚上好!

娜拉:克里斯蒂娜!

海默:这么晚了你还来,林德夫人?

林德夫人:是的,请你别见怪。我一心想看看娜拉是怎么打扮的。

娜拉:你一直在这儿等我们?

林德夫人:是的,我不幸来迟了一步,来时你们已经上楼了。我觉得自己不看你一眼就无法离去。

海默:(把娜拉的披肩取下来)看吧,你好好看看她吧。我认为她值得一看。林德夫人,她是不是很迷人?

林德夫人:迷人,的确很迷人。

海默:她简直漂亮极了!舞会上人人都这么说。不过,这个可爱的小家伙就是太任性了。你说该怎么办?你恐怕难以相信,我差不多是硬把她拽回来的。

娜拉:托瓦尔德,你哪怕让我再待半个小时也好,将来你一定会后悔。

海默:你听听她的话,林德夫人!她跳完了塔兰泰拉舞,大家热烈鼓掌,这也是应该的,她跳得确实不错。只不过她的表演有点儿太逼真了——我的意思是,严格地说,有点儿超过了艺术标准。不过,这些不必计较。重要的是,她获得了成功,大家都夸她。你觉得大家鼓完掌之后,我还能让她待着不走,削弱那种轰动效应吗?不,绝对不能!于是,我拽住我迷人的意大利小姑娘,或者应该说是任性的意大利小姑娘,挽起她的胳膊,很快地绕场一周,向观众鞠躬致谢——然后,就像小说里描绘的那样,美丽的小精灵突然消失了。退场应该讲究效应,林德夫人。可我就是无法让娜拉明白这个道理。嗬,这屋里怎么这么热!(将他的舞衣扔到一把椅子上,推开书房的门)哇!里面怎么这么黑!哦,当然喽。失陪了。(他走进书房,点亮了蜡烛。)

娜拉:(急切地喘着粗气问)怎么样啦?

林德夫人:(低声回答)我跟他谈过了。

娜拉:那么——

林德夫人:娜拉,你必须把一切都告诉你丈夫。

娜拉:(平淡地)我早就知道会这样。

林德夫人:至于克罗格斯塔德那里,你一点儿都不用担心。但你必须把实情都告诉你丈夫。

娜拉:我绝不告诉他。

林德夫人:那么,那封信会告诉他的。

娜拉:谢谢你,克里斯蒂娜。我知道自己该怎么做。嘘!

海默:(从书房出来)怎么样,林德夫人,你把她仔细欣赏过没有?

林德夫人:欣赏过了。现在我得走了。

海默:怎么,这就要走?这块编织的东西是你的吧?

林德夫人:(把编织活计接过来)是的,谢谢,我差点儿忘了。

海默：你会编织？

林德夫人：当然。

海默：你应该学刺绣，知道吗？

林德夫人：是吗？为什么？

海默：因为刺绣的时候姿态要好看得多。容我做给你看。你左手拿绣片，右手拿绣花针，就像这样，一针又一针，动作飘逸。看见了吧？

林德夫人：看见了。也许——

海默：可是编织东西就不一样了，姿势难看得要命。瞧，就这样，把两条胳膊夹得紧紧的，织针一上一下，有点儿中国味儿。刚才喝的香槟酒味道真是不错。

林德夫人：是吗？再见，娜拉，你可不要再任性了。

海默：说得对，林德夫人！

林德夫人：再见，海默先生。

海默：（送她到门口）再见，再见。祝你一路平安。你住的地方不远，不然我很乐意送送你。再见，再见。（她走了出去；海默关上大门，又回到了房间里。）唉！总算把瘟神送走了。这个女人真是讨厌极了。

娜拉：你累坏了吧，托瓦尔德？

海默：一点儿都不累。

娜拉：也不瞌睡？

海默：一点儿都不瞌睡。恰恰相反，我觉得精神头儿特别大。你呢？你看上去倒是又累又困。

娜拉：是的，我非常累，真想马上就去睡觉。

海默：你看！我不让你再跳舞是正确的决定吧？

娜拉：你所做的一切都非常正确，托瓦尔德。

海默：（亲她的前额）现在我的小云雀说出的话倒是很合乎情理哟。今天晚上兰克兴高采烈的，你注意到了没有？

娜拉：真的？他很高兴？我没跟他说话，所以没注意到。

海默：我跟他说的话也很少，但我好久都没见他有这么高的兴致了。（对她看了一会儿，把身子凑过去）回到自己家里，和你单独在一起，真是令人高兴，你这个叫人心醉、迷人心窍的小宝贝！

娜拉：别那么瞧我，托瓦尔德。

海默：我为什么就不能瞧一瞧我最亲爱的人儿？为什么就不能瞧一瞧我的美人，一个只属于我的美人？

娜拉：（走到桌子的另一侧）今天晚上你可不要对我说这样的话。

海默：（跟过来）看得出，你血管里还在跳塔兰泰拉舞，这让你看上去比以往任何时候都更加迷人。你听，楼上的客人要走了。（声音放低些）娜拉，这整幢楼房很快就会静下来的。

娜拉：是的，但愿如此。

海默：我亲爱的娜拉，每当咱们出去参加这样的聚会，我都很少跟你说话，而是远离你身旁，只是时不时朝你那儿偷看一眼。你可知道原因何在？你知道我为什么那样做吗？那是因为我坚信你我彼此在心里暗暗爱着对方，你就像是和我私订终身的情侣，咱们之间的感情是不容置疑的。

娜拉：是的，是的，我非常清楚你的心一直都和我在一起。

海默：到了要回家的时候，我把披肩搭上你那散发出青春魅力的美丽肩膀，围住你那可爱的脖颈，这时我会浮想联翩，觉得咱们就像是新婚宴尔，刚刚举办过婚礼，我头一次把你带回家——头一次单独跟你待在一块儿，头一次跟我害羞的小宝贝单独在一起！今天晚上，我心里什么都没有想，只想着你。看看你那性感的塔兰泰拉舞姿，我热血沸腾，于是早早就拉你下了楼。

娜拉：走开，托瓦尔德！松开我。我不愿意——

海默：什么？你这是在开玩笑吗，我的小娜拉？你不愿意，你不愿意？我可是你的丈夫呀！（外边传来了敲门声。）

娜拉：（吃惊）你听见没有？

海默：（走到大厅里）谁呀？

兰克：（在外面）是我。我能不能进去坐一会儿？

海默：（低声嘀咕）咦，这时候他还来干什么？（高声）等一等！（开门）进来吧，你可是不请自来。

兰克：我似乎听见你们在说话，就觉得还是进来看看的好。（飞快地环视一周）啊，多好啊！多么熟悉的地方啊！你们俩住在这里可真是又开心又舒服啊！

海默：刚才在楼上，我觉得你好像也很幸福哟。

兰克：一点儿不错。我为什么就不该幸福一些？人生在世，就该及时行乐嘛。只要有条件，只要有时间，就应该好好享受。今晚的酒堪称佳酿。

海默：味道尤其好的是香槟酒。

兰克：你也觉得好？我喝了那么多，简直叫人无法相信！

娜拉：托瓦尔德今晚喝的香槟酒也不少。

兰克：是吗？

娜拉：是的，他每次三杯酒落肚，就会兴致勃勃的。

兰克：辛苦了一天，晚上难道不该享受享受吗？

海默：辛苦？这种评价我恐怕担当不起。

兰克：（在他的背上拍了一下）要知道，我可是能担当得起。

娜拉：兰克医生，你今天一定是忙着搞科学研究了。

兰克：一点儿不错。

海默：你听听吧！小娜拉也谈论起科学研究来了！

娜拉：结果怎么样？是不是应该对你表示祝贺？

兰克：的确应该。

娜拉：这么说，结果很好？

兰克：不管对医生还是病人，都好得不能再好啦，这是毋庸置疑的。

娜拉：（很快追问道）毋庸置疑？

兰克：绝对毋庸置疑。有了这样的结果，难道我就不该在晚上快活快活吗？

娜拉：应该，当然应该，兰克医生。

海默：我也认为应该，只要你明天早晨别喊头疼就行。

兰克：这个嘛，在生活中干什么事情都是有代价的。

娜拉：兰克医生，你喜欢今晚的化装舞会吗？

兰克：是的，只要有漂亮的服装，我就喜欢。

娜拉：我问你，下次化装舞会咱们俩该怎么装扮才好？

海默：不懂事的孩子！已经想到下次化装舞会啦？

兰克：你问咱们俩该怎么装扮？我可以告诉你：你应该装扮成仙女。

海默：是的。可你觉得装扮成仙女应该穿什么衣服才合适呢？

兰克：让你妻子穿平时的衣服最合适。

海默：这话说得真好。能不能告诉我们，你准备装扮成什么样的角色？

兰克：可以告诉你们，我的好朋友，我已经有了自己的打算。

海默：什么打算？

兰克：下次开化装舞会的时候，我要扮隐身人。

海默：这话真逗！

兰克：有一种硕大的黑帽子可以叫人隐身，你没听说过吗？你只要一戴上那种帽子，别人就看不见你了。

海默：（忍住笑）是呀，一点儿不错。

兰克：哦，我忘了进来要干什么了。海默，给我一支雪茄——要那种黑黑的哈瓦那雪茄。

海默：请吧！（把雪茄烟盒递过去）

兰克：（拿了一支雪茄，把烟头切掉）谢谢。

娜拉：（给他划火柴）让我给你点着吧。

兰克：谢谢。（娜拉拿着火柴，兰克就着火点烟。）现在我要跟你们告别了！

海默：再见，再见，老伙计！

娜拉：愿你睡个好觉，兰克医生。

兰克：谢谢你的祝愿。

娜拉：你也应该对我有同样的祝愿。

兰克：祝你？那好，也愿你睡个好觉！谢谢你为我点烟。（冲他们，点点头，走了出去）

海默：（压低声音）他不该喝那么多酒。

娜拉：（心不在焉）也许吧。（海默从衣袋里掏出一串钥匙走进大厅。）托瓦尔德，你到那儿干什么？

海默：我去清理一下信箱，里面都满了，明天早晨送报纸来都没地方放了。

娜拉：今晚你工作不工作？

海默：你明明知道我今晚是不会工作的。这是怎么回事？有人动过这锁。

娜拉：动过锁？

海默：是的，是有人动过。这是怎么回事？我想绝不会是女佣——这儿有只断了的发夹。娜拉，这是你的发夹。

娜拉：（急忙接嘴）一定是孩子们干的。

海默：那你得管管他们，叫他们别这么调皮。好啦，终于把信箱打开了。（取出信箱里的东西，冲厨房那儿喊道）海伦！海伦，你去把门厅的灯熄灭！（回到房间里，关上通向大厅的那扇门，把手里的信往前一摊）你瞧，这么一大堆信。（把整叠信件翻过来）哦，这是什么？

娜拉：（在窗口）是那封信。不！托瓦尔德，你别看！

海默：是两张名片——是兰克医生的。

娜拉：兰克医生的？

海默：（看了看名片）是兰克医生的。这两张名片放在最上头，一定是他出门时扔进去的。

娜拉：名片上写着什么没有？

海默：他的名字上头有个黑色的十字。你瞧，多么不吉利！看上去就好像他自报死讯。

娜拉：他正是这意思。

海默：什么？你知道这事？他跟你说过什么没有？

娜拉：他说了，说给咱们这样的名片就意味着他要跟咱们永别了。他打算把自己关在屋里，悄悄地死去。

海默：我可怜的老朋友呀！我早就知道他将不久于人世，但没想到会这么快！他就像一只受了伤的动物，悄悄地爬进窝里藏了起来。

娜拉：一个人到了非死不可的时候，最好还是静悄悄地死。托瓦尔德，你说对不对？

海默：（走来走去）他已经融入了咱们的生活，简直无法想象他会永远地离开。他的痛苦和孤独跟咱们阳光灿烂的幸福生活相比，就好像是乌云衬托着太阳。唉，也许这是最好的结局，至少对他来说如此。（站住）大概对咱们也是如此，娜拉。现在只剩下咱们俩了。（张开双臂搂住她）我亲爱的妻子，我怎么搂你都觉得搂得不够紧。你可知道，娜拉，我常常希望你会遇到大灾大难，好让我冒着生命危险，不顾一切地冲上前去救你。

娜拉：（从他怀里挣出来，语气坚定地说）现在你可以看信了，托瓦尔德。

海默：不，不，今晚我不看信。今晚我要陪着你，我亲爱的妻子。

娜拉：你的朋友就要死了，你还有心情陪我？

海默：你说得对。这件事对你我都是打击，是咱们必须面对的丑陋事实——一想到死亡就让人不寒而栗。咱们必须努力忘掉这件事情。睡觉吧，都各自回房间睡觉吧。

娜拉：（搂住他的脖子）晚安，托瓦尔德，晚安！

海默：（亲她的前额）晚安，我的小鸟儿。祝你睡个好觉，娜拉。我要去看信了。（他拿着那些信走进书房，随手关上了门。）

娜拉：（茫然地四处摸索，抓起海默的舞衣穿在身上，以快速、沙哑、断断续续的声音低声说道）再也见不着他了！永远，永远也见不着啦！（把披肩蒙在头上）永远见不着我的孩子们啦！永远，永远见不着啦！啊，就要沉入冰冷、漆黑、深不见底的水里了！但愿灾难会烟消云散！现在他已经拿着信了，正在看！别了，托瓦尔德！别了，我的孩子们！（她正要举步穿过大厅跑出去，却见海默哗啦一声将书房的门拉开了，手里拿着一封信站在那里。）

海默：娜拉！

娜拉：啊！

海默：这是什么？你知道这封信里说的是什么吗？

娜拉：知道，我知道。快让我走！让我出去！

海默：（拉住她）你上哪儿去！

娜拉：（竭力想脱身）你救不了我的，托瓦尔德！

海默：（惊慌地倒退）这是真的吗？信里写的事情是真的吗？太可怕了！不，不，这不可能是真的。

娜拉：全是真的。我爱你胜过这个世界上的一切。

海默：哼，别这么花言巧语的了！

娜拉：（走近他一步）托瓦尔德！

海默：你这个可怜虫——瞧你干的好事！

娜拉：让我走。一人做事一人当，我不会连累你的。

海默：请别再演戏，摆出一副大义凛然的样子了。（把大厅的门锁上）不许你出去，给我好好解释一下。你知道自己捅了多么大的娄子吗？回答我！你知道自己捅了多么大的娄子吗？！

娜拉：（目光坚定地望着他，脸上的表情越来越冷静）是的，现在我才彻底知道了。

海默：（走来走去）真像是做了一场噩梦醒过来！整整八年——我一直最喜欢、最得意的女人——原来是个伪君子，是个骗子——甚至比这更坏，是个罪犯！真是太丑恶了！可耻！可耻！（娜拉不作声，目光坚定地望着他。他走到她面前，停了下来。）我早就应该想到会出这种事，早就应该有所预见。你父亲就缺乏做人的原则——你给我住嘴！——上梁不正下梁歪，有其父必有其女嘛。不信宗教，不讲道德，缺乏责任心！当初我为他遮掩，现在遭到了报应！那时为了你，我出手相助，而这就是你对我的报答！

娜拉：不错，是这样的。

海默：你毁掉了我的幸福，葬送了我的前程。想一想真是令人毛骨悚然！现在，我被一个不择手段的人握在了手心里，他想怎么摆布我就怎么摆布我，他要什么我就得给什么,要我干什么我就得干什么——我哪里敢拒绝。因为一个缺心眼儿的女人,我就沦落到如此悲惨的境地!

娜拉:我死了你就解脱了。

海默:别说漂亮话了。你父亲也是这样,说起话来天花乱坠。如你所说,即便你死了,对我又有什么好处?一点儿好处都没有。他照样可以把事情公布出去,弄得我背黑锅,让人家怀疑我和你沆瀣一气,参与了你干的坏事。人们很可能还会认为我是幕后主使,是我唆使你那么干的!这些事情我都得感谢你——结婚这么多年,我一直疼你爱你,想不到你就这样感谢我!你现在明白你的所作所为给我带来多么严重的后果了吗?

娜拉:(冷静地、不动声色地)我明白。

海默:真是意想不到,让我实在接受不了。当务之急是必须商量出个对策来。你把披肩摘下来。摘下来,听见没有!我先得想个办法稳住他。这件事无论如何都必须压下来。至于你和我,必须跟从前一样过日子——那自然只是做给别人看的。当然,你还得继续住在我家里。不过,我不会允许你再教育孩子;我不敢再把他们交给你教育。想不到我不得不对一个我深深爱着的人说这种话,一个我仍然——算啦,一切都完了。从现在起,不会有什么幸福可言了,你我要操心的是如何挽救这个家,如何收拾残局、保住颜面——

〔前门的门铃响了。〕

海默:(吓了一跳)怎么回事?都这么晚了!难道发生了最坏的情况——?难道他会——?你快藏起来,娜拉!

我就说你病了。

〔娜拉站着没动。海默走过去打开大厅的门。〕

女佣:(披着衣服走到门口)有一封信是给夫人的。

海默:交给我吧。(把信接过来,关上了门)是的,真是他来的信。不能把它给你,我要先看看。

娜拉:好吧,那你就看吧。

海默:(站到灯旁)我真有点儿不敢看,说不定咱俩都得完蛋。不行,我必须看。(拆开信,看了几行之后发现信里夹着一张纸,马上快活得叫了起来)娜拉!(娜拉莫名其妙地看着他。)娜拉!别急,让我再看一遍!不错,这是真的!我得救啦!娜拉,我得救啦!

娜拉:我呢?

海默:你当然也得救了,咱们俩都得救了,你和我都平安无事了。瞧,他把借条还你了。他说他为此事感到很抱歉,后悔得不得了,还说他的生活柳暗花明,发生了可喜的转变——算啦,别管他说什么了!咱们没事啦,娜拉!任何人都不能威胁你啦!啊,娜拉,娜拉!等一等,先让我把这害人的东西烧了再说。噢,让我再看看——(朝着借条瞟了一眼)不,不,我不想再看它。这件事对我来说简直就是一场噩梦。(把借条和克罗格斯塔德的两封信全都撕碎扔进炉子里,看着它们化为灰烬)好啦,它们已不复存在啦。他说自从圣诞节前夕你就——这三天对你而言一定非常可怕,娜拉。

娜拉:这三天我过得就像是打了一场恶仗。

海默:你痛苦万分,找不到出路,只能——那些可怕的事情咱们就不要再想了，应该欢呼雀跃才对，多说几遍："一切都过去了！一切都过去了！"听我说，娜拉，你似乎还不明白暴风雨已经过去了。你为什么绷着脸，一副冷冰冰的表情？我可怜的小娜拉，我非常理解你——你好像还无法相信我已经宽恕你了。但这是真的，娜拉，我发誓，我宽恕你所做的一切。我知道你那样做是为了我，是因为爱我。

娜拉：是这样的。

海默：你对我的爱是一个妻子对丈夫应有的爱。只不过由于缺乏经验，你采用了错误的方式。不过，不要以为你自作主张，采取了错误的行动就会减少我对你的爱！不会的，不会的。以后你尽管依赖我，我会为你出谋划策，为你指明方向。正因为你无助，所以在我眼里你格外迷人，要不然我还算什么男子汉大丈夫？刚才我觉得好像天都要塌下来了，心里一害怕，就说了一些难听的话，你千万别放在心上。我已经宽恕你了，娜拉，我发誓已经宽恕你了。

娜拉：谢谢你的宽恕。（从右边的门走出去）

海默：别走！（向门里张望）你在那儿干什么？

娜拉：（在里屋）脱掉化装舞会服装。

海默：（站在敞开的门旁）好，脱掉吧。我的小鸟儿受到了惊吓，现在就冷静冷静，把心静下来吧。你放心好啦，不会有事的，我的翅膀又宽又大，能够为你遮风挡雨。（在门口来回踱步）咱们的家多暖和，多舒适啊，娜拉。这里就是你的避风港。在这里，我会保护你，就像保护一只从鹰爪下救出来的小鸽子一样。我会让你那颗扑扑乱跳的心平静下来——你的心会逐渐恢复平静的,娜拉,相信我好啦。明天早晨,你的精神面貌就会焕然一新,一切很快便会恢复常态。过不了多久,就不用我再重复地说我已经宽恕你了,因为那时你将切切实实感受到我的宽恕。你以为我真的会撵你,或者责备你吗?那你是不明白一个男人心里真正的感受,娜拉。如果一个男人宽恕了自己的妻子——完全彻底、真心实意地宽恕了她,那他就会有一种无法形容的甜蜜、满足的感觉。他会觉得是他塑造了她,觉得她对他的依附感会加倍;可以说他给了她新的生命,因而从某种程度而言,她既是他的妻子又是他的孩子。从今往后,你既是我的妻子又是我的孩子,我吓坏了的可怜的小宝贝。以后什么都不要你操心,娜拉,你只要对我开诚布公就可以了,我将全心全意、鞠躬尽瘁地为你效力——怎么?你还不睡觉?又换衣服做什么?

娜拉:(穿着平时的衣服)不错,托瓦尔德,我换了衣服。

海默:为什么?天都这么晚了!

娜拉:今晚我不睡觉。

海默:可是,我亲爱的娜拉——

娜拉:(看看自己的手表)还不算太晚。请坐下,托瓦尔德,你我之间有许多话要谈谈。(她在桌子的一头坐下。)

海默:娜拉,这是什么意思?你的脸色又冰又冷,像一块铁板。

娜拉:你坐下,三言两语是说不完的。我心里有很多话要对你讲一讲。

海默:(在桌子另一头坐下)你把我吓了一大跳,娜拉!我实在不了解你。

娜拉:是的,一点儿不错,你的确不了解我,我也是直到今晚才真正了解你。请你不要插话,你只管听就行了,等我把话说完。托瓦尔德,今天咱们就来个彻底了结吧。

海默:这话是什么意思?

娜拉:(沉吟片刻)咱们像这样坐在一起,你不觉得反常吗?

海默:怎么反常?

娜拉:咱们结婚已经八年了,你和我,丈夫和妻子,这还是第一次坐下来认真交谈,你不觉得反常吗?

海默:你说的"认真"是什么意思?

娜拉:这八年里——要是从咱们认识的时候算起,其实还不止八年,你我从未就任何正经的事情交流过。

海默:难道要我经常对你说一些你帮不上忙的麻烦事吗?

娜拉:我指的不是你工作上的事情。我是说,咱们从未一起坐下来,认真商量过任何事情。

海默:可是,我至亲至爱的娜拉,那样做对你有好处吗?

娜拉:问题就出在这里。你从来就没了解过我。我受尽了委屈,托瓦尔德——先是受爸爸的委屈,接下来又受你的委屈。

海默:这是什么话!你父亲和我——我们俩爱你胜过

这个世界上的任何人，你还说受了委屈？

娜拉：（摇摇头）你们从未爱过我，只是觉得爱我会给你们带来愉悦。

海默：娜拉，你在说什么？

娜拉：这完全是事实，托瓦尔德。在我出嫁前我跟爸爸一起生活，他说什么就是什么，我必须服从，即便心里有看法也不敢说出来，因为那会叫他不高兴。他把我叫作"宝贝娃娃"，将我当作一个玩具，就像我对待我的布娃娃一样。后来我和你在一起生活——

海默：你怎么能用这样的语言形容咱们的夫妻生活呢？

娜拉：（不为所动）我是说，我从爸爸手里转移到了你手里。所有的一切都按照你的喜好进行安排，你的好恶就是我的好恶，或者说我得假装是我的好恶。实际上我已不确定自己的真实感受了，有时是这样，有时是那样。回想起来，我觉得自己活得就像一个可怜的女人，只能靠别人的施舍过日子。我活着仅仅是为了取悦你们，托瓦尔德，为了表演把戏给你们看。你们喜欢看到我这样。你和我爸爸可把我害苦了。由于你们的过错，我的生活毫无意义。

海默：你真是不讲道理、忘恩负义，娜拉！难道你在这里生活得不幸福吗？

娜拉：是的，我从来就没有幸福过。我曾经觉得自己很幸福，其实根本不幸福。

海默：什么！你不幸福！

娜拉：不错，只是有些快活罢了，因为你一直对我都很好。不过,咱们家只不过是个游戏室——我是你的"布娃娃"妻子,正如我出嫁前是我爸爸的"布娃娃"孩子那样,而咱们的孩子则是我的"布娃娃"。你逗我玩儿的时候,我感到很快活;而我逗他们玩儿的时候,他们同样感到十分快活。这就是咱们的夫妻生活,托瓦尔德。

海默:你的话虽然有点儿夸大其词,按你自己的看法扭曲了事实,但也不无道理。不过,以后会有所改观——玩耍游戏将会结束,授课时间将会开始。

娜拉:给谁授课?给我还是给孩子们?

海默:既给你授课,也给孩子们授课,我亲爱的娜拉。

娜拉:唉,托瓦尔德,你不配教我做一个乖顺的贤妻良母。

海默:你怎么能这么说!

娜拉:我——我配教育孩子们吗?

海默:娜拉!

娜拉:这是你刚刚说过的话,说你不敢把他们交给我教育,难道不是吗?

海默:那是气头上的话!为什么老提这句呢?

娜拉:其实你的话一点儿都没说错,我不配教育孩子。还有一件事情是我必须做的,那就是自我教育。在这方面你是帮不了我的,我得自己去完成。所以,现在我必须离开你。

海默:(跳起来)你说什么?

娜拉:要想了解我自己和我周围的环境,我就得一个人过日子。正是出于这个原因,我不能再留在你身边了。

海默：娜拉！娜拉！

娜拉：我现在就走，立刻就走。我相信克里斯蒂娜一定会留我过夜的。

海默：你疯了！我不让你走！不许你走！

娜拉：不许我走已经不顶用了。我只带自己的东西。你的东西我一件都不要，现在不要，以后也不要。

海默：你怎么疯到这般田地！

娜拉：明天我要回家去——回到从前的老家去。在那儿找点事情做是极其容易的。

海默：好一个盲目的、没脑子的女人！

娜拉：我会努力做一个有脑子的女人的，托瓦尔德。

海默：就这么丢下你的家庭、丈夫和儿女！你不想想外人会怎么说！

娜拉：我考虑不了这么多，只知道自己应该这么做。

海默：实在叫人吃惊。对于自己最为神圣的职责，你怎么能就这样抛下不管呢？

娜拉：依你看，我最为神圣的职责是什么？

海默：那还用我说？对你的丈夫和儿女尽职，不就是你最为神圣的职责吗？

娜拉：我还有别的职责，也同样神圣。

海默：绝对不会有的。你说那是什么职责？

娜拉：是对我自己尽职。

海默：你首先要尽的是妻子之职、母亲之职。

娜拉：这些话现在我再也不相信了。我相信的是：首先，我是一个有理性的人，跟你是一样的——因而我无论如何都要努力争取做一个有独立人格的人。我心里很清楚，托瓦尔德，大多数人都认为你是对的，书本上也是这么说的，但我再也不会满足于听从大多数人的观点以及书本上所讲的道理，而要独立思考，亲自去了解。

海默：难道你不明白你在家里有着多么重要的地位吗？难道在诸如此类的问题上，没有颠扑不破的道理可以作为你的向导吗？难道你不信仰宗教吗？

娜拉：托瓦尔德，恐怕我真的不明白宗教为何物。

海默：你说什么？

娜拉：除了受坚信礼①时牧师说的那些话，对于别的方面我一无所知。牧师时而说宗教是这样的，时而又说是那样的，没有个定数。当我离开这里一个人静下心来时，也要好好思考思考宗教问题，看看牧师的话是否正确，或者说看看宗教是否适合我。

海默：想不到你这个岁数的人还说这种话！不过，假如宗教不能作为你的指路明灯，那就让我试试别的办法吧，看看能不能唤醒你做人的良心。你大概还有点儿道德观念吧？如果你没有的话，就说没有。请回答我的问题。

娜拉：请相信我，托瓦尔德，这个问题不容易回答。我实在不明白什么是道德观念，仅仅对此感到迷茫和困惑。我只知道你我看待这个问题时，有着完全不同的角度。我还知道，所谓的法律跟我所想的大相径庭，我无法让自己相信这样的法律是正确的。按照这样的法律，一个女人无

---

① 一种基督教仪式。根据基督教教义，孩子十三岁时受坚信礼。只有被施坚信礼后，才能成为教会正式教徒。

权为自己生命垂危的老父亲省去麻烦,也无权挽救自己丈夫的性命。这样的法律叫我无法相信。

海默:你说这些话像个小孩子。你不了解你所生存的这个世界是个什么样的世界。

娜拉:是的,我不了解。但我现在要努力了解它。我要看看自己是否能搞清楚,究竟是这个世界正确,还是我正确。

海默:你病了,娜拉,在发烧说胡话。我看你好像精神错乱了。

娜拉:我的脑子从来没有像今天晚上这么清醒过。

海默:你丢下丈夫和儿女离家出走,能说是脑子清醒吗?

娜拉:是的,一点儿没错。

海默:这么说,这其中可能只有一个原因。

娜拉:什么原因?

海默:那就是你不再爱我了。

娜拉:是的,正是这样。

海默:娜拉!你怎么能说出这话!

娜拉:我这样说,心里是很痛苦的,托瓦尔德,因为你一直对我都很好,但不这样说又不行。我的确不再爱你了。

海默:(恢复了镇静)你说这话,脑子也是清醒的吗?

娜拉:是的,非常清醒。所以我不能再在这儿待下去了。

海默:是否能说一说我究竟做错了什么,才使得你放弃了对我的爱?

娜拉:可以,完全可以。今天晚上,那件奇妙的事情没有发生。也就是在那个时候,我发现你并非我想象中的那种人。

海默:我听不明白,请你再说清楚点。

娜拉:我耐着性子整整等了八年——我当然非常清楚,奇迹不会天天有。后来大祸临头的时候,我却十分肯定奇迹终于要发生了。克罗格斯塔德把信扔在信箱里以后,我怎么也想不到你会同意接受他的条件。我满以为你一定会对他说:你愿意把此事公布于众,那就公布吧。而且说完这句话之后,你还会——

海默:还会怎样?难道我要让自己的妻子出丑丢脸,让她蒙羞受辱?

娜拉:你说了那句话之后,我满以为你会挺身而出,自己承担一切责任,说一句:一人做事一人当,都是我干的。

海默:娜拉!

娜拉:你想说我是绝不会同意让你做自我牺牲吧?是的,我当然不会。可是,我说的话怎么比得上你说的话那么能令人相信!那正是我既盼望发生又害怕发生的奇迹——为了阻止它的发生,我想过自杀。

海默:我愿意为你不分日夜地工作,娜拉,愿意为你受穷受苦。可是,没有一个男人愿意为他所爱的女人牺牲自己的荣誉。

娜拉:而千千万万的女人则为男人牺牲了她们的荣誉。

海默:噢,你思考问题和说话都像一个冒冒失失的孩子。

娜拉：也许是吧。而你思考问题和说话则不像一个我可以托付终身的男子汉。你的恐惧感一消失——不是为我受到威胁而恐惧，而是怕你自己会受到牵连，当威胁到你的暴风雨一停息，你就恢复了原样，就好像什么事情都没发生过一样。一切又跟从前一样了——我又成了你的小云雀、布娃娃，今后你会加倍地精心照料我，因为我太脆弱了。（站起来）托瓦尔德，直到那个时候我才明白，原来我和一个陌生人在一起生活了八年，还给他生了三个孩子。唉！真是想都不敢想！我真恨不得把自己撕成碎片！

海默：（伤心地）我明白了，我明白了，在咱们中间出现了一道深沟——这是不可否认的。可是，娜拉，难道就不能填平这道沟吗？

娜拉：照我现在这样子，我不能再做你的妻子了。

海默：我一定会洗心革面、重新做人的。

娜拉：也许吧——你的布娃娃离开你之后，也许你会。

海默：要我跟你分手？要我跟你分手？不，不，娜拉，我不明白为什么要这样做。

娜拉：（走向右边的房间）不管你明白不明白，都必须这样做。（回来时，她手里拿着外套、帽子和一个小包。她把这些东西搁在桌子旁边的椅子上。）

海默：娜拉，娜拉，现在别走！明天再走吧。

娜拉：（穿外套）我不能在陌生人家里过夜。

海默：难道咱们不能像兄妹那样在这儿过日子吗？

娜拉：（戴帽子）你很清楚那种日子长不了。（围披肩）

托瓦尔德，再见。我不去看孩子了。我知道现在照管他们的人比我强。照我现在这样子，我对他们一点儿用处都没有。

　　海默：可是，将来总有一天，娜拉，将来总有一天，对吧？

　　娜拉：我怎么能知道呢？我心里没数，不知道自己将来会怎么样。

　　海默：不管将来怎么样，你仍然是我的妻子。

　　娜拉：托瓦尔德，我告诉你，我听人说，要是一个女人像我这样离开夫家，按法律讲，就解除了丈夫对她的所有义务。反正不管怎样，我现在把你对我的义务全部解除了。你可千万不要觉得受到我的哪怕一丁点儿的约束，我也不受你约束。双方都有绝对的自由。拿去，这是你的戒指。把我的也还我。

　　海默：连戒指都要还？

　　娜拉：要还。

　　海默：那拿去吧。

　　娜拉：好。现在一切都结束了。我把钥匙放在这儿。家里的事，用人都知道——她们比我更熟悉。明天，我离开克里斯蒂娜那儿之后，她会到这里来，把我从娘家带来的东西打包带走。到时候，我会叫她把东西寄到我的落脚地。

　　海默：一切都结束了！一切都结束了！娜拉，你永远也不会再想念我了吧？

　　娜拉：我会时常想到你，想到孩子们和这个家。

海默：我可以给你写信吗，娜拉？

娜拉：不，千万别写信。

海默：可是，至少容我给你寄点儿——

娜拉：不用，什么都不用寄。

海默：如果你遇到困难，请允许我帮助你。

娜拉：不必，我不接受陌生人的帮助。

海默：娜拉，对你来说，难道我永远只是个陌生人？

娜拉：（拿起手提包）唉，托瓦尔德，那就要等奇迹中的奇迹发生了。

海默：请告诉我，那究竟是什么！

娜拉：你我都必须脱胎换骨，变成完全不同的人——唉，托瓦尔德，我现在已不再相信会有奇迹发生了。

海默：可是我信。你说下去！咱们俩都得改变到什么样子？

娜拉：改变到你我能成为举案齐眉、相敬如宾的夫妻！再见。（她穿过大厅走了出去。）

海默：（瘫倒在靠门的一把椅子上，双手捂住脸）娜拉！娜拉！（四面望望，站起身来）屋子空了。她走了。（心头闪过一线希望）奇迹中的奇迹——？

〔楼下的大门砰的一声关上了。〕

（剧终）

人民公敌

人物表

托马斯·斯托克曼医生，市政温泉浴场的卫生官员

斯托克曼夫人，医生的妻子

佩特拉，教师，医生夫妇的女儿

叶利夫和墨顿，医生夫妇的两个儿子，一个十三岁，一个十岁

彼得·斯托克曼，医生的哥哥，市长，兼任警察局长和浴场委员会主席等职

墨顿·基尔，斯托克曼夫人的养父，制革厂厂主

霍夫斯塔德，《人民信使报》编辑

比林，助理编辑

霍斯特船长

阿斯拉克森，印刷厂老板

参加市民大会的群众，各种身份、各行各业的人，几位妇女，一群学生

（故事发生在挪威南部的一座沿海城市里）

第一幕

布景:斯托克曼医生家的客厅。傍晚。室内陈设虽然朴素,却布置得简单而整洁,家具齐全。右墙有两扇门,靠后的一扇通到大厅,靠前的一扇通到医生的书房。左面墙上,到大厅去的那扇门的正对面有一道门通向其他的房间——家庭成员各自的卧室。贴着左墙正中,有一只火炉。再往前走,有一张沙发。沙发上方挂着一面镜子,前面放着一张椭圆形的桌子。桌上点着一盏带罩的灯。后墙有扇敞着的门通往餐厅。餐桌上有一盏灯,只见比林坐在桌旁,下巴那儿披着餐巾,而斯托克曼夫人站在桌旁,正在把一大盘烤牛肉递给他。其他的位子都空着,桌上杯盘狼藉,显然是有人刚吃过饭。

斯托克曼夫人:瞧,比林先生,你晚来了一个小时,就只好吃冷肉了。

比林:(大嚼大咽)这肉味道很好,简直好极了,香喷喷的。

斯托克曼夫人：你知道，我丈夫是掐着钟点吃饭的，非常准时。

比林：没关系的。其实，我倒觉得这么一个人坐着，没人干扰，吃饭更香。

斯托克曼夫人：那就好，只要你高兴就行——（转过身去听大厅里的动静）大概霍夫斯塔德先生也来了。

比林：很可能是的。

〔彼得·斯托克曼市长走了进来，身上穿着外套，头上戴着礼帽，手里拿着手杖。〕

彼得·斯托克曼：晚上好，凯瑟琳。

斯托克曼夫人：（迎上前，进了客厅）啊，晚上好——原来是你！谢谢你来看我们！

彼得·斯托克曼：我碰巧路过这儿，所以——（眼睛望着餐厅）看得出你们在请客。

斯托克曼夫人：（有点儿窘迫）不是请客——他只是碰巧赶上，随便吃点儿。（急忙又说）你也进去吃点儿吧？

彼得·斯托克曼：我？不了，谢谢。嗬，我怎敢晚上吃烤肉！哪能消化得了！

斯托克曼夫人：噢，偶尔吃一点儿也没什么。

彼得·斯托克曼：不行，不行，我的好弟妹。我晚上只喝茶以及吃面包夹黄油，长此以往有利于养生嘛，再说也比较节约。

斯托克曼夫人：（笑了笑）你可千万别把我和托马斯当成乱花钱的人啊。

彼得·斯托克曼：哪儿的话，我的好弟妹。我再怎么也不会把你们当成那号儿人。（用手指了指医生的书房）他不在家吗？

斯托克曼夫人：是的。刚吃过晚饭，他带孩子们出去溜达溜达。

彼得·斯托克曼：刚吃过饭就散步恐怕不好。（侧耳细听）我想我听见他回来的声音了。

斯托克曼夫人：不会的，不可能是他。（外边传来了敲门声。）请进！（霍夫斯塔德从大厅走了进来。）哦，是你，霍夫斯塔德先生！

霍夫斯塔德：是我。请原谅，我在印刷厂有事缠身，耽搁了一点儿时间。晚上好，市长先生。

彼得·斯托克曼：（微微欠了欠身子）晚上好。你这次来，肯定儿是有事吧？

霍夫斯塔德：是有一点儿事，是关于报上的一篇文章。

彼得·斯托克曼：我猜就是的。听说我弟弟是《人民信使报》的撰稿人，而且投了不少稿子。

霍夫斯塔德：是的，他一旦觉得有"逆耳的忠言"，就为《人民信使报》撰稿发声，的确写了不少文章。

斯托克曼夫人：（冲着霍夫斯塔德）你不进去——？（用手指指餐厅）

彼得·斯托克曼：是啊，是啊，他向读者发声表达自己的想法，以期获得共鸣，作为撰稿人是无可非议的。再说，我本人没有任何理由会对贵报产生恶意，霍夫斯塔德先生。

霍夫斯塔德：我和你的想法完全一致。

彼得·斯托克曼：不管在任何方面，这座城市里的居民都有一种相互包容的崇高精神——一种令人敬佩的城市精神。这种精神的根源在于咱们大家的利益高度一致，这使得大家能够团结起来——这种集体利益也是每一位具有正义感的市民最为关心的。

霍夫斯塔德：你在说温泉浴场吧？

彼得·斯托克曼：一点儿不错。我说的正是咱们新建的美丽、舒适的温泉浴场。霍夫斯塔德先生，请记住我的话：它将会成为整个城市生活中的一个亮点！这是毋庸置疑的！

斯托克曼夫人：托马斯也这么说。

彼得·斯托克曼：想想吧，在过去短短的一两年里，这地方发展得多么快！真是财源滚滚、生意兴隆，整个城市焕发出了勃勃生机！房价和地租天天往上涨。

霍夫斯塔德：失业率也在下降。

彼得·斯托克曼：是的，这也是一个可喜之处。有产阶级应交的贫困人口救济税随之减少，这大大减轻了他们的负担。如果今年夏天能成为真正的旺季，这种减负力度甚至还会加大。游客多了，来疗养的人多了，他们口口相传，会令温泉浴场美名远扬。

霍夫斯塔德：听说这是一项前景广阔的事业。

彼得·斯托克曼：前景非常广阔。我们每天都能接到打听租房事宜的咨询。

霍夫斯塔德：斯托克曼医生的文章此时面世正是好

时机。

彼得·斯托克曼：是他最近写的吗？

霍夫斯塔德：是他去年冬天写的，是宣传温泉浴场的，说这儿的卫生条件是如何如何好。不过，我暂时把文章搁置了起来，没有发表。

彼得·斯托克曼：啊——我想大概是因为有不妥之处吧？

霍夫斯塔德：不是，完全不是的。是因为我觉得在春季发表比较好，因为春季正是人们认真考虑到何处避暑的季节。

彼得·斯托克曼：非常正确，你的判断正确极啦，霍夫斯塔德先生。

斯托克曼夫人：只要是浴场的事，托马斯真的是呕心沥血。

彼得·斯托克曼：别忘了，他可是浴场的卫生官员哟。

霍夫斯塔德：是的。不仅如此，他还是浴场的创办人呢。

彼得·斯托克曼：他是创办人？真的吗？不错，我时而会听到有些人会这么说。不过，恕我直言，我觉得我在这件事上是有一些小功劳的。

斯托克曼夫人：是的，托马斯也常这么说。

霍夫斯塔德：你的功劳谁敢否认，斯托克曼先生？你推动了这项事业，为它操碎了心，这是有目共睹的。我刚才只是说，办浴场的点子是斯托克曼医生头一个提出来的。

彼得·斯托克曼：啊，点子固然很好！我弟弟倒是有不少的点子，但遗憾的是，到了付诸实施的时候，就得借助他人之力，借助具有另外一种气质的人，霍夫斯塔德先生。我坚信至少在这个家里——

斯托克曼夫人：亲爱的彼得——

霍夫斯塔德：你怎么会认为——？

斯托克曼夫人：你不进餐厅吃点儿东西吗，霍夫斯塔德先生？我丈夫肯定快回来了。

霍夫斯塔德：谢谢。那我就吃几口吧。（走进餐厅）

彼得·斯托克曼：（压低声音）真怪，这些农家子弟似乎总是这么不知进退。

斯托克曼夫人：不必这么斤斤计较！你和托马斯有手足之情，难道就不能分享这份荣誉吗？

彼得·斯托克曼：我倒是想分享，但有些人显然贪心不足，不愿意分享嘛。

斯托克曼夫人：这就是胡扯了！你跟托马斯一直都相处得不错嘛。（竖起耳朵静听）我想，这回真是他回来了。（走过去打开通向大厅的那扇门）

斯托克曼医生：（在外面大声说笑）凯瑟琳，瞧，又来了一位客人。真是叫人高兴！请进，霍斯特船长，把外套挂在那只钩子上。啊，看我这人，你就没穿外套。你都想不到，凯瑟琳，我是在大街上碰见他的，好不容易才把他拉进来！（霍斯特船长走进来，向斯托克曼夫人问好。斯托克曼医生紧随其后。）进来吧，孩子们。要知道，走了一圈，他们又饿了。霍斯特船长，来，你一定得尝尝我们的烤牛肉。（他把霍斯特拉进餐厅。叶利夫和墨顿也跟了进去。）

斯托克曼夫人：托马斯，你没看见——

斯托克曼医生：（在餐厅门口转过身来）哦，是你，彼得，你在这儿！（走过去和彼得握手）真是太叫人高兴啦。

彼得·斯托克曼：可惜我马上就要走——

斯托克曼医生：胡说！马上就要喝棕榈酒了。你没忘了热一热棕榈酒吧，凯瑟琳？

斯托克曼夫人：当然没忘。水都开了。（走进餐厅）

彼得·斯托克曼：还有棕榈酒？！

斯托克曼医生：是的。请你坐下来，咱们好好干上一杯。

彼得·斯托克曼：谢谢，我向来不参加酒会。

斯托克曼医生：这不是酒会。

彼得·斯托克曼：我却觉得像是。（朝餐厅那儿望了一眼）真是了不起，他们竟能吃那么多的东西。

斯托克曼医生：（搓搓手）是啊，瞧着年轻人吃东西真痛快，你说是不是？要知道，他们的胃口总是那么好！就应该这样。一分食物，一分力气嘛！他们是推动社会未来发展的潜在力量，彼得。

彼得·斯托克曼：你说到"推动"，那么请问，在这个地方他们会推动什么呢？

斯托克曼医生：哦，那你就得问他们年轻人了——到时候他们会施展神通的。咱们当然看不出来。像你我这样的老顽固，跟不上形势了。

彼得·斯托克曼：真的？你真的这么想吗？我得说，你用这个词形容咱们着实奇怪——

斯托克曼医生：嘿，你可别太抠字眼，彼得。我只是想说我感到十分高兴，非常满足。社会发展日新月异，而我生逢盛世，觉得自己幸运极了。生活在这样一个时代，本身就是一件幸事！仿佛一个新的世界正在咱们周围形成。

彼得·斯托克曼：你真的这么想？

斯托克曼医生：啊，你当然不如我看得这么真切。你一直生活在这种环境之中，感觉已经麻木了。我则不然——我这么多年住在北方的一个偏僻的角落里，几乎与世隔绝，看不到有新思想的人。而今来到这里，我觉得自己就好像来到了一个兴旺的大都市。

彼得·斯托克曼：嗬，还大都市呢！

斯托克曼医生：我不是不知道，跟许多别的地方相比较，这儿只是个弹丸之地。可是，这儿有蓬勃的朝气，有辉煌的未来，有许许多多你可以为之工作和奋斗的事业，而这才是最关键的。（叫喊）凯瑟琳，邮递员来过没有？

斯托克曼夫人：（在餐厅里）没来过。

斯托克曼医生：还有，这儿的生活舒适、安逸，彼得！咱们可是吃过苦、挨过饿的人，应该学会珍视这种生活。

彼得·斯托克曼：噢，当然——

斯托克曼医生：实不相瞒，我们在北方经常是饥寒交迫，而到了这里，就觉得日子过得像王公贵族。就拿今天说吧，我们午饭吃的是烤牛肉，而且晚饭也能吃上烤牛肉。难道你不愿意尝一点儿吗？或者，你不妨进去看看也可以嘛。来吧——

彼得·斯托克曼：不了，不了，免了吧！

斯托克曼医生：进去坐坐总可以吧？我们买了块桌布，你看到了吧？

彼得·斯托克曼：是的，我注意到了。

斯托克曼医生：我们还买了个灯罩。你看见了没有？这些都是用凯瑟琳省下的钱买的。现在，家里看上去是多么舒适啊。你说是不是？你走到这边来——不，不，不是那边——是这儿！对，就是这里！瞧，灯罩把光线都聚到这里了。我觉得这灯罩棒极了，你说是不是？

彼得·斯托克曼：如果能买得起这种奢侈品的话——

斯托克曼医生：能买得起，现在我能买得起了。凯瑟琳说，我挣的钱差不多够开销了。

彼得·斯托克曼：差不多够了——是呀！

斯托克曼医生：一个科学家的生活应该讲究一点儿格调。我十分肯定，一个普通公务员每年的开销是比我大的。

彼得·斯托克曼：当然喽！一个公务员，一个薪酬高的公务员——

斯托克曼医生：哦，任何一个普通公务员都是如此！那种身份的人每年的开销要比我高出两三倍——

彼得·斯托克曼：那得取决于职位的高低。

斯托克曼医生：不管怎样吧，我可以告诉你：我并非漫无目的地乱花钱。招待朋友对我而言是一种欢乐，是我无论如何也不肯放弃的。要知道，我需要交朋友。在一个闭塞的地方我一住就是许多年，而今需要结交一些充满热情、怀揣理想、思想开放、活跃积极的年轻人，此刻正在餐厅里吃饭的那几个正是这样的人。希望你能多了解了解霍夫斯塔德——

彼得·斯托克曼:噢,对啦,霍夫斯塔德告诉我,说他又准备发表你的一篇文章了。

斯托克曼医生:我的文章?

彼得·斯托克曼:是的,是关于浴场的文章,你去年冬天写的。

斯托克曼医生:噢,是那篇!目前我不愿意让它见报。

彼得·斯托克曼:为什么不愿意?我觉得目前正是应该发表的时候。

斯托克曼医生:在正常的情况下,也许是这样的。(走到房间的另一头)

彼得·斯托克曼:(目光跟随着他)现在的情况有什么反常之处吗?

斯托克曼医生:(站定)实不相瞒,彼得,有些话我现在还不能说,反正今晚是不便说的。若论目前的情形,可能反常之处是有很多的,或者也许压根儿就没有,纯属我个人的臆想。

彼得·斯托克曼:我得说,你的话听上去神神秘秘的。难道出了什么事情,非得瞒着我不成?我可是浴场委员会主席,我觉得——

斯托克曼医生:而我倒觉得——。算了,算了,咱们不必为此动肝火,彼得。

彼得·斯托克曼:胡言乱语!我可不是你说的那号儿人,动不动就生气。不过,我有权强调一点:所有的事情都必须拿到桌面上解决,都必须通过正规渠道解决,必须由合法的政府当局经手,决不允许在背后搞小动作,采用见不得人的手段。

斯托克曼医生:我几时背着你搞过小动作?

彼得·斯托克曼:反正你有一种根深蒂固的毛病,做事我行我素,这在一个讲究秩序的社会里,几乎同样叫人无法接受。个人无疑应该服从社会,或者说得更具体些,应该服从照管集体利益的政府当局。

斯托克曼医生:你这话也许有理。可是,这跟我有什么干系呢?

彼得·斯托克曼:这个道理你好像永远都弄不懂,亲爱的托马斯。不过,我可告诉你,早晚有一天你会栽跟头的。这就是我对你的忠告。再见吧。

斯托克曼医生:莫非你疯啦?你把事情完全弄错了。

彼得·斯托克曼:我一般是不会弄错的。现在我得告辞啦——(冲着餐厅里高声说)再见,凯瑟琳!再见,先生们!(走了出去)

斯托克曼夫人:(走出餐厅)他走啦?

斯托克曼医生:是的,气呼呼地走了。

斯托克曼夫人:你又把他怎么了,亲爱的托马斯?

斯托克曼医生:没什么。反正不到恰当的时候,他别想让我向他汇报。

斯托克曼夫人:你有什么事要向他汇报?

斯托克曼医生:噢,你别管,叫我处理好啦,凯瑟琳。咦,这就怪了,邮递员竟然没来。

〔霍夫斯塔德、比林和霍斯特从餐桌旁站起,走进客厅。

叶利夫和墨顿也跟着进来。〕

比林：（伸懒腰）啊！饱餐一顿，就像是换了个人。

霍夫斯塔德：今天晚上市长似乎不大高兴。

斯托克曼医生：他胃口不好，消化力差。

霍夫斯塔德：我倒觉得是我们这两个《人民信使报》的刺儿头让他消化不了。

斯托克曼夫人：我还以为你们跟他和好了，不再闹别扭了呢。

霍夫斯塔德：和好是和好了，但这只是暂时休战而已。

比林：正是如此！这四个字就将当前的局势说了个明明白白。

斯托克曼医生：咱们不该忘了，彼得是个孤零零的光棍儿，怪可怜的。他没有家庭乐趣，一天到晚没完没了地处理公务，吃饭也只是点儿粗茶淡饭！小伙子们，把椅子搬到桌子跟前去！是不是能喝杯棕榈酒，凯瑟琳？

斯托克曼夫人：（走向餐厅）我正要去拿呢。

斯托克曼医生：霍斯特船长，你挨着我坐在沙发上。你可是难得一见呀。请坐，我的朋友们。（大家围桌而坐。斯托克曼夫人端着一只托盘进来，盘子上摆着酒精灯、酒杯和几瓶酒等物。）

斯托克曼夫人：酒来啦！这是亚力酒，这是朗姆酒，这是白兰地。大家随意点儿，别客气。

斯托克曼医生：（拿起一只杯子）我们自己来。（他们各自给自己调棕榈酒。）一边喝酒，一边抽雪茄吧。叶利夫，你知道雪茄烟盒在哪里，去拿过来。墨顿，你去给我拿烟斗。(两个孩子进了右首的房间。)我怀疑叶利夫时不时会偷上一根我的雪茄,而我假装不知道。(高声叫喊)墨顿,把我的吸烟帽[①]也拿来!凯瑟琳,你去告诉他我把吸烟帽放在什么地方了。噢,他找着了。(孩子们把东西都拿了来。)好,朋友们,你们抽雪茄,我抽烟斗。在北方的时候,这只烟斗不知陪伴我经历了多少风风雨雨。(跟大家碰杯)祝诸位健康!啊,坐在这儿,又舒适又暖和,感觉真好!

斯托克曼夫人:(坐着打毛衣)你们快开船了吧,霍斯特船长?

霍斯特:很可能在下个星期。

斯托克曼夫人:是不是去美国?

霍斯特:是的,是这么打算的。

比林:那你不能参加这次的选举了吧?

霍斯特:要举行选举吗?

比林:你不知道?

霍斯特:不知道。我不太关心这种事情。

比林:你对公共事务不感兴趣?

霍斯特:是的。这种事情我一点儿都不了解。

比林:这也没什么。无论如何,参加选举投票都是应该的。

霍斯特:甚至连对此完全不了解的人也应该去投票?

比林:完全不了解?此话怎讲?一个社会就像一艘船,人人都应该有当舵手的准备。

---

① 男性在吸烟时戴的帽子。

霍斯特：这话在岸上也许说得过去，但在船上却是行不通的。

霍夫斯塔德：大多数海员对岸上的事物都漠不关心，实在叫人感到惊讶。

比林：也叫人感到极为反常。

斯托克曼医生：海员就像候鸟一样，以四海为家。这就要求咱们更加努力，投入更大的热情，霍夫斯塔德。明天的《人民信使报》有没有关于公益事业的新闻？

霍夫斯塔德：没有关于本市的新闻。不过，后天我打算登你那篇文章——

斯托克曼医生：我的文章？千万别登！暂时别登，必须等一等。

霍夫斯塔德：真的吗？我们的报纸上留有地方，我觉得现在正是发表的好时机——

斯托克曼医生：是呀，是呀，你很可能是对的，但还是等一等为好。我以后再跟你解释原因。（佩特拉戴着帽子，穿着外套，腋下夹着一叠练习本从大厅里走进来。）

佩特拉：晚上好。

斯托克曼医生：晚上好，佩特拉。你过来吧。

〔大家和佩特拉相互问好。佩特拉把外套、帽子连同练习本一起放在靠门的一把椅子上。〕

佩特拉：你们坐在这儿享清福，而我却在外边吃苦受罪！

斯托克曼医生：那你就过来也享享清福吧！

比林：我给你调杯酒吧？

佩特拉：（走到桌前）谢谢你，我还是自己来吧——每次让你调，你都调得特别浓。噢，我想起来了，爸爸，这儿有你一封信。（走到放东西的椅子那儿取信）

斯托克曼医生：有封信？谁来的？

佩特拉：（在外套口袋里摸索）是我出门时邮递员交给我的。

斯托克曼医生：（站起来，走过去）你这时候才交给我？

佩特拉：我当时忙着去上课，没时间跑回来交给你。噢，找到啦！

斯托克曼医生：（把信抢过来）快让我看，快让我看，孩子。（看了看发信人的地址）对，一点儿不错！

斯托克曼夫人：你盼星星盼月亮，盼的就是这封信，托马斯？

斯托克曼医生：是的，就是这封。我现在必须到书房里去——哪里有灯，凯瑟琳？书房有灯吗？

斯托克曼夫人：有，灯早点上了，放在写字桌上了。

斯托克曼医生：好，好，失陪一会儿——（走进了书房）

佩特拉：究竟是什么事，妈妈？

斯托克曼夫人：不知道。这一两天他就跟掉了魂儿一样，老问邮递员来了没有。

比林：也许是乡下病人的信吧。

佩特拉：可怜的老爹！过不了多久他就会累垮的。（为她自己调酒）好啦，这下味道肯定很好！

霍夫斯塔德：今天你又到夜校教课了吗？

佩特拉：（端着酒杯呷了一口）上了两个小时的课。

比林:上午在学校上了四个小时?

佩特拉:五个小时。

斯托克曼夫人:看得出,你还要改作业。

佩特拉:是的,要改一大堆作业。

霍斯特:我觉得你也太忙了。

佩特拉:是的,但忙一点儿好,虽然累点儿,可是心里高兴。

比林:你喜欢这样的生活?

佩特拉:是的。白天累,夜里就睡得香。

墨顿:你一定是个罪孽深重的人,佩特拉。

佩特拉:罪孽?

墨顿:是的,你拼命工作就是罪孽深重。诺伦德先生说过,工作是对罪孽的惩罚。

叶利夫:得了吧,你可真是个笨蛋,竟相信那样的鬼话!

斯托克曼夫人:别这样说话,叶利夫!

比林:(大笑)精彩!精彩!

霍夫斯塔德:你不愿意拼命工作吗,墨顿?

墨顿:是的,我不愿意。

霍夫斯塔德:那么,你长大了干什么?

墨顿:我想当海盗。

叶利夫:那你就是异教徒喽。

墨顿:好呀,我就当异教徒吧,难道不行吗?

比林:我和你真是英雄所见略同,墨顿!我也是这么想的。

斯托克曼夫人：（给他使眼色）我敢说这不是你的真心话，比林先生。

比林：是真心话，我发誓！我是异教徒，并为此感到自豪。信我的话吧，用不了多久，咱们所有人都会成为异教徒的。

墨顿：到了那时候，咱们就可以想干什么就干什么啦？

比林：是这样的，等着瞧吧，墨顿。

斯托克曼夫人：你们得回自己的房间了，孩子们。我知道你们都要预备明天的功课呢。

叶利夫：我想再待一会儿——

斯托克曼夫人：不行，不行，你们俩都给我回房间去。

（孩子们道了晚安，走进左边的房间。）

霍夫斯塔德：你真的认为孩子们听了这些话会有坏处吗？

斯托克曼夫人：不知道。但我不愿意叫他们听这种话。

佩特拉：恕我直言，妈妈，我觉得你这样就大错特错了。

斯托克曼夫人：也许是吧。可是我不愿意让他们在家里听到这些话。

佩特拉：家里和学校都一样，都非常虚假——在家里不许说真话，在学校则对着孩子们撒谎。

霍斯特：对着孩子们撒谎？

佩特拉：是的。我们站在讲台上讲的都是些连我们自己都不相信的东西，难道你不知道吗？

比林：一点儿不错。

佩特拉：要是有条件，我就自己办学，以完全不同的教育理念办学。

比林：是啊，要是有条件就好了！

霍斯特：哦，要是你真想办学，斯托克曼小姐，我很乐意为你提供教室。家父留给我一套房子，虽然旧点儿，但面积很大，空着没有什么用处，楼下还有一个宽敞的餐厅——

佩特拉：（大笑）非常感谢。不过，恐怕我不是那块料。

霍夫斯塔德：据我看，佩特拉小姐将来很可能会干新闻报道这一行。顺便问一句，你答应为我们翻译的那篇英文小说，是不是已经动笔了？

佩特拉：还没有呢。不过，到时候会交给你的。

〔斯托克曼医生手里拿着一封拆开的信从书房走了过来。〕

斯托克曼医生：（晃着那封信）新闻来了。告诉你们吧，市民们这下子可有谈资啦！

比林：有新闻？

斯托克曼夫人：什么新闻？

斯托克曼医生：一个重大发现，凯瑟琳！

霍夫斯塔德：真的吗？

斯托克曼夫人：是你发现的？

斯托克曼医生：对，是我发现的。（走来走去）就让他们骂吧，骂我疯头疯脑、胡思乱想吧！实话告诉你们，这一次他们要是再骂我，可就要小心点儿了！

佩特拉：爸爸，快告诉我们到底是怎么回事吧。

斯托克曼医生：好的，好的。别着急，我会把事情全都告诉你们的。可惜彼得不在这儿！这件事可以证明，有时候人们发表议论会罔顾事实，实际上就像瞎眼的鼹鼠——

霍夫斯塔德：此话怎讲，医生？

斯托克曼医生：（在桌旁站住）是不是大家普遍认为这座城市是一个非常卫生的地方？

霍夫斯塔德：当然。

斯托克曼医生：实际上大家都认为此处是一个极其卫生的地方，应该大力宣传，说它不仅有益于病人疗养，也适合健康的人养生——

斯托克曼夫人：是呀。可是，亲爱的托马斯——

斯托克曼医生：咱们一直在宣传这座城市，为它大唱赞歌——我更是不遗余力，又是在《人民信使报》上发表文章，又是撰写宣传小册子——

霍夫斯塔德：是呀。怎么啦？

斯托克曼医生：这个浴场——咱们称它是"这座城市的经济命脉"以及"我市的神经中枢"，鬼知道还有什么美名——

比林：记得在一个重要的场合，我曾称它是"这座城市充满活力的心脏"。

斯托克曼医生：的确如此。可是你们知道这个浴场的真实面目吗？知道这个规模宏大、富丽堂皇、有口皆碑、耗费了不知多少钱财的浴场究竟是什么东西吗？

霍夫斯塔德：不知道。究竟是什么东西？

斯托克曼夫人：是呀，究竟是什么东西？

斯托克曼医生：那地方整个儿就是传染病的温床！

129

佩特拉：你在说温泉浴场，爸爸？

斯托克曼夫人：（同时）你在说咱们的浴场？

霍夫斯塔德：可是，医生——

比林：简直叫人无法相信！

斯托克曼医生：整个浴场就像一座外面刷得雪白、里头流淌着毒液的坟墓，实不相瞒，对公共健康造成的危害要多大有多大！莫里达尔那儿的污物，那儿臭气熏天的脏水流入通向城市蓄水池的管道，污染了水源。这还不够，那股可恶、肮脏、有毒的水还慢慢渗入了海滩——

霍夫斯塔德：就在浴场那儿？

斯托克曼医生：一点儿不错。

霍夫斯塔德：你怎么能如此肯定，医生？

斯托克曼医生：我一直在认认真真调查此事。我早就有了疑心——去年来这儿的客人中出现了几种非常奇怪的病症，有的人患的是伤寒，有的人患的是胃热症——

斯托克曼夫人：是的，的确有这种情况。

斯托克曼医生：当时我们还以为是客人没来之前就已经患病了。可是到了冬天，我开始有了不同的看法，于是就竭尽全力着手检查那儿的水质。

斯托克曼夫人：原来你一天到晚忙的就是这个？

斯托克曼医生：是的，我实际上一直在忙这事，凯瑟琳。我手头没有检验水体所需的科学仪器，于是就把这儿的饮用水和海水都取了些样品送到大学，请一位化学专家做精准的分析。

霍夫斯塔德：化验报告你收到没有？

斯托克曼医生：（把信给他看）这就是！化验报告证明水里含有腐烂性有机物，充满了纤毛虫，无论是饮用还是外用，都会极大地威胁人的健康。

斯托克曼夫人：幸亏你发现得早。

斯托克曼医生：你完全可以这么说。

霍夫斯塔德：现在你打算怎么办呢，医生？

斯托克曼医生：自然是着手整顿喽。

霍夫斯塔德：能整顿好吗？

斯托克曼医生：这一步棋必须走。否则温泉浴场就完全用不成了，就会荒废。不过，大家也不必担心。我已胸有成竹，知道该采取什么样的措施。

斯托克曼夫人：可你为什么要将此事瞒得密不透风呢，亲爱的？

斯托克曼医生：难道你让我在未获得确凿证据之前就跑到大街上，弄得满城风雨不成？对不起，这可不行，我可没那么傻。

佩特拉：话虽如此，你总可以告诉我们——

斯托克曼医生：谁都不能告诉。不过，你明天可以跑去见那位"老獾"[①]——

斯托克曼夫人：托马斯！别这么说话，托马斯！

斯托克曼医生：噢，我是说你可以去见你的外公。你说了，那老头儿会吓一跳的！我知道他觉得我是个疯子，许多人都这么看我，我并不是没有留意到。不过，现在就

---

① 斯托克曼医生给自己的岳父墨顿·基尔起的绰号，意思是说他是个老顽固。

让那些聪明人瞧瞧吧——到时候他们就知道我是怎样一个人了！（一边搓手，一边走来走去）这座城市里就要有一场轩然大波了，凯瑟琳。你都想象不到事态有多严重。所有的管道都必须重新铺设！

霍夫斯塔德：（站起来）所有的管道？

斯托克曼医生：是的，当然是所有的。管道的入水口太低了，必须抬高，要比原来的位置高出许多。

佩特拉：你以前就是这么建议的，看来你是对的。

斯托克曼医生：是的，佩特拉，你还记着这事呢。当初他们动工之前，我就写文章反对他们的规划。可是，那时候没人理睬我。现在，他们自己酿的苦果，就让他们自己尝吧。当然，我已经写好了报告，准备交给浴场委员会，报告在我手里搁了有一个星期了，专等这份化验报告出来。（指指那封信）现在总算可以提交报告了。（走进书房，拿来了几页纸）瞧瞧吧！写了满满四页！我要把这封信连同报告书一起交上去。给我找张旧报纸，凯瑟琳，用来包这些东西。万事俱备，只欠东风！你把这包东西交给——交给——（急得跺了跺脚）——她叫什么来着？——你把东西给女佣，让她马上送到市长那儿。

〔斯托克曼夫人拿起那包东西，穿过餐厅走了。〕

佩特拉：你看彼得伯伯会怎么说呢，爸爸？

斯托克曼医生：那有什么可说的！这么重要的事情浮出了水面，他要是不高兴才怪呢。

霍夫斯塔德：对于你的发现，能不能让我写篇短的报道，登在《人民信使报》上？

斯托克曼医生：如果你这样做，我将感激不尽。

霍夫斯塔德：此事刻不容缓，让公众尽早了解真相乃为上策。

斯托克曼医生：当然。

斯托克曼夫人：（回来）女佣把东西送走了。

比林：我敢说，医生，这下子你就要成为这座城市的风云人物了！

斯托克曼医生：（高兴地来回踱步）哪儿的话！说到底，我只不过是尽到了自己的职责罢了。我只不过有幸发现了一些问题罢了，仅此而已。不过，话又说回来——

比林：霍夫斯塔德，你不觉得这座城市应该给斯托克曼医生颁发一份奖状什么的吗？

霍夫斯塔德：到时候我会提议的。

比林：我去找阿斯拉克森谈一谈。

斯托克曼医生：使不得，我的好朋友，千万别那样做。我可不愿意那样招摇过市。要是浴场委员会考虑给我加薪水，我也是不会接受的。听见了吗，凯瑟琳？即使他们给我加薪，我也不会接受。

斯托克曼夫人：你这样做很对，托马斯。

佩特拉：（举杯）为你的健康干杯，爸爸！

霍夫斯塔德和比林：为你的健康干杯，医生！祝你身体健康！

霍斯特：（跟斯托克曼医生碰杯）希望这件事会给你带来好运。

斯托克曼医生：谢谢，谢谢，我亲爱的朋友们！我感到幸福极了!一个人能为自己的家乡,能为自己的乡亲们做点事情,那种感觉简直棒极啦!太好啦,凯瑟琳!(他张开双臂搂住妻子,抱着她转圈圈。而她笑着,叫着,要从他怀里挣脱出来。大伙儿哄堂大笑,给医生鼓掌喝彩。两个孩子在门口探进头来瞧热闹。)

第二幕

布景：同上。通向餐厅的门关着。上午。斯托克曼夫人打开餐厅的门走出来，手里拿着一封密封的信，走到医生书房的门口，探头向里面瞧了瞧。

斯托克曼夫人：你在屋里吧，托马斯？

斯托克曼医生：（从书房里）在呢，我刚回来。（走出来）什么事？

斯托克曼夫人：有你哥哥一封信。

斯托克曼医生：啊哈，咱们瞧瞧里面写了什么！（拆开信封，念信）"手稿退还"，（接着往下念，声音低得听不清念的是什么）哼！

斯托克曼夫人：他说什么？

斯托克曼医生：（把信往衣袋里一塞）没什么，只说今天中午要过来一下。

斯托克曼夫人：是吗？这次你可要记住待在家里等他。

斯托克曼医生：没问题。反正上午的出诊病人我都看完了。

斯托克曼夫人：我心里没谱，不知道他是怎么个态度。

斯托克曼医生：你瞧着吧，问题是我发现的，而不是他，所以他肯定会不高兴的。

斯托克曼夫人：难道你不为此感到担心吗？

斯托克曼医生：噢，要知道，其实他心里还是挺高兴的。不过，话又说回来，彼得这个人除了他自己，不愿意其他人对这座城市有所贡献。

斯托克曼夫人：听我一句，托马斯，你应该心平气和地跟他分享这份荣誉。难道你就不明白，正是因为有了他的任命，你才有了今日的发现？

斯托克曼医生：我十分愿意跟他分享荣誉，只要能够把错误纠正过来就行——

〔墨顿·基尔出现在通向大厅的那扇门的门口，探头朝房间里四周看了看，嘿嘿一笑。〕

墨顿·基尔：（诡秘地）是——是真的吗？

斯托克曼夫人：（迎上去）爸爸！是你呀！

斯托克曼医生：啊，基尔先生！上午好，上午好！

斯托克曼夫人：请进。

墨顿·基尔：要是真的，我就进来。要是假的，我就不进了。

斯托克曼医生：要是什么是真的？

墨顿·基尔：关于水源之说是不是真的？

斯托克曼医生：当然是真的。不过，你是怎么知道的？

墨顿·基尔：（走进来）佩特拉上学校去，路过我那儿——

斯托克曼医生：是吗？

墨顿·基尔：是的。是她告诉我的。起初我以为她只是跟我开个玩笑——可她又不是那号儿人。

斯托克曼医生：当然不是。你怎么能想到她会骗你呢！

墨顿·基尔：这个嘛，最好不要轻易相信人，因为一不小心你就会上当受骗。不管怎么样吧，难道她说的都是真的？

斯托克曼医生：确切无疑，都是真的。请坐下来说话。（拉他坐在沙发上）对这座城市而言，难道这不是一件幸事吗——

墨顿·基尔：（几乎笑出来）对这座城市而言是一件幸事？

斯托克曼医生：是啊，幸亏我发现得及时。

墨顿·基尔：（还是忍着笑）是啊，是啊，是啊！可是我万万想不到，你竟然有胆量给你哥哥来一个这样的下马威！

斯托克曼医生：给他来个下马威？

斯托克曼夫人：其实，爸爸——

墨顿·基尔：（把两只手和下巴颏儿都贴在手杖柄上，眯着眼睛狡黠地瞧着医生）让我猜猜到底是怎么回事。是不是有什么有害的东西钻到了水管里？

斯托克曼医生：是的，是纤毛虫。

墨顿·基尔：根据佩特拉的说法，这种有害的东西数量很多，数也数不清。

斯托克曼医生：的确如此，也许不止千万。

墨顿·基尔：不过，这种东西肉眼是看不到的，对不对？

斯托克曼医生：是的，人的肉眼是看不到的。

墨顿·基尔：（低声咯咯一笑）有意思——这是我听过的最有意思的事情！

斯托克曼医生：这话是什么意思？

墨顿·基尔：即便这是真的，你也别想让市长相信这种事情。

斯托克曼医生：那就等着瞧吧。

墨顿·基尔：你以为他会那么傻——？

斯托克曼医生：但愿全城的人都会那么傻。

墨顿·基尔：全城的人？哦，那倒也不是件坏事。他们这是自作自受，应该叫他们尝尝苦头。他们自以为是，觉得自己比我们这些老家伙高明，竟然把我赶出了市议会。这就是他们的所作所为——像撵一条狗一样把我撵了出来！现在他们总算遭到报应了。你也给他们来个下马威，托马斯！

斯托克曼医生：其实，我——

墨顿·基尔：给他们点儿颜色瞧瞧！（站起来）要是你有本事让市长和他的狐朋狗友自食其果，我就捐十英镑给慈善机构，说到做到！

斯托克曼医生：那好极了。

墨顿·基尔：我得告诉你，我可不是钱多得不得了，随便捐钱的。不过，你要是能将此事办妥，圣诞节我一定捐五英镑给慈善机构。

〔霍夫斯塔德从大厅的门走进来。〕

霍夫斯塔德：上午好！（站住）噢，对不起——

斯托克曼医生：没关系。请进，请进。

墨顿·基尔：（又咯咯一笑）啊哈！他也参与了此事？

霍夫斯塔德：你指的是什么事？

斯托克曼医生：当然，他也参与了。

墨顿·基尔：我猜就是这样的！此事必须见报才行。你们自有锦囊妙计，托马斯！利用你的才智好好干！我得告辞了。

斯托克曼医生：你不再坐一会儿？

墨顿·基尔：不了，我必须走了。这是件有价值的事情，你就放开手干吧，你不会后悔的。

〔他走出去，斯托克曼夫人送他到大厅。〕

斯托克曼医生：（大笑）想想看，关于水源出问题之事，这老头儿压根儿就不相信。

霍夫斯塔德：哦？你们在说这件事？

斯托克曼医生：是的，我们在说这件事。大概你也是为此事而来的吧？

霍夫斯塔德：正是。你能腾出几分钟时间吗，医生？

斯托克曼医生：多长时间都行，我亲爱的朋友。

霍夫斯塔德：市长那儿有回音没有？

斯托克曼医生：还没有。他一会儿就来。

霍夫斯塔德：打昨天晚上起，我一直在想这问题。

斯托克曼医生：怎么样？

霍夫斯塔德：你是医生和科学家，讲究的是科学，在你看来，水源问题仅仅是孤立事件。你可能没有意识到里面还牵扯许多其他的事情。

斯托克曼医生：此话怎讲？我亲爱的朋友，咱们坐下来说。别坐在那儿，坐在沙发上吧。（霍夫斯塔德坐在了沙发上。斯托克曼医生坐在了桌子另一侧的一把椅子上。）现在说吧。你的意思是——？

霍夫斯塔德：你昨天说水源受到污染是因为土壤出了问题。

斯托克曼医生：是的。毫无疑问，祸根就是莫里达尔的那个充满了毒液的臭水坑。

霍夫斯塔德：对不起，医生，我看祸根恐怕是另外一个臭水坑。

斯托克曼医生：什么臭水坑？

霍夫斯塔德：就是那个咱们全市市民赖以为生却正在腐蚀咱们生活的臭水坑。

斯托克曼医生：你究竟想说什么，霍夫斯塔德？

霍夫斯塔德：整座城市的利益一点儿一点儿地落到一群官僚手里。

斯托克曼医生：言重了！他们不一定都是官僚。

霍夫斯塔德：是的。不过，有些人虽然不是官僚，却是官僚的狐群狗党。富人和古老世家操纵着咱们，把咱们完全攥在了手心。

斯托克曼医生：不错，可是他们有才干、有眼光嘛。

霍夫斯塔德：当初铺设管道的时候他们表现出来的才干和眼光，现在跑到哪儿去了？

斯托克曼医生：当然，他们的决策愚蠢至极，但现在纠正为时不晚。

霍夫斯塔德：你以为纠正起来会一帆风顺吗？

斯托克曼医生：不管是否能一帆风顺，反正非纠正不可。

霍夫斯塔德：不错，只要报社能有所担当就行。

斯托克曼医生：我觉得不必兴师动众，我亲爱的朋友。我坚信我哥哥——

霍夫斯塔德：对不起，医生，我觉得自己必须告诉你：我打算对此事发难。

斯托克曼医生：在报纸上登出来？

霍夫斯塔德：是的。当初我接管《人民信使报》的时候，我就拿定主意要打击那个刚愎自用、抱残守缺的利益集团，不让他们操纵咱们的生活。

斯托克曼医生：可是后来你亲口告诉过我，说结果不尽如人意，弄得报社差点儿关门大吉。

霍夫斯塔德：是的。那时候我们不得不委曲求全，这也是事实，因为他们如果出面干涉，温泉浴场的项目就会受到威胁，很可能会泡汤。但如今，浴场已经落成，我们可以跟那些大人物分道扬镳了。

斯托克曼医生：固然可以跟他们分道扬镳，但说起来，咱们还欠他们一份情呢，一份大大的人情。

霍夫斯塔德：这一点无可否认。但我是个具有民主思想的记者，对这样的现象不能坐视不管。说什么官员无过错，这样的神话必须被打破；这样的迷信，跟其他的迷信一样，必须被扫除。

斯托克曼医生：我完全同意你的看法，霍夫斯塔德先生。如果是迷信，一定得扫除！

霍夫斯塔德：我实在不愿意将市长列为口诛笔伐的对象，因为他是你哥哥。不过，我坚信你跟我看法相同——真理比什么都重要。

斯托克曼医生：那还用说。（声调突然变得激昂）可是——可是——

霍夫斯塔德：你可千万别把我看错了。跟大多数人比起来，我的私心并不重，野心也不大。

斯托克曼医生：我亲爱的朋友——谁会说你这种话！

霍夫斯塔德：你是知道的，我出身贫寒，所以有机会了解下层社会的人最迫切需要的是什么。他们最需要的是允许他们参与公共事务，医生，从而发展才干，增长智慧，赢得尊严——

斯托克曼医生：我非常理解。

霍夫斯塔德：我认为，一个新闻记者如果能为民众排忧解难，为底层的被压迫民众排忧解难，而他却坐失良机，那他就是严重失职。我很清楚，那些身居高位的人会骂我是煽风点火者，或者别的什么，那就随他们骂吧。只要问心无愧，我就——

斯托克曼医生：完全正确！完全正确，霍夫斯塔德先生！只要身子正，就不怕影子斜！（外边传来了敲门声。）请进！

〔阿斯拉克森出现在了门口。他一身黑，穿着有点儿寒碜,但很体面,脖子上的白领带有些发皱,戴着手套,手里拿着一顶呢帽。]

阿斯拉克森:(鞠躬)对不起,恕我冒昧打搅,医生——

斯托克曼医生:(站起来)哎呀,是你呀,阿斯拉克森!

阿斯拉克森:是我,医生。

霍夫斯塔德:(站起来)你是不是找我,阿斯拉克森?

阿斯拉克森:不是的,我并不知道你在这儿。我是来找医生的——

斯托克曼医生:愿意为你效劳。找我什么事?

阿斯拉克森:听比林先生说,你打算改进供水管道,此话当真?

斯托克曼医生:是的,是为了改善浴场的水质。

阿斯拉克森:我明白,我明白。噢,我来这儿是想说,我会尽我所能地支持这项计划,有多少力就出多少力。

霍夫斯塔德:(冲着医生)看到了吧!

斯托克曼医生:对此我深表感激,不过——

阿斯拉克森:有我们这些小本生意人的支持,毕竟是件好事。在这座城市里我们可是多数派,人多力量大嘛。有多数派的支持,对你来说是有好处的,医生。

斯托克曼医生:这是毋庸置疑的。只不过,我觉得此事不必采取非常措施。在我看来这是一件光明正大的事情——

阿斯拉克森:不管怎么说,害人之心不可有,防人之心不可无嘛。我对咱们的政府当局了如指掌——他们对别人的建议通常是听不进去的。所以我觉得咱们来个小小的示威，也没有什么不妥当的。

霍夫斯塔德：一点儿不错。

斯托克曼医生：你说示威？到底示什么威呀？

阿斯拉克森：就是以极为有节制的方法表达一下愿望，医生。有节制一直都是我努力的目标，也是一个公民最可贵的美德——至少这是我的想法。

斯托克曼医生：众所周知，你就具有这种品质，阿斯拉克森先生。

阿斯拉克森：是的。我觉得自己可以为此而感到自豪。实际上，水源对我们小本生意人来说极为重要。浴场前景广阔，要是做好了的话，可以说，将会成为本城的一座金矿。咱们都要靠它吃饭呢，尤其是我们这批有房产的人。所以，我们坚决支持这项规划。我既然是房主联合会的主席——

斯托克曼医生：是呀。

阿斯拉克森：我也是节制运动协会的秘书——我一直在致力于这项事业，你大概知道吧，先生？

斯托克曼医生：当然，当然。

阿斯拉克森：噢，你知道，我接触的人多，人脉广。鉴于我有个好名声，人们都知道我是个有节制的守法公民——就跟你一样，医生——所以在地方上有一定的影响力，如果允许我这么说的话，应该是个有点儿权力的人。

斯托克曼医生：这一点我非常清楚，阿斯拉克森先生。

阿斯拉克森：所以，如果有必要，我可以准备一篇公开感谢信，这是轻而易举的事情。

斯托克曼医生：公开感谢信？

阿斯拉克森：是的，代表全体市民对你表示感谢，感谢你对这项极为重要的公共事务所做出的杰出贡献。不用说，那篇文章的措辞必须非常谨慎，免得得罪当权者——他们毕竟是决策者嘛。依我之见，只要注意到这一点，就绝对不会得罪人！

霍夫斯塔德：这个嘛，即便那些当官的不买账——

阿斯拉克森：不，不，不。千万不要跟当权者唱对台戏，霍夫斯塔德先生。那些人牢牢掌握着咱们的命运，是得罪不起的。我曾经跟他们唱过反调，结果一点儿好处都没有。不过，咱们有理有节地公开表达一下市民们的观点，是任何人都不会反感的。

斯托克曼医生：（跟他握手）市民们如此热心地支持我，我简直说不出心里有多高兴，亲爱的阿斯拉克森先生。我高兴极了，高兴极了！来，咱们干上一小杯雪莉酒，好吗？

阿斯拉克森：不了，谢谢。我滴酒不沾。

斯托克曼医生：哦，那么，来杯啤酒怎么样？

阿斯拉克森：谢谢，啤酒也不喝，医生。这么早，我是什么都不喝的。我现在就去找一两个房主谈谈，把事情落实下来。

斯托克曼医生：非常感谢你的热心肠，阿斯拉克森先生。不过，我倒觉得没必要这么兴师动众。依我看，就顺其自然好啦。

阿斯拉克森：官僚们做事总是慢吞吞的，医生。我这里没有责怪他们的意思——

霍夫斯塔德：咱们可以撰文，在明天的报上催促他们一下。

阿斯拉克森：我相信，火药味儿不会很大的，霍夫斯塔德先生。对待他们，每一步都应该有节制，否则就寸步难行。你得听我的劝告，这都是社会这所学校教给我的经验。噢，我得走了，医生。现在你已经知道：我们这些小本生意人坚决支持你，不惜赴汤蹈火，就像是一道铜墙铁壁，愿意给你做靠山——大多数民众站在你这边，医生。

斯托克曼医生：感激不尽，感激不尽，阿斯拉克森先生。（和他握手）再见，再见。

阿斯拉克森：你是不是要跟我一起走，到印刷厂去，霍夫斯塔德先生？

霍夫斯塔德：我过一会儿去，手头有点儿事需要先处理一下。

阿斯拉克森：那好。（鞠躬，向外走。斯托克曼送他到大厅）

霍夫斯塔德：（待斯托克曼回来后）你看应该怎么做，医生？你不觉得现在正是时候，应该给犹疑不决、优柔寡断、畏首畏尾的人注入一点儿活力吗？

斯托克曼医生：你指的是阿斯拉克森？

霍夫斯塔德：不错，我指的正是他。他这种人也许是正派人，但老在泥潭里挣扎，就是拔不出脚来。这儿的大多数人都跟他一样，就像墙头草，东摇西摆的，遇事前怕狼后怕虎，从不敢坚定不移地往前走。

斯托克曼医生：是这样的。不过，我觉得阿斯拉克森的心眼儿特别好。

霍夫斯塔德：而我认为比这更重要的是，一个人应该自力更生，要对自己有信心。

斯托克曼医生：我完全同意你的观点。

霍夫斯塔德：鉴于此，我想抓住这个机会，看能不能给这些好心的人注入一点儿男子汉的大无畏精神。这座城市里的那种敬畏当权者的现象必须彻底消除。他们在水源上犯的过失很严重，是不可原谅的，这一点必须让本城的每一位选民都知道。

斯托克曼医生：很好。如果你认为这有益于集体利益，那就这么办吧。不过，得让我先跟哥哥谈一谈再说。

霍夫斯塔德：反正我得先把这篇意义重大的文章准备好。万一市长拒绝采取措施——

斯托克曼医生：你怎么能这么想？这怎么可能呢？

霍夫斯塔德：并非没有这种可能。万一出现这种情况——

斯托克曼医生：万一出现这种情况，我答应你——万一出现这种情况，你可以把我的文章登出来，一字不改地登出来。

霍夫斯塔德：君子一言，驷马难追。你可不要反悔。

斯托克曼医生：（把手稿递给他）喏，我把稿子交给你。你看一看也无妨，过后还给我就是了。

霍夫斯塔德：很好，很好！我一定谨遵吩咐。我得告辞啦，医生。

斯托克曼医生：再见，再见。你会看到一切都会顺顺利利、一帆风顺的，霍夫斯塔德先生。

霍夫斯塔德：是吗？那就等着瞧吧。(鞠躬，走出去)

斯托克曼医生：(推开餐厅的门，往里瞧)凯瑟琳！哦，你回来了，佩特拉？

佩特拉：(进来)是的，刚从学校回来。

斯托克曼夫人：(进来)他还没来？

斯托克曼医生：你是说彼得？还没来呢。我倒跟霍夫斯塔德谈了半天。他对我的发现很热心。原来，这件事的意义比我最初料想的重大得多。如果有必要的话，他的报纸会为我摇旗呐喊。

斯托克曼夫人：你们觉得会出现那种情况吗？

斯托克曼医生：绝对不会。不过，不管怎么说吧，有一家思想开放、独立自主的报社站在我这边，还是挺叫人感到自豪的。对啦，想一想吧，就连房主联合会的主席刚才也来找我了！

斯托克曼夫人：真的吗？他来干什么？

斯托克曼医生：也是来表示支持的。如果有必要，他们会抱成团支持我的。凯瑟琳，你知道我身后站着些什么人吗？

斯托克曼夫人：你背后？不知道。你说你背后站着些什么人？

斯托克曼医生：站的是广大的民众。

斯托克曼夫人：真的？这对你有好处吗，托马斯？

斯托克曼医生：我觉得是有好处的。(来回踱步和搓手)啊，和地方上的人同心协力，和他们建立兄弟般的情谊，这种感觉真好！

佩特拉：能够为民众谋福利，做有价值的事情，的确很好，爸爸！

斯托克曼医生：而且是为自己的故乡出力，孩子！

斯托克曼夫人：有人拉门铃。

斯托克曼医生：一定是他来了。(响起了敲门声)进来！

彼得·斯托克曼：(从大厅里进来)上午好。

斯托克曼医生：很高兴见到你，彼得！

斯托克曼夫人：上午好，彼得。你怎么样？

彼得·斯托克曼：还可以。谢谢。(转向医生)昨天下班之后，我收到了你写的那篇有关浴场水质的报告。

斯托克曼医生：是吗？你看了没有？

彼得·斯托克曼：我看了。

斯托克曼医生：你的意见怎么样？

彼得·斯托克曼：(往旁边瞥了一眼)唔！——

斯托克曼夫人：咱们走，佩特拉。(母女一同走进左边的房间)

彼得·斯托克曼：(沉吟片刻)你背着我搞调查，有这个必要吗？

斯托克曼医生：有这个必要。因为没有绝对的把握，我——

彼得·斯托克曼：意思是你现在有绝对的把握了？

斯托克曼医生：你看了报告，肯定已经很清楚了。

彼得·斯托克曼：你是不是打算把报告当作正式文件提交给浴场委员会？

斯托克曼医生：当然。必须采取应对措施，而且越快越好。

彼得·斯托克曼：跟平常一样，你在报告里的措辞还是那么激烈。除了好些别的话，你还说咱们浴场供给疗养病人的是一种慢性毒药。

斯托克曼医生：还能怎么说呢，彼得？想一想吧，无论是饮用水还是浴场里的水，全都是有毒的！可怜的病人们信赖咱们，花那么多钱来疗养，为的是恢复健康，可是咱们却向他们提供这样的水！

彼得·斯托克曼：根据你的结论，咱们必须修一道污水沟，把你所说的从莫里达尔流出的污水排走，还得重新铺设饮用水管道。

斯托克曼医生：是的。你有别的什么良策吗？反正我是想不出来别的办法。

彼得·斯托克曼：今天早晨，我找了个借口去见市政工程师，以半真半假的语气谈到了这些改建计划，说以后很可能会考虑动工。

斯托克曼医生：以后！

彼得·斯托克曼：他付之一笑，说他觉得那是不必要的浪费。你所提出的改建工程得花多少钱，这些你仔细想过没有？根据我掌握的情况，工程的耗资可能会高达一万五千或两万英镑。

斯托克曼医生：会有这么多？

彼得·斯托克曼：是的。更为糟糕的是，工程的工期至少需要两年。

斯托克曼医生：两年？需要整整两年？

彼得·斯托克曼：起码得两年。在这段时间里，浴场该怎么办？关掉它？实际上，也唯有如此。人们知道了水里有毒，你以为还有人敢来吗？

斯托克曼医生：可是，彼得，实情的确如此。

彼得·斯托克曼：浴场办得正风生水起，为世人所知，在这关键时刻却偏偏出了这事。邻近别的城市也有办浴场的条件。你不觉得他们会乘虚而入，大张旗鼓地干起来，将客流吸引到他们那儿去吗？毫无疑问，他们一定会毫不犹豫那么干的。那时，咱们将何去何从？也许就只好关门大吉了，那么多的钱便打了水漂。你的故乡小城将会葬送在你的手里！

斯托克曼医生：葬送在我手里！

彼得·斯托克曼：只有将浴场办好，这座城市才有前途，才有指望。这一点你和我一样清楚。

斯托克曼医生：那你说该怎么办？

彼得·斯托克曼：我看了你的报告，不相信浴场的情况真像你说的那么严重。

斯托克曼医生：老实告诉你，也许比报告里说的更严重！到了夏天，天气一热，情况一定会进一步恶化的。

彼得·斯托克曼：如我方才所言，我觉得你是夸大其词了。退一步说，假如情况明显恶化，一个能干的医生也应该知道怎么做，应该能够阻止不良影响的扩散，或者采取补救措施。

斯托克曼医生：是吗？还有什么？

彼得·斯托克曼：浴场的供水情况已成既定事实，因而就必须按既定事实对待。不过，浴场委员会也许将来出于谨慎，也不是不可能考虑拿出合理数目的工程款来改善水质。

斯托克曼医生：你以为我会参与这种瞒天过海的勾当？

彼得·斯托克曼：瞒天过海？！

斯托克曼医生：是的。这是阴谋诡计——是欺骗，是谎言，是对公众、对整个社会的重大犯罪！

彼得·斯托克曼：刚才我已经说过了，我不信事态会那么严重，会有那么大的危险。

斯托克曼医生：你不信？这是事实，容不得你不信！我的报告事实清楚、真实可信。你自己心知肚明，彼得，只是你不愿承认罢了。正是由于你的错误决策，浴场和输水管道的选址才出现了问题，而你却死不认错。哼，都是因为你那可怕的错误决策！你心里的小九九以为我看不出来？

彼得·斯托克曼：即便你说的情况属实，那又怎么样？就算我有意维护自己的名誉，也是为了这座城市的利益着想。丧失了威望，我就无法处理好公共事务——依我看，处理好公共事务对民众才是最有价值的。鉴于此，以及其他的一些原因，我觉得不便将你的报告提交给委员会——这一点至关紧要。为了公众的利益，这份报告不能上交。以后找个时间我会把这个问题提出来，悄悄地按最恰当的方法处理。不过，这件倒霉的事情万万不可走漏风声，一个字都不能让民众知道。

斯托克曼医生：恐怕纸包不住火，不让人知道是不可能的，我亲爱的彼得。

彼得·斯托克曼：无论如何也不能走漏风声。

斯托克曼医生：恕我直言，这是不顶用的。已经有许多人知道了。

彼得·斯托克曼：此话当真？谁知道了？不会是《人民信使报》的那批人吧？

斯托克曼医生：是他们——他们知道了。那家思想开明、独立自主的报社将会监督你履行你的职责。

彼得·斯托克曼：（沉吟片刻）你可真是个我行我素的人，托马斯。你也不想想，这件事会给你带来什么样的后果？

斯托克曼医生：后果？给我带来后果？

彼得·斯托克曼：不错，它会给你以及你的家庭带来严重后果。

斯托克曼医生：你这话是什么意思？

彼得·斯托克曼：我觉得我一直都在尽我做兄长的责任——难道我不是一直在尽我的力量帮助你吗？

斯托克曼医生：是的，的确如此。对此我深表感激。

彼得·斯托克曼：没必要感激。其实，从某种程度而言，我这样做也是有目的的——是为了我自己。我一直希望，我如果能帮你改善家里的经济状况，对你说话就可以有些分量。

斯托克曼医生：什么！你帮我是为你自己打算！

彼得·斯托克曼：从某种程度而言，是这样的。如果一个人当上了政府官员，而他的近亲却时不时做些叫人尴尬的事情，会令这位官员苦不堪言的。

斯托克曼医生：你认为我做了叫你尴尬的事情？

彼得·斯托克曼：是的。不幸的是，你做了，可是你自己都不知道。你天性不安分守己、好斗，喜欢做叛逆的事情。你有一个糟糕透顶的嗜好，那就是发表文章指点江山，不管对不对，都要议论一通。你心里一旦有什么想法，就要付诸笔端，或为报社撰文，或发行宣传册。

斯托克曼医生：一个公民有了新思想，难道没有责任跟公众分享吗？

彼得·斯托克曼：噢，公众并不需要新思想。公众只要有了大家公认的旧观念，对他们而言就已经非常好了。

斯托克曼医生：你真的这么想？

彼得·斯托克曼：是的。今天，我索性跟你打开天窗说亮话吧。之前，我尽量把话藏在心里，因为我知道你是个火暴脾气，听不进忠言，但现在我必须实话实说了，托马斯。你都不知道你那喜欢冲动的脾气对你的危害有多大。你抱怨当权者，甚至责怪政府，总是把他们说得一无是处，硬是认为你受到了冷淡，受到了迫害。你这么难相处，究竟想让别人怎么对待你？

斯托克曼医生：还有什么话，请尽管说！说我难相处？

彼得·斯托克曼：是的，托马斯。你是个极难相处的人，对此我深有体会。你蔑视一切，该珍视的东西你却置之不理，似乎全然忘了正是由于我的努力，你才得以被任命为浴场的卫生官员——

斯托克曼医生：那是因为我有资格当那儿的卫生官员！我比任何人都有资格！第一个发现这座城市有条件造疗养浴场的人就是我。当时，只有我看到了这一点。我单枪匹马为之奋斗了许多年，连篇累牍撰写宣传文章——

彼得·斯托克曼：此话毋庸置疑。不过，尽管计划很好，但条件并不成熟——你住在北方一个偏僻的小地方，当然看不到这一点。后来，条件一成熟，我——还有其他的一些人——立刻将计划付诸了实施。

斯托克曼医生：实施倒是实施了，然而却把我那么漂亮的计划搞得一团糟。显而易见，你们是些缺心眼儿少智慧的饭桶！

彼得·斯托克曼：据我看，你又犯了老毛病，在为你的好战之心找个发泄口。你喜欢跟你的上司唱对台戏——这可是你多年的习惯。谁要是权力比你大，你就无法容忍。你蔑视任何一个地位比你高的人，将他们视为仇敌，千方百计挑他们的刺、找他们的毛病。现在我必须提请你注意：你的一意孤行可能会威胁到这座城市的利益，也可能会损害我的利益。因此，我必须郑重警告你，托马斯，你必须按我的意思去做。

斯托克曼医生：做什么？

彼得·斯托克曼：这件事非常敏感，应该郑重对待，严加保密，可是你却不知轻重，竟告诉了外人，现在显然想瞒也瞒不住了。形形色色的谣言很快就会四处流传，而对咱们有成见的人会对此添油加醋地大做文章。所以你必须站出来，公开驳斥那些飞短流长。

斯托克曼医生：让我驳斥？怎么驳斥？我听不懂你的话。

彼得·斯托克曼：希望你站出来说你又做了进一步调查，得出的结论是：事态根本没有你最初所想象的那么危险，那么严重。

斯托克曼医生：啊哈？你想让我表这样的态？

彼得·斯托克曼：不仅如此，我们还希望你公开表示信任委员会，相信无论浴场有什么缺陷，他们一定会全心全意、认真负责地采取必要的应对措施。

斯托克曼医生：千不该，万不该，你就不该遮遮掩掩，隐瞒真相！请相信我的话，彼得，我这话可是认真的、毫不含糊的。

彼得·斯托克曼：作为浴场委员会的一名官员，你无权只考虑个人的想法。

斯托克曼医生：（感到意外）是吗？

彼得·斯托克曼：作为公职人员，是这样的。如果作为个体，那就是另外一码事了。而身为浴场的一名基层官员，你无权发表与你的上司相左的看法。

斯托克曼医生：岂有此理！我是个医生，一个科学家，竟无权——

彼得·斯托克曼：此事并不是简单的科学问题，而是一个复杂的问题，还牵扯技术和经济层面。

斯托克曼医生：我才不管牵扯什么层面呢，在任何问题上，我都要自由地发表自己的看法。

彼得·斯托克曼：悉听尊便。不过，凡是涉及浴场的事情，决不允许胡言乱语。我们不准你那样做。

斯托克曼医生：（提高了嗓门）你们不准——！哼！你们只不过是一群——

彼得·斯托克曼：这是我的禁令！我是你的上司——我的命令你必须服从。

斯托克曼医生：（压住胸中的怒火）彼得，假如你不是我哥哥的话——

佩特拉：（猛地推开门）爸爸，别忍这口气！

斯托克曼夫人：（追进来）佩特拉！佩特拉！

彼得·斯托克曼：哦！原来你们在外头偷听！

斯托克曼夫人：你们说话声音那么大，我们不听都不行！

佩特拉：不错，我就是在偷听。

彼得·斯托克曼：哦，不管怎么说吧，我非常高兴——

斯托克曼医生：（逼近一步）你在说"不准"和"服从"什么的，对不对？

彼得·斯托克曼：我那样说话也是你逼的。

斯托克曼医生：难道我非得隐瞒真相，对公众撒谎不成？

彼得·斯托克曼：我们认为你必须按照我刚才说的那样，发表个声明。

斯托克曼医生：要是我不照办呢？

彼得·斯托克曼：那我们就自己发表个声明，好让公众安心。

斯托克曼医生：那好，我将奉陪到底，用我的笔说话，坚持我的观点。我要让公众看到我是对的,你们是错的。那时候,你们会怎么样?

彼得·斯托克曼:到那时候,他们要免你的职的话,我可就想拦也拦不住了。

斯托克曼医生:你说什么?

佩特拉:爸爸——免你的职!

斯托克曼夫人:免职!

彼得·斯托克曼:他们会撤掉你在浴场的职务。到那时候,我将不得不提议马上让你走人,以后不准过问浴场的事务。

斯托克曼医生:你真敢那么做!

彼得·斯托克曼:是你自己铤而走险,逼我们这样做的。

佩特拉:伯伯,用这样的手段对付我爸爸这般正直的人,简直可耻!

斯托克曼夫人:少说话,佩特拉!

彼得·斯托克曼:(瞧着佩特拉)嘀,咱们窝里斗,一家人不认一家人了,是不是?当然是喽。(转向斯托克曼夫人)凯瑟琳,我觉得在你们家你是最有头脑的。你不妨动用一下你的影响力劝劝你丈夫,让他明白一个道理:他的一意孤行将会连累他的家人以及——

斯托克曼医生:我的家庭是我自己的事,不用你管!

彼得·斯托克曼:——不仅会连累他的家人,还会连累这座他休养生息的城市。

斯托克曼医生:真正关心这座城市利益的人是我!我要做的只不过是揭露早晚都会暴露于光天化日之下的弊

病。我要用实际行动表明我对自己故乡的赤子之心。

彼得·斯托克曼：你又盲目又顽固，难道想把这座城市最重要的财源一刀砍断？

斯托克曼医生：是毒源，伙计！你是不是疯了？咱们这是在靠贩卖污水和腐败发财致富！整个城市的繁荣昌盛全是靠谎言维持的！

彼得·斯托克曼：这些都是你个人的臆想，或者说是别有用心的杜撰。一个造谣污蔑自己故乡的人必将成为社会公敌。

斯托克曼医生：（冲上前去）你竟敢——！

斯托克曼夫人：（跨前一步，用身子把他们隔开）托马斯！

佩特拉：（拉住她父亲的胳膊）爸爸，别生气！

彼得·斯托克曼：我犯不上跟你动武。反正我警告过你了。仔细想想，怎么才对得起你自己和你的家庭吧。再见。（走了出去）

斯托克曼医生：（走来走去）这口气我怎么能咽得下去！他竟然跑到我家里来对我指手画脚，凯瑟琳！你说气人不气人！

斯托克曼夫人：的确既可耻又荒唐，托马斯——

佩特拉：我真想让伯伯听听我的看法——

斯托克曼医生：这也怪我自己有点儿优柔寡断。我早就应该跟他摊牌——让他尝尝我的厉害——叫他看看我不是好惹的！他竟然骂我是社会公敌！他骂我！是可忍，孰不可忍！

斯托克曼夫人：可是，亲爱的托马斯，你哥哥掌握着权力呀。

斯托克曼医生：他有权力，我有公理。

斯托克曼夫人：是呀，你有公理，你有公理。可是，你手中没有权力，公理又有什么用呢？

佩特拉：噢，妈妈，你怎么能说这种话！

斯托克曼医生：难道你认为在一个自由的国家里，手中掌握着公理会没有用处？你可真荒谬，凯瑟琳。再说，我不是还有一家思想开放、独立自主的报社在前边冲锋陷阵吗？不是还有广大民众给我做后盾吗？依我看，这就是最大的权力！

斯托克曼夫人：可是，托马斯，你不会真的那么干吧？

斯托克曼医生：真的怎么干？

斯托克曼夫人：针锋相对地跟你哥哥作对。

斯托克曼医生：上帝呀，不叫我坚持正义和真理，那叫我干什么？

佩特拉：不错，这也正是我心里的话。

斯托克曼夫人：可这不会给你带来任何好处。他们如果不高兴，就一定会给你小鞋穿。

斯托克曼医生：啊哈，等着瞧吧，凯瑟琳！到时候你会看到我将把战火烧到他们的大本营里去。

斯托克曼夫人：你把战火烧到他们的大本营里去，他们就把你解雇，看你怎么办。

斯托克曼医生：他骂我是社会公敌！即便天塌下来，我也要对公众尽责，对社会尽责！

斯托克曼夫人：可是，你的亲人怎么办，托马斯？你的家人怎么办？难道你就不应该想想怎样对自己的妻子儿女尽责吗？

佩特拉：妈妈，你不该遇事先考虑自己家。

斯托克曼夫人：你说得倒是容易！遇到风浪，你倒是有能力应付。托马斯，你得为年幼的儿子着想，为你自己着想，也为我——

斯托克曼医生：我想你是疯了，凯瑟琳！你要我成为一个可怜的懦夫，跪在地上向彼得以及他的狐群狗党乞怜，那我以后怎么做人，心里怎会有片刻的安宁？

斯托克曼夫人：这套道理我不懂，我只知道你如果跟他对着干，咱们家是不会有安宁日子的！到时候，没有了固定收入，咱们又会过上愁吃愁穿的苦日子。那种度日如年的生活，我已经过够了。托马斯，想想那是什么滋味，千万不能忘记过去！

斯托克曼医生：（控制住情绪，攥紧拳头）他们竟然让一个自由的、有尊严的人对他们奴颜婢膝！这还不可怕吗，凯瑟琳？

斯托克曼夫人：是很可怕。他们这般对待你，的的确确就是犯罪。可是，天下不公平的现象比比皆是，能忍就忍了吧。噢，孩子们来了，托马斯。你看看他们吧！往后他们该怎么办？唉，别那样做，别那样做！难道你忍心叫他们——（叶利夫和墨顿拿着课本已经走了进来，听着妈妈说话。）

斯托克曼医生：孩子们——我——（忽然表情变得坚

定起来）不行，即便整个世界都支离破碎了，我也决不低头让步。（走向书房）

斯托克曼夫人：（跟了过去）托马斯，你要干什么？

斯托克曼医生：（在书房门口）我要坚持正义——等孩子们长大成人后，我得有脸见他们。（走进书房）

斯托克曼夫人：（潸然泪下）上帝呀，帮帮我们吧！

佩特拉：爸爸是个有气节的人，绝不会屈服的！

〔两个男孩一脸迷茫地在一旁观看，佩特拉使眼色叫他们别作声。〕

第三幕

布景：《人民信使报》编辑室。后方左首是通向外面的正门。右首是一扇玻璃门，透过玻璃可以看见排字间。右墙上又有一门。屋子当中摆着一张大桌子，桌上堆满了稿件、报纸和书籍。前边左首有一扇窗户，靠窗摆着一张写字台，台前放着一只高凳子。桌子旁边有两把扶手椅，另外还有几把椅子靠墙摆放。屋子里光线暗淡，让人感到不舒服；家具是旧的，那些椅子又破又脏。可以看见排字间里有几个工人在忙着排字，而一个印刷工正在操作一台手摇印刷机。霍夫斯塔德在写字台前写东西。比林拿着斯托克曼医生的手稿从右边走进来。

比林：喂，我说！
霍夫斯塔德：（仍在写东西）你看完啦？
比林：（把手稿搁在写字台上）看完了，仔仔细细地看完了。

霍夫斯塔德：你看医生的话是不是很激烈？

比林：何止激烈！简直就是重磅炸弹！文章里的每一句话——怎么说呢？——每一句话都像是大铁锤在重重敲击。

霍夫斯塔德：是的。不过，他们那伙人一锤子是打不倒的。

比林：此话不假。所以，咱们必须一锤接一锤地砸，非得将那个官僚世界彻底砸碎不可。刚才我坐着看这份稿子的时候，我好像觉得一场革命正在孕育之中。

霍夫斯塔德：(转过身来)嘘！别让阿斯拉克森听见。

比林：(放低声音)阿斯拉克森胆小如鼠，是个草包，没有一点儿男子汉气概。不过，这次你是不是会坚持自己的主张，坚决不让步？是不是一定刊登医生的文章？

霍夫斯塔德：是的，假如市长不低头，咱们就登。

比林：那会掀起轩然大波的。

霍夫斯塔德：幸运的是，不管出现什么情况，形势都会对咱们有利。如果市长不同意医生的建议，就会惹恼那些小本生意人——房主联合会以及其他的一些人。要是他同意了医生的建议，则会得罪浴场的那些大股东——那些大股东一直都拥护他，是他的主要支持者——

比林：是的，那是用刀子割那些大股东的肉，让他们拿出真金白银来——

霍夫斯塔德：是的，那是一定的。等他们那个小集团一破裂，咱们就连篇累牍地发表文章，列举市长的诸多失职之处，号召民众擦亮眼睛，让他们看到应该叫自由派唱主角,将城市里的重要位置交给自由派,让自由派完全掌控城市事务。

比林:的确应该这样!于无声处听惊雷,我看见了,我看见革命的暴风雨就要来了!

〔外边有人敲门。〕

霍夫斯塔德:嘘!(大声)进来!(斯托克曼医生从临街的大门走了进来。霍夫斯塔德迎上前去。)啊,原来是你呀,医生!有何吩咐?

斯托克曼医生:赶快发表,霍夫斯塔德先生!

霍夫斯塔德:事情已经发展到这般田地啦?

比林:好极了!

斯托克曼医生:是的,赶快发表吧!毫无疑问,事情确实发展到这般田地了。他们酿的苦果,就让他们自己尝吧。这座城市里就要有一场刀光剑影的战斗了,比林先生!

比林:但愿是一场白刃战!咱们会把利剑刺向他们的喉咙,医生!

斯托克曼医生:这篇文章只是头一炮。我已经打好腹稿,准备再写四五篇。阿斯拉克森在哪儿呢?

比林:(向印刷室喊叫)阿斯拉克森,上这儿来一趟!

霍夫斯塔德:你说还要写四五篇文章?都是谈这件事?

斯托克曼医生:不是的,与此事关系不大,我亲爱的朋友,是另一件事,只不过都涉及供水和排水问题。要知道这是环环相扣的,走完一步棋就再走下一步棋。准确点儿说,跟拆旧房子一样,要一步一步来。

比林：完全正确。不把那些破破烂烂、又脏又旧的房子拆掉，咱们就绝不收兵。

阿斯拉克森：（走进屋来）拆掉？难道你们真的想拆掉浴场，医生？

霍夫斯塔德：不是那回事，别担心。

斯托克曼医生：对，我们谈的完全是另外一件事。霍夫斯塔德先生，你觉得我这篇文章怎么样？

霍夫斯塔德：我觉得写得简直太好了。

斯托克曼医生：真的吗？我太高兴了，简直高兴极了。

霍夫斯塔德：文章写得清晰易懂，不是专家也看得懂它的中心思想。明白事理的人一定会站在你这边。

阿斯拉克森：但愿稳健的人也会赞成。

比林：不管稳健的还是不稳健的，全城的人都会赞成的。

阿斯拉克森：这么说，咱们可以大胆把它登出来。

斯托克曼医生：我想是可以的！

霍夫斯塔德：那就让它明天早晨见报吧。

斯托克曼医生：当然，一天都不能耽搁。我想问你一声，阿斯拉克森先生，你肯不肯亲自监印这篇文章？

阿斯拉克森：非常乐意。

斯托克曼医生：要像对待宝贝一样对待它，仔仔细细地排印！不能出现一个错字——每一个字都很重要。回头我再来一趟，也许你可以让我看看校样。你们不知道我的心情有多么急迫，只盼着它马上见报，盼着它马上出现在公众面前——

比林：犹如一道闪电一样出现在公众面前！

斯托克曼医生：到时候就让眼睛雪亮的市民们看看孰是孰非吧。你们想象不到我今天蒙受了多么大的冤屈——他们用各种各样的手段威胁我，甚至企图剥夺我做人的基本权利——

比林：什么！剥夺你做人的权利！

斯托克曼医生：——他们企图贬低我的人格，让我成为一个懦夫，逼着我把个人利益放在最神圣的信念之上。

比林：岂有此理！是可忍，孰不可忍！

霍夫斯塔德：那帮人丧心病狂，什么事都做得出来。

斯托克曼医生：那好，我会叫他们吃不了兜着走的，一定要让他们尝尝我的厉害。我要把《人民信使报》作为阵地，天天写文章抨击他们，一篇接着一篇，就像一颗颗投向他们的炸弹——

阿斯拉克森：是的。不过——

比林：万岁！向他们宣战！向他们宣战！

斯托克曼医生：我要当着公众的面将他们打翻在地，把他们彻底击垮，我要把他们的一道道防线全都击破！不达目的誓不罢休！

阿斯拉克森：是的。不过，一定要稳一点儿，医生——稳健地步步推进。

比林：坚决不能四平八稳地做事，而应该雷厉风行！对他们绝不能心慈手软！

斯托克曼医生：要知道现在要解决的不仅仅是供水和排水的问题了，而且要使整个社会生活都得到净化和消毒——

比林：这话说到点子上了！

斯托克曼医生：应该明白，所有碌碌无为者都必须被撵出去——各行各业都是如此！一幅广阔无边的壮丽画卷已经展现在我的面前，只是目前还看不太清楚，但总有一天会看清的。咱们需要的和必须寻找的是年轻有为、充满活力的旗手，我的朋友们，让他们在各行各业领导人们前进。

比林：对，对！

斯托克曼医生：只要大家团结一致，咱们的大事就能够顺利完成。这场革命就会像一艘巨轮一样顺利地扬帆起航。你们说是不是？

霍夫斯塔德：依我看，这样做就有希望让有能力的人掌握城市的管理权。

阿斯拉克森：只要每一步都走得稳，我看就不会有什么危险。

斯托克曼医生：我才不管有没有危险呢！我所做的一切都是为了公理，为了做人的良心。

霍夫斯塔德：你光明磊落，应该得到民众的拥护，斯托克曼医生。

阿斯拉克森：是的，斯托克曼医生无可否认是这座城市真正的朋友，是真心实意为社会谋福利的人。

比林：信我的话，阿斯拉克森，斯托克曼医生是人民真正的朋友。

阿斯拉克森：我想，用不了多久，房主联合会就会用这样的美名称呼他的。

斯托克曼医生：（非常感动，跟大家握手）谢谢你们，谢谢你们，我亲爱的忠诚的朋友。听了你们的话，我感到极为振奋。我哥哥送给我的是一个完全相反的名称。我发誓一定要加倍回敬他！现在我得告辞了，要去看一位可怜的病人，回头再到这儿来。阿斯拉克森先生，我那篇文章排版印刷时一定要千小心万小心，可不要出错，不要漏掉一个感叹号！再加上一两个倒情有可原！千万，千万！诸位，暂时告别了！再见，再见！

〔大家送他到门口，互道珍重。〕

霍夫斯塔德：他对咱们大有用处。

阿斯拉克森：是的，只要他管的事情仅限于浴场就行了。可是，如果他越过雷池，咱们再跟着他摇旗呐喊，便非明智之举了。

霍夫斯塔德：唔！——这要看情况而定——

比林：阿斯拉克森，你这人掉个树叶都怕砸破头！

阿斯拉克森：说我胆小？不错，跟地方当局作对，我的胆子是很小，比林先生。让我告诉你吧，这是我从经验里得来的教训。不过，要是让我参与高层政治，参与政府的决策，那时候你看我还胆小不胆小。

比林：不错，我承认那时候你不会胆小的。可这正是你自相矛盾的地方。

阿斯拉克森：我是个有觉悟的人，这才是问题的所在。要是你攻击政府，对他们一点儿影响都没有，你会看到他们连理你都不理，该干什么照样干什么。而地方当局就不一样了——你可以把他们撵下台,换上一批新人手,但也许新人手狗屁不懂,结果会给房主及所有其他的人造成无法挽回的损失。

霍夫斯塔德:不过,公民自治也是一种锻炼嘛。难道你不觉得这很重要吗?

阿斯拉克森:一个人如果要维护自己的利益,就不能面面俱到,霍夫斯塔德先生。

霍夫斯塔德:但愿我永远都不会有自己的利益,也就不需要维护了。

比林:对,对!

阿斯拉克森:(笑了笑)哼!(指着写字台)谢里夫·斯坦斯卡德先生是你的前任,曾经坐在那张编辑桌前。

比林:(啐了一口)呸!那是个叛徒。

霍夫斯塔德:我可不是变色龙,永远不会是的。

阿斯拉克森:政坛上风云变幻,谁都说不准会出现什么情况,霍夫斯塔德先生。至于你,比林先生,鉴于你正在谋求市议会秘书的职位,我奉劝你还是把船帆稍微收一收的好。

比林:我——!

霍夫斯塔德:真有这事吗,比林?

比林:噢,是的——不过你必须清楚,我只是想给那些大人物制造点儿麻烦。

阿斯拉克森:反正这些跟我无关。不过,要是有人指责我在原则问题上胆小怕事和自相矛盾,那我就得强调一点:我的政治历史是公开透明的。我可不是个说变就变的人,要说变也只是变得更稳健了一些。我的心始终和人民在一起,但我不否认,我的理智多少有点儿偏向当局那方面——我说的是地方当局。(走进印刷室)

比林:这种人,是不是不要再跟他打交道了,霍夫斯塔德?

霍夫斯塔德:你看还有什么别的人愿意为咱们垫付纸张费和印刷费吗?

比林:没有资本真麻烦!

霍夫斯塔德:(在写字台前坐下)是啊,只要咱们有资本——

比林:是不是可以去找斯托克曼医生想想办法?

霍夫斯塔德:(翻阅稿件)找他有什么用?他一个子儿也没有。

比林:他没钱,可他背后有个有钱的人——墨顿·基尔老头儿,人称"老獾"。

霍夫斯塔德:(一边写)你敢肯定那老头儿有钱吗?

比林:百分之百地肯定!他的一部分钱一定会给斯托克曼一家子的。不管怎么说,他会把钱用在孩子们的身上,这是极有可能的。

霍夫斯塔德:(身子转过一半来)你在打这个算盘?

比林:打算盘?我什么算盘也没有打。

霍夫斯塔德:那就好。我要是你,就连议会秘书职位的算盘也不打。你就是有那个打算,我可以向你保证,也一定会竹篮打水一场空的。

比林:你当我不知道?我的真正目的不是得到那个职

位，而是想让他们给我个钉子碰碰——碰钉子能激起一个人的战斗力，给人增添一种战天斗地的劲头儿。我坚信，在这座无波无澜、缺乏刺激的偏僻小城里，迫切需要的就是这种精神和劲头儿。

霍夫斯塔德：(手不停挥地写着)是这样的，是这样的。

比林：好啦，等着瞧吧！——我得去写那篇告房主联合会之书了。(走进右边的房间)

霍夫斯塔德：(坐在写字台前，咬着笔杆，慢吞吞地自言自语)对，就这样，就这样！(有人敲门)请进！(佩特拉从外边的那扇门走进来。霍夫斯塔德站了起来。)哦，是你？有事吗？

佩特拉：是的。恕我打搅——

霍夫斯塔德：(拉过一把椅子来)坐下谈好不好？

佩特拉：谢谢，不坐了，我马上就走。

霍夫斯塔德：你来这儿是不是为你父亲捎话？

佩特拉：不，我为自己的事而来。(从外套口袋里掏出一本书)这是那本英文小说。

霍夫斯塔德：为什么你又把它拿回来了？

佩特拉：我不翻译了。

霍夫斯塔德：可是你答应过我——

佩特拉：不错，可那是因为我没看过。恐怕你也没看过吧？

霍夫斯塔德：是的。你知道我不懂英文，可是——

佩特拉：我知道。正因如此，所以我要你另找点儿别的材料。(把书搁在桌子上)这篇小说不能登在《人民信使报》上。

霍夫斯塔德：为什么不能登？

佩特拉：因为它的内容跟你们的观念是矛盾的。

霍夫斯塔德：哦，说到这一点——

佩特拉：你没明白我的意思。这篇小说的意思是说，冥冥之中有一种超自然的力量保佑着世界上的所谓好人，使他们事事如意；而另一方面，所有的所谓坏人都受到了惩罚。

霍夫斯塔德：这些话没说错啊，因为读者想看到的正是这种现象。

佩特拉：难道你相信这样的鬼话？反正我是绝对不相信的。你心里很清楚，现实世界里是没有这种事的。

霍夫斯塔德：你说的一点儿不错。不过，编辑不能总是按照自己的意愿行事，在不重要的事情上要迎合公众的趣味。在社会生活中，政治是最要紧的问题——反正对报纸而言就是这样。如果我想宣传我的政治主张，沿着一条通往自由和进步的道路走下去，就不能把读者吓跑。倘若将这样一篇道德小说连载于我报的文艺版，读者赞成书中的伦理观念，他们就愿意看前边几版登载的内容——可以说，这样一来他们就更安心了。

佩特拉：不害臊！你不该设这样的圈套引读者上钩！你又不是只蜘蛛！

霍夫斯塔德：（含笑）谢谢你如此高看我。其实，这不是我的主意，而是比林的锦囊妙计。

佩特拉：是比林出的馊主意？

霍夫斯塔德:是的。不管怎么说,那天是他推出了这套理论,就是在这个地方。急于连载这篇小说的也是比林,而我对这本书的内容一无所知。

佩特拉:可是,比林的思想那么进步,怎么会——

霍夫斯塔德:噢,比林是个很复杂的人。听说他还想进议会,当议会的秘书呢。

佩特拉:我简直不敢相信,霍夫斯塔德先生。他怎么能干那种事?

霍夫斯塔德:啊,这你得问他自己了。

佩特拉:我真没想到比林是这种人。

霍夫斯塔德:(仔细打量她)没想到?你真的感到很意外吗?

佩特拉:是的。或者说,也许并不意外。真的,我就是不太明白——

霍夫斯塔德:我们当记者的没有多大价值,斯托克曼小姐。

佩特拉:你真这么想吗?

霍夫斯塔德:我有时候这么想。

佩特拉:报道一些家长里短的普通小事也许价值不大,这我是可以理解的。不过,你们现在要报道一件重大事情了——

霍夫斯塔德:你指的是你父亲那件事吧?

佩特拉:正是。我想你现在一定觉得自己身价百倍了吧?

霍夫斯塔德:是的,我今天的确有这种感觉。

佩特拉：这是当然的，对不对？你选择了一个光荣的职业——为即将出现的真理鸣锣开道，为勇敢的新思想铺平道路。最为重要的是，你敢于仗义执言，和一个蒙冤受屈的人站在一起——

霍夫斯塔德：尤其因为那个蒙冤受屈的人是——唉！——我不知道该怎么说才好——

佩特拉：你要说那个蒙冤受屈的是个正直、诚实的人？

霍夫斯塔德：（柔声细语）我的意思是说，尤其因为他是你父亲。

佩特拉：（突然愣住了）你为的是这个？

霍夫斯塔德：是的，佩特拉——佩特拉小姐。

佩特拉：难道你首先考虑的是这个？而不是事情本身？不是真理？也不是我父亲的那颗伟大、正义的心？

霍夫斯塔德：当然，这些我也是考虑的。

佩特拉：谢谢你的直言不讳。霍夫斯塔德先生，你暴露了你的真实想法，从今往后我再也不会信任你了。

霍夫斯塔德：难道我说主要看你的面子，你就这么生我的气——

佩特拉：我生你的气是因为你对我父亲不诚实。你曾对他慷慨陈词，仿佛你最关心的是公理和民众的福祉，欺骗了我的父亲，也蒙蔽了我的双眼。你表里不一，说一套做一套，让人无法原谅，永远也无法原谅！

霍夫斯塔德：你说话不该如此刻薄，佩特拉小姐——尤其在这种时刻。

佩特拉：为什么说尤其在这种时刻？

霍夫斯塔德：因为你父亲没有我的帮助将寸步难行。

佩特拉：（从上到下打量他）难道你真会袖手旁观？实在可耻！

霍夫斯塔德：不，不，我不是那号儿人。刚才的话完全是有口无心，请你务必相信。

佩特拉：我心里清楚应该相信什么。再见。

阿斯拉克森：（从印刷室走进来，一副急急忙忙、稀奇古怪的样子。）见鬼了，霍夫斯塔德！——（一眼看见了佩特拉）唉，真是尴尬——

佩特拉：书在桌子上，你找别人翻译吧。（向门口走去）

霍夫斯塔德：（跟了过去）听我说，佩特拉小姐——

佩特拉：再见。（走了出去）

阿斯拉克森：我说，霍夫斯塔德先生——

霍夫斯塔德：听着呢！怎么啦？

阿斯拉克森：市长来了，在印刷室里。

霍夫斯塔德：你说市长来了？

阿斯拉克森：是的。他想跟你谈谈。他是从后门进来的，因为他不愿叫人看见，这你明白。

霍夫斯塔德：他想跟我谈什么呢？等一等，我去见他。（走到印刷室门口，开门，鞠躬，请彼得·斯托克曼进来。）瞧着点儿，阿斯拉克森，别让人——

阿斯拉克森：我懂得。（走进印刷室）

彼得·斯托克曼：你大概没想到我会来找你吧，霍夫斯塔德先生？

霍夫斯塔德：是的，的确没想到。

彼得·斯托克曼：（四面一望）你这儿很舒服，实在让人感到惬意。

霍夫斯塔德：是吗？

彼得·斯托克曼：事先也没有打个招呼我就跑了来，多有打搅！

霍夫斯塔德：哪里的话，市长先生。有什么事只管吩咐。你把帽子和手杖交给我吧。（把东西接过来，搁在一把椅子上）请坐。

彼得·斯托克曼：（在桌旁坐下）谢谢。（霍夫斯塔德也坐了下来。）今天遇到一件事，实在把我烦透了，霍夫斯塔德先生。

霍夫斯塔德：真的吗？你日理万机，难免会——

彼得·斯托克曼：今天叫我心烦的是那位浴场卫生官员。

霍夫斯塔德：是吗？是斯托克曼医生？

彼得·斯托克曼：他给浴场委员会写了个报告，说浴场存在问题。

霍夫斯塔德：他真这么说？

彼得·斯托克曼：是的。他没告诉你吗？我还以为他说过——

霍夫斯塔德：噢，对啦，他的确提到过——

阿斯拉克森：（从印刷室出来）我来拿那篇稿子。

霍夫斯塔德：（气呼呼地）噢！在写字台上。

阿斯拉克森：（把稿子拿到手里）有了。

彼得·斯托克曼：等等，这是不是就是我刚才说的那篇稿子?

阿斯拉克森:是的,是医生写的那篇,市长先生。

霍夫斯塔德:哦?你们刚才谈论这篇稿子啦?

彼得·斯托克曼:是的,一点儿不错。你看写得怎么样?

霍夫斯塔德:噢,我是个外行,只是随便扫了一眼。

彼得·斯托克曼:扫了一眼就决定刊登?

霍夫斯塔德:对于出自一个杰出才俊的文章,我是无法拒登的。

阿斯拉克森:编辑稿件的事情跟我无关,市长先生——

彼得·斯托克曼:这我知道。

阿斯拉克森:我只是负责把交给我的稿件印出来。

彼得·斯托克曼:是这样的。

阿斯拉克森:所以我必须——(动身走向印刷室)

彼得·斯托克曼:等一等,阿斯拉克森先生。能让我说句话吗,霍夫斯塔德先生?

霍夫斯塔德:但说无妨,市长先生。

彼得·斯托克曼:你是个谨慎细心、善解人意的人,阿斯拉克森先生。

阿斯拉克森:承蒙夸奖,市长先生。

彼得·斯托克曼:而且是一个很有影响力的人。

阿斯拉克森:主要是在小本生意人群体里有点儿影响力。

彼得·斯托克曼:小本生意人是纳税的中流砥柱——世界各地全都如此。

阿斯拉克森:这话不假。

彼得·斯托克曼：毫无疑问，他们当中的主流看法你是了解的，对不对？

阿斯拉克森：是的，我想是这样的，市长先生。

彼得·斯托克曼：在这座城市里，正是这么一个市民群体，经济上并不十分宽裕，然而却有一种值得称赞的自我牺牲精神——

阿斯拉克森：什么精神？

霍夫斯塔德：自我牺牲精神！

彼得·斯托克曼：这是一种集体精神的表现，令人感到高兴，实在令人感到高兴。实话说，这种情况是我始料未及的。对于民意，你了解得比我清楚。

阿斯拉克森：可是，市长先生——

彼得·斯托克曼：这一次，这座城市要做出的牺牲确实不小。

霍夫斯塔德：这座城市？

阿斯拉克森：我不明白你的意思。是不是浴场——？

彼得·斯托克曼：我们粗略估计了一下，那位卫生官员提出的几项改建工程要花费大约两万英镑。

阿斯拉克森：这数目可不小。不过——

彼得·斯托克曼：当然，有必要发行一批市政公债。

霍夫斯塔德：（站起来）难道你要全体市民出这笔钱？

阿斯拉克森：你是说这笔钱必须市民众筹？从小本生意人干瘪的钱包里掏钱？

彼得·斯托克曼：我亲爱的阿斯拉克森先生，难道还能从别的地方筹到钱吗？

阿斯拉克森：这笔钱应该由浴场的股东出。

彼得·斯托克曼：浴场的股东是不会再出一分钱的。

阿斯拉克森：你敢肯定吗，市长先生？

彼得·斯托克曼：我自认为是有这个把握的。如果这座城市想进行大规模改建，钱就应该由城市出。

阿斯拉克森：哼，真他妈的——对不起！——如果是这样，就另当别论了，霍夫斯塔德先生。

霍夫斯塔德：是的，的确如此。

彼得·斯托克曼：最糟的是，浴场必须停业，两年开不了门。

霍夫斯塔德：停业？彻底不能营业？

阿斯拉克森：要停两年？

彼得·斯托克曼：是的，工程得耗时两年——最起码两年。

阿斯拉克森：见鬼，那怎么能叫人受得了，市长先生！让我们这些房主吃什么、喝什么？

彼得·斯托克曼：不幸的是，这个问题太难回答了，阿斯拉克森先生。你叫我们怎么办？假如咱们对外宣布，说咱们的水受到了污染，周围瘟疫流行，整个城市都——

阿斯拉克森：这都是些没有根据的空想吧？

彼得·斯托克曼：我想来想去，想不出丝毫的根据。

阿斯拉克森：这么说，斯托克曼医生的话完全是空穴来风、无中生有了——请原谅我这么说他，市长先生。

彼得·斯托克曼：不幸都被你言中了，阿斯拉克森先生。我弟弟一向都很任性，做事欠考虑。

阿斯拉克森：既然是这样，你还打算支持他吗，霍夫斯塔德先生？

霍夫斯塔德：谁能想得到——

彼得·斯托克曼：我写了一篇短文，用理智的眼光分析了当前的形势，特意指出，即便出现问题，浴场委员会也有能力加以解决。

霍夫斯塔德：你把文章带来了没有，市长先生？

彼得·斯托克曼：（在衣袋里摸索）带来了。我把它拿来是觉得你可能会——

阿斯拉克森：天呀，他来了！

彼得·斯托克曼：谁？我弟弟吗？

霍夫斯塔德：在哪儿？在哪儿？

阿斯拉克森：他刚走过排字间。

彼得·斯托克曼：真是太糟糕了！我不想在这儿见他，可是还有几件事要跟你们说呢。

霍夫斯塔德：（指着右面的门）你到那里头坐一坐。

彼得·斯托克曼：可是——

霍夫斯塔德：里头除了比林没别人。

阿斯拉克森：快，快，市长先生。他就要进来了。

彼得·斯托克曼：好，就这么办。不过，你们可要想办法赶快将他打发走。（阿斯拉克森为他推开右面的门，等他进去后，就又把门拉上了。）

霍夫斯塔德：你装着很忙的样子，阿斯拉克森。（他坐下写字。阿斯拉克森翻弄搁在椅子上的一堆报纸。）

斯托克曼医生：（从排字间进来）我回来了。（放下帽

子和手杖)

霍夫斯塔德:(一边写字)这么快,医生?刚才说的事,你可要加紧办,阿斯拉克森。今天的时间非常紧迫。

斯托克曼医生:(冲着阿斯拉克森)听说校样还没出来?

阿斯拉克森:(没回身)哪能这么快,医生。

斯托克曼医生:是啊,是啊。不过,我心急如焚,希望你能理解。那篇文章不见报,我的心一刻也得不到安宁。

霍夫斯塔德:哦?文章印出来得花些时间呢,是不是,阿斯拉克森?

阿斯拉克森:是的,恐怕是这样的。

斯托克曼医生:好吧,我亲爱的朋友们,回头我再来吧。如果有必要的话,我多跑两趟也没关系。此事关系重大——城市的福祉受到了威胁——怕麻烦是不行的。(转身离去,但刚走两步就停下,又走了回来)噢,我想起来了,还有件事要跟你说。

霍夫斯塔德:对不起,改天再说行不行?

斯托克曼医生:一两句话就完了。是这么回事:明天大家在报上看了我的文章,就会知道我一冬天都在为这座城市的福祉埋头工作——

霍夫斯塔德:是的。可是医生——

斯托克曼医生:我知道你想说什么。你觉得这不过是我的责任——显然也是一个公民的责任。当然,这一点我也很明白。可是,要知道,我的市民同胞们可能会——你不妨想一想那些好心人会怎么样吧,他们可一直都是非常看重我的!

阿斯拉克森:市民们一向非常看重你,医生。

斯托克曼医生:我担心的正是这一点,也是非常关键的一点。这消息一传到他们耳朵里,尤其是那些穷人,可能会觉得这是在号召他们将来把地方政权掌握在他们自己手中——

霍夫斯塔德:(站起来)是啊。医生,不瞒你说——

斯托克曼医生:看看,我就知道有这种事!不过,我不愿意听到这种事。如果这种事情已经在酝酿——

霍夫斯塔德:酝酿什么事情?

斯托克曼医生:不管是什么事情都不行——为我举办游行、宴会或颁发奖章什么的,这些都是不行的。你可要发誓,庄严、诚挚地发誓,一定要出面阻止这种事情的发生。你也要站出来阻止,阿斯拉克森先生,明白吗?

霍夫斯塔德:请你原谅,医生,我们必须把实际情况告诉你,反正早晚都是要说的——

〔斯托克曼夫人从临街的门走进来,使得他没能说下去。〕

斯托克曼夫人:(一眼看见了丈夫)我就想到你在这儿。

霍夫斯塔德:(迎上去)斯托克曼夫人,你也来了?

斯托克曼医生:你来这儿干什么,凯瑟琳?

斯托克曼夫人:你当然知道我来干什么。

霍夫斯塔德:坐下说,好不好?也许——

斯托克曼夫人:谢谢,不用客气。我来找我丈夫,请你别见怪。你知道,我可是三个孩子的母亲。

斯托克曼医生：废话！这谁都知道。

斯托克曼夫人：是吗？恐怕没人知道你今天做的事情好像并没有将你的妻子儿女放在心上。你要是真的关心我们，就不会把我们拖入灾难之中了。

斯托克曼医生：你疯了吧，凯瑟琳？难道一个人因为有了妻子儿女，就不该宣传真理了吗？就不该做个积极有用的公民了吗？就不该为自己的家乡尽责效力了吗？

斯托克曼夫人：该是该，托马斯，但一定要合乎人情。

阿斯拉克森：这正是我的观点。做任何事情都要稳健。

斯托克曼夫人：这就是你的不对了，霍夫斯塔德先生。你怂恿我丈夫离开他的家人，设下圈套愚弄他。

霍夫斯塔德：我可没有愚弄任何人——

斯托克曼医生：愚弄我？你以为我是傻瓜，是好愚弄的吗？

斯托克曼夫人：你就是好愚弄的！我很清楚你是这座城市里最有头脑的人，但也最容易上当受骗，托马斯。（转向霍夫斯塔德）你可要知道，如果你把他写的文章登出来，他就会丢掉浴场的工作。

阿斯拉克森：什么？

霍夫斯塔德：听我说，医生！

斯托克曼医生：（大笑）哈哈！让他们试试！谅他们也不敢。告诉你吧，我身后有广大市民的支持！

斯托克曼夫人：这就更糟了——他们支持你就是害你。

斯托克曼医生：胡说，凯瑟琳。你回去把家里的事管好就是了，社会上的事让我管吧。我信心十足，高高兴兴的，你害怕个啥劲儿？（来回踱步，搓手）你放心，真理和人民一定会胜利的！我仿佛看见思想开明的中产阶级浩浩荡荡地走了过来——像一支凯旋的军队在前进！（在一把椅子旁边站住）咦，这是什么东西？

阿斯拉克森：糟糕！

霍夫斯塔德：唉！

斯托克曼医生：这可是最高权力的象征呀！（用两个指尖儿把市长的官帽小心夹着，高高举起）

斯托克曼夫人：是市长的帽子！

斯托克曼医生：这儿还有一根权杖！这两件宝贝怎么会——

霍夫斯塔德：噢，你知道——

斯托克曼医生：噢，我明白了。他来过这儿，是要做你的思想工作。哈哈！这回他可把算盘打错了！他一看见我在印刷室，撒腿就跑了。（放声大笑）他是不是跑了，阿斯拉克森先生？

阿斯拉克森：（急忙）不错，他跑掉了，医生。

斯托克曼医生：顾不得拿手杖和——令人无法置信！彼得是绝不会把自己的东西丢下的！你们把他藏在哪儿了？啊，一定在那个房间里。你瞧着，凯瑟琳！

斯托克曼夫人：托马斯，求你别胡来！

阿斯拉克森：别鲁莽，医生！

〔斯托克曼医生戴了市长的帽子，拿了市长的手杖，走到那扇门前，把门推开，行了个军礼。彼得·斯托克曼走了出来，脸气得通红。比林跟在后面。〕

彼得·斯托克曼：这是搞什么鬼名堂？

斯托克曼医生：说话放尊重些，我的好彼得。现在我是这座城市的当权派。（大摇大摆地走来走去）

斯托克曼夫人：（几乎要哭）别闹了，托马斯！

彼得·斯托克曼：（跟在他后面）把帽子和手杖还给我！

斯托克曼医生：（还是那副口气）你也许是警察局长，但我是市长——全城市民的主人，请你务必明白这一点！

彼得·斯托克曼：把帽子摘下来！别忘了这是政府官员戴的帽子。

斯托克曼医生：得了吧！觉醒的人民是无所畏惧的，难道你以为他们会害怕一顶官帽？告诉你吧，明天这座城市里将会爆发一场革命。你以为可以解雇我，现在就让我解雇你吧——撤销你的全部职务！你以为我做不到吗？等着瞧吧，强大的社会力量是支持我的。霍夫斯塔德和比林将会在《人民信使报》上开炮，而阿斯拉克森会一马当先，率领房主联合会加入战斗——

阿斯拉克森：我恐怕干不了，医生。

斯托克曼医生：你当然可以——

彼得·斯托克曼：哈哈！我想问一声：霍夫斯塔德先生是不是愿意煽阴风点鬼火？

霍夫斯塔德：不愿意，市长先生。

阿斯拉克森：霍夫斯塔德先生又不是个傻瓜，不会愿意为了一件捕风捉影的事毁了自己以及他的报纸的。

斯托克曼医生：（四面一望）这是怎么回事？

霍夫斯塔德：你的文章论据不足，有些虚妄，所以我不能支持你。

比林：市长给我解释了情况，恕我也不能——

斯托克曼医生：有些虚妄？我可以负全责！你们只要把文章登出来就是了，我完全有能力为我的证据辩护。

霍夫斯塔德：恕我不能登——我不能登，不愿意登，也不敢登。

斯托克曼医生：你不敢登？这是什么话？你是编辑，我觉得在报社是编辑说了算的！

阿斯拉克森：差矣。是订户说了算，医生。

彼得·斯托克曼：幸而如此。

阿斯拉克森：说了算的是公众舆论，是开明的公众，是房主和其他老百姓。支配报纸的是这些人。

斯托克曼医生：（不动声色）难道这些力量都会反对我？

阿斯拉克森：是的，是这样的。如果登载了你的文章，全城都会跟着遭殃。

斯托克曼医生：原来是这么回事。

彼得·斯托克曼：请你把帽子和手杖还给我！（斯托克曼医生摘下帽子，连手杖一道搁在桌上。彼得·斯托克曼把它们拿在手里。）你这短命市长完蛋了。

斯托克曼医生：鹿死谁手还不知道呢。（转向霍夫斯塔德）这么说你不能在《人民信使报》上刊登我的文章了？

霍夫斯塔德：是的，这也是为你的家人考虑。

斯托克曼夫人：谢谢你，霍夫斯塔德先生，你不必为他的家人考虑。

彼得·斯托克曼：（从衣袋里掏出一篇稿子）一旦有情况发生，用这个来引导公众应该足够了。这是一份官方声明，可以麻烦你登在报上吗？

霍夫斯塔德：（把稿子接过来）当然可以。马上就登。

斯托克曼医生：我的文章你不登！你以为压住我的稿子就能压住我，就能扼杀真理吗！事情恐怕不会像你想的那么简单。阿斯拉克森先生，请你马上把我的文章印成小册子——费用由我出。我要印四百册——不，印五百册或六百册。

阿斯拉克森：即便你给我几百册小册子那么重的黄金，我也不能让我的印刷机印这样的文章，医生——这可是冒天下之大不韪。这座城市里没有一家印刷厂会给你印的。

斯托克曼医生：那就把稿子还给我吧。

霍夫斯塔德：（把稿子交还给他）给，拿去吧。

斯托克曼医生：（拿起自己的帽子和手杖）文章反正是要公布出去的。我要在市民大会上把它念出来，让市民同胞们听到真理的声音！

彼得·斯托克曼：全城没有一个团体肯把会场借给你做这么一件事的。

阿斯拉克森：我敢说会是这样的。

比林：是的。你要是能找到会场，那才真是活见鬼呢。

斯托克曼夫人：这简直太可耻了！为什么他们都要跟你对着干？

斯托克曼医生：（生气地）我告诉你为什么。因为咱们这儿的男人都是老太婆——都跟你一样，只关心自己家里人,不关心公众的利益。

斯托克曼夫人:(挽起丈夫的胳膊)那么,这回我要让他们看看,一个老太婆也能做个大丈夫。我和你站在一起,托马斯!

斯托克曼医生:这话说得有胆量,凯瑟琳!我只要有一口气,就一定要将文章公布出去!找不到会场,那我就找一面鼓来,敲着鼓游街,在街头巷尾念我的文章。

彼得·斯托克曼:你不至于疯到那种地步吧!

斯托克曼医生:我会那样做的。

阿斯拉克森:全城没有一个人会跟你走的。

比林:是的。要是有人跟你走,那才是活见鬼了。

斯托克曼夫人:别泄气,托马斯,我会叫咱家的孩子跟你走。

斯托克曼医生:这主意好极了!

斯托克曼夫人:墨顿一定很高兴跟你走,叶利夫也会很乐意的。

斯托克曼医生:对,佩特拉也会去!还有你,凯瑟琳!

斯托克曼夫人:我不去。我要站在窗口看着你们,我将在那儿为你们打气。

斯托克曼医生:(搂住她亲吻)谢谢你,亲爱的!先生们,那咱们就较量较量吧!我倒要看看,一群懦夫是不是能够压制住一个渴望净化社会的爱国者!(他和妻子一道走出了临街的大门。)

彼得·斯托克曼:(表情凝重地摇摇头)现在,他把自己的妻子也带疯了。

第四幕

布景:霍斯特船长家一间旧式大屋子。后面的双扇合页门开着,通到一个小套间。左边墙上有三扇窗。对面墙壁的正中间搭了个台子,台上摆着一张小桌子,桌上有两支蜡烛、一个水瓶、一只玻璃杯和一个铃。窗与窗之间点着几盏灯。前方左首有张桌子,桌上有几支蜡烛,桌旁有把椅子。右首有扇门,门跟前放着几把椅子。屋子几乎是满满当当的,挤满了来自各行各业的市民,其中夹着几个女人和男学生。仍有人不断从后面涌入,很快就连个插脚的地方也没有了。

市民甲:(和另一个市民打招呼)喂,拉姆斯塔德!你也来了?

市民乙:是的。每逢公众集会我都参加。

市民丙:我想你肯定把哨子也带来了!

市民乙:那还用说。你呢?

市民丙:当然也带来了!埃文森老伙计说要拿一只牛

角号来呢。

市民乙:埃文森那家伙真逗人!(大家笑起来。)

市民丁:(靠拢来)喂,请问,今晚到底开的是什么会呀?

市民乙:斯托克曼医生要发表演说,抨击市长。

市民丁:市长可是他哥哥呀。

市民甲:那有什么!斯托克曼医生可不是个胆小怕事的人。

市民丙:可他错了——《人民信使报》上是这么说的。

市民乙:是的,我觉得这次他肯定错了,因为无论是房主联合会还是市民俱乐部都不愿借场地给他,让他开这个会。

市民甲:他甚至连浴场的大厅也借不到。

市民乙:是的,我想他是借不到的。

人群中另一个角落的一个与会者:我说——这件事咱们该支持谁呀?

他身旁的另一个与会者:看着阿斯拉克森好啦,他支持谁咱们就支持谁。

比林:(腋下夹着一个文具盒挤过人群)对不起,先生们,能不能叫我过一过?我在为《人民信使报》写新闻报道。十分感谢!(他在会场左侧的桌旁坐下。)

一个工人:他是谁呀?

第二个工人:你不认识?他叫比林,为阿斯拉克森的报纸撰稿。

〔霍斯特船长带着斯托克曼夫人以及佩特拉从右边的

门走进了会场,叶利夫和墨顿紧随其后。〕

霍斯特:我想你们都坐在这里比较好,万一场面过于激烈,便于溜出去。

斯托克曼夫人:你认为这儿会出乱子吗?

霍斯特:天有不测风云,有这些人在场,谁都说不准。不过,你坐下就是了,不必为此感到不安。

斯托克曼夫人:(落座)你借会场给我丈夫,真是叫人感激不尽。

霍斯特:噢,要是没人愿意——

佩特拉:(在母亲身旁坐下)这可是件需要勇气的事情,霍斯特船长。

霍斯特:噢,小事一桩,哪有那么了不起。

〔霍夫斯塔德和阿斯拉克森挤过人群走了过来。〕

阿斯拉克森:(走到霍斯特跟前)医生还没来吧?

霍斯特:他在隔壁的房间等着呢。(后边大门那儿的人群里出现了一些动静。)

霍夫斯塔德:瞧,市长来啦!

比林:是的。他要是再不来,会把人急死的!

〔彼得·斯托克曼一点儿一点儿挤过人群,走到左侧的墙根,彬彬有礼地冲众人鞠了一躬,然后坐了下来。须臾,斯托克曼医生从右首的那扇门入场,身穿黑颜色的双排扣长礼服,脖系白领结。这时响起了稀稀拉拉的几声掌声,随后掌声便消失了。会场上恢复了平静。〕

斯托克曼医生:(低声)你感觉怎么样,凯瑟琳?

斯托克曼夫人:还好,谢谢。(压低嗓门)你可一定不要发脾气，托马斯。

斯托克曼医生：噢，我心里有数，会控制好自己的。（看看表，然后走上主席台，冲众人鞠躬致敬）现在已经过一刻钟了……所以，我就开始了。（从口袋里掏出他的讲演稿）

阿斯拉克森：我觉得应该先选出大会主席再开会。

斯托克曼医生：不，完全没这个必要。

几个与会者：有必要！有必要！

彼得·斯托克曼：斯托克曼医生的报告很可能会招致不同的看法，引得众说纷纭。

人群中有几个声音：选大会主席！选大会主席！

霍夫斯塔德：这是人心所向——与会者似乎普遍希望能选出大会主席。

斯托克曼医生：（克制住情绪）好吧，那就按大家的意思办吧。

阿斯拉克森：诸位看，市长是否能胜任这个职务？

人群中的第三位与会者：（鼓掌）好极啦！好极啦！

彼得·斯托克曼：诸位，由于某些大家很容易理解的原因，我就不主持会议了。幸运的是，咱们中间有一位主持会议的合适人选，我想大家一定都赞成。那就是房主联合会主席阿斯拉克森先生。

许多声音：赞成，赞成阿斯拉克森主持！拥护阿斯拉克森！

〔斯托克曼医生拿起稿子，在台上走来走去。〕

阿斯拉克森：既然市民同胞们信任我，让我主持，我也就不推辞了。

〔大家鼓掌欢呼。阿斯拉克森走上讲台。〕

比林：（记录）"与会群众一致欢迎阿斯拉克森先生任会议主席。"

阿斯拉克森：既然大家选我当主席，那我就简单说几句吧。我是个喜欢平静生活、过安稳日子的人，讲求的是谨慎和稳重，也就是信奉中庸之道。对于这一点，我的朋友可以做证。

许多声音：没错！没错，阿斯拉克森！

阿斯拉克森：从生活经验中我体会到，稳重是一个公民应该具有的最宝贵的品质——

彼得·斯托克曼：说得好，说得好！

阿斯拉克森：而且，这种谨慎和稳重的品质可以让一个人最为有效地服务于社会。因而，我奉劝那位召集了这次会议的可敬的公民，一定要慎重行事，绝不应该超越底线。

门口的一个人：节制运动协会万岁！

一个声音：见鬼！

许多声音：嘘！嘘！

阿斯拉克森：先生们，请肃静！有没有人要发言？

彼得·斯托克曼：主席先生！

阿斯拉克森：市长要发言了。

彼得·斯托克曼：鉴于我跟浴场的那位卫生官员是近亲，今天晚上我本不打算发言。可是我是浴场委员会主席，并且有责任关心这座城市的重大利益，于是就不得不说几句了。我敢说，今天到会的公民没有一个赞成传播负面新闻，把那些关于浴场卫生状况的不靠谱的、夸大其词的传闻公布出去。

许多声音：不赞成！当然不赞成！

彼得·斯托克曼：所以我要提个建议：不允许那位卫生官员宣读他的报告书，不允许他妄加评论。

斯托克曼医生：(大怒)不允许？搞什么鬼！

斯托克曼夫人：(咳嗽)呃哼！呃哼！

斯托克曼医生：(压住心头的怒火)好吧，你继续说吧！

彼得·斯托克曼：我在《人民信使报》发表的声明已经把重要事实说得很清楚了，任何一个公正的公民看了都会一目了然，都能看得到那位卫生官员提出的建议将会产生怎样的严重后果——他不仅对本市领导层横加指责，还会给纳税人增加至少数千英镑的不必要的负担。

〔人群中响起了不满的声音和叽里呱啦的乱叫声。〕

阿斯拉克森：(摇铃)肃静，请肃静，先生们！我拥护市长提出的建议，同意他的观点，认为医生的调查报告是醉翁之意不在酒，明着是说浴场的事情，其实意在发动一场革命，要变更这座城市的管理权。没人会怀疑医生有什么不良动机——对于这一点，大家的看法恐怕是一致的。我本人也是赞成人民自治的，但有一个原则——不能给纳税人增加过于沉重的负担。所以，我死也不能——对不起——在这件事情上，我不能跟他站在一起。有的时候，你得为一件事情付出高昂的代价，这就是我的看法。

〔鼓掌喝彩声四起。〕

霍夫斯塔德：在此，我觉得有必要解释一下我的处境。

起初，斯托克曼医生的建议似乎引起了一些共鸣，我也全心全意、毫无保留地支持他。可后来不久我们就觉得自己有理由怀疑受到了误导，怀疑实情并非如此——

斯托克曼医生：受到了误导！

霍夫斯塔德：好吧，就算是让我们相信了一些并非完全靠得住的表述吧。市长发表的声明澄清了事实。我坚持自由开放的原则，我想今晚到会的人谁都不会对此感到怀疑的。而《人民信使报》对重大政治问题的公正态度，也是众所周知的。不过，一些有阅历、有见识的人曾对我提出过忠告：在纯粹地方性的问题上，报纸必须采取相当谨慎的态度。

阿斯拉克森：我完全同意这位发言人说的话。

霍夫斯塔德：这件事摆在大家面前，毫无疑问，斯托克曼医生违背了民意。请问诸位，报纸编辑首要的、最基本的职责是什么？难道不是跟读者保持一致行动吗？难道他不是无形中受了群众的委托，应该勤勤恳恳、坚持不懈地为那些他所代表的人谋幸福吗？难道我这种看法错了吗？

许多声音：没错，没错！你说得很对！

霍夫斯塔德：跟这样一个人决裂，我心里别提有多难过了。岂不知最近我还是他家的常客呢！截至目前，这个人一直都是有口皆碑的好人——这个人唯一的缺点，或者说主要的缺点，是受感情的驱使，而非受理性的支配。

稀稀拉拉的几个声音：对！斯托克曼是个好人！

霍夫斯塔德：我必须对社会负责，所以只好跟他决裂。

此外，还有个原因逼着我反对他的主张，要是可能的话，使他离开他所选择的那条危险的道路——那就是为他的家人着想——

斯托克曼医生：别偏离主题，只说水源和排水的问题！

霍夫斯塔德：我重复一遍：他无法赡养自己的妻子儿女，我得为他们考虑。

墨顿：他在说咱们吗，妈妈？

斯托克曼夫人：嘘！

阿斯拉克森：现在我宣布对市长的建议进行表决。

斯托克曼医生：没有这个必要！今天晚上我不打算谈浴场那些脏东西。这个搁下不提。我要谈的完全是另外一件事。

彼得·斯托克曼：（低声自言自语）又有什么新鲜玩意儿来了？

一个醉汉：（在入口处）我是个纳税人，也有权利说话！我的观点不容置辩，我坚定不移地认为——

几个声音：后边的那个，少说话！

另外几个声音：他喝醉了！把他轰出去！（醉汉被人轰了出去。）

斯托克曼医生：能允许我发言吗？

阿斯拉克森：（摇铃）斯托克曼医生要发言了。

斯托克曼医生：要是在前几天，我倒很想看看有谁敢像今天晚上一样压制我，不许我说话！要是那样的话，我会勇敢地捍卫我的神圣权利，像雄狮一样扑上前去！可是现在我不计较了，因为我有更重要的事情要告诉大家。（人群朝他跟前挤,墨顿·基尔也在其中。)

斯托克曼医生:(接着说)这几天我脑子里想了许多许多事情,考虑了各种各样的因素,最后脑子似乎都快要爆炸了。

彼得·斯托克曼:(咳嗽)呃哼!

斯托克曼医生:不过,末了我还是想清楚了,将整个形势看了个透亮。这就是我今晚要发言的原因。我要向你们公布一项重大发现,市民同胞们!与这一发现相比较,什么水源受到污染,什么浴场所处的位置是疾病的温床,全都是微不足道的小事了。

许多声音:(大声叫嚷)别提浴场的事!我们不听!别再说了!

斯托克曼医生:我刚说过,我要公布的是最近的一项重大发现,那就是:咱们精神生活的根源全都中了毒,整个城市的社会机构都建立在害人的虚伪基础上。

几个惊惶的市民:他说什么?

彼得·斯托克曼:他在含沙射影!

阿斯拉克森:(手按着铃)我要求发言人说话要有节制。

斯托克曼医生:我心里一直爱着我的故乡——在这儿我度过了自己的青春岁月。离开故土时我尚年轻,一个人漂泊在外,思乡之情愈加浓烈,想念家乡以及这儿的人们。(有几个人鼓掌欢呼。)在遥远的北方,我在一个荒僻的地方一待就是许多年,接触到的是一些散居在群山里的山民。我心里常想,与其派我这么个人来,不如派个兽医,对于这些吃不饱的穷人也许更有好处。(大家窃窃私语。)

比林:(把笔搁下)怎么能说这种话!

霍夫斯塔德:这是在侮辱一个可敬的群体!

斯托克曼医生:等一等!我虽然漂泊在外,但是恐怕没人会指责我忘掉了自己的故乡。我在那儿就像绒鸭孵蛋一样,最后孵出了温泉浴场的规划。(称赞和反对的声音同时响起。)后来,由于命运的安排,我又回到了故乡,心里别提有多高兴了——先生们,这可是我在这个世界上最大的心愿。当时,我还有一个心愿,那就是满怀激情地、热忱地、不知疲倦地为我的故乡和社区造福。

彼得·斯托克曼:(眼望天花板)哼,以这种方式造福可真是荒诞离奇!

斯托克曼医生:于是,我罔顾真实情况,沉迷于幻想之中。直到昨天上午,确切地说是昨天下午,我才如梦方醒,发现的第一件事就是地方当局昏聩到了极点——(人们大吼大叫,哈哈大笑。斯托克曼夫人连声咳嗽。)

彼得·斯托克曼:主席先生!

阿斯拉克森:(摇铃)我以主席身份——!

斯托克曼医生:可别因为一句话就揪我的小辫子,阿斯拉克森先生。我只是想说,咱们的领导层愚蠢得令人无法置信,他们应该为浴场的事情负责。反正我是无法容忍这样的领导!——这样的人我已经受够了!他们就像一群山羊闯进庄稼地里,到处糟蹋庄稼。他们会成为自由人的绊脚石,让自由人寸步难行,因而最好彻底消灭掉,就像消灭害虫一样——(一阵喧嚷)

彼得·斯托克曼:主席先生,难道允许发表这样的言论吗?

阿斯拉克森:(手按着铃)医生!——

斯托克曼医生:我的哥哥彼得就是这个领导层的好样本,大脑迟钝,有着根深蒂固的偏见,成天在我眼前晃来晃去,可我就是不明白自己怎么现在才认清这些上流人士的真正嘴脸——(笑嚷声和嘘声乱成一片。斯托克曼夫人使劲咳嗽。阿斯拉克森拼命摇铃。)

醉汉:(又进来了)他是不是在说我?我叫彼得森,好吧——要是说我——

一片愤怒的声音:把那个酒鬼赶出去!把他赶出去!(醉汉又被人轰了出去。)

彼得·斯托克曼:那个人是谁?

市民甲:我不认识他,市长。

市民乙:他是别处来的。

市民丙:他大概是个挖土工人——(接下来的话听不清了)

阿斯拉克森:那家伙显然是喝多了。医生,往下说,不过请你把话说得有节制一些。

斯托克曼医生:好吧,先生们,我就不再评价咱们的领导层了。听了我刚才的一席话,如果有谁以为我今晚的目标是抨击这些上流人士,那他就错了,大错特错了。因为我坚信:这些寄生虫,这些抱残守缺的残渣余孽,只是作茧自缚,正在加速自己的灭亡,不需要别人催促他们。其实,对社会危害最大的不是他们,兴风作浪、毒害咱们精神生活的根源以及污染咱们赖以生存的家园的也不是他们,真理和自由最险恶的敌人也不是他们。

叫喊声四起:那么是谁?是什么人?把名字说出来!把名字说出来!

斯托克曼医生:你们放心,我当然要说!我昨天的重大发现指的就是这个。(提高嗓音)真理和自由最险恶的敌人不是别人,而是咱们当中的多数派——被标榜为思想开放的该死的多数派!现在你们明白了吧?

〔会场哄堂大乱。大多数人都在高声叫喊,以跺脚和发嘘声表示反对。几个年长者彼此交换眼色,似乎有点儿幸灾乐祸。斯托克曼夫人站了起来,一脸担忧的表情。叶利夫和墨顿走过去想动手打几个正在起哄的小学生。阿斯拉克森摇铃,叫大家肃静。霍夫斯塔德和比林在交头接耳,却听不见他们在说什么。最后,会场安静了下来。〕

阿斯拉克森:作为主席,我要求发言人收回刚才那些考虑不周的话。

斯托克曼医生:办不到,阿斯拉克森先生!因为剥夺了我说话的自由、不让我讲真话的正是社会上的多数派。

霍夫斯塔德:历来都是多数派掌握着公理。

比林:并且,还掌握着真理!

斯托克曼医生:公理从来就不在多数派一方。从来就不在他们一方!面对这样的谎言,凡是有思想、有见识的人必须站出来揭穿。社会上的多数派是由什么样的人组成的?智者,还是愚者?就目前而言,普天之下愚者占了绝大多数,我想诸位对这一点是不会否认的。苍天在上!让愚者统治智者,难道你们认为这就是公理吗?(吼叫声和辱骂声响成一片。）是呀，你们可以用吼叫声压住我，然而却无法回答我的问题。多数派拥有强大的力量，这是很不幸的，可是他们手中并不掌握公理。公理在我的手里，在我和其他一些少数派的手里。少数派总是正确的！（又是一阵喧嚷声。）

霍夫斯塔德：哈哈！从前天起，斯托克曼医生变成贵族了！

斯托克曼医生：我已经说过，我不想在一些心胸狭窄、见风使舵的小人身上浪费口舌——我和他们已一刀两断。蓬勃的生命不能再跟僵死的人纠缠在一起。我所关心的是那些数量虽少，但掌握着新思想和鲜活的真理的人。这些人是社会的排头兵，远远地走在前边，让多数派想赶都赶不上。他们披荆斩棘，为真理浴血奋斗——真理刚刚萌芽，认识它和支持它的人还不多。

霍夫斯塔德：这么说，医生现在是革命家了！

斯托克曼医生：当然是的，霍夫斯塔德先生！我要发动一场革命，向"多数派掌握着真理"的谎言宣战。多数派拥护的究竟是什么样的真理？他们拥护的所谓真理其实是腐朽的、正在土崩瓦解的旧道理。如果一种道理成了老皇历，就很可能会变为骗人的谎言。（大笑声和讥讽的叫声）是这样的，信不信由你们。真理绝对不可能像一些人想象的那样，跟玛士撒拉①一样长寿！按照规律，一般的真理只有十七八年的寿命，充其量也只有二十年的寿命，基本

---

① 《旧约·创世记》中人物，据传享年969岁。

不会比这更长了。年老的真理历来都是体弱多病的,而多数派却奉为至宝,作为滋补精神的营养品推荐给社会。恕我直言,这样的东西里没有什么营养价值——我是医生,应该是很了解的。这些"多数派真理"好像隔年的腌猪肉,又似腐烂的臭火腿——正是因为这些东西,社会上才有了道德坏血病。

阿斯拉克森:我觉得发言人偏离主题太远了。

彼得·斯托克曼:我完全同意主席的话。

斯托克曼医生:难道你疯了,彼得?我句句都紧扣主题。我的主题就是:群众,即多数派——那些可恨的多数派——在毒害着人们精神生活的根源,在污染人们赖以生存的家园。

霍夫斯塔德:广大民众是伟大的民众,是胸襟宽广的民众,难道就因为他们明智地捍卫确定无疑并得到公认的真理,就让你如此怀恨在心?

斯托克曼医生:嗐,我的好霍夫斯塔德先生,请你别奢谈什么确定无疑的真理!多数派现在所拥护的真理早已过时,是咱们爷爷辈的先驱坚持过的真理,当今的社会排头兵已经不再承认它们是真理。我坚信当今社会确定无疑的真理只有一条,再无其他,那就是:一个社会如果以这种陈腐、苍白的所谓真理为准则,人们就不能过上健康的生活。

霍夫斯塔德:与其无端指责,你还不如举例说明社会奉为准则的陈腐、苍白的所谓真理究竟是什么。

〔很多人赞成这提议。〕

斯托克曼医生：噢，我可以举出一大堆例子来说明那些垃圾是什么。不过，现在我只谈所谓的公认的真理——这样的真理归根结底只是可恶的谎言，而霍夫斯塔德先生、《人民信使报》以及拥护《人民信使报》的人却将其奉为准则。

霍夫斯塔德：你指的是什么？

斯托克曼医生：我指的是你们从祖宗手里继承下来的一种教条，即公众、群众、普通人是人口的重要组成部分——他们构成了"人民"——没有知识、没受过培养的平民跟少数智力超群、出类拔萃的人物同样有权裁判、批准、领导和管理。

比林：这种话我要是说过才怪呢！

霍夫斯塔德：（同时大声喊）市民同胞们，你们好好听听吧！

许多愤怒的声音：去他的！难道我们不算人？难道只让那些上等人掌握统治权？

一个工人：把这个胡说八道的家伙赶出去！

另一个人：把他轰出去！

又有一个人：（大声嚷）埃文森，快吹你的牛角号！

〔在嘘声和愤怒的叫喊声中响起了震耳的牛角号声。〕

斯托克曼医生：（等声音平静了一点儿）理智点吧！难道你们就不能听一听真理的声音吗？我并不指望你们立刻就能同意我的观点，但我得承认，刚才我确实以为，霍夫斯塔德先生只要心平气和点儿，就会同意我的说法。他自称是个自由思想家①——

许多声音：（低声，惊讶）他说什么？自由思想家？霍夫斯塔德是自由思想家？

霍夫斯塔德：（大声嚷）拿证据来，斯托克曼医生！我在报上说过这话吗？

斯托克曼医生：（想了一想）不，该死，你没说过，因为你从来没那份胆量。算啦，我就不让你难堪了，就算我是自由思想家吧。我要以科学的方法向诸位证明的是：《人民信使报》说你们这些平常人，这些普普通通的老百姓是人民的精华，那是用可耻的方法误导你们，是报纸编造出的弥天大谎！老百姓只是普通人，是原材料，只有经过加工培养才能成为人民。（嘲笑声和怒吼声）难道不是这样吗？良种动物和劣种动物之间有着巨大差异，难道不是吗？拿一只平常的乡下老母鸡说吧。它瘦得跟干柴棒一样，能有多少肉给你吃？没有多少肉！它下的蛋小得可怜——恐怕就连乌鸦也能下那样的蛋。可是，良种西班牙母鸡或者日本母鸡，抑或良种的野鸡和火鸡，情况就大不一样了！还可以将人类最熟悉不过的狗拿来举例子。先说说普通的狗吧——我指的是那种粗毛癞皮的劣等狗，那种满街乱窜、在墙根撒尿的狗。拿它们跟贵宾犬比一比就可以比出高下来——贵宾犬生活在上等人家，吃的是美食，听的是高雅的说话声和音乐声，是经过了不知多少代的繁殖才培育出的良种狗。难道你们不觉得贵宾犬的大脑比普通狗要

---

① 主要指不信上帝的人。

发达得多吗？当然要发达得多！良种的贵宾犬自小就受训练——人们教它们学各种伶俐的把戏。那种把戏，就是把普通的狗累死，它们也学不会。

〔会场上响起一片吼叫声和嘲笑声。〕

一个市民：（大声）你是说我们只不过是些狗？

另一个市民：我们不是畜生，医生！

斯托克曼医生：朋友，不骗你，咱们都是畜生，只不过是最高等的畜生而已——即便在咱们这些高等畜生中，真正优秀的也只是凤毛麟角。精英犬和普通犬之间有着天壤之别！有意思的是，只要说的是四条腿畜生，霍夫斯塔德先生大概就会完全赞成我的看法的——

霍夫斯塔德：不错，只要指的仅仅是畜生，我就赞成。

斯托克曼医生：很好。可是只要我把这条规律应用到两条腿的畜生身上，霍夫斯塔德先生恐怕马上就会打住，不敢再独立思考了，不敢坚持自己的主张，得出合乎逻辑的结论了。于是，他把整个理论完全倒了个个儿，在《人民信使报》上硬说乡下老母鸡和街上的野狗才是这个种群里最优良的品种。不过这也不能怪他——凡是没有脱离平庸的境界、没有达到大智大慧高度的人都是如此。

霍夫斯塔德：我承认自己并非什么大智大慧的人，而是地位低下的庄户人家的儿子。他侮辱普通人，而我的根就在普通人中间，我为此感到自豪。

众人的声音：说得好，霍夫斯塔德！说得好！说得好！

斯托克曼医生：我说的普通人并不限于下层社会。在咱们周围爬来爬去的——甚至包括一些在社会上身居高位的人，都是平庸的人。只要看看你们这位自鸣得意、气派十足的市长就知道了！我哥哥彼得跟其他用两条腿走路的人别无两样，都是平庸之辈——（嘲笑声和嘘声）

彼得·斯托克曼：对于这种人身攻击我表示抗议！

斯托克曼医生：（不为所动）——我说他平庸，并非因为他和我一样，是波美拉尼亚①那一带的海盗的子孙——那些平庸的海盗是我们的祖先——

彼得·斯托克曼：无稽之谈，胡编乱造！

斯托克曼医生：——我说他平庸，是因为他对上级唯命是从，认为上级的话都是对的。客观地说，这样的人就属于平庸之辈。所以，我哥哥彼得虽然身份显赫，但实际上距离精英能差十万八千里——也就根本谈不上什么思想解放了。

彼得·斯托克曼：主席先生——！

霍夫斯塔德：这么说，在这座城市里，只有杰出人物才会有开明的思想？这种新观点可真叫人大开眼界哟！（哈哈大笑）

斯托克曼医生：不错，这也是我的新发现中的一部分内容。还有一部分内容是：思想开明几乎等同于道德。所以我认为：《人民信使报》天天宣传歪理罪不容恕，说什么只有群众，只有多数派才思想开明，才讲究道德，还说什么罪恶、腐败和精神上的各种堕落都是从文化里渗出来的，正像浴场的脏水是从莫里达尔的制革厂流出来的一样！

---

① 欧洲历史地区名。指西起奥得河下游以西地带，东迄维斯瓦河之间的波罗的海沿岸地区。现在大部分归属波兰，仅最西部属德国。

（有人在大叫大嚷，有人在插嘴。斯托克曼医生不为所动，面带笑容、满怀激情地说了下去。）《人民信使报》还鼓吹什么应该提高多数派的社会地位！可是岂不知，如果把《人民信使报》的理论付诸实践，所谓的提高多数派的社会地位其实是在害他们，是把他们送上堕落的不归之路。幸而"文化败坏道德"之说只不过是咱们的祖先曾经相信过的老皇历，是从旧时代流传下来的。其实，真正的罪魁祸首是愚昧、贫穷以及肮脏的生活条件！房子如果不通风，不天天打扫——我妻子凯瑟琳坚持说，地板也得天天擦洗，这种说法值得商榷——但我敢说你住在这样的房子里，就一定会在两三年内丧失按道德标准思考和行动的能力。氧气一缺少，良心就会衰弱。在这座城市里，肯定有许多户人家都严重缺氧，因为绝大多数人都良心衰弱，竟然希望把城市的繁荣建立在虚假和欺骗的基础之上。

阿斯拉克森：我们不能允许他用这样的言辞污蔑整个社会。

一个市民：我提议，主席叫发言人坐下。

许多声音：（愤怒地）对！对！让他坐下！让他坐下！

斯托克曼医生：（控制不住情绪）不让我说话，那我就到大街上把真相喊出来！我就到别的城市发表文章，让全国都知道这里的黑幕！

霍夫斯塔德：看来，斯托克曼医生非得把这座城市毁掉而后快。

斯托克曼医生：不错，正因为我非常爱自己的家乡，所以宁可毁掉它，也不愿看到它将繁荣建立在谎言之上。

阿斯拉克森：这话实在言重了。

〔一片吼叫声和喝倒彩声。斯托克曼夫人咳嗽了几下，但不管用——她丈夫不再理睬她的警示。〕

霍夫斯塔德：(高声喊叫，压住了其他的声音)一个有意毁掉整个社会的人就是人民公敌！

斯托克曼医生：(越来越激昂)一个依靠谎言生存的社会，毁掉又有何妨？应该把它夷为平地！告诉你们吧，所有靠欺骗过日子的人都应该像害虫一样被彻底消灭掉！否则，全国都得中毒，照这样下去，全国都得毁灭。假如全国都中了毒，我会说一句心里话：让这个国家灭亡吧，让人民都毁灭吧！

人群中许多声音：听这家伙说的话，完完全全就是一个人民公敌！

比林：他是人民公敌，这就是人民的呼声！

整个会场：(大声)对！对！他是人民公敌！他仇视这个国家，仇视全体人民！

阿斯拉克森：作为一个市民，作为一个有良心的人，我感到十分震惊，想不到会听到这样的言论。斯托克曼医生竟是这样一个人，这叫我做梦都想不到。怀着沉痛的心情，我不得不同意刚才那几位可敬的市民所说的话，并且建议通过表决形成结论。我提出这样的结论供表决："大会宣布浴场卫生官员托马斯·斯托克曼医生为人民公敌。"

〔会场响起一片鼓掌喝彩声。好些人围着斯托克曼医生叫骂。斯托克曼夫人和佩特拉站起身来。墨顿和叶利夫跟几个起哄的小学生打架。几个大人把他们拉开。〕

斯托克曼医生：（转向叫骂的人）喂，你们这些傻瓜！我告诉你们——

阿斯拉克森：（摇铃）我们不能再听你说了，医生，就要进行正式投票了。不过，看在私人的情分上，我宣布采用书面不记名投票方式，而非口头表决。你有空白纸没有，比林先生？

比林：蓝的和白的我这儿都有。

阿斯拉克森：（向他走去）好极了。既然有纸，很快就可以完成。你把纸裁成小纸条——对，就这么裁。（转向群众）蓝纸条是反对，白纸条是赞成。回头我自己过来收票。

〔彼得·斯托克曼走出会场。阿斯拉克森和另外一两个人帽子里盛着纸条绕行会场。〕

市民甲：（冲着霍夫斯塔德）医生到底怎么啦？这让人怎么理解？

霍夫斯塔德：噢，他这个人太顽固。

市民乙：（冲着比林）比林，你常到他家去，是不是发现他有酗酒的习惯？

比林：酗酒不酗酒我不知道，反正每次去，他家的桌子上都摆着酒。

市民丙：我倒觉得他有时候脑子不正常。

市民甲：不知道这是不是他家族遗传的一种病。

比林：恐怕真是遗传的病。

市民丁：不是的。他肯定是因为什么事情对某人怀恨在心，借此泄恨而已。

比林：是了。最近他提出要给他加薪，结果没有加成。

几个市民：（异口同声）难怪呢！这就叫人容易理解了！

醉汉：（又混入了人群中）我要一张蓝票！我也要一张白票！

若干个声音：那个醉鬼又来了！快把他轰出去！

墨顿·基尔：（走近斯托克曼医生）斯托克曼，瞧，你一意孤行，尝到苦头了吧？

斯托克曼医生：我尽了我的责任。

墨顿·基尔：刚才你说莫里达尔的制革厂怎么啦？

斯托克曼医生：你应该听得很清楚。我说它们是污染水质的根源。

墨顿·基尔：也包括我的制革厂？

斯托克曼医生：不幸的是，你的制革厂污染最严重。

墨顿·基尔：你是不是也要把这件事发表在报纸上？

斯托克曼医生：我什么事都不能隐瞒。

墨顿·基尔：你也许要为此付出高昂的代价，斯托克曼！（走了出去）

一个胖子：（走近霍斯特船长，对旁边的女士看也没看）船长，你把房子借给人民公敌开会啦？

霍斯特：房子是我的财产，我想自己是有权借出去的，维克先生。

胖子：我要是以同样的方式支配我的财产，那你也就不能有什么话说了。

霍斯特：这话是什么意思，先生？

胖子：明天你就明白了。（转身走开）

佩特拉：他是你的船老板吧，霍斯特船长？

霍斯特：是的。他是船主维克先生。

阿斯拉克森：（手里拿着表决票走上讲台，摇铃）诸位！现在我宣布投票结果。所有投票的人，除了一个——

一个年轻人：就是那醉汉！

阿斯拉克森：除了一个喝醉酒的人，到会的公民一致同意浴场卫生官员托马斯·斯托克曼医生为人民公敌。（人群鼓掌，欢呼）咱们这古老光荣的城市万岁！（欢呼声）咱们精明强干、大义灭亲的市长万岁！（欢呼声）散会！（下台）

比林：主席万岁！

全体群众：阿斯拉克森万岁！万岁！

斯托克曼医生：把帽子和外套给我，佩特拉！船长，你的船上有上新大陆的舱位没有？

霍斯特：医生，你和你的家人去的话，我们会想办法的。

斯托克曼医生：（佩特拉帮他穿外套）好。咱们走，凯瑟琳！咱们走，孩子们！

斯托克曼夫人：（低声）托马斯，亲爱的，咱们走后门出去吧。

斯托克曼医生：不走后门，凯瑟琳！（高声）你们等着吧，这个人民公敌不会跟你们结束的，非要跟你们见个分晓不可！我可不像某个大人物[①]一样轻易宽恕人。我决不说："我宽恕你们，因为你们不知道自己干的是什

[①] 指耶稣。

么事!"①

阿斯拉克森:(大声)这是亵渎神明的话,斯托克曼医生!

比林:上帝啊!这话叫一个虔诚的人听上去真是太可怕了。

一个粗暴的声音:他说这话是在威胁咱们!

另外几个声音:(愤慨地)走,砸他家的窗户去!把他扔到海峡里!

又有一个声音:吹响你的牛角号,埃文森!吹,使劲吹!

〔牛角号声、嘘声和狂喊声乱成一片。斯托克曼医生带着全家人穿过厅堂朝外走。霍斯特给他们开路。〕

全体群众:(在他们后头叫骂)人民公敌!人民公敌!

比林:(把记录的稿纸整理在一起)今晚我要愿意去斯托克曼家喝酒才见鬼呢!

〔人群朝出口涌去。到了外边,叫骂声仍不绝于耳,到处都有人在喊:"打倒人民公敌!"〕

---

① 见《新约·路加福音》二十三章三十四节。

第五幕

布景:斯托克曼医生的书房。靠墙摆着一些书架和盛标本的玻璃柜。后面有扇门通向大厅,前面左首有扇门通向客厅。右墙有两扇窗,玻璃都被打碎了。屋子当中摆着医生的写字桌,桌上堆着书籍和稿件。屋子里乱七八糟的。时间是早晨。斯托克曼医生穿着睡衣、拖鞋,戴着吸烟帽,弯着腰用伞柄在一个柜子底下掏东西,掏了半天,掏出一块石头来。

斯托克曼医生:(对着敞开的客厅的门)凯瑟琳,我又找着了一块。

斯托克曼夫人:(在客厅里)是吗?恐怕还会找到许多呢。

斯托克曼医生:(把那块石头搁在桌上的一堆石头里)我要把这堆石头珍藏起来,让叶利夫和墨顿天天看。他们长大后,这就是给他们的传家宝。(又在一个书架下掏石块)那个女孩子——她叫什么来着!——你知道那个女孩——

她去找过玻璃匠了吧？

斯托克曼夫人：(走进书房)去过了，玻璃匠说他不知道今天能不能来。

斯托克曼医生：瞧着吧，他是不敢来的。

斯托克曼夫人：是的，兰迪妮①就是这么想的，说他怕街坊邻里说闲话，不敢到这里来。(冲着客厅里)什么事，兰迪妮？交给我吧。(进客厅，马上又拐了回来)这儿有你一封信，托马斯。

斯托克曼医生：我看看。(拆信和读信)哈哈！我早就料到了。

斯托克曼夫人：谁的信？

斯托克曼医生：是房东的，让咱们搬家呢。

斯托克曼夫人：这怎么可能呢？他可是个大好人呀！

斯托克曼医生：(眼睛瞧着信)房东说不敢不叫咱们搬家。他自己并不愿意，可是不敢不这么办。他说众怒难犯，害怕遭到别人的谴责，实在是身不由己，还说得罪了某些有势力的人他可担当不起。

斯托克曼夫人：看到了吧，托马斯？

斯托克曼医生：看到了，看到了，我看得清清楚楚。这座城市里的人都是懦夫，前怕狼后怕虎，没有一个勇敢的人。(把信扔在桌子上)不过，这跟咱们没有关系了，凯瑟琳，因为咱们就要远走高飞，到新大陆去了——

斯托克曼夫人：可是，托马斯，你敢肯定这样做是明

---

① 女佣的名字。

智之举?

斯托克曼医生:他们公开侮辱我,给我扣帽子,视我为人民公敌,砸我的玻璃窗,难道你还让我在这儿待下去不成?你瞧这里,凯瑟琳,他们还在我这条黑裤子上撕了个大口子。

斯托克曼夫人:哎呀,天呀!这是你最好的一条裤子啊!

斯托克曼医生:一个人站出来为捍卫自由和真理战斗的时候,是不该穿好裤子的。要知道,我倒不是心疼裤子——裤子破了,你可以为我补一补嘛。可恨的是,那些人竟敢攻击我,就好像他们有资格跟我交手一样——这口气我到死都咽不下去!

斯托克曼夫人:毫无疑问,他们不该那样对待你,托马斯。可是,难道就因为这,咱们就离开故土,一去不复返了吗?

斯托克曼医生:即便到别的城市生活,恐怕也还会遇到蛮横的人,跟这里的人没什么两样。看着吧,他们半斤八两,都是一样的货色。就让那些疯狗撕咬吧,没什么了不起的。最糟的是,全国各地都一样,所有的人都奴性十足。在自由的西方,情形也许会好一点儿,但也好不到哪里去——在那儿,也会有多数派,会有所谓开明的社会舆论,也会有阴谋诡计和见不得人的勾当。不过,那儿的人也许处事果断,一刀把你杀死了事,而不是将你慢慢折磨死。这儿的人则不然——这儿的人会用老虎钳把自由人的灵魂拧得紧紧的。如果有必要的话,还不如隐居。(来回踱步)

要是我知道哪里有以低价出售的一片原始森林或者一个南海小岛就好了——

斯托克曼夫人：可是，应该多为孩子们想一想，托马斯！

斯托克曼医生：(停了下来)你这人真怪，凯瑟琳！你愿意让孩子们生活在这样的社会环境里？昨晚你也亲眼看到了：这儿的人有一半是疯子，另一半是连一点儿理性都没有的畜生。

斯托克曼夫人：可是，亲爱的托马斯，那是因为你说话不注意，惹恼了他们。

斯托克曼医生：是吗？难道我说的不是大实话吗？怪就怪他们颠倒黑白，分不清是非曲直，明明是真理，却被他们说成是谎言！最荒唐的是，那些自诩为自由派的人，明明都是成年人，却有不懂事的行径，声称自己是什么思想开明的人！这样的现象你见过没有，凯瑟琳？

斯托克曼夫人：是的，是的，他们的确昏了头，这是肯定的。可是——(佩特拉从客厅走了进来。)这么早就从学校回来了？

佩特拉：是的。我被告知他们要解聘我。

斯托克曼夫人：要解聘你？

斯托克曼医生：你也被解聘了？

佩特拉：巴斯克夫人通知了我。我觉得最好还是马上走吧。

斯托克曼医生：你做得很对！

斯托克曼夫人：没想到巴斯克夫人那么坏！

佩特拉：巴斯克夫人一点儿也不坏，妈妈。我看得很清楚，她心里很难受。可是，她说她不敢不这么办，所以只好把我解聘了。

斯托克曼医生：（大笑和搓手）她也是不敢触犯众怒呀！太有意思了！

斯托克曼夫人：唉，昨晚剑拔弩张，出现了那么可怕的场面——

佩特拉：不单纯是因为昨晚。还另有原因呢，爸爸！

斯托克曼医生：什么原因？

佩特拉：巴斯克夫人还给我看了她今天早晨收到的三封信——

斯托克曼医生：恐怕是匿名信吧？

佩特拉：是的。

斯托克曼医生：我猜就是的，因为他们没那个胆量，是不敢署名的，凯瑟琳！

佩特拉：两封匿名信里都说，有个常上咱们家来的人昨天晚上在俱乐部说，在好些问题上我的主张都非常激进——

斯托克曼医生：你没否认吧？

佩特拉：没否认，你知道我是不会否认的。巴斯克夫人平日跟我私下谈话的时候，她的主张也很激进。可是现在他们在说我的坏话，她就不敢再留我了。

斯托克曼夫人：说坏话的竟然是个常上咱们这儿来的人！托马斯，你看，这就是你好客的下场！

斯托克曼医生：这种令人恶心的地方咱们不能再住下

去了。赶紧收拾行李，凯瑟琳，越早离开越好。

斯托克曼夫人：别出声——我好像听见有人在大厅里。你去看看是谁，佩特拉。

佩特拉：（开门）哦，是你，霍斯特船长！快请进！

霍斯特：（走了进来）早上好。我觉得应该来看看你们怎么样了。

斯托克曼医生：（跟他拉手）真的很感谢你的关心。

斯托克曼夫人：还得感谢你昨晚帮我们挤出了人群，霍斯特船长。

佩特拉：后来你是怎么回的家？

霍斯特：噢，没什么难的。我力气大，那些家伙只会叫骂，不敢动手。

斯托克曼医生：是啊，他们都是些卑鄙的懦夫，是些可怜虫！你过来，我给你看点儿东西！这些石头是他们从窗户扔进来的。你瞧瞧吧！这么一堆石头，只有两块是大的，其余的都是小石子——都是些小得可怜的石子。那些家伙站在外边大吼大叫，说什么要给我点儿颜色瞧瞧，可是却雷声大雨点小——这里的人只不过是些缩头缩脑的鼠辈。

霍斯特：这一次他们没敢把你怎么样，医生。

斯托克曼医生：的确如此。可我还是气得不行。有朝一日，如果全国掀起了大风大浪，你就会看到所谓的公众舆论转向，而多数派就会像一群绵羊一样夹着尾巴逃窜，霍斯特船长。想一想就让人感到伤心。我所担心的是——算啦，我可真是咸吃萝卜淡操心！他们说我是人民公敌，我就做人民公敌好了!

斯托克曼夫人:你绝不会是人民公敌,托马斯。

斯托克曼医生:别说这话,凯瑟琳。背上这么一个骂名,一个可憎的骂名,就像心头扎了一根针,取都取不掉。它就扎在我的心尖上,像一种腐蚀性的酸一样渗入我的胃里,什么泻药都治不好。

佩特拉:嗤!对他们你只能付之一笑,爸爸。

霍斯特:总有一天他们会改变看法的,医生。

斯托克曼夫人:对,托马斯,这是一定的。

斯托克曼医生:也许吧。但愿不要太迟了。就让他们自作自受吧!让他们在猪圈里打滚吧,早晚有一天他们会后悔不该把一个爱国者轰出去的。你什么时候开船,霍斯特船长?

霍斯特:唉!——我来就是想说这事的——

斯托克曼医生:是吗?是不是船出了故障?

霍斯特:不是的。问题在于,他们不让我上船了。

斯托克曼医生:你是说他们不让你当船长了?

霍斯特:(笑了笑)正是这样。

佩特拉:你也被解聘了?

斯托克曼夫人:你瞧,我说什么来着,托马斯!

斯托克曼医生:这是为捍卫真理所付出的代价!噢,要是我早知道会——

霍斯特:你不必放在心上。此处不留人,自有留人处,我一定能在别处找到工作的。

斯托克曼医生:这就是维克那家伙干的事——一个有

钱人，又不靠别人吃饭，也干这种缺德的事！可耻！

霍斯特：其实他是个大好人。他告诉我，说他很愿意留下我，只是不敢——

斯托克曼医生：他真的不敢？是啊，他当然不敢。

霍斯特：他说作为一个有党派的人，实在不容易——

斯托克曼医生：那个可敬的人说的是大实话！政党就像一部做香肠的机器，把各种脑子搅碎了拌在一块儿，把什么猪脑子、驴脑子都做成了一个大杂烩！

斯托克曼夫人：别说了，别说了，亲爱的托马斯！

佩特拉：（冲着霍斯特）要是昨晚你不送我们回家，事情也许还不至于这么糟。

霍斯特：我并不后悔。

佩特拉：（伸手给他）谢谢你！

霍斯特：（转向斯托克曼医生）我来还想告诉你：要是你们决意要离开这儿的话，我还有一种安排——

斯托克曼医生：好极了！——只要能立刻离开就行。

斯托克曼夫人：嘘！是不是有人敲门？

佩特拉：肯定是伯伯来了。

斯托克曼医生：啊哈！（大声喊）进来！

斯托克曼夫人：亲爱的托马斯，你千万别——

〔彼得·斯托克曼从大厅走了进来。〕

彼得·斯托克曼：哦，你们有事。那么，我——

斯托克曼医生：没关系，进来吧。

彼得·斯托克曼：可是，我想单独跟你谈谈。

斯托克曼夫人：我们上客厅去就是了。

霍斯特：我回头再来吧。

斯托克曼医生：你别走，请你跟她们到客厅坐一坐，霍斯特船长。我还想再听听你——

霍斯特：好吧，那我就等等吧。（他跟着斯托克曼夫人以及佩特拉进了客厅。）

斯托克曼医生：我敢说，你今天一定觉得这儿风很大。那就把帽子戴上吧。

彼得·斯托克曼：谢谢，那我就戴上了。（戴上帽子）昨天晚上我大概着了凉，站在那里直哆嗦——

斯托克曼医生：真的吗？我倒觉得昨天晚上热得很。

彼得·斯托克曼：我很抱歉，昨晚没能制止那些过火的举动。

斯托克曼医生：除了这个，没别的什么话要说吗？

彼得·斯托克曼：（从衣袋里掏出一个大信封）这是浴场委员会给你的一份公文。

斯托克曼医生：是我的解聘书？

彼得·斯托克曼：是的。日期从今天算起。（把信封搁在桌上）这样做让我们很难过。可是，恕我直言，为了舆论，我们不敢不这么办。

斯托克曼医生：（含笑）不敢？这两个字今天我似乎听见有人说过了。

彼得·斯托克曼：请你务必明白自己的处境。以后你不能再在本地行医了。

斯托克曼医生：鬼才想再在这儿行医呢！不过，你怎么说话语气如此肯定？

彼得·斯托克曼：房主联合会正在挨家挨户找人签名，号召所有正直的市民别找你看病，我敢说，没有一户会不签的——他们不敢不签！

斯托克曼医生：是啊，是啊，对此我毫不怀疑。可是，那又怎么样呢？

彼得·斯托克曼：我劝你最好还是上别处暂时避避风头——

斯托克曼医生：是的，我已经在考虑离开此地了。

彼得·斯托克曼：很好。你可以用半年的时间好好想一想，等到想通了，就写一份检讨书，三言两语的，承认自己的错误——

斯托克曼医生：那时候我也许可以复职，是不是？

彼得·斯托克曼：也许吧，这并不是完全做不到的事。

斯托克曼医生：到那时候舆论怎么办？你们肯定会考虑公众的感情，不敢那么做的。

彼得·斯托克曼：舆论是极其易变的。不瞒你说，最要紧的是，我们要拿到一份你亲笔写的检讨书。

斯托克曼医生：哦，原来你们处心积虑，就是为了这个！我不妨提醒你一句，你可别忘了我不久前的奉劝，让你们不要耍这种狡猾的花招！

彼得·斯托克曼：那时候，你的处境会大为改观的。你到时候将完全有理由相信全城的人都会支持你——

斯托克曼医生：不错，可现在我觉得全城的人都在攻击我（怒从心头起）绝不，绝不写！你就是让魔鬼来攻击我，我也绝不低头！绝不低头，我告诉你！

彼得·斯托克曼:一个有妻儿的人不该像你这么固执。你没有权利这么做,托马斯。

斯托克曼医生:我没有权利!世界上只有一件事是一个自由人没有权利做的。你知道是什么吗?

彼得·斯托克曼:不知道。

斯托克曼医生:你当然不知道。不过,我可以告诉你。一个自由人没有权利让自己蒙垢,没有权利做他连自己都要唾骂的肮脏事情!

彼得·斯托克曼:这种话听上去义正词严、冠冕堂皇。假如没有别的原因,你恐怕也不会这么一意孤行了吧?问题在于,这其中另有原因。

斯托克曼医生:什么原因?

彼得·斯托克曼:你自己心知肚明。不过,我是你的哥哥,做事历来谨慎小心,我奉劝你不要抱过高的期望,免得到头来空欢喜一场。

斯托克曼医生:你这话到底是什么意思?

彼得·斯托克曼:难道你真的想让我相信你对基尔先生遗嘱里的条款一无所知?

斯托克曼医生:我知道他有一点儿钱,打算捐给贫困的、年老的体力劳动者。这和我有什么关系?

彼得·斯托克曼:首先,基尔先生可不是只有一点儿钱,而是有许多钱。

斯托克曼医生:这我可不知道!

彼得·斯托克曼:唔,真的吗?那我就认为你也不知道他的财富有相当大的一部分将留给你的孩子,而你和你的妻子可以动用那笔钱的利息。这些他从没告诉过你吗？

斯托克曼医生：他从没有告诉过我！他非但对此只字不提，还成天发脾气，抱怨苛捐杂税太重，让他负担不起。你敢完全肯定这是真的，彼得？

彼得·斯托克曼：我这消息的来源绝对靠得住。

斯托克曼医生：这么一来，谢天谢地，凯瑟琳的生活有着落了——孩子们的生活也有着落了！我必须马上告诉她——（大声喊）凯瑟琳，凯瑟琳！

彼得·斯托克曼：（拦住他）嘘，暂时先别说。

斯托克曼夫人：（开门）什么事？

斯托克曼医生：噢，没什么，没什么。你回去吧。（斯托克曼夫人又关上了门。斯托克曼医生激动得来回走动。）生活有着落了！——想想吧，我们的生活有保障了！一辈子都不用愁了！生活无忧无虑，这种感觉真好！

彼得·斯托克曼：好是好，但事情正相反，你们的生活并没有保障——基尔先生随时都可以修改遗嘱。

斯托克曼医生：他绝不会那样做的，我亲爱的彼得。我抨击你和你的那些聪明透顶的朋友，那个"老獾"高兴都来不及呢。

彼得·斯托克曼：（吃了一惊，仔细打量他）啊哈，一句话让人明白了许多事情。

斯托克曼医生：什么事情？

彼得·斯托克曼：看得出你和他串通一气，原来有着不可告人的目的。你打着捍卫真理的幌子，不顾一切地猛烈攻击这座城市的领导层，原来是——

斯托克曼医生:原来是什么?

彼得·斯托克曼:看得出,你的所作所为只不过是为了取悦那个仇恨社会的老头儿,为了拿到他的遗嘱。

斯托克曼医生:(气得几乎说不出话来)彼得——你是我平生所见过的最卑鄙无耻的小人。

彼得·斯托克曼:咱们从此一刀两断。你解聘的事不能挽回了——现在我们手里有了对付你的武器了。(出去)

斯托克曼医生:可耻!可耻!(大声喊)凯瑟琳,他走后,你们一定要把地板好好擦一擦!叫那个鼻子上老有煤灰的女孩——该死,她叫什么来着?

斯托克曼夫人:(在客厅里)嘘!托马斯,小声点儿!

佩特拉:(来到门口)爸爸,外公来了。他问能不能跟你单独说句话。

斯托克曼医生:当然可以。(迎到门口)请进,基尔先生。(墨顿·基尔走进屋来。斯托克曼医生随手把门关上。)坐下来说好吗?

墨顿·基尔:我就不坐了。(四面一望)今天你们这儿看上去挺舒服的,托马斯。

斯托克曼医生:是呀,的确很舒服!

墨顿·基尔:非常舒服——新鲜空气也挺充足。昨天你提到过的氧气今天一定足够了。我想,今天你的良心一定很宽慰。

斯托克曼医生:是这样的。

墨顿·基尔:我猜就是的。(拍拍自己的胸脯)你知道我怀里揣的是什么吗?

斯托克曼医生：希望也是一颗清白的良心。

墨顿·基尔：哼，良心算什么！这比良心管用。（从胸前口袋里掏出一个大皮夹子，把它打开，露出一叠纸来）

斯托克曼医生：（诧异地看着他）莫非是浴场的股票？！

墨顿·基尔：今天买那儿的股票不费吹灰之力。

斯托克曼医生：你一直在买——？

墨顿·基尔：我倾其所有，能买多少就买多少。

斯托克曼医生：可是，亲爱的基尔先生——你也不想想现在浴场是什么样一种状况！

墨顿·基尔：如果你理智行事，很快就可以叫浴场重见光明。

斯托克曼医生：你也看到了，我尽了一切力量挽救浴场，可是——这座城市里的人都疯了！

墨顿·基尔：昨天你说，最脏的东西是从我的制革厂流出来的。假如此话属实，那我祖父、我父亲和我自己简直像三个瘟神恶煞，这些年一直在用脏水污染这座城市。面对这样的责难，你说我能甘心忍受吗？

斯托克曼医生：可惜你不甘心也没办法。

墨顿·基尔：对不起，我不甘心。我的名誉不准别人白白糟蹋。听说有人叫我"老獾"。我知道，獾是一种猪。我不能容忍他们这样称呼我——我就是死也要做一个干干净净的人。

斯托克曼医生：你打算怎么办？

墨顿·基尔：我要你给我洗刷干净，托马斯。

斯托克曼医生：我？！

墨顿·基尔：你知道不知道我买这些股票用的是什么钱？你当然不知道，但我可以告诉你。这是一笔我死后将留给凯瑟琳、佩特拉和那两个男孩子的钱。不瞒你说，我手里还是攒了一些钱的。

斯托克曼医生：(大怒)你竟然把留给凯瑟琳的钱用来炒股！

墨顿·基尔：不错，现在所有的钱都投在了浴场上。我倒想看看你是不是还会那样固执，那样缺乏理智，托马斯！如果你仍坚持认为那些细菌以及其他的脏东西是从我的制革厂流出来的，那就等于是在剥凯瑟琳的皮，剥佩特拉和那两个男孩子的皮——除了疯子，谁也不会干那种蠢事。

斯托克曼医生：(来回踱步)不错。可我就是疯子！我是疯子！

墨顿·基尔：这跟你的妻儿利益相关，你不可能丧心病狂到那种地步的。

斯托克曼医生：(在他面前站住)在买那些垃圾股之前，你为什么就不能和我商量商量？

墨顿·基尔：现在木已成舟，覆水难收了。

斯托克曼医生：(走来走去，心神不定)要是这件事我没有绝对把握倒也罢了！可是，我百分之百肯定我是对的。

墨顿·基尔：(掂掂手里的皮夹子)要是你一味蛮干，一味地固执，这些股票就不值什么钱了。(把皮夹子揣在衣袋里)

斯托克曼医生：不过，应该有解决办法的！也许可以用科学的方法寻找到一种预防的药剂什么的——或者某种解毒的药——

墨顿·基尔：你是说用药把那些细菌杀死？

斯托克曼医生：是的。或者说使它们不再害人。

墨顿·基尔：能不能用老鼠药试一试？

斯托克曼医生：别胡说！他们不是说水源受到污染仅仅是我的臆想嘛，那就让他们说好啦！他们愿意怎么样就怎么样吧！那些愚昧无知、心胸狭窄的人不是骂我是人民公敌吗？他们不是恨不得把我的衣服也撕烂吗？

墨顿·基尔：他们还把你家的窗户都砸坏了！

斯托克曼医生：出于对家庭的责任，我必须跟凯瑟琳仔细谈一谈——在这些事情上她很在行。

墨顿·基尔：这就对啦。她是个懂道理的人，应该听她的。

斯托克曼医生：（逼近他）想不到你竟然能干出这种荒唐事！你用凯瑟琳的钱冒风险，弄得我骑虎难下、左右为难！看着你，我就像见到了魔鬼——

墨顿·基尔：那我最好还是走吧。不过，下午两点钟之前，不管行不行，我都必须听到你的回信。如果不行，我就把股票都捐给慈善机构，今天就去捐。

斯托克曼医生：能给凯瑟琳留多少？

墨顿·基尔：一分也不留。（通向大厅的门开了。霍夫斯塔德和阿斯拉克森出现了。）瞧，这两个宝贝来了！

斯托克曼医生：（怒视两个不速之客）真是活见鬼！你

229

们怎么还有脸来我家?

霍夫斯塔德:当然。

阿斯拉克森:我们无事不登三宝殿。

墨顿·基尔:(低声)行还是不行——下午两点之前给我回信!

阿斯拉克森:(瞟了霍夫斯塔德一眼)啊哈!

〔墨顿·基尔走了出去。〕

斯托克曼医生:你们找我什么事?有话快说。

霍夫斯塔德:昨晚开会我们态度不好,让你生气了,对此我完全理解——

斯托克曼医生:你在说你们的态度?你们的态度简直棒极了!我称之为胆小鬼的态度、老太婆的态度——厚颜无耻的态度!

霍夫斯塔德:你爱怎么说就怎么说吧,反正我们是迫不得已。

斯托克曼医生:是不敢不那么办,对不对?

霍夫斯塔德:你要这么说也可以。

阿斯拉克森:可是,你为什么对我们只字不提呢?——对我或霍夫斯塔德先生哪怕是暗示一下也可以嘛。

斯托克曼医生:暗示?暗示什么?

阿斯拉克森:暗示一下幕后的情况。

斯托克曼医生:你这话叫我摸不着头脑。

阿斯拉克森:(神秘地点了点头)你心里是有数的,斯托克曼医生。

霍夫斯塔德:别绕圈子了,瞒是瞒不住的。

斯托克曼医生：(看看这个，又看看那个)你们俩搞什么鬼！

阿斯拉克森：请问，你岳父是不是满城地跑，四处购买浴场的股票？

斯托克曼医生：是的，他今天是在大量收购浴场股票，可是——

阿斯拉克森：其实应该避嫌，找一个跟你关系不那么密切的人去收购才对。

霍夫斯塔德：至于浴场的那场风波，你不该抛头露面，不该让别人知道攻击浴场的始作俑者是你。事先你应该跟我商量一下才对，斯托克曼医生。

斯托克曼医生：(直着眼瞪了半晌，接着好像如梦方醒，惊愕地说道)难道真有这种事吗？天下会有这种事？

阿斯拉克森：(笑了笑)显然是有的。不过，要知道，手法稍微细腻点儿，效果会更好。

霍夫斯塔德：这种事，多叫几个人参与——每人分担一份责任，担子就减轻了。

斯托克曼医生：(表情凝重)先生们，不妨直说吧，你们究竟想干什么？

阿斯拉克森：也许，最好请霍夫斯塔德先生说——

霍夫斯塔德：不，阿斯拉克森，还是你说吧。

阿斯拉克森：噢，事情是这样的，我们已经掌握了那桩案子的底细，愿意竭诚效力，让《人民信使报》听你的调度。

斯托克曼医生：怎么？你们现在敢这么做了？不怕公

众舆论的压力吗?不怕招来狂风暴雨吗?

霍夫斯塔德:咱们同心协力,就可以化险为夷。

阿斯拉克森:你必须有两手打算,医生,一旦攻击获胜,就——

斯托克曼医生:你是说,等我们翁婿俩把浴场股票用贱价一买到手就转向?

霍夫斯塔德:依我看,你想把浴场控制在手里,这种愿望大体而言是合情合理、无可挑剔的。

斯托克曼医生:当然,为了这一合情合理的愿望,我把"老獾"拉来入伙。我们只是把输水管随便修一修,在海滩上挖几个坑应应景,不让市民们掏一分钱,敷衍了事。是不是应该这样做,嗯?

霍夫斯塔德:我想是的——《人民信使报》可以做你的后盾。

阿斯拉克森:在自由社会里,报纸是一股强大的力量,医生。

斯托克曼医生:对。舆论也是一股强大的力量。而你,阿斯拉克森先生,我想,房主联合会方面你可以负责吧?

阿斯拉克森:是的。还有节制运动协会我也可以负责。你尽管放心好啦。

斯托克曼医生:可是,先生们——有句话我实在不好意思问——可是,你们想得到什么回报呢?

霍夫斯塔德:请相信我,我们只想助你一臂之力,并无意得到回报。不过,《人民信使报》的状况很不稳定,实在令人担忧,现在政治方面需要做的事情有很多,而我又不愿意停刊。

斯托克曼医生：是啊，你是人民肝胆相照的朋友，这一次的确面临着巨大考验。（忽然发作）可是，你别忘了我是人民的公敌！（大步来回走）我的手杖呢？该死！我的手杖跑哪儿去了？

霍夫斯塔德：你找手杖干什么？

阿斯拉克森：难道你要——

斯托克曼医生：（站住）要是我把钱拿到手，一分钱都不给你们，你们该做何感想？别忘了，让我们这些富人掏腰包不是那么容易的！

霍夫斯塔德：你也别忘了，抢购股票之事可以有两种说法。

斯托克曼医生：不错，或褒或贬都在你的掌握之中。如果我不出钱拯救《人民信使报》，你肯定会抹黑我，对我穷追猛打，可以想象得到——一定会像狗撵兔子一样，非把我咬死不可。

霍夫斯塔德：这是自然界的规律——为了生存，所有的动物都会拼死一搏的。

阿斯拉克森：哪里有食物就到哪里去。人为财死，鸟为食亡嘛。

斯托克曼医生：（在屋里走来走去）好，那么你们就到臭水沟里找食物吧！因为我要让你们看看，咱们这三只动物，究竟谁最厉害。（找着了一把伞，将伞举过头顶）喂，现在来吧——！

霍夫斯塔德：君子动口不动手！

阿斯拉克森:小心别让伞伤着人!

斯托克曼医生:从窗户里滚出去,霍夫斯塔德先生!

霍夫斯塔德:(向门外移步)你是不是疯了?

斯托克曼医生:你也从窗户里滚出去,阿斯拉克森先生!快给我跳!我让你跳你就跳!

阿斯拉克森:(绕着写字桌跑)你要稳重一些,医生。我可是个弱不禁风的人——受不了这么——(大呼小叫)救命啊!救命啊!

〔斯托克曼夫人、佩特拉和霍斯特从客厅走了过来。〕

斯托克曼夫人:天啊,托马斯!到底是怎么回事?

斯托克曼医生:(把伞在空中挥舞)我叫你跳出去!滚到臭水沟里去!

霍夫斯塔德:他无缘无故打人!霍斯特船长,我请你做见证。(慌忙从大厅里逃走)

阿斯拉克森:(犹豫不决)我对这里的路径不太熟悉——(从客厅溜出去)

斯托克曼夫人:(拉住她丈夫)消消气,托马斯!

斯托克曼医生:(把伞扔下)可恶,让那两个家伙跑掉了!

斯托克曼夫人:他们找你干什么?

斯托克曼医生:回头告诉你。现在我心里还有别的事。(走到写字桌前,在一张名片上写了几个字)凯瑟琳,你看,我写的是什么?

斯托克曼夫人:三个大大的"不"字。这是什么意思?

斯托克曼医生:回头一齐告诉你。(把名片递给佩特拉)

佩特拉,叫那个脸上有煤灰的女孩赶紧送到"老獾"家里去,越快越好。刻不容缓!(佩特拉拿起名片奔向大厅。)

斯托克曼医生:很好,我想今天魔鬼的手下都来过了!现在,我要把笔锋削得尖尖的,让他们尝尝笔尖扎在身上的滋味。我要饱蘸毒液,写几篇辛辣文章!我要将墨水瓶砸在他们的头上!

斯托克曼夫人:是很可恨,可你忘了咱们就要走了,托马斯。

〔佩特拉回到屋里。〕

斯托克曼医生:怎么样?

佩特拉:她送去了。

斯托克曼医生:很好。你刚才说咱们就要走了,凯瑟琳?不走,咱们绝不走!咱们要在这儿待下去!

佩特拉:在这儿待下去?

斯托克曼夫人:在这座城市待下去?

斯托克曼医生:是的,就待在这儿!战场在这儿,这儿就是双方交锋的地方。我将在这儿打赢他们!我的裤子一补好,我就出去另外找房子。必须有一处过冬的地方。

霍斯特:你们可以搬到我家去。

斯托克曼医生:可以吗?

霍斯特:当然可以。我家有的是空地方,我又几乎常年不在家。

斯托克曼夫人:那就太感谢你了,霍斯特船长。

佩特拉:谢谢你!

斯托克曼医生:(紧紧握住他的手)谢谢!谢谢!一

个难关渡过去了!现在我可以腾出手立刻干正事了。在这里有许多事等着我去干,干都干不完,凯瑟琳!幸好我现在的时间由我自己支配,因为我被浴场解雇了,无官一身轻嘛。

斯托克曼夫人:(叹气)是的,这我知道。

斯托克曼医生:他们还想把我的病人都抢走。好,让他们抢吧!反正有穷人会来找我看病的——他们付不起医疗费;而且,毕竟最需要我的也是这些人。来看病,我就给他们讲大道理,向他们宣传真理,一年到头向他们宣讲!

斯托克曼夫人:可是,亲爱的托马斯,我觉得你经历了几场风波,应该知道演讲会有什么结果。

斯托克曼医生:你这话真可笑,凯瑟琳。难道你让我退出战场,甘心败给那些舆论,败给结实的多数派,败给那些阎王小鬼吗?不,绝不!我的目的简单明了。我只想让那些糊涂虫明白一点:自由派是自由最阴险的敌人;他们的党纲在扼杀一切新生的、朝气蓬勃的真理;权宜之计只会叫道德沦丧、是非颠倒,早晚会让大家的日子没法儿过的。霍斯特船长,难道你不觉得我应该让人们明白这个道理吗?

霍斯特:你很可能是对的。我对这种事情知道得不多。

斯托克曼医生:是这样的,容我解释给你听吧!当务之急是要消灭政党的党魁,因为他们就像饿狼,像贪得无厌的饿狼,要活下去,每年就得吃掉好些小动物。只要看看霍夫斯塔德和阿斯拉克森你就明白了!他们不知杀害过多少小动物——即使不杀害,也会将它们变成残废,也会咬得它们血肉模糊,除了乖乖地当俯首帖耳的房主以及《人民信使报》的订户之外,别的事都干不了!(坐在桌沿上)凯瑟琳,你过来,看看今天的太阳多么灿烂!清新芬芳的空气真是叫人沉醉!

斯托克曼夫人:是啊,要是能靠灿烂的阳光和清新的空气过日子就好了,托马斯。

斯托克曼医生:噢,得勒紧裤带过几天紧巴日子——以后会好起来的。我担心的不是这个,而是一种更为严重的情况——怕只怕将来缺乏思想开放、品德高尚的人才继承我的事业。

佩特拉:爸爸,不必担心,日子还长得很呢。噢,孩子们已经回来了!

〔叶利夫和墨顿从客厅走了进来。〕

斯托克曼夫人:今天学校放假吗?

墨顿:不是的。课间休息时,我们跟同学打了一架——

叶利夫:不对,是他们挑衅要跟我们打架来着。

墨顿:后来诺伦德先生说我们最好在家待两天。

斯托克曼医生:(打了个响指,从桌沿上跳下来)有了!有了!以后你们就不要再到学校去了!

两个孩子:再不上学了?

斯托克曼夫人:托马斯,这怎么能行——

斯托克曼医生:不必再去了!我自己教你们——也就是说你们不用再学那些味如嚼蜡的东西了——

墨顿:万岁!

斯托克曼医生:——不过我要把你们培养成思想开放、

品德高尚的人。佩特拉，你可得帮我的忙。

佩特拉：好的，爸爸，请你放心好啦。

斯托克曼医生：咱们的学校就设在他们侮辱我、骂我是人民公敌的那间屋子里。不过，学生人数太少，起码得有十二个学生才可以开课。

斯托克曼夫人：在这座城市里你别想招到学生。

斯托克曼医生：会招到的。（转向两个儿子）你们认识不认识街上的那些野孩子——也就是那些小叫花子？

墨顿：认识，爸爸，我认识好多呢！

斯托克曼医生：好极了，给我找几个来。我要给他们做一个测试，看看他们当中有没有可塑之才。

墨顿：你把我们培养成思想开放、品德高尚的人，打算让我们做什么？

斯托克曼医生：让你们把国内的饿狼赶走，全都赶走，孩子们！

〔叶利夫听了半信半疑。墨顿则高兴得蹦了起来，高呼"万岁"。〕

斯托克曼夫人：但愿别让饿狼把你赶走，托马斯。

斯托克曼医生：凯瑟琳，难道你疯了？把我赶走？现在我可是这座城市里最有力量的人！

斯托克曼夫人：你是最有力量的人——现在？

斯托克曼医生：是的。我甚至还敢说，现在我是全世界最有力量的人。

墨顿：是这样的！

斯托克曼医生：（低声）嘘！先别吭声。我还有一个重大发现呢。

斯托克曼夫人：还有发现？

斯托克曼医生：是的。（让大家都到他跟前来，悄悄地说道）让我告诉你们吧——世界上最强大的人就是最孤独的人！

斯托克曼夫人：（笑了笑，摇了摇头）噢，托马斯呀，托马斯！

佩特拉：（鼓励似的抓紧她父亲的两只手）爸爸！

（剧终）

群 鬼

人物表

海伦·阿尔文（曾经担任国王侍从的阿尔文上尉的遗孀）

奥斯瓦德·阿尔文（她的儿子，画家）

曼得斯牧师

雅各布·恩格斯特兰德（木匠）

莱吉娜·恩格斯特兰德（阿尔文夫人的女佣）

（故事发生在挪威西部阿尔文夫人的乡间别墅，旁边有一条大峡湾）

第一幕

布景:一间宽敞的花园房,左边有一扇门,右边有两扇门。屋子当中有一张圆桌,桌子周围有几把椅子。桌上有书籍、杂志和报纸。左前方有一扇窗,靠窗有一张小沙发,沙发前面有一张缝纫桌。后方连接着一间比较狭窄的温室,四面都是落地大玻璃窗。温室右边有一扇门通向花园。透过大玻璃窗,在连绵不绝的雨水的遮掩下,一条峡湾若隐若现。

木匠恩格斯特兰德站在通向花园的门边。他的左腿有点儿瘸,左脚靴子底下加了一块木头。莱吉娜手里拿着一把空的喷水壶,拦着不许他进去。

莱吉娜:(低声)你来干什么?站着别动。你身上净是雨水,直往下滴。

恩格斯特兰德:这是上帝下的好雨,我的孩子。

莱吉娜:我说这是魔鬼下的雨。

恩格斯特兰德:天呀,这是什么话,莱吉娜。(瘸着腿朝前走了一两步,要进屋去)我有事要跟你说呢——

莱吉娜:别把你脚下的木头弄得咯吱咯吱响,听见没有!少爷在楼上睡觉呢。

恩格斯特兰德:睡觉?大中午还睡觉?

莱吉娜:这不关你的事。

恩格斯特兰德:昨晚我出去喝了个痛快——

莱吉娜:这话我倒信。

恩格斯特兰德:是啊,我们是可怜蛋,是堕落的人,我的孩子——

莱吉娜:似乎的确如此。

恩格斯特兰德:——要知道,在这个世界上,诱惑来自四面八方。不过,我干活儿很辛苦,也得放松放松。天晓得,今天早晨我五点半就开始干活儿了。

莱吉娜:很好,很好。你还是快走吧。我不愿意站在这儿,好像跟你有 rendez-vous①似的。

恩格斯特兰德:你说好像跟我有什么?

莱吉娜:我不愿意让人瞧见你在这儿。所以,快去做你自己的事情吧。

恩格斯特兰德:(趋前一两步)我得跟你说完话再走。今天下午孤儿院里的活儿就干完了,我打算乘今晚的船回城里的家。

莱吉娜:(嘴里咕哝)祝你一路顺风!

---

① 法文,意思是"约会"。莱吉娜喜欢说法文,表示她是上流社会的人。

恩格斯特兰德：谢谢你，我的孩子。明天孤儿院开张，不用说，一定热闹得很，少不了饮酒狂欢。我不能让人说雅各布·恩格斯特兰德经不起美酒的诱惑。

莱吉娜：哼！

恩格斯特兰德：你瞧着吧，明天会来一大群有头有脸的人物。听说曼得斯牧师也要从城里赶来。

莱吉娜：他今天就来。

恩格斯特兰德：瞧，我没说错吧！要是让他看到我有什么不体面的地方，我会感到非常抱歉的，明白吗？

莱吉娜：嗤！这就是你的小算盘？

恩格斯特兰德：我的什么小算盘？

莱吉娜：(仔细打量他）这次，你打算怎么欺骗曼得斯牧师？

恩格斯特兰德：嘘！嘘！你是不是疯了？怎么会说我欺骗曼得斯牧师呢？那是绝对不可能的！曼得斯牧师是我肝胆相照的朋友，我怎么能欺骗他！我来这儿只是想跟你说，你知道——我打算今晚回家。

莱吉娜：依我说，回去得越早越好。

恩格斯特兰德：是的。可是，我想带你一起走，莱吉娜。

莱吉娜：(吃惊）你要带我一起走？你在说什么呀？

恩格斯特兰德：我在说，我想带你一起回家。

莱吉娜：(轻蔑地）就是再怎么样，你也别想让我跟你回家。

恩格斯特兰德：噢，咱们瞧着吧！

莱吉娜：你死了这条心吧，我是绝不会回去的！我在阿尔文夫人这样的大户人家长大,她待我像亲闺女一样,你还指望我跟你回去?——回到一个寒酸的家里?真不害臊!

恩格斯特兰德:你到底想干什么?难道你要和你老子对着干,臭丫头?

莱吉娜:(嘴里咕哝,连看也不看他)你老说我不是你亲生的。

恩格斯特兰德:呸!提这干什么——

莱吉娜:你不是老骂我是什么——骂我是杂种吗!

恩格斯特兰德:我敢赌咒没用过这么脏的词。

莱吉娜:我清清楚楚记得你就是这样骂我的。

恩格斯特兰德:是吗?那一定是我当时喝多了,这你不知道吗?在这个世界上,诱惑来自四面八方,莱吉娜。

莱吉娜:哼!

恩格斯特兰德:再说,当时你妈妈正在发火,那我就得找点儿话回击她,我的孩子。她老是装腔作势,自以为是上等人。(学他老婆说话)"别惹我,恩格斯特兰德!别惹我!别忘了我在罗森沃尔德庄园国王侍从阿尔文老爷家里待过三年呢。"(大笑)真肉麻!她老忘不了她在这儿当用人时,阿尔文上尉受封,当上了国王侍从。

莱吉娜:苦命的妈妈!没过多久你就把她折磨死了。

恩格斯特兰德:(把肩膀一耸)哼,鬼话!不用说,什么都是我的错!

莱吉娜:(转过身去,声音不大)哼!还有那条腿呢!

恩格斯特兰德:你说什么腿,我的孩子?

莱吉娜：Pied de mouton[①].

恩格斯特兰德：你说的是英国话？

莱吉娜：是的。

恩格斯特兰德：好嘛，好嘛，你在这儿学了不少东西，现在可用上了，莱吉娜。

莱吉娜：（沉吟片刻）你要我进城干什么？

恩格斯特兰德：我一个孤苦伶仃、无依无靠的老人，只有你这么一个孩子，亏你还问我要你回去干什么！

莱吉娜：得啦，别跟我说这种废话！你究竟要我回去干什么？

恩格斯特兰德：好吧，那我就告诉你吧——我想改行，换换工作。

莱吉娜：（不屑地）你老改行，可是哪一行都干得没什么起色。

恩格斯特兰德：不错。但这一次你就瞧着吧，莱吉娜！我他妈的要是——

莱吉娜：（跺脚）别说脏话！

恩格斯特兰德：嘘，嘘。你批评得很对，我的孩子。我只是想跟你说——这次在孤儿院干活儿，我挣了许多钱。

莱吉娜：是吗？那不是挺好。

恩格斯特兰德：在这偏僻的乡下，有钱都没处花。

莱吉娜：是吗？你打算怎么办？

恩格斯特兰德：噢，是这样的——我想搞点儿挣钱的

---

① 法文，意思是"羊腿"。

买卖,打算开一家水手酒馆——

莱吉娜:呸!

恩格斯特兰德:当然是开一家档次高的酒馆,不是接待普通水手的那种猪圈。不是的,绝不是那种乱七八糟的地方!我的酒馆专门接待船长和大副,以及——以及达官贵人。

莱吉娜:你要我去——

恩格斯特兰德:当然要你去帮忙喽。要知道,你去也只是做些面子上的事,脏活儿累活儿不让你干,我的孩子。你愿意怎样就怎样。

莱吉娜:噢,原来是这么回事!

恩格斯特兰德:开酒馆嘛,总得有个女掌柜,这是明摆着的事。我想让酒馆充满生气,晚上有歌有舞。别忘了,在海上漂泊的人,日子是很单调的。(凑近一些)你可不要死脑筋,把自己给耽误了,莱吉娜。在这里会有什么结果?你的女主人倒是教给你不少东西,可这对你有什么好处?听说她要你上孤儿院照管小孩子。这样的事你也愿意干,是吗?难道你这么死心眼儿,愿意将你的大好年华耗费在一群脏孩子身上?

莱吉娜:不会的。只要事情能像我希望的那样——唉,很难说呀——很难说。

恩格斯特兰德:"很难说"?这是什么意思?

莱吉娜:你不用管了。你究竟攒了多少钱?

恩格斯特兰德:算到一块儿,大概有七八百克朗[①]。

[①] 1 克朗 =1 先令 3.5 便士。(原注)

莱吉娜：倒也不算少。

恩格斯特兰德：够开张用的了，我的孩子。

莱吉娜：你愿意不愿意给我一点儿？

恩格斯特兰德：这可不行，想都别想！

莱吉娜：甚至连买件新衣服的钱都不愿意给？

恩格斯特兰德：跟我到城里去，我的孩子，有你新衣服穿的。

莱吉娜：得了吧！我要想进城，自己会去的。

恩格斯特兰德：你应该听你老爹的话，让你老爹为你指引方向，莱吉娜。我在小港街看中了一幢大房子，不用付多少现钱就能租下来，可以作为水手酒馆的所在。

莱吉娜：我才不愿意跟你在一起生活呢。咱俩井水不犯河水，你走吧！

恩格斯特兰德：你和我在一起住不长，我的孩子。我没有这种福气！这一两年你越长越漂亮，如果你能把握住自己的命运——

莱吉娜：怎么样？

恩格斯特兰德：你很快就能钓上一条大鱼——一个大副——甚至可能是一个船长——

莱吉娜：我才不愿意嫁那等人呢——他们一点儿 savoir-vivre①都没有。

恩格斯特兰德：你说他们没有什么？

莱吉娜：告诉你吧，我知道水手是什么样的人。嫁人

---

① 法文，意思是"修养"。

绝不能嫁给他们!

恩格斯特兰德:不愿意嫁就不嫁吧,但你照样能够从他们口袋里掏钱。(换上一副更为推心置腹的面孔)他——那个英国人——那个坐着游艇来的家伙——在她身上就花了三百美元,而她长得一点儿也不比你漂亮。

莱吉娜:(逼近他)滚出去!

恩格斯特兰德:(后退)好啦,好啦!你不至于打我吧?

莱吉娜:你要再敢污蔑妈妈,我非打你不可。我说了,让你快滚!(把他朝着通向花园的门口推去)关门时声音小点儿,阿尔文少爷在——

恩格斯特兰德:他在睡觉,这我知道。你对小阿尔文先生倒是挺关心的——(声音放低了些)哦嗬!你不会说他——

莱吉娜:你马上给我滚!你净说疯话!不,别从那条路走,曼得斯牧师从那边过来了。你从厨房台阶那里下去吧。

恩格斯特兰德:(向右走)好,好,我走就是了。见了他,你应该听听他的教诲。他会告诉你一个孩子应该怎样为父亲尽孝。要知道,我再怎么也是你的父亲呀。教堂登记簿上的记载可以证明这一点。

〔他从莱吉娜给他打开的右边第二道门走出去,随手关上了门。莱吉娜匆匆忙忙在镜子里照了一照,用手帕把身上掸一掸,整一整领巾,然后就忙着浇花了。〕

〔曼得斯牧师从通往花园的门里走进温室来。他穿着外套,拿着雨伞,背着个双肩背的小旅行包。〕

曼得斯:早晨好,恩格斯特兰德小姐。

莱吉娜:(转过身来,露出一副又惊又喜的样子)呀,原来是您呀!早安,曼得斯牧师!轮船来得这么早?

曼得斯:刚到。(走进客厅)最近的天气可真是糟糕。

莱吉娜:(跟了进来)这样的雨天对庄稼大有好处,先生。

曼得斯:毫无疑问,你说得一点儿不错。我们城里人很少考虑到庄稼。(动手脱外套)

莱吉娜:噢,我帮您一把好吗?——脱下来了!哇,怎么湿成这样子了!我给您挂在大厅里。还有那把伞,我拿去撑开,让它晾干。

〔莱吉娜拿着外套和雨伞从右边第二道门出去了。曼得斯牧师把旅行包从肩膀上卸下来,连帽子一起放在一把椅子上。这时,莱吉娜又回来了。〕

曼得斯:啊,从外头进来真舒服。这里一切都好吧?

莱吉娜:托您的福,都好,先生。

曼得斯:为明天的事做准备,你们大概都忙得不可开交吧?

莱吉娜:是的,要干的事情真多。

曼得斯:阿尔文夫人大概在家吧?

莱吉娜:噢,瞧我,她在家呢,刚上楼给少爷预备巧克力去了。

曼得斯:噢,对啦,刚才我在码头上听说奥斯瓦德回来了。

莱吉娜:是的。他前天回来的。我们原以为他今天才能到家。

曼得斯：他身体很好，健健康康的吧？

莱吉娜：是的，都托您的福了。不过，由于旅途劳顿，他简直累坏了。他是从巴黎一路赶过来的，坐了一整天火车，中间也没有休息。这会儿他大概正在小憩。咱们说话最好将声音压低些。

曼得斯：对，越低越好。

莱吉娜：（将一把扶手椅拉到桌子旁边）请坐，曼得斯牧师，别客气！（他坐下，莱吉娜把一个脚凳放在他脚下。）好啦！这下子舒服了吧，先生？

曼得斯：谢谢，谢谢，非常舒服。（瞧着她）知道吗，恩格斯特兰德小姐，自从我上回看见你之后，你好像长高了。

莱吉娜：是吗，先生？阿尔文夫人说我也长胖了。

曼得斯：长胖了？噢，也许是胖了一点儿，但正合适。

〔沉默了一会儿。〕

莱吉娜：我是不是去向阿尔文夫人通报一声，就说您来了？

曼得斯：谢谢，谢谢，不忙，好孩子。噢，顺便问一句，莱吉娜，我的好姑娘，你爸爸在这儿过得怎么样？

莱吉娜：多谢您的关心，先生，他过得很好。

曼得斯：他上回进城时找过我。

莱吉娜：是吗？他一直都很喜欢跟您交谈，先生。

曼得斯：你大概常到工地瞧他吧？

莱吉娜：我？噢，当然，我只要有时间就——

曼得斯：恩格斯特兰德小姐，你爸爸是个没主见的人，特别需要有个人引导他。

莱吉娜：噢，是的，我觉得他的确需要。

曼得斯：他需要的是一个跟他亲近的人，一个他所关心的人，一个能给他出主意的人。他上次去找我，把这些心里话都跟我说了。

莱吉娜：是的，他也跟我说过这种话。可是我不知道阿尔文夫人能不能让我走。目前，孤儿院刚建成，非常需要人手。再说，阿尔文夫人对我那么好，我真舍不得离开她。

曼得斯：可是，好孩子，做女儿的应该——当然，咱们先得问你主人愿意不愿意。

莱吉娜：可是，我一个女孩子家，都这么大了，给一个单身汉料理家务，真不知道合适不合适。

曼得斯：什么话，恩格斯特兰德小姐！那单身汉是你自己的爸爸呀！

莱吉娜：是的，就算是吧。可是，如果那是一个温馨的家，那个人是一位真正的绅士——

曼得斯：唉，我亲爱的莱吉娜——

莱吉娜：——如果他是一个值得我爱和敬重的人，一个配得上当父亲的人——

曼得斯：是的。可是我亲爱的好孩子——

莱吉娜：如果是那样的话，我是很愿意进城的，因为这儿的日子太冷清了。你应该知道一个人孤苦伶仃地生活是什么滋味，先生。我要是有一个温馨的家，我肯定愿意立刻就回去。你能为我找到一个这样的安身之地吗，先生？

曼得斯：我？我办不到。

莱吉娜：亲爱的先生，假如你找到了，可要记着我——

曼得斯：（站起来）好的，好的，当然会的，恩格斯特兰德小姐。

莱吉娜：因为，要是我——

曼得斯：麻烦你去通报你的女主人一声，就说我来了，好吗？

莱吉娜：好，我这就去，先生。（从左边走出去）

曼得斯：（背着手在屋子里来回走了几步，在后边的窗口前停下，将目光投向窗外的花园。随后，他又回到桌子旁边，随手拿起一本书，看看封面，吓了一跳，再看看另外的几本书。）哈，竟然看这种书！

〔阿尔文夫人从左边的门走进来。莱吉娜跟在后面，可是马上就又从右边的第一道门走出去了。〕

阿尔文夫人：（伸出手来）欢迎，我亲爱的牧师。

曼得斯：你好，阿尔文夫人！我答应过来，现在如约而来。

阿尔文夫人：你历来都很准时。

曼得斯：请你相信，我杂事缠身，实在不容易抽出空。我要参加那么些教区会和董事会——

阿尔文夫人：你拨冗来见，而且来得这么早，就更应该感谢你了。咱们可以在吃饭前把事情了结掉。你的行李呢？

曼得斯：（急忙回答）我的行李在旅馆里，今晚我住那儿。

阿尔文夫人：(忍着没笑出来)甚至到了现在，难道还不能说服你留在我家过夜？

曼得斯：不了，不了，多谢你的美意，阿尔文夫人！我还是像往常一样住旅馆的好。那儿离码头近，上轮船最方便。

阿尔文夫人：那就随你了。可是我觉得实在没关系，现在咱们都老了——

曼得斯：你这话怪逗人的。也难怪你今天兴致这么好——孤儿院明天开幕，奥斯瓦德又刚回家。

阿尔文夫人：的确如此。你都不知道我心里有多高兴！他有两年多没回家了，这次回来说要陪我过冬呢。

曼得斯：真的吗？这是他孝顺你，要不然他怎么肯扔下罗马和巴黎的繁华生活，跑到这冷冷清清的乡下来呢。

阿尔文夫人：是啊，谁叫他妈妈偏偏要住在这儿呢。我那儿子是个孝子，总惦记着他老妈！

曼得斯：假如他不回家，而是一门心思钻研艺术什么的，置母子亲情于不顾，那就太说不过去了。

阿尔文夫人：是呀，就是这个道理。不过，关于这些，不必为我儿子担心。真不知你见了他还能不能认出他。他在楼上呢，要在沙发上稍微休息休息，马上就下来。请坐，亲爱的牧师。

曼得斯：谢谢。你有时间吗？

阿尔文夫人：当然有。(在桌子旁边坐下)

曼得斯：很好。那么让我拿样东西给你看。(走到搁旅行包的椅子边，从包里拿出一包文件来，在阿尔文夫人对面坐下,想在桌子上找块空地方搁文件)先说几句,这是——(把话打住)阿尔文夫人,请你告诉我,桌子上怎么有这种书?

阿尔文夫人:怎么啦?这是我看的书呀。

曼得斯:你还看这种书?

阿尔文夫人:不错。

曼得斯:你看这种书是为了解闷还是为了寻开心?

阿尔文夫人:说起来,我觉得看了这些书,心里多了点儿把握。

曼得斯:真怪!此话怎讲?

阿尔文夫人:噢,我平时思考的那些问题在这些书中似乎都找到了答案,得到了证实。曼得斯牧师,奇妙之处在于,这些书里虽然没有惊世骇俗的论断,却有大多数人所思所想的道理。只不过,大多数人想是想了,却没有将自己的想法提升为理论,要不就是他们有理论却没有说出来。

曼得斯:天呀!难道你真相信大多数人——

阿尔文夫人:是的,我真相信。

曼得斯:不过,这个国家平常人的那套道理你肯定不会相信吧?你总不会相信咱们这儿的凡夫俗子的话吧?

阿尔文夫人:当然相信喽。这里和别的地方没什么两样。

曼得斯:好吧,我真得说——

阿尔文夫人:顺便问一句,你为什么讨厌这些书?

曼得斯:讨厌?你以为我有闲工夫看这种书吗?

阿尔文夫人:这就是说你并不了解这些你所不屑的书喽?

曼得斯:我读过好些批评这些书的文章,所以对它们嗤之以鼻。

阿尔文夫人:是的,可是你自己的看法——

曼得斯:亲爱的阿尔文夫人,在好些事情上,一个人必须要看看别人怎么说。世间万般事都是这样安排的,这样才有井然的秩序。否则,社会真不知会乱成什么样子!

阿尔文夫人:是呀,是呀,我敢说你的高论很有点儿道理。

曼得斯:再者,我当然不否认这种书可能很吸引人。而且,你渴望能跟得上国外据说正在进行的思想运动,还让你儿子到那儿去,一待就是许多年,对此我也不能责怪你。可是——

阿尔文夫人:可是什么?

曼得斯:(声音低下来)可是,不能跟别人谈论这件事,阿尔文夫人。自己在家里看什么书,思考什么问题,千万不能逢人便讲。

阿尔文夫人:这是当然的。我完全同意你的观点。

曼得斯:曾几何时,你一门心思要办孤儿院,而今孤儿院落成,真希望你能以孤儿院的福祉为重——要是我没看错的话——你那时对宗教的看法跟现在很不一样。

阿尔文夫人:噢,是的,这我承认。不过,咱们刚才要说的是孤儿院的事情——

曼得斯:不错,正是要说孤儿院的事呢。亲爱的夫人,我只强调一点：小心驶得万年船！现在咱们就言归正传吧。（打开文件袋，取出几页纸来）看到了吧？

阿尔文夫人：是不是文件？

曼得斯：全都办妥了，一点儿不含糊。实话告诉你，为了不误事，我可是费了九牛二虎之力，一点儿不放松地催他们。一到关键时刻，那些管事的人就谨慎得要命。不过，总算把手续都办齐了。（翻看文件）你瞧！这是罗森沃尔德庄园索尔维克那块地的过户契约——连地带新盖的学生宿舍楼、教室、教师住宅和教堂都包含在里面了。这是捐赠法律文书以及孤儿院章程的批准书。你看一遍好吗？（念道）"阿尔文上尉孤儿院章程"。

阿尔文夫人：（眼睛看着那些文件）现在都办妥了。

曼得斯：我选择用"上尉"这个词，而没有用"国王侍从"一词，是因为我不愿太招摇。

阿尔文夫人：哦，是吗？你觉得怎么妥当就怎么办吧。

曼得斯：这是银行存款簿，存款利息用来支付孤儿院的日常开销。

阿尔文夫人：谢谢。不过，还是由你掌管吧，那样方便些。

曼得斯：乐于效劳。我觉得可以暂时把钱存在银行里，利息当然并不理想，只有百分之四，要提款还得提前六个月通知，但这只是权宜之计。如果以后可以找到好的抵押贷款——当然，抵押品一定得来历分明，咱们再另做打算。

阿尔文夫人：当然，亲爱的曼得斯牧师。在这种事情上，你是最有眼光的。

曼得斯：我一定会尽量留意的。不过还有一件事，我好几回都想问你呢。

阿尔文夫人：什么事？

曼得斯：孤儿院的房子要不要上保险？

阿尔文夫人：当然喽，这是必须的。

曼得斯：嗯，别忙，阿尔文夫人，此事得仔细斟酌斟酌。

阿尔文夫人：我们家所有的东西都上了保险——什么动产不动产，什么牲畜和庄稼，都有保险。

曼得斯：你的私有财产上保险是无可非议的。我家的东西也都上了保险。不过，孤儿院就另当别论了——孤儿院是出于崇高的目的而创建的，是神圣的。

阿尔文夫人：是的，可是不能因为这个就——

曼得斯：就我个人而言，我觉得上保险以防不测没有丝毫不妥之处——

阿尔文夫人：是呀，我也是这么想的。

曼得斯：可是，普通民众会有怎样的想法呢？这一点你当然比我更清楚。

阿尔文夫人：这个嘛——若论大家的想法——

曼得斯：会不会有一批人——一批真正重要的人物，会站出来反对？

阿尔文夫人：你指的"真正重要的人物"是哪些人？

曼得斯：我指的是那些有地位、有势力的人，他们的意见你不重视都不行。

阿尔文夫人：此处倒是有一些这样的人，也可能会大惊小怪——

曼得斯：正是这个道理！在城里，这样的人也大有人在。你只要想想我的同僚就知道了！他们一定会怪你我不相信上帝。

阿尔文夫人：可是，你自己问心无愧就行了，我的好牧师——你至少该明白——

曼得斯：是的，我明白——我明白；我是问心无愧的，良心是清白的。可是，遭别人误解是在所难免的，这很可能会对孤儿院带来不利的影响。

阿尔文夫人：假如真是这样——

曼得斯：另外，我对自己所面临的困难也不能完全不考虑——我甚至可以说是痛苦，我也许会陷入尴尬的处境。城里有头有脸的人物非常关注孤儿院的情况，当然有一部分原因是因为他们关注城里人的利益，希望孤儿院的创建能够大大减轻富人所应该缴纳的贫民救济税。鉴于我一直在为你出谋划策，为你运筹帷幄，怕就怕他们会将矛头指向我——

阿尔文夫人：噢，怎么也不能叫你担这风险。

曼得斯：别的不说，报纸杂志肯定会对我口诛笔伐——

阿尔文夫人：这可不行，亲爱的曼得斯牧师。这么一说，咱们得把事情定下来。

曼得斯：你不打算给孤儿院上保险啦？

阿尔文夫人：是的，上保险的事就算啦。

曼得斯：（靠在椅背上）可是，万一有灾难发生该怎么办？天有不测风云，人有旦夕祸福！一旦出事，你有能力赔偿损失吗？

阿尔文夫人：没有。不妨直说吧，我绝不会做那种事的。

曼得斯：那我得告诉你，阿尔文夫人，咱们肩负的责任可是不轻啊。

阿尔文夫人：你看有没有别的办法？

曼得斯：没有。问题就出在这儿——咱们实在没有别的办法。咱们既不能让别人产生误会，又不便得罪教友。

阿尔文夫人：你是牧师，当然不能得罪他们。

曼得斯：我真心觉得咱们应该相信孤儿院一定会吉星高照、无灾无难的，因为上天特别眷顾它。

阿尔文夫人：但愿如此，曼得斯牧师。

曼得斯：那就顺其自然，不必为它牵肠挂肚了。

阿尔文夫人：是的，的确是这样的。

曼得斯：很好。就这么决定了。（记下来）那就不上保险了。

阿尔文夫人：怪就怪在，你早不提晚不提，偏偏在今天提到了此事——

曼得斯：我想问你这件事已不是一天两天了。

阿尔文夫人：——我说怪，是因为就在昨天，孤儿院差点儿发生火灾。

曼得斯：真的吗？

阿尔文夫人：真的，不过并无大碍，只是木工场里有堆刨花着了火。

曼得斯：是恩格斯特兰德干活儿的地方？

阿尔文夫人：是的。据说他划火柴不注意，喜欢随地乱扔。

曼得斯：他心里事情太多，那个人——他要战胜的逆境太多了。谢天谢地，现在好了，听说他要过体面的日子了。

阿尔文夫人：真的吗？谁说的？

曼得斯：是他自己告诉我的。说来，他可是个很不错的工匠。

阿尔文夫人：噢，是的，只要不酗酒，的确如此。

曼得斯：唉，那可是个让人伤心的缺点！不过，他说那是因为腿疼，经常需要喝点儿酒压一压。上次他进城时找我，说出的话叫我深受感动。他对我千恩万谢，说我帮他在这儿找到工作，使他能够跟莱吉娜在一起。

阿尔文夫人：他不常见莱吉娜。

曼得斯：他们父女常见面呢，天天说话哩。这是他亲口告诉我的。

阿尔文夫人：唔，也许是吧。

曼得斯：他深切感受到身边必须有个人，当诱惑来临时，好管住他。雅各布·恩格斯特兰德就是这么一个人：可怜巴巴地找到你，一味谴责自己，怪自己缺点多，让你不由得就会喜欢他。上次他找我说话——请相信我的话，阿尔文夫人，他的确需要莱吉娜，让莱吉娜回家去——

阿尔文夫人：（腾地站了起来）莱吉娜！

曼得斯：——你可别反对。

阿尔文夫人：我一定反对。再说，莱吉娜将来要在孤儿院工作。

曼得斯：可是你别忘了，他毕竟是莱吉娜的父亲——

阿尔文夫人：哼，他是什么样的父亲我很清楚。此事行不通！出于好心，我绝不让莱吉娜到他身边去。

曼得斯：（站起来）亲爱的夫人，别生气。你错怪了可怜的恩格斯特兰德，好像很担心——

阿尔文夫人：（平静了些）错怪不错怪跟这没关系。我既然收留了莱吉娜，就要继续收留下去。（竖起耳朵听）嘘！亲爱的曼得斯先生，此事就别再说了。（高兴得容光焕发）你听！奥斯瓦德下楼来了。现在应该以他为重，要想就只想关于他的事。

〔奥斯瓦德·阿尔文身上穿一件薄外套，手里拿着帽子，嘴里叼着一只海泡石大烟斗，从左边门进来，在门口停住了脚步。〕

奥斯瓦德：噢，对不起，我以为你在书房里。（走上前来）早上好，曼得斯牧师。

曼得斯：（瞪着眼瞧他）哦！真怪！

阿尔文夫人：你看他怎么样，曼得斯先生？

曼得斯：我——我——难道真是——

奥斯瓦德：不错，我正是那回头的浪子，先生。

曼得斯：（意欲解释）我亲爱的年轻朋友——

奥斯瓦德：噢，那就是迷路的羔羊回来了。

阿尔文夫人：奥斯瓦德这样说话是因为他想起了当初你坚决反对他学绘画的事。

曼得斯：有些事乍一看似乎不可取，可是后来却证明——（握紧奥斯瓦德的手）不管怎么样，欢迎你回家！欢迎！亲爱的奥斯瓦德，你可不要觉得——我能叫你奥斯瓦德吗?

奥斯瓦德:不叫我奥斯瓦德,还能叫我什么呢?

曼得斯:很好。亲爱的奥斯瓦德,我想说的是,你可不要觉得我对绘画深恶痛绝。我毫不怀疑,有许多人虽然学的是绘画,但跟学别的东西一样,还能不损伤自己的内心。

奥斯瓦德:但愿如此。

阿尔文夫人:(喜形于色)我就知道他里里外外都没受过损伤。你仔细瞧瞧他就知道了,曼得斯先生。

奥斯瓦德:(心神不定,走来走去)是啊,是啊,亲爱的妈妈。咱们还是说点儿别的吧。

曼得斯:噢,当然——这是谁都无法否认的。你现在已经小有名气了。报上常常能看到对你的评论,大多数都是正面的。可是近来我好像不大能看见你的名字了。

奥斯瓦德:(朝温室走去)近来我抽不出空,画得不多。

阿尔文夫人:就是画家,时而也得休息休息呀。

曼得斯:对,对。休息的时候可以养精蓄锐,为的是画出伟大的作品来。

奥斯瓦德:对。妈妈,快开饭了吧?

阿尔文夫人:再等不到半个小时就开饭。他食欲特别好,真是要感谢上帝。

曼得斯:还喜欢抽烟斗。

奥斯瓦德:这是家父的烟斗,是在我的房间里找到的——

曼得斯：哦，怪不得！

阿尔文夫人：怪不得什么？

曼得斯：刚才奥斯瓦德出现在门口那儿，嘴里叼着这烟斗，样子活像他父亲。

奥斯瓦德：真的吗？

阿尔文夫人：噢，怎么能这样说！奥斯瓦德长得像我。

曼得斯：不错，可是他嘴角那股神气——那两片嘴唇——的确让我想起了他的父亲——特别是他现在抽烟的样子，父子俩简直像极了。

阿尔文夫人：一点儿都不像。我倒觉得奥斯瓦德的嘴弯弯的，有点儿牧师的神气。

曼得斯：对，对，我有几个同事的嘴都是这个样子。

阿尔文夫人：好孩子，你能不能把烟斗收起来？我这儿不许抽烟。

奥斯瓦德：（放下烟斗）好吧。我小时候抽过烟斗，现在只不过想再尝尝它的滋味。

阿尔文夫人：你抽过烟？

奥斯瓦德：是的，那时候我还是个小不点儿。记得有天晚上我到爸爸的房间里去，正赶上他兴致很高。

阿尔文夫人：哦，那时候的事情你哪里能记得。

奥斯瓦德：能记得，记得一清二楚。他让我坐在他膝上，把烟斗塞给我说："抽一口，孩子，使劲抽！"于是我就使劲抽了一口，结果呛得我脸色苍白，额头上的汗珠有黄豆那么大。乐得他哈哈大笑——

曼得斯：那样做实在是太出格了。

阿尔文夫人：亲爱的朋友，别当真，那只不过是奥斯瓦德梦中的情景。

奥斯瓦德：不，妈妈，不是我做梦梦见的。难道你不记得了吗？当时，你走过来把我抱到了我自己的房间。后来我就病了，我还看见你哭呢。爸爸是不是常爱这么开玩笑？

曼得斯：他年轻的时候的确兴致很高，觉得生活充满了欢乐——

奥斯瓦德：可是他还是做了不少事，做了许多又好又有用的事，可惜英年早逝。

曼得斯：是的。亲爱的奥斯瓦德·阿尔文，你有一个精力充沛、令人钦佩的父亲。毫无疑问，这对你而言一定是一种激励——

奥斯瓦德：是的，的确是这样的。

曼得斯：你能回家参加你父亲的纪念会，是你的孝心。

奥斯瓦德：纪念我爸爸，我不能不回来。

阿尔文夫人：他在家陪伴我那么久，这才是最令我高兴的。

曼得斯：我听说你要在家里过冬。

奥斯瓦德：还说不定要在这儿待多长时间呢，先生。不过，啊，待在家里的感觉真是太好啦！

阿尔文夫人：（喜笑颜开）是吗，亲爱的？

曼得斯：（同情地望着奥斯瓦德）我亲爱的奥斯瓦德，你小小年纪就出门闯荡世界了。

奥斯瓦德：是啊。有时候我心里在想是不是太早了点儿。

阿尔文夫人：噢，一点儿都不早。一个身体健康的孩子，尤其是独生子，还是早一点儿出去闯荡的好——在父母的羽翼下生活，非被惯坏不可。

曼得斯：这一点值得商榷，阿尔文夫人。一个小孩子所在的合适的地方应该是，而且一定是他自己的家。

奥斯瓦德：我完全同意你的观点，曼得斯牧师。

曼得斯：你看看你自己的儿子吧——咱们不妨当着他的面说——他早早出门闯荡的结果怎么样？他今年二十六七岁了，还不知道一个秩序井然的家庭究竟是什么样子。

奥斯瓦德：对不起，牧师，这话你可完全说错了。

曼得斯：是吗？我还以为你差不多老在艺术圈儿里过日子，接触的净是艺术家呢。

奥斯瓦德：是这样的。

曼得斯：接触的主要是青年艺术家，是不是？

奥斯瓦德：是的，的确如此。

曼得斯：我一直都觉得年轻人没有能力成家，没有能力养家糊口。

奥斯瓦德：许多年轻人的确是娶不起老婆的。

曼得斯：是呀，我说的正是这个意思。

奥斯瓦德：可是，尽管他们娶不起老婆，却可以有个家。实际上，他们当中很多人都有家，而且是非常舒适、秩序良好的家。

〔阿尔文夫人聚精会神地听儿子说话,不住点头赞成,可是没说什么。〕

曼得斯:我所说的家可不是单身汉住的那种地方,而是指一个男人带着老婆孩子过日子的地方。

奥斯瓦德:是的,是一家几口住的地方,里面住着一个男子和他的孩子,还有孩子的母亲。

曼得斯:(吃惊,双手绞在一起)可是,那不就是——

奥斯瓦德:怎么啦?

曼得斯:跟他住在一起的——是孩子的母亲?

奥斯瓦德:是啊,难道你要他把孩子的妈妈撵出去吗?

曼得斯:原来你说的是非法同居!人们称之为"不正常婚姻"!

奥斯瓦德:我看不出那些人过的日子有什么特别不正常的地方。

曼得斯:如果是有廉耻之心的青年男女,怎么能那样过日子?也不怕别人说闲话?

奥斯瓦德:你让他们怎么办?年轻的艺术家一贫如洗,女孩也没钱,而婚礼开销巨大。他们能有别的办法吗?

曼得斯:我让他们怎么办?那我就说说他们应该怎么办吧,阿尔文先生。他们应该从一开始就管住自己——这才是他们应该做的事。

奥斯瓦德:热恋中的青年男女几乎是不可能遵循这一规矩的。

阿尔文夫人:是的,几乎是不可能的!

曼得斯:(接着说下去)政府当局怎么能容忍这种事

情！怎么能允许他们公然非法同居！（转向阿尔文夫人）当初我深深为你儿子担忧，难道是多余的吗？在某种圈子里，不道德的现象四处可见，甚至得到了人们的某种认可！

奥斯瓦德：实不相瞒，先生，我有个习惯，几乎每逢星期天都会到一两户这样的不正常人家做客——

曼得斯：还偏偏挑星期天去！

奥斯瓦德：星期天是休息日，难道不可以放松一下吗？在他们家里，我没听到过一句脏话，更没看见过所谓的不道德现象。在艺术圈儿，你知道我在什么时候、什么地方看见过不道德的现象吗？

曼得斯：不知道。谢天谢地，我怎么能知道！

奥斯瓦德：那好，让我告诉你吧。有些所谓的模范丈夫和模范父亲偷偷溜到巴黎开眼界，还屈尊跑到艺术家的寒碜住所。这些见过世面的绅士，大讲特讲他们去过的藏污纳垢之地以及做过的肮脏事情，真是叫你做梦都想不到——这就是我见过的不道德现象。

曼得斯：什么！你是不是说体面人一离开家就会——

奥斯瓦德：这些体面人离开家后是一种样子，回到家则慷慨激昂地批评国外伤风败俗的现象十分严重。难道你没听到过他们的这些议论吗？

曼得斯：听是肯定听到过——

阿尔文夫人：我也听到过。

奥斯瓦德：这样的议论你们也许会信以为真，因为他们会说得有鼻子有眼！（双手抱头）唉！想不到国外的那种伟大、自由、光辉的生活竟然让人糟蹋成了这种样子！

阿尔文夫人:别激动,奥斯瓦德,这对你不好。

奥斯瓦德:是的,你说得很对,妈妈。我知道这对我不好。你瞧,我累坏了,想在吃饭前出去溜达溜达。失陪了,牧师。我知道你不会同意我的看法,但我还是要说出来。(从右边第二道门里出去)

阿尔文夫人:可怜的孩子!

曼得斯:你可以说他可怜。想不到他成了这种样子!

〔阿尔文夫人瞧着他,一声不吭。〕

曼得斯:(走来走去)他说自己是个浪子。唉!唉!

〔阿尔文夫人仍然瞧着他。〕

曼得斯:你怎么看?

阿尔文夫人:我看奥斯瓦德是对的,句句在理。

曼得斯:(站住不动)在理?在什么理?

阿尔文夫人:曼得斯牧师,当我一个人独处的时候,心里也有他那种想法。只是我不敢说出来。这下好啦!现在有我儿子替我发言了。

曼得斯:阿尔文夫人,你真可怜。我得认真跟你谈一谈了。此时此刻,站在你面前的不再是你的生意经理和顾问,也不再是你和你丈夫的老朋友,而是一位牧师——这位牧师曾在你步入迷途的关键时刻为你指点过迷津。

阿尔文夫人:这位牧师现在对我有何指教?

曼得斯:首先,我要提醒一下你,不能忘记过去。此时提醒正是时候。明天是你丈夫逝世十周年的忌日,他的纪念碑要在明天揭幕。明天我要在全体到会的人面前发言,而现在得先跟你单独谈谈。

阿尔文夫人：很好，曼得斯牧师。有话请讲！

曼得斯：你可记得，结婚不到一年你就跑到悬崖边打算轻生？可记得你曾抛弃了自己的家庭，从你丈夫身边逃走？是的，阿尔文夫人，你从你丈夫身边逃走了，你逃走了，任他怎么苦苦哀求，你都拒绝回去。

阿尔文夫人：难道你忘了我结婚头一年，内心是多么痛苦？

曼得斯：想要追求现世幸福就是反叛精神的表现。咱们有什么权利享受幸福？咱们只能尽自己的义务，阿尔文夫人！那时你的义务就是坚定地守在你选择的这个男人身边，你和他缔结了神圣的婚姻。

阿尔文夫人：那时，阿尔文的生活有多么放荡，日子过得有多么荒唐，你不是不知道。

曼得斯：那些有关他的传闻我一清二楚。假如那些传闻属实，他年轻时候的生活方式我是最不赞成的。不过，你作为妻子，不该评判丈夫的是与非，因为你的职责是谦卑地背负大智大慧的上帝交给你的十字架。可是，你却逆天行事，扔掉十字架，抛弃了那个你本该扶持的罪人，一走了之，置你自己的名誉于不顾，甚至还差点儿让别人的名誉也毁于一旦。

阿尔文夫人：别人的名誉？你大概是说某一个人的名誉吧？

曼得斯：你所做的最轻率的一件事就是跑去找我寻求庇护。

阿尔文夫人：找我们的牧师难道不应该吗？找我们的

知己朋友难道不应该吗?

曼得斯：正是出于这个原因，你才不该找我。你应该感谢上帝，亏得我有主见，苦口婆心地劝说你，使你放弃了你的荒唐计划——我受命于上帝，引导你回到恪尽职守的阳光大道上，回到了你丈夫的身边。

阿尔文夫人：是的，曼得斯牧师，你当然功不可没。

曼得斯：我只不过是上帝的一个卑贱的仆人。我引导你回到尽职和尽忠的岗位上，后来证明，这对你的一生而言有着多么大的好处！我的预言难道没有实现吗？阿尔文难道没有痛改前非、重新做人吗？难道自那以后他没有跟你在一起规规矩矩、清清白白地过日子吗？难道他没有成为一个为整个地区造福的恩人吗？难道他没有帮助你、勉励你，使你逐渐成为他的助手，和他一道为民众造福吗？你不但是个助手，还是非常得力的助手——我很清楚，阿尔文夫人，这样的赞扬你受之无愧。不过接下来，我要说说你人生当中犯的第二个大错误。

阿尔文夫人：什么意思？

曼得斯：正像你曾经抛弃过做妻子的义务，后来你又抛弃了做母亲的义务。

阿尔文夫人：啊——！

曼得斯：你一生吃了固执任性的大亏，心里老有叛逆的念头，不守规矩，历来都不愿意受任何束缚，对于生活中的所有负担你都不管三七二十一，一推了之，仿佛愿意撂挑子就可以撂挑子一样。你不高兴做妻子，就一拍屁股离开了你的丈夫。后来，你嫌做母亲太麻烦，索性就把孩子送走,让他跟陌生人住在一起。

阿尔文夫人:不错,我是这么做的。

曼得斯:所以,你和你儿子就疏远了。

阿尔文夫人:不是的!不是的!我们没有疏远。

曼得斯:是的,你们疏远了,肯定疏远了。现在他回到你身边,心里该是什么滋味?你好好反思反思吧,阿尔文夫人。你曾经对不起你丈夫,于是你为他建立纪念碑以示悔过。至于对不起你儿子,你也应该悔过才对。当务之急是要引导他,让他迷途知返。我劝你赶紧回头,趁着还来得及,挽救挽救他。说实在的,阿尔文夫人,(竖起食指)你是个难逃罪责的母亲!我觉得自己有责任提醒你。

〔静默。〕

阿尔文夫人:(慢条斯理,控制着情绪)你把心里话都说出来了,曼得斯牧师。明天你要在大会上发言悼念我丈夫。我明天不发言,但现在我想对你说几句心里话,像你一样开诚布公。

曼得斯:不用说,你一定会寻找理由为自己的行为辩护——

阿尔文夫人:不是的。我只是想说一说往事。

曼得斯:什么往事?

阿尔文夫人:你刚才提到了我和我丈夫的情况,说到了你引导我回到恪尽职守的阳光大道上之后——这是借用你的话——我们的生活情况,还说到了你只是耳闻并非亲眼见过的传闻。你曾经是我们的心腹之交,可是从那以后你就再也没有踏进过我家的房门。

曼得斯：那是因为后来不久你和你丈夫就搬出了城。

阿尔文夫人：是的。我丈夫在世的时候，你也没再来看过我们。后来你负责孤儿院的事务，出于工作你才不得不来见我。

曼得斯：（声音低柔、踌躇）海伦——假如你有责怪我的意思，我只能请你想一想——

阿尔文夫人：是啊，想一想你的职位，再想一想我是离家出走的妻子。面对我这种不守规矩的女人，当然躲得越远越好。

曼得斯：亲爱的——阿尔文夫人，你这话说得太过火了——

阿尔文夫人：好吧，就算我说得过火了。我的意思是说，你对于我婚后生活的评价，只是根据一些常理和听到的传闻做出的。

曼得斯：这我承认。你还有什么要说的？

阿尔文夫人：那么，曼得斯牧师——我就把真实情况都说出来吧。我发过誓，总有一天会把实情对你讲的——只告诉你一个人！

曼得斯：真实情况是什么？

阿尔文夫人：真实情况就是我丈夫一生都荒淫无度，至死都没有改变。

曼得斯：（用手摸索，想找一把椅子）你说什么？

阿尔文夫人：婚后的十九年里，他依旧荒淫无度——为所欲为——就跟你为我们证婚之前的他，是一个样儿。

曼得斯：生活有点儿放荡，有点儿不守规矩，有些越轨行为，你就说他"荒淫无度"？

阿尔文夫人：这是我们的医生说的。

曼得斯：我不明白你的意思。

阿尔文夫人：你也不必明白。

曼得斯：你的一席话听得我头晕。这么说，婚后这些年你看上去生活幸福美满，而实际上却在一个看不见的深渊中挣扎？

阿尔文夫人：差不多是这样的。现在你总算明白了。

曼得斯：这种事情——这种事情在我看来简直不可思议。我无法理解！无法相信！这怎么可能呢？这种情况怎么瞒得过人呢？

阿尔文夫人：我日复一日地苦苦挣扎，总害怕家丑外扬。奥斯瓦德出生后，我觉得阿尔文似乎收敛了一些。可没过多久，他又故态复萌了。于是我又陷入了痛苦之中，而且是加倍的痛苦，就好像在进行一场殊死搏斗，生怕别人知道我孩子的父亲竟然是那种人。你知道，阿尔文知道怎样能赢得人心，所以所有的人都坚信他是个好人，绝不会有不当行为。有些人的生活方式不会损害他们的名誉。阿尔文就是这样一个人。可是到最后，曼得斯先生——我必须让你知道一件往事——一件最丑陋的事情。

曼得斯：比你刚才说的那些还要丑陋吗？

阿尔文夫人：他在外边拈花惹草，我一忍再忍，只当不知。可是后来他竟然把丑事闹到我们家里来了——

曼得斯：不可能吧？就在这里？

阿尔文夫人：是的，就是在我们这个家里。就在那儿

（用手指着右边第一道门），我头一回发现就是在那个餐厅里。当时，我在那儿有点事做，房门开了一条缝。我听见我们家的女佣从花园里走了过来，到温室给花浇水。

曼得斯：后来怎么样？

阿尔文夫人：不一会儿，我听见阿尔文也进了温室，接着就听见他柔声细语地对女佣说话。那话真肉麻！（一声冷笑）哦！他的话至今还在我的耳边回响，既可恶又可笑——我听见女佣低声央求他："放开我，阿尔文先生！让我走！"

曼得斯：想不到他那么轻浮！不过，那只是逢场作戏，不会有严重后果的，请相信我好啦，阿尔文夫人。

阿尔文夫人：没过多久，我就知道自己应该相信什么了。阿尔文先生把那女孩子弄到了手，而且还结了果实，曼得斯先生。

曼得斯：（如遭雷击）竟有这种事情发生在这儿——发生在这幢房子里！

阿尔文夫人：就是在这幢房子里，我忍辱负重。为了晚上能把他留在家里我强装笑颜，陪着他寻欢作乐。我坐在他身边陪他碰杯喝酒，听他说又肮脏又愚蠢的话，末了还得费很大的劲儿把他硬拉上床睡觉——

曼得斯：（受到触动）这种日子你怎么能忍受得了！

阿尔文夫人：为了孩子，我不得不忍受。可是到了后来我简直忍无可忍，因为就连我的贴身女佣都——于是我发誓要结束这种局面。我将控制权一把抓过来——所有的事情——无论是他的事还是别的事——都归我管。这下子，我有了对付他的武器，令他不敢肆意胡来了。随后，我把奥斯瓦德送出了家门。那时他快七岁了，跟别的孩子一样开始懂事，开始问这问那了。我无法让他在家里再待下去，因为我觉得家里受到了污染，就连呼吸空气都会叫孩子中毒。这就是我送他走的原因。现在你该明白了，为什么他父亲在世的时候我不允许他进这个家门。我的心里有多痛苦，只有苍天知道！

曼得斯：你过的的确是一种水深火热的日子。

阿尔文夫人：要不是有事情做，那种日子我是忍受不了的。可以毫不夸口地说，我的确干出了一番成绩！我呕心沥血地置田买地，大刀阔斧地进行改革，节省了不少人力物力，而人们却交口称赞阿尔文——你想，他哪里有这些精力！——他就知道成天躺在沙发上看一本破旧的士绅录！没有的事。告诉你吧，在他头脑清楚的时候，是我鼓励他振作起来重新做人的。在他故态复萌或者怨天尤人、牢骚满腹的时候，是我挑着千斤重担，一个人受罪。

曼得斯：这么一个人你还为他竖立纪念碑？

阿尔文夫人：这就是内心不安所带来的后果。

曼得斯：内心不安？此话怎讲？

阿尔文夫人：我总担心他的真实情况早晚会暴露，被人们知道。创办孤儿院就是为了平息外头的谣言，使人们不起疑心。

曼得斯：你的目的可真是达到了，阿尔文夫人。

阿尔文夫人：另外，我还有个理由。我打定主意不让我自己的孩子奥斯瓦德继承他父亲一丝一毫的产业。

曼得斯：这么说，你用阿尔文的产业——？

阿尔文夫人：是的。年复一年，我投在创办孤儿院的项目上的钱——我仔细算过——刚好跟他的产业价值相等，这就让阿尔文中尉[①]成了当时的"大善人"。

曼得斯：我不明白——

阿尔文夫人：我把钱投在那里，是不愿意让它传入奥斯瓦德的手中。我儿子的一切都得由我给他——一切。

〔奥斯瓦德·阿尔文从右边第二道门里进来。他已经摘了帽子，脱了外套，把它们放在大厅里。〕

阿尔文夫人：（迎上去）这么快就回来了，我的宝贝儿子？

奥斯瓦德：是的。老是下不完的雨，在外头什么都干不成。听说饭已经好了。棒极了！

莱吉娜：（手里拿着个小包裹，从餐厅里进来）有你一个包裹，阿尔文夫人。（把包裹递给她）

阿尔文夫人：（看了曼得斯先生一眼）肯定是明天开幕典礼用的颂歌歌本。

曼得斯：噢——

莱吉娜：饭准备好了。

阿尔文夫人：很好。我们马上就来。我先看看——（动手拆包裹）

莱吉娜：（冲着奥斯瓦德）阿尔文先生喝红葡萄酒还是白葡萄酒？

[①] 那时他还是中尉。

奥斯瓦德:麻烦你了,两样都要。

莱吉娜:Bien①,先生。(走进餐厅)

奥斯瓦德:我帮你开酒瓶吧。(跟着她走进餐厅,让餐厅的门半敞着)

阿尔文夫人:(已经把包裹拆开)果然是歌本。我想就是的。这是开幕典礼用的颂歌歌本,曼得斯牧师。

曼得斯:(双手合在一起)明天发言,真不知怎么个样子才好。

阿尔文夫人:噢,你一定会顺顺利利的。

曼得斯:(低声,为的是不让餐厅里的人听见)是的,再怎么也不能叫人听出其中有什么蹊跷!

阿尔文夫人:(低声,但口气很坚决)是的。这出又臭又长、令人可憎的丑剧就要落幕了。从后天起,我将开始一种新生活,就好像我那个丈夫压根儿就没有在这幢房屋里居住过一样。这户人家只有我和我的儿子,再无他人。

〔餐厅里传来一把椅子倒地的声音,同时听见〕

莱吉娜:(严厉但很微弱的声音)奥斯瓦德,别这样!你疯了吗?让我走!〕

阿尔文夫人:(惊恐万状)啊——!

〔她狂乱地将目光转向餐厅的那扇半开半掩的门。只听见奥斯瓦德在那里嘻嘻哈哈地笑着,接着就听见拔酒瓶塞子的声音。〕

曼得斯:(不安地)怎么回事?怎么啦,阿尔文夫人?

---

① 法文,意思是"好的"。

阿尔文夫人：(声音嘶哑)鬼！鬼！温室里的那两个鬼又出现了！

曼得斯：这怎么可能！你是说莱吉娜——？难道她——？

阿尔文夫人：是的。走，咱们过去。别作声！

〔她抓着曼得斯牧师的胳膊，摇摇晃晃地朝着餐厅走去。〕

第二幕

布景:同上。外边的景致仍然笼罩在浓雾里。
曼得斯和阿尔文夫人从餐厅里回来。

阿尔文夫人:(在门道那儿)Velbekomme①,曼得斯先生。(转过身去朝着餐厅)奥斯瓦德,你也进来,好不好?

奥斯瓦德:(在餐厅里)不,谢谢。我想出去走走。

阿尔文夫人:好,去吧。天气似乎好点儿了。(关上餐厅门,走到大厅门口,叫道)莱吉娜!

莱吉娜:(在外头)什么事,阿尔文夫人?

阿尔文夫人:你到洗衣房去,把那些花环收拾收拾。

莱吉娜:好的,阿尔文夫人。

〔阿尔文夫人等莱吉娜走后,急忙把门关上。〕

曼得斯:他大概听不见咱们说话吧?

阿尔文夫人:关上门是听不见的。再说,他就要出去了。

---

① 一句相当于德语"Prosit die Mahlzeit"的短语:但愿食欲好,消化得快。(原注)

曼得斯：我还是觉得心乱如麻，真不知刚才那顿饭是怎么咽下去的。

阿尔文夫人：（走来走去，竭力控制不安的情绪）我也是。现在该如何是好？

曼得斯：是啊，该如何是好？我简直有点儿不知所措，因为我从未经历过这种事情。

阿尔文夫人：我相信目前还没有闹出乱子来。

曼得斯：闹出乱子可天理不容！可是，谁知道会有什么可怕的事情发生呢？

阿尔文夫人：你放心，这只是奥斯瓦德一时糊涂，行为有些不当罢了。

曼得斯：噢，我刚说过，这种事情我外行。不过我想应该——

阿尔文夫人：必须让莱吉娜离开这里，马上就得离开。这一点是毫无疑问的。

曼得斯：是的，当然必须让她离开。

阿尔文夫人：可是，让她到哪儿安身呢？不应该——

曼得斯：到哪儿安身？当然到她爸爸那儿去了。

阿尔文夫人：你说到谁那儿？

曼得斯：到她——难道恩格斯特兰德真的不是她的——？天呀，阿尔文夫人，怎么会有这种事！你一定是搞错了。

阿尔文夫人：可惜我并没有搞错——乔安娜[①]把一切

---

① 莱吉娜的生母。

都对我坦白了,阿尔文想赖也赖不掉。我万般无奈,只好将事情隐瞒了起来。

曼得斯:是啊,你也只好那么办了。

阿尔文夫人:我们立刻就把乔安娜打发走了,还给了她一大笔钱堵住她的嘴。后来,她到城里谋生,跟恩格斯特兰德重修旧好,肯定让他看了她那鼓起的钱包,对他撒了谎,说那年夏天有个坐游艇的外国人到这儿来。于是,她跟恩格斯特兰德就急急忙忙地结了婚。说起来,他们的婚礼还是你主持的呢。

曼得斯:可是,又该如何解释——?我清楚记得恩格斯特兰德有一天来找我,说他要结婚。他后悔得不得了,一味地自责,怪自己不该跟未婚妻干那种丑事。

阿尔文夫人:当然,出于无奈,他只好替别人背黑锅了。

曼得斯:想不到他竟然那么不老实,对我也撒谎!雅各布·恩格斯特兰德竟是这么一种人,简直叫我无法相信!回头我一定得狠狠地教训他一顿,让他吃不了兜着走。他们的结合简直就是一种道德的沦丧!为了几个钱——!你们给了乔安娜多少钱?

阿尔文夫人:三百块。

曼得斯:想一想吧!为了区区三百块钱,他竟然跟一个堕落的女人结婚!

阿尔文夫人:那么,你怎么说我呢?我是跟一个堕落的男人结了婚。

曼得斯:唉,什么话!你怎么会说这种话!他怎么会是堕落的男人!

阿尔文夫人：你以为跟我结婚时的阿尔文比跟恩格斯特兰德结婚时的乔安娜要清白些吗？

曼得斯：这两件事完全不一样——

阿尔文夫人：其实并没什么不一样——唯一的区别在于价格的高低：一个是区区三百块钱，一个是全部家产。

曼得斯：你怎么能把两件天差地别的事情相提并论呢？你结婚是心甘情愿的，也是跟家里人商量过的。

阿尔文夫人：（眼睛不瞧他）我还以为你了解我当时的心意呢。

曼得斯：（冷淡地）我要是了解，就不会天天到你丈夫家里去了。

阿尔文夫人：实际情况是——反正我自己并没考虑过结婚的事。

曼得斯：那么，你一定跟你最亲近的人商量过，跟你母亲和两个姑姑商量过——这是你应该做的。

阿尔文夫人：是的，我的确跟她们商量过。她们三个替我做了决定。啊，她们可真是独具慧眼，说拒绝这样的亲事真是糊涂透顶。要是妈妈能看到我现在的下场，看到这门亲事给我带来的后果就好了！

曼得斯：有这样的后果，不能让任何人负责。至少有一点是很清楚的——你们的婚姻完全合法，完全合规。

阿尔文夫人：（在窗口）唉，老是什么法律和规矩！我经常心想害人不浅的正是这两样东西。

曼得斯：阿尔文夫人，说这话就是一种罪过。

阿尔文夫人：哦，此话我不说不行。跟这些压制人的虚伪东西我势不两立——对它们我再也无法忍受了。我必须采取措施，争取自由。

曼得斯：什么意思？

阿尔文夫人：（轻轻敲着窗框）千不该万不该，我不该隐瞒阿尔文过的是什么样的生活。当时，我胆小怕事，不敢一走了之，前怕狼后怕虎，怪就怪我是个懦夫。

曼得斯：懦夫？

阿尔文夫人：我担心外人知道我离家出走的话，会说什么"可怜的人！妻子跑了，难怪他会胡作非为"。

曼得斯：这样说也有一定的道理。

阿尔文夫人：（眼睛盯着他）要是我有胆量的话，就会去找奥斯瓦德，对他说："听我说，孩子，你父亲是个荒淫无耻的人——"

曼得斯：天呀，怎么能说这种话！

阿尔文夫人：我要把今天跟你说的事情一五一十地全都告诉他，一字不漏地告诉他。

曼得斯：你真是太让我吃惊了，阿尔文夫人。

阿尔文夫人：是的，我知道，知道得很清楚。连我自己对这想法都吃惊不小。（离开窗口）我是个彻头彻尾的懦夫。

曼得斯：你把尽职尽责视为懦夫行为？难道你忘了做儿子的应该敬爱父母吗？

阿尔文夫人：咱们不必空谈。我只问你一句：奥斯瓦德应该敬爱国王侍从阿尔文这样的父亲吗？

曼得斯：你为人之母，难道忍心让你儿子心中的理想毁于一旦吗？

阿尔文夫人：那么，真相怎么办呢？

曼得斯：顾了真相，理想怎么办？

阿尔文夫人：唉，什么理想不理想！我要不是胆小怕事，就一定会说出真相！

曼得斯：你可不要小看了理想的力量，阿尔文夫人，不然会惹出事来的。就拿奥斯瓦德说吧，不幸的是，他似乎心中没多少理想，而我看得出他父亲就是他的一个理想。

阿尔文夫人：是的，此话不假。

曼得斯：他之所以会把父亲当作典范，是你给他写信时给他灌输的思想，使他有了这种观念。

阿尔文夫人：不错。我迷信于尽自己的义务，又有诸多顾虑，于是就年复一年地对儿子撒谎。唉，怪就怪我是个懦夫——一个胆小怕事的懦夫！

曼得斯：你在你儿子心里树立了一个虚幻的光辉形象，而今不该将它贬得一文不值。

阿尔文夫人：哼！谁知道那究竟是什么样的光辉形象！不管怎么说吧，反正我不能让他跟莱吉娜纠缠下去，不能让他毁了那个可怜女孩的一辈子。

曼得斯：是啊，那是绝对不行的！那样后果太可怕了！

阿尔文夫人：要是我知道他是认真的，知道他会因此而获得幸福的话——

曼得斯：怎么？你打算怎么样？

阿尔文夫人：不过，那是行不通的；因为不幸的是，莱吉娜绝非他的佳偶。

曼得斯：什么？你这话是什么意思？

阿尔文夫人：若非我是个可悲的懦夫，我就会对他说："要娶就娶她吧，或者随你怎么样，只要别干偷偷摸摸的事情就行。"

曼得斯：苍天在上，你竟然会想到让他们结婚！简直太可怕了！简直闻所未闻！

阿尔文夫人：你真的"闻所未闻"？老实说，曼得斯牧师，你以为咱们这一带，像他们这样近亲结婚的例子还少吗？

曼得斯：我一点儿都不懂你的意思。

阿尔文夫人：其实你是懂的。

曼得斯：噢，你觉得有可能——唉！有些人家的家庭生活的确不太清白，可是像你说的这种事我闻所未闻，起码不能肯定说有。再说，你身为母亲，怎么会想到让自己的儿子——

阿尔文夫人：不，我不能——无论如何我也不同意这样的事情发生——这就是我的回答。

曼得斯：是啊，因为你是个"懦夫"嘛，这是你自己说的。可是，假如你不是"懦夫"，那会——？天呀！这样的结合实在太荒唐！

阿尔文夫人：据说咱们的祖宗就是这么结合的。你说是谁做出了这样的安排，曼得斯牧师？

曼得斯：我不能跟你讨论这种大道理，阿尔文夫人，因为你的情绪很不稳定。但我要说，你不该把良心的不安称为"胆小"——！

阿尔文夫人：请容我解释一下，我胆小，我怯懦，全是因为我被一群鬼缠住了，怎么也摆不脱。

曼得斯：你说什么把你缠住啦？

阿尔文夫人：一群鬼！我听见莱吉娜和奥斯瓦德在餐厅里说话的时候，我觉得眼前好像出现了一群鬼。我几乎觉得咱们都是鬼，曼得斯牧师。非但咱们从祖宗那里继承下来的东西在咱们身上又出现，而且形形色色陈腐的思想、僵死的观念也纷纷在咱们心里作怪。它们没有生命力，但仍然死缠着咱们，想甩都甩不掉。我只要拿起一张报纸，好像就会看见字里行间有鬼在游荡。天下之人一定都变成了鬼，多如大海里的沙子。咱们每一个人都是鬼，可怜巴巴，怕见光明。

曼得斯：唉，这都是因为你看书中了毒。我敢说，你中毒不浅！哼，都是那些鼓吹革命、鼓吹自由思想的可怕书籍害了你！

阿尔文夫人：你错了，我亲爱的牧师。启发我的不是书籍，而是你本人，为此我深表感谢。

曼得斯：感谢我？

阿尔文夫人：是的。你强迫我履行所谓的义务和职责，把我深恶痛绝的事情说成是正确及合理的——正是这样的时刻启发了我的思考。也正是在这时，我开始深入研究你的学说。原来只想解开一个疙瘩，谁知一个疙瘩解开了，所有的东西都散开了。我这才恍然大悟，发现整个东西都是机器缝制的。

曼得斯：（低声，伤心）这就是我一生中最艰苦的一场战斗取得的战果?

阿尔文夫人:不如说那是你一生中最大的失败。

曼得斯:那是我最大的胜利,海伦——是战胜自我的胜利。

阿尔文夫人:对于咱们俩而言,那是罪恶。

曼得斯:那时候你误入歧途,跑来找我,对我说:"我来了!收留我吧!"我吩咐你:"女人,快回到自己丈夫那儿去!"难道这是罪恶吗?

阿尔文夫人:是的,我认为是的。

曼得斯:你我都不了解对方。

阿尔文夫人:是的,至少此时此刻是不了解的。

曼得斯:即使在内心最隐秘的深处,我也从来没有不把你视为他人之妻。

阿尔文夫人:哦,真的吗?

曼得斯:海伦!

阿尔文夫人:对于过去的事情,一个人是很容易忘记的。

曼得斯:我没忘记。我还是我,跟从前一样。

阿尔文夫人:(换话题)好吧,好吧,好吧,过去的事,不说也罢。目前,董事会的事以及教区会的事已经让你忙得不可开交了,而我忙于跟群鬼作战,要应付心里的鬼以及外头的鬼。

曼得斯:外头的鬼我可以帮你驱除。今天听你说了这些可怕的事情,我的良心不允许我坐视不管,让一个没人保护的女孩子在你家里住下去。

阿尔文夫人：你不觉得最好的办法是给她找个安身之处吗？我的意思是说，给她找一门好亲事。

曼得斯：这是肯定的。我认为从各方面来说，这对于她都不失为良策。莱吉娜的年纪已经——当然，我对这些事情知之甚少，不过——

阿尔文夫人：莱吉娜成熟得很早。

曼得斯：不错，我也这么想。记得我为她行坚信礼的时候，就觉得她的身体已经发育得很成熟了。当务之急，应该赶快把她送回家去，让她父亲照管她——哦，对啦，恩格斯特兰德不是她的——真是人心隔肚皮，想不到他竟然会对我隐瞒真相！

〔有人敲大厅外边的门。〕

阿尔文夫人：这是谁呢？请进！

恩格斯特兰德：（穿得很齐整，站在门口）对不起，我——

曼得斯：正说着呢！哼！

阿尔文夫人：原来是你，恩格斯特兰德！

恩格斯特兰德：跟前没有用人，于是我就冒昧敲了门。

阿尔文夫人：噢，没关系。进来吧。你是不是有事找我？

恩格斯特兰德：（走进来）不是，谢谢您，夫人。我想跟牧师说一两句话。

曼得斯：（在屋里走来走去）哼，真有你的！你想跟我说话，是不是？

恩格斯特兰德：是的，我很想——

曼得斯：（在他面前站住）好吧。能问问你有什么事吗？

恩格斯特兰德：噢，是这样的，牧师：多亏阿尔文夫人，我们把工钱都拿到手了，所有的手续都办完了，我想是不是应该跟那些一直在一起干活儿的工友——今晚在一起开个小小的祷告会作为了结？

曼得斯：开祷告会？在孤儿院开？

恩格斯特兰德：噢，要是你觉得不合适的话——

曼得斯：合适是合适，只不过——嗯——

恩格斯特兰德：我自己有个习惯，晚上要做祷告——

阿尔文夫人：是吗？

恩格斯特兰德：是的。说起来，也只不过是时不时做点儿小功德。可惜我是个平常人，没什么德行，上帝可怜我！——所以，我想趁着可敬的曼得斯牧师恰好在这儿，开一个——

曼得斯：哦，你听我说，恩格斯特兰德，我先得问你一个问题：你目前的心境适合做祷告吗？你是否良心清白、心境安宁？

恩格斯特兰德：噢，愿上帝饶恕我们，牧师！最好还是不谈良心了吧。

曼得斯：要谈，这是一个不容回避的问题。你怎样回答我刚才的问题？

恩格斯特兰德：若说良心，我的良心有的时候非常难受。

曼得斯：唔，你自己承认了。也许你可以来个竹筒倒豆子，将关于莱吉娜的真实情况都告诉我。

阿尔文夫人：（急忙拦阻）曼得斯先生！

曼得斯：（安慰地）请允许我——

恩格斯特兰德：你问莱吉娜的事？上帝呀，你这一问，真是吓了我一跳！（瞧着阿尔文夫人）她没做错什么事情吧？

曼得斯：但愿没有。我要问的是你和莱吉娜之间的真实情况。你真的是她的生身父亲吗？嗯？

恩格斯特兰德：（支支吾吾）噢——这个嘛——我和可怜的乔安娜之间的情况你是很了解的。

曼得斯：得了，别再闪烁其词了！你妻子离开这里之前把一切都对阿尔文夫人讲了。

恩格斯特兰德：哦，这个嘛——她真的讲了？

曼得斯：看到了吧？你们的情况我们都掌握了，恩格斯特兰德。

恩格斯特兰德：她可是发过誓的，是手按《圣经》发的誓——

曼得斯：她真的是手按《圣经》发的誓？

恩格斯特兰德：没有手按《圣经》，只是发了个誓，但她言之凿凿，很是认真。

曼得斯：这些年你一直对我隐瞒真相，而我却一味信任你，毫无保留地信任你！

恩格斯特兰德：好吧，这一点我无可否认。

曼得斯：你这样做对得起我吗，恩格斯特兰德？只要我能做到的，无论是在语言上还是在行动上，我历来都倾尽全力帮助你，难道不是吗？你说，是不是这样？

恩格斯特兰德：有许多次，要不是你出手相助，我就走投无路了。

曼得斯：你就这么报答我！你害我在教会登记簿上填写假材料；你原本应该对我讲出真相，可是你却年复一年地隐瞒着。你的所作所为完全不可饶恕，恩格斯特兰德。从今以后我再也不管你的事了！

恩格斯特兰德：(叹口气)罢了！事已至此，我也没办法了。

曼得斯：对于你的行为，你还有什么可为自己辩护的？

恩格斯特兰德：难道你让我把乔安娜的事说出来，使她的境况雪上加霜不成？你不妨设想一下，假如你跟可怜的乔安娜一样身陷困境——

曼得斯：我？

恩格斯特兰德：对不起，我不是说你做了她那样的事情。我的意思是，假如你行为欠妥，在世人面前抬不起头来，那该怎样？对于一个可怜的女人，咱们男人不应该太刻薄，尊敬的牧师。

曼得斯：我并没有对她刻薄，只是在责备你。

恩格斯特兰德：我能不能冒昧地问你一个问题？

曼得斯：要问你就问吧。

恩格斯特兰德：帮助一个堕落的人，应该不应该，正确不正确？

曼得斯：当然是应该的、正确的。

恩格斯特兰德：一个人该不该信守自己神圣的誓言？

曼得斯：当然应该，可是——

恩格斯特兰德：乔安娜跟那英国人弄出了乱子之

后——有人说是美国人,也有人说是俄国人——你知道的,她就进城来了。那个苦命的女人曾经叫我碰过一两次钉子,因为她眼里只有英俊的男人,我偏偏长着这条倒霉的腿。你该记得,有一次我走进一家舞厅,看见一群水手喝醉酒在发酒疯,于是上前想劝他们改邪归正——

阿尔文夫人:(在窗口旁)哦——?

曼得斯:这些我都知道,恩格斯特兰德——那群畜生把你从楼上推了下来。这件事你以前跟我说过。你的腿就是那次给摔断了,这是你的荣耀。

恩格斯特兰德:我可不是想炫耀,尊敬的牧师。我只是想说,乔安娜当时跑来找我,一把鼻涕一把泪地向我忏悔,你都不知道我听了以后心里有多难过,尊敬的牧师。

曼得斯:你真的很难过吗,恩格斯特兰德?好吧,你继续说吧。

恩格斯特兰德:于是我对她说:"那个美国佬是个到处为家的家伙,靠不住。至于你呢,乔安娜,你犯了大罪,是个堕落的女人。不过有我呢——雅各布·恩格斯特兰德是个两条腿长得结结实实的、顶天立地的——"我这样说只是打个比方,你知道的,尊敬的牧师。

曼得斯:我完全理解。你继续说吧。

恩格斯特兰德:我就这么救了她,跟她结了婚,为的是不让别人知道她曾经误入歧途,跟外国人有过风流韵事。

曼得斯:这些事你做得都很对。我只是不赞成你收下那笔钱——

恩格斯特兰德:什么钱?我收下钱?我一分钱也没收

下过!

曼得斯:(将询问的目光投向阿尔文夫人)可是——

恩格斯特兰德:哦,等一等!我想起来了。乔安娜手里是有几个钱,可是我没要,而是说:"这是罪恶的脏钱,不管它是臭金币——或是钞票还是什么的——都应该摔到那个美国人的脸上!"可是,他漂洋过海,早已走得没影儿了,尊敬的牧师。

曼得斯:他真的走得没影儿了吗,我的好朋友?

恩格斯特兰德:是真的,先生。乔安娜和我说好了要把那笔钱留给孩子做教育费。后来那笔钱都花在了孩子身上——每一分钱,我都可以说出明细。

曼得斯:照你这么说,情况可就大不相同了。

恩格斯特兰德:实际情况就是如此,尊敬的牧师。我敢说我对莱吉娜尽到了一个父亲应尽的责任!只要我微薄的力量能办得到的事我都会去做,可惜我是个拿不定主意的人!

曼得斯:好,好,我的朋友——

恩格斯特兰德:不管有什么样的委屈,我都可以无愧地说是我一手把孩子养大的,我以一颗善心对待苦命的乔安娜,像《圣经》上说的那样安安心心过日子。可我从未想过要去找你夸耀自己,说一说像我这样的人也能做好事。不会的,我雅各布·恩格斯特兰德积德行善,是不会向人吹嘘的。可惜好事不常有,糟糕的事、倒霉的事却有一大堆——每次我见你,净谈这些糟糕的事、倒霉的事。我过去说过,现在还要说:一个人的良心有时候不是那么太清白。

曼得斯：把手伸过来，雅各布·恩格斯特兰德。

恩格斯特兰德：噢，使不得！尊敬的牧师，你——

曼得斯：来，别客气。（握紧他的手）这才对了！

恩格斯特兰德：尊敬的牧师，要是能得到你的原谅——

曼得斯：原谅你？恰好相反，我倒应该请你原谅我——

恩格斯特兰德：这可使不得，先生！

曼得斯：当然应该这样。我真心实意地请求你原谅，原谅我错怪了你。真希望我能证明我的诚意，证明我是真心后悔了，证明我对你的好意——

恩格斯特兰德：你果真愿意证明，尊敬的牧师？

曼得斯：非常乐意。

恩格斯特兰德：那好，现在就有个机会。我在这儿积攒了一点儿钱，想在城里建立一个"水手之家"。

阿尔文夫人：你？

恩格斯特兰德：是的。从某种角度来说，也算是个孤儿院吧。水手们一上岸，免不了会受到各种各样的诱惑。到了我这个"水手之家"，我要让他们有归家之感，觉得有父母在照拂他们。

曼得斯：你看这事怎么样，阿尔文夫人？

恩格斯特兰德：说来惭愧，我的启动资金不太充裕。如果有人能帮我一把——

曼得斯：很好，很好，以后咱们详谈。你的计划我完全赞成。但现在，你先回孤儿院，把一切都准备好，点亮蜡烛，营造出喜庆的气氛。然后，咱们再在一块儿做祷告——我坚信你现在的心境已经适合做祷告了。

恩格斯特兰德：是的，我相信是这样的。我得告辞了，夫人，谢谢您的好心，求您替我好好照顾莱吉娜——（擦眼泪）苦命的乔安娜的孩子。说起来也怪，我越来越疼她，觉得她简直就是我的掌上明珠。这是真的。（鞠躬，从大厅走了出去）

曼得斯：现在你觉得这个人怎么样，阿尔文夫人？他的陈述跟别人说的完全不同，是不是？

阿尔文夫人：是的，的确不一样。

曼得斯：由此看来，评判一个人必须慎之又慎。不过，发现自己错怪了一个人，心里还是感到挺痛快的！你说是不是？

阿尔文夫人：我说你就像是个纯真的孩子，永远也不会改变你的纯真，曼得斯。

曼得斯：你说我吗？

阿尔文夫人：（把两只手搭在他的肩上）我真有点儿想搂着你的脖子，亲一亲你。

曼得斯：（赶紧往后退）使不得，使不得！上帝保佑我！你怎么会有这种念头！

阿尔文夫人：（笑了笑）哈哈，你用不着怕我。

曼得斯：（在桌子旁边）你有时候说话有点儿太夸张了。现在让我把文件收拾到一起，放进包里。（一边说一边收拾）好，一切就绪。现在，我该跟你告别了。奥斯瓦德回来后，你可要多留点儿神。我回头再来看看。（他拿了帽子，从大厅的门出去了。）

阿尔文夫人：（叹口气，对着窗口出了会儿神，把屋子稍稍整理了一下,正要走进餐厅,却低低地惊叫一声,在门口站住)奥斯瓦德,你怎么还在餐桌旁坐着?

奥斯瓦德:(在餐厅里)我在抽雪茄。

阿尔文夫人:我还以为你出去散步了呢。

奥斯瓦德:这样的天气还能散步吗?

〔一只酒杯"当"地响了一下。阿尔文夫人让门敞着,拿起编织活计坐在挨着窗口的沙发上。〕

奥斯瓦德:刚出去的是不是曼得斯牧师?

阿尔文夫人:是的,他上孤儿院去了。

奥斯瓦德:唔。(酒杯和酒壶相碰,又"当"地响了一下。)

阿尔文夫人:(眼神不安)亲爱的奥斯瓦德,当心点儿,那酒的酒劲儿很大。

奥斯瓦德:喝点儿酒能去湿气。

阿尔文夫人:你过来陪我坐坐好吗?

奥斯瓦德:我过去就不能抽烟了。

阿尔文夫人:你很清楚,抽雪茄是可以的。

奥斯瓦德:噢,那好吧,我过去就是了。让我再喝一小口。来啦!(抽着雪茄走进房间,随手把门关上。沉默了一会儿)牧师上哪儿去了?

阿尔文夫人:我刚说过,他上孤儿院去了。

奥斯瓦德:噢,不错,你是说过。

阿尔文夫人:你不该在餐桌旁一坐就坐那么久,奥斯瓦德。

奥斯瓦德:(把拿着雪茄的手背到身后)我觉得坐在那

儿心情特别愉快,妈妈。(用手拍拍她,轻抚着她)回到家里,坐在妈妈的餐桌旁,待在妈妈的屋子里,吃着妈妈给我准备的美味佳肴,简直是神仙过的日子哟。

阿尔文夫人:我的乖孩子,我的宝贝!

奥斯瓦德:(一边走一边抽烟,突然变得有点儿不耐烦)不过这种日子,我又能怎样?我又画不成画。

阿尔文夫人:为什么画不成?

奥斯瓦德:天气这么坏,整天见不着一丝阳光!(在屋子里走来走去)唉,无法作画简直是——!

阿尔文夫人:也许你这次回家并非明智之举,对不对?

奥斯瓦德:噢,明智倒是明智,妈妈。回家是必须要回的。

阿尔文夫人:你知道,我情愿放弃有你相伴的欢乐而不愿让你——

奥斯瓦德:(在桌子旁边站住)妈妈,实话实说,我回家你是不是心里真的很高兴?

阿尔文夫人:我怎么能不高兴!

奥斯瓦德:(搓弄一张报纸)我还以为有没有我在你跟前,对你来说都一个样儿呢。

阿尔文夫人:你怎么忍心对你妈妈说这种话,奥斯瓦德?

奥斯瓦德:可是,这些年没有我,你不是过得挺好吗?

阿尔文夫人:是的,没有你,我的生活很宁静。这是实情。

〔二人半晌无声。暮色慢慢降临。奥斯瓦德放下雪茄,在屋子里来回踱步。]

奥斯瓦德：（在阿尔文夫人身旁站住）妈妈，我能在沙发上坐下来，坐在你身边吗？

阿尔文夫人：（让出点儿地方）当然可以，我的好孩子。

奥斯瓦德：（坐下）有件事必须告诉你，妈妈。

阿尔文夫人：（忧虑）什么事？

奥斯瓦德：（凝视前方）我不能再瞒下去了。

阿尔文夫人：瞒什么？什么事？

奥斯瓦德：（还是那样）我想写信告诉你，但怎么也做不到。自从我回家以后——

阿尔文夫人：（抓住他的胳膊）奥斯瓦德，到底是什么事？

奥斯瓦德：昨天和今天，我试图将那些心事忘掉——把它们驱赶出心房，然而却功亏一篑。

阿尔文夫人：（站起来）现在，你必须把一切都告诉我，奥斯瓦德！

奥斯瓦德：（拉着她又在沙发上坐下）坐着别动，容我说给你听——这次回来，我感到十分疲倦——

阿尔文夫人：是吗？怎么啦？

奥斯瓦德：我并非为这而感到苦恼，我的这种疲倦跟普通的疲倦不一样——

阿尔文夫人：（站起来）你该不是病了吧，奥斯瓦德？

奥斯瓦德：（又拉她重新坐下）坐着别动，妈妈。别担心，我这不是真病，不是普通意义上的"病"。（双手抱头）妈妈，我的脑子出了毛病，成了废品，恐怕再也画不成画

了!(双手捂脸,伏在她的膝上,呜咽出声,几度哽咽)

阿尔文夫人:(脸色发白,浑身哆嗦)奥斯瓦德!看着我!不会的,不会的,这是不可能的!

奥斯瓦德:(抬起头,目光绝望)我再也画不成画了!完了!完了!我成了行尸走肉!妈妈,你想象得出这有多么可怕吗?

阿尔文夫人:我可怜的孩子!这种可怕的病怎么跑到了你的身体里?

奥斯瓦德:(重新坐直身子)我也百思不得其解,百般琢磨不透,因为无论从哪方面说,我都没有过放纵行为。请你务必相信我,妈妈。我从未做过荒唐事!

阿尔文夫人:我坚定不移地相信你,奥斯瓦德。

奥斯瓦德:即便如此,这种怪病还是降临在了我身上,实在是倒霉透顶!

阿尔文夫人:噢,这种病一定会治好的,我亲爱的好孩子。这只不过是过度劳累留下的病根。相信我,不会错的。

奥斯瓦德:(沮丧)起初我也这么想,可实际并非如此。

阿尔文夫人:你从头到尾把一切都讲给我听。

奥斯瓦德:好的,我会的。

阿尔文夫人:你是什么时候发现的?

奥斯瓦德:是上次从家里刚回到巴黎后发现的。当时我觉得头疼得厉害,后脑勺疼得最厉害,一阵一阵的,就好像脖子上套了铁箍,箍得紧紧的,一直往上拧。

阿尔文夫人:是吗?后来呢?

奥斯瓦德:最初我以为那只是发育时期常犯的那种头

痛病——

阿尔文夫人:是的,是的——

奥斯瓦德:但不久我就发现并非如此。结果,我无法再作画。我有心画一幅大的新作,然而却力不从心,所有的力量都消失了。我的思想集中不起来,眼前的东西在旋转,转啊转的。唉,那种状况简直糟糕透了!最后,我请了个医生来给我看病,终于了解了实情。

阿尔文夫人:此话怎讲?

奥斯瓦德: 给我看病的是巴黎的一位名医。我把病症告诉他,接着他就仔细问了一大串我觉得跟这病毫不相干的问题。我不明白他为什么要那样问——

阿尔文夫人:后来呢?

奥斯瓦德:末了他说:"你生下来就带有一种有虫子的病。"他用的是法语词 vermoulu[①]。

阿尔文夫人:(提心吊胆)他说这话该怎么理解?

奥斯瓦德:我听了也不懂,就请他再仔细讲一讲。那个家伙竟然说——(握紧拳头)噢——!

阿尔文夫人:他说什么?

奥斯瓦德:他说:"父亲造孽,儿女遭报应。"

阿尔文夫人:(慢慢站起来)父亲造孽?

奥斯瓦德:我差点儿没给他脸上来一巴掌——

阿尔文夫人:(走到屋子另一头)父亲造孽——

奥斯瓦德:(苦笑一声)是啊,你说气人不气人?我没客气,立刻予以反驳,说他的话毫无根据。可你猜他怎

---

① 意思为"虫蛀的"。

样?他一口咬定他是对的。后来,我把你写给我的信拿出来,将有关爸爸的地方翻译成法语念给他听——

阿尔文夫人:后来呢?

奥斯瓦德:后来,他当然只好承认他的分析是错的,继而换了一种说法,让我了解到了实情——一种匪夷所思的事实。原来,我不该跟朋友们一道逍遥自在,不该跟他们一道狂欢,那样的生活让我的体力严重透支。所以说,一切都是我咎由自取!

阿尔文夫人:奥斯瓦德!不是的,不是的,别信那些鬼话!

奥斯瓦德:他说不可能有别的原因。最让我痛心的是,是我自己不小心,断送了自己的一生!原来我希望自己能大有作为——如今想都不敢想了,也不能再去想了。唉,假如我的人生能够重新开始,我绝对不会再做那样的蠢事!

〔他把脸埋在沙发里。阿尔文夫人双手紧紧绞在一起,默默地走来走去,心里在斗争着。〕

奥斯瓦德:(过了一会儿,把头抬起来,用一个胳膊肘撑住身子)要是这是遗传病,而非我自己行为不慎造成的,那倒也罢了。可是,这些只能怪我自己!是我自己头脑糊涂,怪我自己莽撞、草率,断送了我的幸福、我的健康,所有这一切——我的前程以及我的生命——!

阿尔文夫人:不,不,我的好孩子,情况不可能会那么糟糕!(俯下身子看他)情况不可能像你想的那样,糟到了无法挽回的地步。

奥斯瓦德：唉，那是你不知道——（跳起来）妈妈，我不该惹你为我难过！有时候我真希望你不要为我操心，不要为我如此牵肠挂肚。

阿尔文夫人：不为你操心为谁操心，奥斯瓦德？我只有你这么一个儿子！你是我在这个世界上的一切，是我唯一关心的人！

奥斯瓦德：（抓住她的两只手，用嘴去亲）是的，是的，这我知道。我在家的时候，当然看得到，感受得到，而这也是最叫我难过之处。现在，你把所有的情况都了解了，咱们今天就不再说了，因为这件事我不敢多想。（走到房间的另一侧）能不能给我点儿喝的东西，妈妈？

阿尔文夫人：喝的东西？你想喝什么？

奥斯瓦德：噢，什么都行。家里应该有冰镇潘趣酒①吧？

阿尔文夫人：有是有，可是，亲爱的奥斯瓦德——

奥斯瓦德：别拒绝我的请求，妈妈。行行好吧！我心里愁绪万千，必须喝几口酒把它们冲走。（说着话走进温室）噢，这里怎么这么黑！（阿尔文夫人拉了拉挂在右边的铃绳。）这场雨下得没完没了，恐怕会下几个星期，甚至会下几个月！连一丝阳光都见不到！数次回家，我都记不得有太阳露过脸。

阿尔文夫人：奥斯瓦德——你是不是心里在想着要离开我？

---

① 一种用酒、果汁、香料等调和的饮料。

奥斯瓦德：唉！（深深叹了口气）——我心里什么都没想，什么也不能想！（低声）随它去吧。

莱吉娜：（从餐厅里进来）你拉铃了吗，夫人？

阿尔文夫人：是的，给我们把灯拿进来。

莱吉娜：好的，夫人。灯早就点好了。（出去）

阿尔文夫人：（走到奥斯瓦德身边）奥斯瓦德，你要跟我说老实话。

奥斯瓦德：噢，我说的都是老实话，妈妈。（走到桌子跟前）我觉得我说的已经够多的了。

〔莱吉娜把灯拿进来，放在桌子上。〕

阿尔文夫人：莱吉娜，请你给我们拿一小瓶香槟酒来。

莱吉娜：好的，夫人。（出去）

奥斯瓦德：（一只胳膊搂住阿尔文夫人的脖子）这正是我想喝的。我就知道妈妈是不会让自己的儿子失望的。

阿尔文夫人：我可怜的宝贝儿子奥斯瓦德，你现在不管有什么样的请求，我都不会拒绝的。

奥斯瓦德：（热切地）真的吗，妈妈？这是不是你的心里话？

阿尔文夫人：怎么？什么心里话？

奥斯瓦德：我不管有什么样的请求，你都不会拒绝。

阿尔文夫人：我亲爱的奥斯瓦德——

奥斯瓦德：嘘！

莱吉娜：（用托盘送来了一小瓶香槟酒和两只玻璃杯，将酒和杯子放在桌子上）需要我开瓶吗？

奥斯瓦德：不用了，谢谢。我自己来吧。

〔莱吉娜又走了出去。〕

阿尔文夫人：（在桌子旁边坐下）刚才你说要我有求必应——究竟是什么请求？

奥斯瓦德：（忙着开酒瓶）咱们先喝上一两杯再说。

〔瓶塞"砰"的一声被拔掉。他先斟满一杯，刚要斟第二杯时却被母亲拦住了。〕

阿尔文夫人：（用手捂住酒杯口）谢谢，别给我斟。

奥斯瓦德：哦，你不喝？那我就喝了！（他把一杯酒一饮而尽，又斟满一杯，再次一饮而尽，然后才在桌旁坐下。）

阿尔文夫人：（焦急地等待）究竟是什么请求？

奥斯瓦德：（眼睛不看她）刚才吃饭时我觉得你和曼得斯牧师神情古怪——沉默寡言的。告诉我，究竟怎么啦？

阿尔文夫人：你注意到啦？

奥斯瓦德：是的。唔……（沉吟片刻）能不能告诉我：你觉得莱吉娜怎么样？

阿尔文夫人：我觉得怎么样？

奥斯瓦德：是的。她是不是很棒？

阿尔文夫人：亲爱的奥斯瓦德，你对她的了解不如我对她了解得这么深——

奥斯瓦德：此话怎讲？

阿尔文夫人：不幸的是，莱吉娜在她的那个家里待得太久了。我应该早点儿把她接到我身边来。

奥斯瓦德：是的。可是，你不觉得她的模样儿很棒吗，妈妈？（斟酒）

阿尔文夫人：莱吉娜有不少毛病——

奥斯瓦德：哦，那有什么关系？（又喝酒）

阿尔文夫人：她有毛病，可我还是喜欢她，要照顾她。无论如何我也不能让她受到伤害。

奥斯瓦德：（一跃而起）妈妈，只有莱吉娜能救我！

阿尔文夫人：（站起来）你这话是什么意思？

奥斯瓦德：面对灵魂的痛苦，我无法再一个人忍受下去。

阿尔文夫人：你不是有你妈妈在分担你的痛苦吗？

奥斯瓦德：是的，我以前也是这么想的，所以我就回家来寻求安慰。可是，回家也不顶用。现在我明白这并非灵丹妙药。在家中浑浑噩噩地过日子，叫我无法忍受。

阿尔文夫人：奥斯瓦德！

奥斯瓦德：我必须换一种活法，妈妈。我必须离开你，因为我不忍心让你看着我受罪。

阿尔文夫人：我可怜的孩子！可是，奥斯瓦德，你病成这个样子——

奥斯瓦德：如果只是身体有病，我就留在你的身边，妈妈，这你放心，因为你是我在这个世界上最好的朋友。

阿尔文夫人：是啊，奥斯瓦德，的确是这样的！

奥斯瓦德：（心神不定，来回走动）可是，最叫人忍受不了的是精神上的折磨，是撕心裂肺的懊悔——是那能要人命的恐惧。啊，我真是害怕得要死！

阿尔文夫人：（跟在他身后走动）害怕？害怕什么？你这话是什么意思？

奥斯瓦德：唉，别再问了。我自己也不知道害怕什么。那种感觉无法形容。

（阿尔文夫人走到右边拉铃。）

奥斯瓦德：你拉铃干什么？

阿尔文夫人：想让我儿子高兴——这就是我的心愿。我可不想让他把事情憋在心里。（莱吉娜刚到门口，就对她说）再拿一瓶香槟酒来——要大瓶的。（莱吉娜答应后出去了。）

奥斯瓦德：妈妈！

阿尔文夫人：你是不是觉得我们这里的人不懂得如何过日子？

奥斯瓦德：难道她长得不漂亮吗？她是多么窈窕妩媚，多么健康啊！

阿尔文夫人：（在桌子旁边坐下）你坐下，奥斯瓦德，咱们母子说几句知心话。

奥斯瓦德：（坐下）妈妈，你大概不知道，我还欠着莱吉娜一份情呢。

阿尔文夫人：你？

奥斯瓦德：都怪我做事欠考虑，或者怎么说都行——不管怎么说，都怪我幼稚吧。那是我上次回家的时候发生的事情——

阿尔文夫人：什么事情？

奥斯瓦德：她常问我巴黎那边的情况，我也就给她介绍了介绍。记得有一天，我随便问了她一句："你想到那儿去看看吗？"

阿尔文夫人：她怎么说？

奥斯瓦德：我见她脸一红，接着说道："是的，我很想去，比什么都想。"我就说："好的，也许办得到。"——或者别的什么应景的话。

阿尔文夫人：后来呢？

奥斯瓦德：我当然把这件事抛在脑后，忘了个干净。可是前天，我无意中问起，她是不是高兴看我在家住这么久——

阿尔文夫人：她怎么说？

奥斯瓦德：她用奇怪的眼光瞟着我，问道："那么我上巴黎的事情怎么办？"

阿尔文夫人：她到巴黎去！

奥斯瓦德：原来她把我以前随便说的话当真了，一直在心里记挂着，而且还认认真真学起了法语——

阿尔文夫人：怪不得——！

奥斯瓦德：妈妈，我以前几乎没有特别留意过她，可是这回看到这个活泼可爱、美丽动人的女孩站在我面前，仿佛张开胳膊准备迎接我——

阿尔文夫人：奥斯瓦德！

奥斯瓦德：我恍然大悟，原来她就是我的救星——我看到她身上充满了生活的乐趣。

阿尔文夫人：（惊讶）充满生活的乐趣？那里头怎么有救星呢？

莱吉娜：（拿着一瓶香槟酒从餐厅里进来）对不起，我去了这么半天，我得到地窖里去拿酒。（把酒瓶搁在桌子上）

奥斯瓦德：再去拿只玻璃杯来。

莱吉娜：（不解地望着他）阿尔文夫人的杯子已经拿来了，阿尔文少爷。

奥斯瓦德：我知道，我说给你自己拿一只来，莱吉娜。（莱吉娜有点儿吃惊，飞快地瞟了一眼阿尔文夫人。）怎么不去拿？

莱吉娜：（低声，犹豫）这是不是阿尔文夫人的意思？

阿尔文夫人：去拿杯子吧，莱吉娜。

〔莱吉娜走进餐厅。〕

奥斯瓦德：（目送着她）你看她走路的姿态多么美！又稳又轻松！

阿尔文夫人：这件事万万行不通，奥斯瓦德！

奥斯瓦德：此事已经决定了。难道你看不出来吗？反对也没用。

〔莱吉娜拿着一只空杯子进来，手里拿着它站在那儿。〕

奥斯瓦德：坐下吧，莱吉娜。

〔莱吉娜以询问的目光望着阿尔文夫人。〕

阿尔文夫人：坐下吧。（莱吉娜在靠近餐厅门的一把椅子上坐下，空杯子仍拿在手里。）奥斯瓦德，你刚才说起了生活的乐趣？

奥斯瓦德：噢，生活的乐趣嘛，妈妈——正是这一带所缺乏的，家里也感受不到。

阿尔文夫人：你在我身边也感受不到吗？

奥斯瓦德：是的，在家里我是感受不到的。这种事情你是不懂的。

阿尔文夫人：我懂，我懂，我觉得自己现在几乎已经全懂了。

奥斯瓦德：这儿也无法享受工作的欢乐！归根结底，这些都是一回事。至于工作的乐趣，你恐怕一无所知。

阿尔文夫人：你的话也许是对的。你不妨给我多讲讲，奥斯瓦德。

奥斯瓦德：我的意思是说，这儿的传统观念是：工作是受罪，是对罪恶的惩罚；生命是一种悲惨的遭遇，应该尽早结束，结束得越早越好。

阿尔文夫人：是的，现世有着"无尽的烦恼"，人们总是想着法子给自己找烦恼。

奥斯瓦德：到了外边的大千世界，你就听不到这样的言论了。在那儿，没人再相信这种骗人的教条。他们觉得只要能活着，就是欢乐，就是幸福。妈妈，你注意到了没有？我的绘画作品反映的都是生活的乐趣——所有的主题都是生活的乐趣——反映的全是光明、太阳、愉快的气氛以及洋溢着幸福的面孔！所以，我害怕留在家中，待在你身旁。

阿尔文夫人：害怕？在我的身边有什么可怕的？

奥斯瓦德：我怕我的天性会受到扭曲，变得丑陋不堪。

阿尔文夫人：（目不转睛地看着他）你真的觉得会出现这样的情况？

奥斯瓦德：是的。虽然在这儿跟外头一样过日子，但毕竟会有所不同。

阿尔文夫人：（一直在用心听他说话，此时站了起来，眼睛睁得大大的，目光茫然，口中念叨着）现在我终于看到事情的严重后果了。

奥斯瓦德：看到什么严重后果？

阿尔文夫人：这是我头一次看到。现在我可以讲出实情了。

奥斯瓦德：（站起来）妈妈，我不懂你的意思。

莱吉娜：（也站起来）也许我该走吧？

阿尔文夫人：不，你留下别走。现在我可以讲出实情了。我的儿子，我就把实情全都告诉你吧。奥斯瓦德！莱吉娜！你们俩听了后可以自己做出选择！

奥斯瓦德：嘘！牧师来了——

曼得斯：（从大厅里走了进来）哇！我们刚才在孤儿院可是大有收益。

奥斯瓦德：我们的收益也不小。

曼得斯：咱们一定得协助恩格斯特兰德开办"水手之家"。莱吉娜必须回到他身旁帮他料理——

莱吉娜：多谢你的美意，我是不会去的，先生。

曼得斯：（这才注意到她）什么？——你也在这儿？手里还拿着酒杯！

莱吉娜：（赶紧放下杯子）对不起！

奥斯瓦德：莱吉娜就要跟我走了，曼得斯先生。

曼得斯：她要走！跟你走！

奥斯瓦德：是的，作为妻子跟我走——要是她愿意的话。

曼得斯：天呀，仁慈的上帝——！

莱吉娜：我没办法，只好这样了，先生。

奥斯瓦德：要不然，我留下来，她也留下来。

莱吉娜：（不由自主）留下来？

曼得斯：阿尔文夫人，你的行为实在叫人费解。

阿尔文夫人：这两条路都不会是他们的选择，因为现在我要把实情讲给他们听。

曼得斯：你不会那样做的！不会的，绝不会的！

阿尔文夫人：会的，我会说出实情的，说出来也碍不着谁的理想。之后，何去何从，可以由他们自己决定。

奥斯瓦德：妈妈——你究竟有什么事瞒着我？

莱吉娜：（竖起耳朵细听）听，夫人，你听！外边有人喊叫，听见了吧？（走进温室，往外瞧）

奥斯瓦德：（走到左边的窗口）出什么事了？那片火光是从哪里来的？

莱吉娜：（大声喊叫）孤儿院着火了！

阿尔文夫人：（冲到窗户旁边）着火了！

曼得斯：孤儿院着火了？不可能！我刚从那儿过来。

奥斯瓦德：我的帽子呢？噢，不管它了——爸爸的孤儿院要紧！（从花园门里跑出去）

阿尔文夫人：拿我的披肩来，莱吉娜！整个孤儿院都烧着了！

曼得斯：多可怕！阿尔文夫人，这是报应，是对无法无天行为的报应。

阿尔文夫人：是的，的确如此。莱吉娜，咱们去看看。（她和莱吉娜急急忙忙从大厅里出去。）

曼得斯：（双手紧紧握在一起）糟糕，没给孤儿院上保险！（也从大厅里出去）

第三幕

布景：仍是那个房间。所有的门都敞着。桌子上的灯还亮着。外面漆黑一团，只有在左边的远处有若隐若现的火光。阿尔文夫人头上蒙着披肩，站在温室里往外瞧。莱吉娜也围着披肩，站得比她略靠后些。

阿尔文夫人：全都烧着了，烧成了一片平地！

莱吉娜：房子的底层还在烧。

阿尔文夫人：奥斯瓦德怎么还不回来？反正救不回来什么东西了。

莱吉娜：是不是需要我把帽子给他送去？

阿尔文夫人：他连帽子都没戴？

莱吉娜：（指着大厅）是的，帽子在那儿挂着呢。

阿尔文夫人：别送了。他马上就会回来的。还是我去找他吧。（从花园门里出去）

曼得斯：（从大厅里进来）阿尔文夫人不在这儿吗？

莱吉娜：她刚到花园那边去了。

曼得斯：我从来没遇到过今晚发生的这种可怕的事情。

莱吉娜：是啊，真是祸从天降，你说是不是，先生？

曼得斯：唉，不说也罢！实在让人想都不敢想。

莱吉娜：怎么会发生这样的事呢？

曼得斯：别问我，恩格斯特兰德小姐！我怎么知道！难道你也——你父亲还不够我受的吗——？

莱吉娜：他又怎么了？

曼得斯：唉，他搅得我心烦意乱——

恩格斯特兰德：（从大厅里进来）尊敬的牧师——

曼得斯：（吓了一跳，转过身来）你也跟着我过来了？

恩格斯特兰德：是的。真该死，可是我不能不——！天呀，天呀！我该说什么好呢？千不该，万不该，不该出这样的事，尊敬的牧师。

曼得斯：（来回踱步）唉！唉！

莱吉娜：到底是怎么回事？

恩格斯特兰德：唉，还不都是今晚做祷告惹的祸。（低声）孩子，这回老头儿可是被咱们拿住了。（高声）怪就怪我出了个馊主意，结果连累牧师惹出了这场大祸！

曼得斯：我敢肯定不是我，恩格斯特兰德——

恩格斯特兰德：除了你，牧师大人，别人手里没有蜡烛。

曼得斯：（站住）你这么说吗？可是我不记得我手里拿着蜡烛。

恩格斯特兰德：我清清楚楚看见你拿着蜡烛，用手指掐了蜡花，将蜡花扔进了刨花堆里。

曼得斯：你在那儿看得清楚吗？

恩格斯特兰德：是的，看得清清楚楚，绝对不会错的。

曼得斯：这实在让我无法理解。再说，我就没有用手指掐蜡花的习惯。

恩格斯特兰德：那个动作实在太危险了！不管怎么说，大祸已经酿成，你说是不是，牧师大人？

曼得斯：（来回走动，六神无主）唉，别再说了！

恩格斯特兰德：（跟着他走）你没有给孤儿院上保险吧，牧师大人？

曼得斯：（继续走来走去）没有，没有，没有。我已经跟你说过了。

恩格斯特兰德：（跟在他后头）没上保险，却放火把那地方烧得干干净净！天呀，天呀，怎么会有这么倒霉的事！

曼得斯：（擦头上的汗）唉，的确很倒霉，恩格斯特兰德。

恩格斯特兰德：孤儿院是慈善机构，据说会给这儿的城镇和乡村带来福音，现在却出了这种事，真是令人惋惜！报纸很可能不会对你手软的，牧师大人。

曼得斯：是的，我正在考虑这个问题呢。最糟糕的恐怕就是这一点。那些恶意的攻击以及各种罪名——！唉，想一想都会叫人不寒而栗！

阿尔文夫人：（从花园里进来）怎么劝他都不愿离开火场。

曼得斯：噢，你回来了，阿尔文夫人。

阿尔文夫人：这下子，你就不用硬着头皮致开幕词了，曼得斯牧师。

曼得斯：唉，我倒宁愿——

阿尔文夫人:(低声)这样倒是最好的结局,反正孤儿院也不会给任何人带来好处的。

曼得斯:你是这么想的?

阿尔文夫人:那你说呢?

曼得斯:不管怎样,这毕竟是一场可怕的惨祸。

阿尔文夫人:咱们不妨直截了当地谈一谈,不妨将它当作一件普通的事情谈一谈——恩格斯特兰德,你是不是在等曼得斯先生?

恩格斯特兰德:(在大厅门口)是的,我是在等他,夫人。

阿尔文夫人:那么你先坐一坐。

恩格斯特兰德:谢谢夫人,我站着就可以了。

阿尔文夫人:(转向曼得斯)你大概要坐轮船走吧?

曼得斯:是的,一个小时内开船。

阿尔文夫人:麻烦你把全部文件都带走吧。关于这件事,我听都不愿再听你说了。我还有别的事要操心呢——

曼得斯:阿尔文夫人——

阿尔文夫人:过几天我把委托书寄给你,你觉得怎么合适就怎么办吧。

曼得斯:非常乐意效劳。这么一来,原来的那份捐赠文本就要彻底改写了!

阿尔文夫人:那是当然的。

曼得斯:我想首先把索尔维克那份产业拨给教区。那块地肯定是有价值的,好歹能派上用场。至于银行存款利息,我想最好拨给一项对本城有好处的事业。

阿尔文夫人:就按你的意思处理吧。这件事我完全不管,不放在心上了。

恩格斯特兰德:应该想一想我的"水手之家",牧师大人。

曼得斯:我敢说这是个不错的建议,应该予以考虑。

恩格斯特兰德:唉,还考虑什么——上帝啊!

曼得斯:(叹气)可惜,这些事情我不知道自己还能管多长时间——说不定迫于公众舆论的压力,我会被迫辞职的。一切都要看官方对火灾调查的结果如何了——

阿尔文夫人:你说什么?

曼得斯:结果如何是无法预料的。

恩格斯特兰德:(走近他)嗯,也许可以预料,因为有我雅各布·恩格斯特兰德呢。

曼得斯:这个嘛,可是——

恩格斯特兰德:(放低声音)雅各布·恩格斯特兰德不是俗话说的在危难时刻见死不救、忘恩负义的那种人。

曼得斯:是的,可我的老朋友——怎么——

恩格斯特兰德:我雅各布·恩格斯特兰德可以为你挺身而出,承担责任,尊敬的牧师。

曼得斯:不行,不行,我不能让你替我担责。

恩格斯特兰德:无论怎么看,这都会是一条妙计。我听说过有人为别人担责的义事,现在轮到我这样做了。

曼得斯:雅各布!(抓紧他的手)像你这样的好人,世间少有。好吧,"水手之家"的事我一定帮忙,你尽管放心。

〔恩格斯特兰德想要向他道谢,可是激动得说不出话来。〕

曼得斯:(把旅行包背到肩上)现在咱们走吧。咱俩一块儿走。

恩格斯特兰德:(站在餐厅门口,低声对莱吉娜)我的孩子,你也跟我一道走吧。一定让你生活得舒舒服服的。

莱吉娜:(把头一扬)Merci①,不过还是不了。(她走进大厅,把曼得斯的外套拿来。)

曼得斯:再见,阿尔文夫人!希望法律和秩序的精神能进入你们家,越快越好。

阿尔文夫人:再见,曼得斯牧师。(她看见奥斯瓦德正从花园门里进来,于是走进温室去迎接他。)

恩格斯特兰德:(和莱吉娜一起帮曼得斯穿外套)再见,孩子。如果遇到困难,你知道上哪儿找我。(低声)记住,小港街,唔——千万记住!(转向阿尔文夫人和奥斯瓦德)那个收留四海漂泊的水手之处,将会被命名为"国王侍从阿尔文上尉水手之家"!假如我能按照自己的意愿经营"水手之家",我就敢说,它一定会无愧于国王侍从阿尔文上尉的荣誉。

曼得斯:(在门口)喂,喂,走吧,亲爱的恩格斯特兰德。再见!再见!(和恩格斯特兰德从大厅里出去)

奥斯瓦德:(走到桌子旁边)他刚才说的是什么水手之家?

阿尔文夫人:噢,那是他和曼得斯牧师打算创办的一个收容所。

---

① 法文,意思是"谢谢"。

奥斯瓦德：将来也会被大火烧光的。

阿尔文夫人：你为什么这么说？

奥斯瓦德：所有一切都会被烧掉的。纪念爸爸的东西都会被大火烧掉，这是命中注定的。就连我也在所难免。(莱吉娜吃了一惊，看了看他。)

阿尔文夫人：奥斯瓦德！刚才你不该在火场待那么久，可怜的孩子。

奥斯瓦德：(在桌子旁边坐下)你的话大概有几分道理。

阿尔文夫人：让我给你擦擦脸，奥斯瓦德，你满脸都是水。(拿自己的手帕给他擦脸)

奥斯瓦德：(目光呆滞地望着前方)谢谢你，妈妈。

阿尔文夫人：你不累吗，奥斯瓦德？想不想睡觉？

奥斯瓦德：(心神不宁)不，不，不想睡！我从不睡觉，要睡也是装睡。(伤心)厄运就要降临了。

阿尔文夫人：(难过地望着他)我的好孩子，你恐怕是病了。

莱吉娜：(关心)阿尔文先生病了吗？

奥斯瓦德：(不耐烦)快去，把所有的门都关上！我害怕得要命！

阿尔文夫人：去把门都关上，莱吉娜。

〔莱吉娜把门都关上，站在大厅门口。阿尔文夫人脱下披肩。莱吉娜也脱下披肩。阿尔文夫人拉过一把椅子，在奥斯瓦德旁边坐下。〕

阿尔文夫人：现在好啦！我守在你身边坐着——

奥斯瓦德：对，就坐在这里。莱吉娜也别走。莱吉娜将会永远陪伴我。你愿不愿意救我一命,莱吉娜?

莱吉娜:我不明白——

阿尔文夫人:救你一命?

奥斯瓦德:是的——在危难时刻救我一命。

阿尔文夫人:奥斯瓦德,难道你母亲不能救你吗?

奥斯瓦德:你?(笑了笑)不,妈妈,你是救不了我的。(凄楚地大笑)你救不了我!哈哈!(郑重地看着她)可是,你不救我又有谁救我呢?(急躁)你为什么就不能直接叫我的名字,莱吉娜?为什么不叫我"奥斯瓦德"?

莱吉娜:(低声)我怕阿尔文夫人不愿意。

阿尔文夫人:不久你就可以这样称呼他了。坐下吧,在我们旁边坐下吧。

(莱吉娜庄重地、有点迟疑地在桌子的另一侧坐了下来。)

阿尔文夫人:可怜的苦命孩子,现在我要把压在你心上的那块石头搬开——

奥斯瓦德:是吗,妈妈?

阿尔文夫人:我要把你说的那些撕心裂肺的懊悔和自责都清除干净。

奥斯瓦德:你真的能做到吗?

阿尔文夫人:是的,现在我能做到了,奥斯瓦德。就在刚才不久,你说到了生活的乐趣,我听后大有感悟,对我的生活以及与之有关的一切往事都有了新的看法。

奥斯瓦德:(摇头)我不明白你的意思。

阿尔文夫人:你该知道你爸爸年轻时当中尉时是怎样

一个人——他浑身上下都充满了生活的乐趣!

奥斯瓦德:是的,这我知道。

阿尔文夫人:人们一看见他就觉得轻松自在。他有着使不完的劲儿,精力充沛!

奥斯瓦德:后来怎么样?

阿尔文夫人:后来,那个快活的孩子——你爸爸那时候就像个小孩子——返回故乡,在这座半封闭的城市里居住下来。在这里,他找不到欢乐——这儿只有花天酒地的堕落。除了在政府部门混混日子,他没有确定的生活目标,没有可以为之全心全意奋斗的理想,只是应付应付差事。他的朋友中没有一个懂得人生的意义,全都是些游手好闲的酒肉朋友——

奥斯瓦德:妈妈——!

阿尔文夫人:因此就发生了那件不可避免的事情。

奥斯瓦德:什么不可避免的事情?

阿尔文夫人:就是今天傍晚你自己说的,要是你在家里待下去也会发生的那种事情。

奥斯瓦德:你是不是说爸爸——?

阿尔文夫人:你可怜的爸爸身上充满了生活的乐趣,只是苦于无处发泄。而我无法给他带来欢乐。

奥斯瓦德:连你也无法使他高兴起来?

阿尔文夫人:我自小学的就是尽义务、守本分那套大道理,后来这就成了我的坚定信条。我不管做任何事情都讲究义务——不是我的义务就是他的义务,再不就是——也用这些义务要求你可怜的父亲,恐怕使他无法忍受这种生活，奥斯瓦德。

奥斯瓦德：你为什么在给我的信里从未提到过这些？

阿尔文夫人：你是他儿子，我以前从未想到过要将这种事情告诉你。

奥斯瓦德：以前你是怎么看他的？

阿尔文夫人：（慢慢地）有一点我看得很清楚：你尚未出生，你爸爸就已经彻底堕落了。

奥斯瓦德：（低声）啊！（站起来走到窗口）

阿尔文夫人：后来，日复一日，有一个念头始终萦绕于我心间：莱吉娜有权住在这儿，以这里为家，像我自己的孩子一样。

奥斯瓦德：（霍地转过身来）莱吉娜——！

莱吉娜：（跳起来，低声）我——？

阿尔文夫人：是的。现在你们俩都明白是怎么回事了。

奥斯瓦德：莱吉娜！

莱吉娜：（自言自语）想不到妈妈竟是那样的女人。

阿尔文夫人：你的母亲有许多优点，莱吉娜。

莱吉娜：不错，可是不管怎样，她毕竟做了那种事情。唉，我早就觉得有点儿不对头，可是——罢了，如果你愿意，夫人，是不是允许我马上离开这儿？

阿尔文夫人：你真的想走，莱吉娜？

莱吉娜：是的，我真的想走。

阿尔文夫人：你当然可以按自己的意愿办事，可是——

奥斯瓦德：（走近莱吉娜）你要走？这里是你的家呀。

莱吉娜：Merci，阿尔文先生！现在我也许可以叫你奥斯瓦德了。实不相瞒，这种生活并非我所期待的。

阿尔文夫人：莱吉娜，都怪我以前没把实情告诉你——

莱吉娜：是的，你的确一直在瞒着我。要是我早知道奥斯瓦德是个病人——唉，算啦，反正我们俩之间也不可能会有什么事情了——我不能再待下去了，不能累死累活地在这荒僻的乡下照料病人。

奥斯瓦德：跟你这么亲近的病人你也不愿照料？

莱吉娜：是的，我不愿意。穷人家的女孩子应该充分利用自己的青春年华，要不然，不等她醒悟过来就会风光不再，成了没人理睬的黄脸婆了！再说，我也有我的生活乐趣，阿尔文夫人！

阿尔文夫人：可惜呀！要走你就走吧。不过，可别把自己宝贵的年华糟蹋掉，莱吉娜。

莱吉娜：噢，事情该怎么样就怎么样吧。假如奥斯瓦德像他爸爸，我也许就像我妈妈。夫人，我能不能问你一句：曼得斯牧师知道我的身世吗？

阿尔文夫人：所有的一切曼得斯牧师都知道。

莱吉娜：（忙着围披肩）既然如此，我还是赶快走人，去赶他那班轮船吧。曼得斯牧师是个好人，容易说话——那个可恶的木匠拿到的钱，我也应该得一份儿。

阿尔文夫人：我衷心希望你能拿到一份儿，莱吉娜。

莱吉娜：（仔细瞧她）夫人，要是从前你把我当成大户人家的女儿抚养，也许对我更合适些。（把头一扬）不过嘛，呸——也没关系！（对那瓶没开的酒狠狠地斜睨一眼）我总有一天能跟上等人在一块儿喝香槟酒的。

阿尔文夫人：如果你需要一个家，莱吉娜，尽管来找我。

莱吉娜：谢谢你，不过用不着，夫人。曼得斯牧师会照料我的，这我很清楚。万一到了山穷水尽的地步，我还有一个安身之地，完全可以到那里去。

阿尔文夫人：什么地方？

莱吉娜："国王侍从阿尔文上尉水手之家"。

阿尔文夫人：莱吉娜——现在我明白了——你打算毁掉你自己。

莱吉娜：哼，哪里的话！再见吧。（对他们点点头告别，从大厅里出去）

奥斯瓦德：（站在窗口朝外看）她走了吗？

阿尔文夫人：走了。

奥斯瓦德：（自言自语）我觉得她离开这儿是错误的选择。

阿尔文夫人：（走到他身后，两手按在他肩膀上）奥斯瓦德，好孩子——你是不是很难过？

奥斯瓦德：（转过脸来对着她）你是不是说我为了爸爸的事情难过？

阿尔文夫人：是的，是为了你那不幸的爸爸。我担心你听了恐怕承受不了。

奥斯瓦德：你怎么会这么想？我听了当然很吃惊，不过跟我没什么关系。

阿尔文夫人：（把手放下）没什么关系？你竟然说你爸爸的不幸遭遇跟你没什么关系！

奥斯瓦德：我当然可怜他，就像我可怜任何一个不幸的人一样。不过——

阿尔文夫人：仅仅是可怜？他可是你的爸爸呀！

奥斯瓦德：（不耐烦）哼，什么"爸爸"不"爸爸"！我对这样的爸爸一无所知，没有任何的记忆，只记得有一次他把我弄病了。

阿尔文夫人：想起来真可怕！不管怎么样，难道做儿子的不应该爱自己的爸爸吗？

奥斯瓦德：如果做父亲的对儿子无教养之恩，而儿子对他一无所知，难道你还要抱着这种古老的迷信思想不放吗？你在别的方面都很开通，为什么在这件事上却糊涂起来了？

阿尔文夫人：难道这仅仅是一种迷信吗？

奥斯瓦德：当然是，你应该可以看得清，妈妈。在当今世界，迷信观念到处流行，这是其中的一种，所以——

阿尔文夫人：（情绪激动）它们是鬼！

奥斯瓦德：（走过去）是的，你可以称它们为鬼。

阿尔文夫人：（狂乱地）奥斯瓦德——莫非你连我也不爱了！

奥斯瓦德：对于你嘛，不管怎样我还是了解的——

阿尔文夫人：是的，你了解我。仅仅如此吗？

奥斯瓦德：当然，我还知道你非常疼我，对此我不能不心怀感激。再说，我现在病了，用得着你的地方多着呢。

阿尔文夫人：是的，我可以照料你，奥斯瓦德。啊，我几乎有点儿感谢你的这场病了，因为正是它使得你回到了家里。我看得很清楚，你的心并没有和我在一起，但我要争取赢得你的心。

奥斯瓦德：(不耐烦)是啊，是啊，是啊，这些自不待言。不过，你别忘了，我是个病人，妈妈。我不能对别人的心情考虑得过多，我自己的病就够我操心的了。

阿尔文夫人：(低声)我会耐心十足的，而且容易满足。

奥斯瓦德：你还应该高高兴兴的，妈妈。

阿尔文夫人：是的，我的好孩子，你说得很对。(走近他)现在我是不是让你的懊悔和自责都消失了？

奥斯瓦德：是的，的确如此。可是谁能消除我心里的恐惧呢？

阿尔文夫人：恐惧？

奥斯瓦德：(在房间里走动)莱吉娜如果在跟前，就可以做得到。

阿尔文夫人：我不明白你的意思。你说的是什么恐惧——莱吉娜怎么帮你消除？

奥斯瓦德：天是不是很晚了，妈妈？

阿尔文夫人：已经是清早了。(从温室的窗口往外看)晨曦笼罩着群山。天已放晴，奥斯瓦德。再过一会儿，你就可以看见太阳了。

奥斯瓦德：我很高兴。啊，生活中也许有许多欢乐，值得为之活下去——

阿尔文夫人：的确如此！

奥斯瓦德：即使我无法画画——

阿尔文夫人：噢，你很快就又能拿起画笔了，我的好孩子——因为你心里不会再有折磨人的烦恼以及沮丧的念头搅扰你了。

奥斯瓦德：是的，我很高兴你帮我赶走了那些怪异的念头。现在还有一件事情需要了结——（在沙发上坐下）咱们能不能好好谈一谈，妈妈？

阿尔文夫人：可以，完全可以。（她将一把扶手椅推到沙发旁边，挨着他坐下。）

奥斯瓦德：太阳快出来了。到那时候你就都明白了。我也不会再有恐惧感了。

阿尔文夫人：我明白什么？

奥斯瓦德：（没听她说话）妈妈，刚才你不是说，只要我求你，你什么事都愿意替我做？

阿尔文夫人：不错，我是这么说的！

奥斯瓦德：你是不是说到做到？

阿尔文夫人：你放心，我的好儿子！在这个世界上，我只有你了，只为你活着了。

奥斯瓦德：很好。现在容我讲给你听——妈妈，我知道你是个有胆量、意志坚强的人。你听完之后可别慌张。

阿尔文夫人：什么事能有那么可怕？

奥斯瓦德：你听了可别吓得叫起来。明白吗？你答应不答应？你我只是静静地坐着，静静地谈话。这你答应吗，妈妈？

阿尔文夫人：好，好，我答应。你说吧！

奥斯瓦德：噢，你要知道，我浑身疲倦，想画画也画不成——这些都不是病根——

阿尔文夫人：那么什么才是病根呢？

奥斯瓦德：我的病是从娘胎里带来的——（用手指指前额，把声音压得很低）——我的病根儿在这儿。

阿尔文夫人：（几乎说不出话来）奥斯瓦德！不会的，不会的！

奥斯瓦德：别嚷！我受不了。确实是这样的，妈妈，我的病根儿就隐藏在这里，随时随地都可能发作。

阿尔文夫人：啊，真可怕！

奥斯瓦德：安静点儿，安静点儿！这是我的实际情况——

阿尔文夫人：（跳起来）不是真的，奥斯瓦德！这是不可能的，绝对不可能！

奥斯瓦德：在外边我曾发过病，所幸很快就过去了。不过，当我意识到自己已经病得很厉害时便怕得要命，心情狂躁、烦闷，于是立刻跑回家来。

阿尔文夫人：这就是你所说的恐惧？

奥斯瓦德：是的。要知道，那是一种难以形容的可怕感觉。如果是平常的绝症倒没什么——虽然我也希望能长寿，但我并不怕死。

阿尔文夫人：是的，是的，奥斯瓦德，你一定能长寿！

奥斯瓦德：可是，那种感觉真是生不如死。让我又变成一个靠人伺候、靠人喂食的小孩——唉，那种苦涩实在难以言传！

阿尔文夫人：又变成小孩，有妈妈照料，有何不可！

奥斯瓦德：（跳起来）不，绝对不行，我可不愿那样苟延残喘。一想到让我常年卧床不起，慢慢老去，变得头发花白,我就无法忍受。在这期间,你也许会先我而去,把我一个人孤零零地留在世上也未可知。(在阿尔文夫人的椅子上坐下)医生说我这病不一定马上就能致死,说它是大脑软化或者这一类的。(苦笑)我觉得他用的术语很好听,总让人想到樱桃色的天鹅绒——软软的,手感很细腻。

阿尔文夫人:(尖声喊叫)奥斯瓦德!

奥斯瓦德:(跳起来,在屋里来回走动)现在,你把莱吉娜从我身边撵走了。如果有她在这儿就好了!我知道她一定会救我的。

阿尔文夫人:(走近他)此话怎讲,我亲爱的孩子?难道你遇到危难,我就不会救你吗?

奥斯瓦德:我在巴黎发病之后,虽然已化险为夷,但医生说以后还会发病的——一旦再次发病——就无药可治了。

阿尔文夫人:他真是太狠心了——

奥斯瓦德:是我要求他说实话的。我告诉他,说我已有所准备——(诡异地一笑)我的确准备好了。(从前胸内衣袋里掏出一只小盒子,把盒子打开)妈妈,你看见没有?

阿尔文夫人:这是什么?

奥斯瓦德:吗啡。

阿尔文夫人:(吓得呆若木鸡,痴痴地看着他)奥斯瓦德——我的孩子!

奥斯瓦德:我一共攒了十二丸。

阿尔文夫人:(伸手抢盒子)把盒子给我,奥斯瓦德!

奥斯瓦德：现在还不能给你，妈妈。（把盒子又藏进前胸内衣袋里）

阿尔文夫人：你真是的，叫我活不下去了！

奥斯瓦德：你一定能活下去的。要是莱吉娜在跟前，我会把实情告诉她，求她最后帮我一次忙。我知道她一定会帮的。

阿尔文夫人：决不会的！

奥斯瓦德：当可怕的时刻到来时，她看见我可怜巴巴地躺在床上，就像一个刚出生的婴儿一样，什么事情也做不了，一脸的迷茫、无助，已经到了不可救药的地步——

阿尔文夫人：莱吉娜无论如何也不会干这种事的！

奥斯瓦德：莱吉娜一定会的。她是一个快乐活泼的女孩，让她照顾我这样的病人，她很快就会厌烦的。

阿尔文夫人：苍天有眼，幸亏莱吉娜不在这儿。

奥斯瓦德：所以，就要靠你来救我了，妈妈。

阿尔文夫人：（大声尖叫）靠我？

奥斯瓦德：你不救我，又有谁会救我呢？

阿尔文夫人：我！我可是你的妈妈呀！

奥斯瓦德：正因为你是我的妈妈啊！

阿尔文夫人：我给了你生命，怎么会夺走它！

奥斯瓦德：我并没有要求你给我生命。再说，你给我的是一条什么命？这样的命我不稀罕，你还是把它收回去吧！

阿尔文夫人：救命！救命！（跑到大厅里）

奥斯瓦德：（跟在她身后）别把我丢下！你上哪儿去？

阿尔文夫人:(在大厅里)我去找医生,奥斯瓦德!让我出去!

奥斯瓦德:(在外面)不许你出去。别人也不许进来。(传来锁门的声音)

阿尔文夫人:(又走进来)奥斯瓦德!奥斯瓦德!我的孩子!

奥斯瓦德:(跟了进来)难道你对我就没有一颗慈母之心吗?难道你就忍心眼睁睁看着我活受罪,生不如死吗?

阿尔文夫人:(静了一会儿,稳定住了情绪,说道)好吧,我答应你。

奥斯瓦德:你真的愿意——?

阿尔文夫人:只要有必要,我就愿意。不过,那一天永远都不会到来的,不,不,绝对不会。

奥斯瓦德:好,但愿如此。但愿你我都能长命百岁。谢谢你,妈妈。

〔他在阿尔文夫人刚才搬到沙发旁边的扶手椅上坐下。天亮起来了。灯还在桌上燃着。〕

阿尔文夫人:(小心翼翼地走近他)现在你心里平静了吧?

奥斯瓦德:是的。

阿尔文夫人:(俯下身子看他)这都是可怕的臆想,奥斯瓦德——其实什么事都没有,只是些臆想。胡思乱想会叫你吃不消的。我要让你好好休息休息,跟妈妈在一起安心过日子,我的好孩子。你要什么我就给你什么,就像你小时候那样。好了,危险的关头已经过去了。你瞧,多么轻松就过去了!噢,我早就知道会这样的——看见了吧,奥斯瓦德,今天是个多么晴朗的日子啊!阳光是多么灿烂啊!现在你可以仔细看看你的家乡了。

〔她走到桌前熄灭了灯。太阳冉冉升起。远方的冰川和雪山在晨光中闪闪发光。〕

奥斯瓦德:(坐在扶手椅上,背对着外头的景致,一动都不动。突然说)妈妈,把太阳给我。

阿尔文夫人:(在桌子旁边,吓了一跳,瞧着他)你说什么?

奥斯瓦德:(声音沉闷、平淡地重复)把太阳给我!把太阳给我!

阿尔文夫人:(走到他身边)奥斯瓦德,你怎么啦?

(奥斯瓦德在椅子上似乎缩成了一团,浑身瘫软,面无表情,目光呆滞。)

阿尔文夫人:(吓得直哆嗦)这是怎么回事?(尖声喊叫)奥斯瓦德!你怎么啦?(跪在他身边,使劲摇他)奥斯瓦德!奥斯瓦德!你瞧瞧我!你认不出我了吗?

奥斯瓦德:(声音依然平淡)把太阳给我!把太阳给我!

阿尔文夫人:(绝望地跳起来,两只手乱抓头发,嘴里喊叫)我受不了了!(好像吓傻了似的,压低了声音)我受不了了!再也受不了了!(突然)他把药搁在哪儿了?(手忙脚乱地在他怀里摸索着)在这儿!(退后几步,喊叫)不!不!不!——也罢!不!不!(站在离他几步的地方,双手揪住自己的头发,瞪着眼看他,吓得说不出话)

奥斯瓦德:(依然坐着不动,嘴里念叨着)把太阳给我!把太阳给我!

(剧终)

(全书完)

图书在版编目（CIP）数据

玩偶之家：易卜生戏剧选：汉英对照／（挪）亨利克·易卜生（Henrik Ibsen）著；方华文译．—南京：译林出版社，2022.4（2024.12重印）
（双语经典）
ISBN 978-7-5447-8884-7

I.①玩… II.①亨… ②方… III.①英语－汉语－对照读物 ②话剧－剧本－挪威－近代 IV.①H319.4：I

中国版本图书馆 CIP 数据核字（2021）第 201917 号

玩偶之家——易卜生戏剧选 〔挪威〕亨利克·易卜生／著 方华文／译

责任编辑	陈绍敏
特约编辑	任佳怡 赵丽娟
装帧设计	鹏飞艺术
校　　对	刘文硕
责任印制	贺　伟

出版发行	译林出版社
地　　址	南京市湖南路 1 号 A 楼
邮　　箱	yilin@yilin.com
网　　址	www.yilin.com
市场热线	010-85376701
排　　版	鹏飞艺术
印　　刷	三河市中晟雅豪印务有限公司
开　　本	889 毫米 ×1194 毫米　1/32
印　　张	22.5
版　　次	2022 年 4 月第 1 版
印　　次	2024 年 12 月第 5 次印刷
书　　号	ISBN 978-7-5447-8884-7
定　　价	69.80 元

版权所有·侵权必究

译林版图书若有印装错误可向出版社调换。质量热线：010-85376178

Bilingual Classics

A DOLL'S HOUSE AND OTHER PLAYS

Henrik Ibsen

CONTENTS

A DOLL'S HOUSE 001

AN ENEMY OF THE PEOPLE 117

GHOSTS 261

A DOLL'S HOUSE

The Characters

Torvald Helmer

Nora, his wife

Dr. Rank

Mrs. Linde

Nils Krogstad

Helmer's three young children

Anne, their nurse

A Housemaid

A Porter

(*The action takes place in Helmer's house.*)

ACT I

Scene.—*A room furnished comfortably and tastefully but not extravagantly. At the back a door to the right leads to the entrance hall; another to the left leads to Helmer's study. Between the doors stands a piano. In the middle of the left-hand wall is a door and beyond a window. Near the window are a round table, armchairs and a small sofa. In the right-hand wall, at the farther end, another door; and on the same side, nearer the footlights, a stove, two easy chairs and a rocking chair; between the stove and the door a small table. Engravings on the wall; a cabinet with china and other small objects; a small bookcase with well-bound books. The floors are carpeted, and a fire burns in the stove. It is winter.*

A bell rings in the hall; shortly afterwards the door is heard to open. Enter Nora, humming a tune and in high spirits. She is in outdoor dress and carries a number of parcels; these she lays on the table to the right. She leaves the outer door open after her, and through it is seen a Porter who is carrying a Christmas Tree and a basket, which he gives to the Maid who has opened the door.

Nora. Hide the Christmas Tree carefully, Helen. Be sure the children do not see it till this evening, when it is dressed. (*To the Porter, taking out her purse.*) How much?

Porter. Sixpence.

Nora. There is a shilling. No, keep the change. (*The Porter thanks her, and goes out. Nora shuts the door. She is laughing to herself as she takes off her hat and coat. She takes a packet of macaroons from her pocket and eats one or two; then goes cautiously to her husband's door and listens.*) Yes, he is in. (*Still humming, she goes to the table on the right.*)

Helmer (*calls out from his room*). Is that my little lark twittering out there?

Nora (*busy opening some of the parcels*). Yes, it is!

Helmer. Is it my little squirrel bustling about?

Nora. Yes!

Helmer. When did my squirrel come home?

Nora. Just now. (*Puts the bag of macaroons into her pocket and wipes her mouth.*) Come in here, Torvald, and see what I have bought.

Helmer. Don't disturb me. (*A little later he opens the door and looks into the room, pen in hand.*) Bought, did you say? All these things? Has my little spendthrift been wasting money again?

Nora. Yes, but, Torvald, this year we really can let ourselves go a little. This is the first Christmas that we have not needed to economize.

Helmer. Still, you know, we can't spend money recklessly.

Nora. Yes, Torvald, we may be a wee bit more reckless now, mayn't we? Just a tiny wee bit! You are going to have a big salary and earn lots and lots of money.

Helmer. Yes, after the New Year; but then it will be a whole quarter before the salary is due.

Nora. Pooh! we can borrow till then.

Helmer. Nora! (*Goes up to her and takes her playfully by the ear.*) The same little featherhead! Suppose, now, that I borrowed fifty pounds today and you spent it all in the Christmas week and then on New Year's Eve a slate fell on my head and killed me and—

Nora (*putting her hands over his mouth*). Oh! Don't say such horrid things.

Helmer. Still, suppose that happened,—what then?

Nora. If that were to happen, I don't suppose I should care whether I owed money or not.

Helmer. Yes, but what about the people who had lent it?

Nora. They? Who would bother about them? I should not know who they were.

Helmer. That is like a woman! But seriously, Nora, you know what I think about that. No debt, no borrowing. There can be no freedom or beauty about a home life that depends on borrowing and debt. We two have kept bravely on the straight road so far, and we will go on the same way for the short time longer that there need be any struggle.

Nora (*moving towards the stove*). As you please, Torvald.

Helmer (*following her*). Come, come, my little skylark must not droop her wings. What is this! Is my little squirrel out of temper? (*Taking out his wallet.*) Nora, what do you think I have got here?

Nora (*turning round quickly*). Money!

Helmer. There you are. (*Gives her some money.*) Do you think I don't know what a lot is wanted for housekeeping at Christmas time?

Nora (*counting*). Ten shillings—a pound—two pounds! Thank you, thank you, Torvald; that will keep me going for a long time.

Helmer. Indeed it must.

Nora. Yes, yes, it will. But come here and let me show you what I have bought. And all so cheap! Look, here is a new suit for Ivar and a sword, and a horse and a trumpet for Bob, and a doll and dolly's bedstead for Emmy—they are very plain, but anyway she will soon break them in pieces. And here are dress lengths and handkerchiefs for the maids; old Anne ought really to have something better.

Helmer. And what is in this parcel?

Nora (*crying out*). No, no! you mustn't see that till this evening.

Helmer. Very well. But now tell me, you extravagant little person, what would you like for yourself?

Nora. For myself? Oh, I am sure I don't want anything.

Helmer. Yes, but you must. Tell me something reasonable that you would particularly like to have.

Nora. No, I really can't think of anything—unless, Torvald—

Helmer. Well?

Nora (*playing with his coat buttons and without raising her eyes to his*). If you really want to give me something, you might—you might—

Helmer. Well, out with it!

Nora (*speaking quickly*). You might give me money, Torvald. Only just as much as you can afford; and then one of these days I will buy something with it.

Helmer. But, Nora—

Nora. Oh, do! Dear Torvald; please, please do! Then I will wrap it up in beautiful gilt paper and hang it on the Christmas Tree. Wouldn't that be fun?

Helmer. What are little people called that are always wasting money?

Nora. Spendthrifts—I know. Let us do as I suggest, Torvald, and then I shall have time to think what I am most in want of. That is a very sensible plan, isn't it?

Helmer (*smiling*). Indeed it is—that is to say, if you were really to save out of the money I give you, and then really buy something for yourself. But if you spend it all on the housekeeping and any number of unnecessary things, then I merely have to pay up again.

Nora. Oh but, Torvald—

Helmer. You can't deny it, my dear, little Nora. (*Puts his arm* *round her waist.*) It's a sweet little spendthrift, but she uses up a deal of money. One would hardly believe how expensive such little persons are!

Nora. It's a shame to say that. I do really save all I can.

Helmer (*laughing*). That's very true—all you can. But you can't save anything!

Nora (*smiling quietly and happily*). You haven't any idea how many expenses we skylarks and squirrels have, Torvald.

Helmer. You are an odd little soul. Very like your father. You always find some new way of wheedling money out of me, and as soon as you have got it it seems to melt in your hands. You never know where it has gone. Still, one must take you as you are. It is in the blood; for indeed it is true that you can inherit these things, Nora.

Nora. Ah, I wish I had inherited many of Papa's qualities.

Helmer. And I would not wish you to be anything but just what you are, my sweet little skylark. But, do you know, it strikes me that you are looking rather—what shall I say—rather uneasy today.

Nora. Do I?

Helmer. You do, really. Look straight at me.

Nora (*looks at him*). Well?

Helmer (*wagging his finger at her*). Hasn't Miss Sweet-Tooth been breaking rules in town today?

Nora. No; what makes you think that?

Helmer. Hasn't she paid a visit to the confectioner's?

Nora. No, I assure you, Torvald—

Helmer. Not been nibbling sweets?

Nora. No, certainly not.

Helmer. Not even taken a bite at a macaroon or two?

Nora. No, Torvald, I assure you, really—

Helmer. There, there, of course I was only joking.

Nora (*going to the table on the right*). I should not think of going against your wishes.

Helmer. No, I am sure of that; besides, you gave me your word—(*Going up to her.*) Keep your little Christmas secrets to yourself, my darling. They will all be revealed tonight when the Christmas Tree is lit, no doubt.

Nora. Did you remember to invite Doctor Rank?

Helmer. No. But there is no need; as a matter of course he will come to dinner with us. However, I will ask him when he comes in this morning. I have ordered some good wine. Nora, you can't think how I am looking forward to this evening.

Nora. So am I! And how the children will enjoy themselves, Torvald!

Helmer. It is splendid to feel that one has a perfectly safe appointment, and a big enough income. It's delightful to think of, isn't it?

Nora. It's wonderful!

Helmer. Do you remember last Christmas? For a full three weeks beforehand you shut yourself up every evening till long after midnight, making ornaments for the Christmas Tree and all the other fine things that were to be a surprise to us. It was the dullest three weeks I ever spent!

Nora. I didn't find it dull.

Helmer (*smiling*). But there was precious little result, Nora.

Nora. Oh, you shouldn't tease me about that again. How could I help the cat's going in and tearing everything to pieces?

Helmer. Of course you couldn't, poor little girl. You had the best of intentions to please us all, and that's the main thing. But it is a good thing that our hard times are over.

Nora. Yes, it is really wonderful.

Helmer. This time I needn't sit here and be dull all alone, and you needn't ruin your dear eyes and your pretty little hands—

Nora (*clapping her hands*). No, Torvald, I needn't any longer, need I! It's wonderfully lovely to hear you say so! (*Taking his arm.*) Now I will tell you how I have been thinking we ought to arrange things, Torvald. As soon as Christmas is over— (*A bell rings in the hall.*) There's the bell. (*She tidies the room a little.*) There's someone at the door. What a nuisance!

Helmer. If it is a caller, remember I am not at home.

Maid (*in the doorway*). A lady to see you, ma'am, —a stranger.

Nora. Ask her to come in.

Maid (*to Helmer*). The doctor came at the same time, sir.

Helmer. Did he go straight into my room?

Maid. Yes, sir.

(*Helmer goes into his room. The Maid ushers in Mrs. Linde, who is in traveling dress, and shuts the door.*)

Mrs. Linde (*in a dejected and timid voice*). How do you do, Nora?

Nora (doubtfully). How do you do—

Mrs. Linde. You don't recognise me, I suppose.

Nora. No, I don't know—yes, to be sure, I seem to—(*Suddenly.*) Yes! Christine! Is it really you?

Mrs. Linde. Yes, it is me.

Nora. Christine! To think of my not recognising you! And yet how could I—(*In a gentle voice.*) How you have altered, Christine!

Mrs. Linde. Yes, I have indeed. In nine, ten long years—

Nora. Is it so long since we met? I suppose it is. The last eight years have been a happy time for me, I can tell you. And so now you have come into the town, and have taken this long journey in winter—that was plucky of you.

Mrs. Linde. I arrived by steamer this morning.

Nora. To have some fun at Christmas time, of course. How delightful! We will have such fun together! But take off your things. You are not cold, I hope. (*Helps her.*) Now we will sit down by the stove, and be cozy. No, take this arm-chair; I will sit here in the rocking-chair. (*Takes her hands.*) Now you look like your old self again; it was only the first moment—You are a little paler, Christine, and perhaps a little thinner.

Mrs. Linde. And much, much older, Nora.

Nora. Perhaps a little older; very, very little; certainly not much. (*Stops suddenly and speaks seriously.*) What a thoughtless creature I am, chattering away like this. My poor, dear Christine, do forgive me.

Mrs. Linde. What do you mean, Nora?

Nora (*gently*). Poor Christine, you are a widow.

Mrs. Linde. Yes; it is three years ago now.

Nora. Yes, I knew; I saw it in the papers. I assure you, Christine, I meant ever so often to write to you at the time, but I always put it off and something always prevented me.

Mrs. Linde. I quite understand, dear.

Nora. It was very bad of me, Christine. Poor thing, how you must have suffered. And he left you nothing?

Mrs. Linde. No.

Nora. And no children?

Mrs. Linde. No.

Nora. Nothing at all, then?

Mrs. Linde. Not even any sorrow or grief to live upon.

Nora (*looking incredulously at her*). But, Christine, is that possible?

Mrs. Linde (*smiles sadly and strokes her hair*). It sometimes happens, Nora.

Nora. So you are quite alone. How dreadfully sad that must be. I have three lovely children. You can't see them just now, for they are out with their nurse. But now you must tell me all about it.

Mrs. Linde. No, no; I want to hear about you.

Nora. No, you must begin. I mustn't be selfish today; today I must only think of your affairs. But there is one thing I must tell you. Do you know we have just had a great piece of good luck?

Mrs. Linde. No, what is it?

Nora. Just fancy, my husband has been made manager of the Bank!

Mrs. Linde. Your husband? What good luck!

Nora. Yes, tremendous! A barrister's profession is such an uncertain thing, especially if he won't undertake unsavory cases; and naturally Torvald has never been willing to do that, and I quite agree with him. You may imagine how pleased we are! He is to take up his work in the bank at the New Year, and then he will have a big salary and lots of commissions. For the future we can live quite differently—we can do just as we like. I feel so relieved and so happy, Christine! It will be splendid to have heaps of money and not need to have any anxiety, won't it?

Mrs. Linde. Yes, anyhow I think it would be delightful to have what one needs.

Nora. No, not only what one needs, but heaps and heaps of money.

Mrs. Linde (*smiling*). Nora, Nora, haven't you learnt sense yet? In our schooldays you were a great spendthrift.

Nora (*laughing*). Yes, that is what Torvald says now. (*Wags her finger at her.*) But "Nora, Nora" is not so silly as you think.

We have not been in a position for me to waste money. We have both had to work.

Mrs. Linde. You too?

Nora. Yes; odds and ends, needlework, crochet-work, embroidery, and that kind of thing. (*Dropping her voice.*) And other things as well. You know Torvald left his office when we were married? There was no prospect of promotion there, and he had to try and earn more than before. But during the first year he overworked himself dreadfully. You see, he had to make money every way he could, and he worked early and late; but he couldn't stand it and fell dreadfully ill, and the doctors said it was necessary for him to go south.

Mrs. Linde. You spent a whole year in Italy, didn't you?

Nora. Yes. It was no easy matter to get away, I can tell you. It was just after Ivar was born, but naturally we had to go. It was a wonderfully beautiful journey, and it saved Torvald's life. But it cost a tremendous lot of money, Christine.

Mrs. Linde. So I should think.

Nora. It cost about two hundred and fifty pounds. That's a lot, isn't it?

Mrs. Linde. Yes, and in emergencies like that it is lucky to have the money.

Nora. I ought to tell you that we had it from Papa.

Mrs. Linde. Oh, I see. It was just about that time that he died, wasn't it?

Nora. Yes, and, just think of it, I couldn't go and nurse him. I was expecting little Ivar's birth every day and I had my poor sick Torvald to look after. My dear, kind father—I never saw him again, Christine. That was the saddest time I have known since our marriage.

Mrs. Linde. I know how fond you were of him. And then you went off to Italy?

Nora. Yes; you see we had money then, and the doctors insisted on our going, so we started a month later.

Mrs. Linde. And your husband came back quite well?

Nora. As sound as a bell!

Mrs Linde. But—the doctor?

Nora. What doctor?

Mrs Linde. I thought your maid said the gentleman who arrived here just as I did, was the doctor?

Nora. Yes, that was Doctor Rank, but he doesn't come here professionally. He is our greatest friend and comes in at least once every day. No, Torvald has not had an hour's illness since then, and our children are strong and healthy and so am I. (*Jumps up and claps her hands.*) Christine! Christine! it's good to be alive and happy! But how horrid of me; I am talking of nothing but my own affairs. (*Sits on a stool near her and rests her arms on her knees.*) You mustn't be angry with me. Tell me, is it really true that you did not love your husband? Why did you marry him?

Mrs. Linde. My mother was alive then and was bedridden and helpless, and I had to provide for my two younger brothers; so I did not think I was justified in refusing his offer.

Nora. No, perhaps you were quite right. He was rich at that time, then?

Mrs. Linde. I believe he was quite well off. But his business was a precarious one, and, when he died, it all went to pieces and there was nothing left.

Nora. And then?—

Mrs. Linde. Well, I had to turn my hand to anything I could find—first a small shop, then a small school and so on. The last three years have seemed like one long working day, with no rest. Now it is at an end, Nora. My poor mother needs me no more, for she is gone; and the boys do not need me either; they have got situations and can shift for themselves.

Nora. What a relief you must feel it—

Mrs. Linde. No, indeed; I only feel my life unspeakably empty. No one to live for anymore. (*Gets up restlessly.*) That is why I could not stand the life in my little backwater any longer. I hope it may be easier here to find something which will busy me and occupy my thoughts. If only I could have the good luck to get some regular work—office work of some kind—

Nora. But, Christine, that is so frightfully tiring, and you look tired out now. You had far better go away to some watering place.

Mrs. Linde (*walking to the window*). I have no father to give me money for a journey, Nora.

Nora (*rising*). Oh, don't be angry with me.

Mrs. Linde (*going up to her*). It is you that must not be angry with me, dear. The worst of a position like mine is that it makes one so bitter. No one to work for and yet obliged to be always on the lookout for chances. One must live, and so one becomes selfish. When you told me of the happy turn your fortunes have taken—you will hardly believe it—I was delighted not so much on your account as on my own.

Nora. How do you mean? Oh, I understand. You mean that perhaps Torvald could get you something to do.

Mrs. Linde. Yes, that was what I was thinking of.

Nora. He must, Christine. Just leave it to me; I will broach the subject very cleverly—I will think of something that will please him very much. It will make me so happy to be of some use to you.

Mrs. Linde. How kind you are, Nora, to be so anxious to help me! It is doubly kind in you, for you know so little of the burdens and troubles of life.

Nora. I——? I know so little of them?

Mrs Linde (*smiling*). My dear! Small household cares and that sort of thing! You are a child, Nora.

Nora (*tosses her head and crosses the stage*). You ought not to be so superior.

Mrs. Linde. No?

Nora. You are just like all the others. They all think that I am incapable of anything really serious—

Mrs. Linde. Come, come—

Nora. —that I have gone through nothing in this world of cares.

Mrs. Linde. But, my dear Nora, you have just told me all your troubles.

Nora. Pooh!—Those were trifles. (*Lowering her voice.*) I have not told you the important thing.

Mrs. Linde. The important thing? What do you mean?

Nora. You look down upon me altogether, Christine—but you ought not to. You are proud, aren't you, of having worked so hard and so long for your mother?

Mrs. Linde. Indeed, I don't look down on anyone. But it is true that I am both proud and glad to think that I was privileged to make the end of my mother's life almost free from care.

Nora. And you are proud to think of what you have done for your brothers.

Mrs. Linde. I think I have the right to be.

Nora. I think so, too. But now, listen to this; I too have something to be proud and glad of.

Mrs. Linde. I have no doubt you have. But what do you refer to?

Nora. Speak low. Suppose Torvald were to hear! He mustn't on any account—no one in the world must know, Christine, except you.

Mrs. Linde. But what is it?

Nora. Come here. (*Pulls her down on the sofa beside her.*) Now I will show you that I too have something to be proud and glad of. It was I who saved Torvald's life.

Mrs. Linde. "Saved"? How?

Nora. I told you about our trip to Italy. Torvald would never have recovered if he had not gone there—

Mrs. Linde. Yes, but your father gave you the necessary funds.

Nora (*smiling*). Yes, that is what Torvald and all the others think, but—

Mrs. Linde. But.—

Nora. Papa didn't give us a shilling. It was I who procured the money.

Mrs. Linde. You? All that large sum?

Nora. Two hundred and fifty pounds. What do you think of that?

Mrs. Linde. But, Nora, how could you possibly do it? Did you win a prize in the Lottery?

Nora (*contemptuously*). In the lottery? There would have been no credit in that.

Mrs. Linde. But where did you get it from, then?

Nora (*humming and smiling with an air of mystery*). Hm, hu! Aha!

Mrs. Linde. Because you couldn't have borrowed it.

Nora. Couldn't I? Why not?

Mrs. Linde. No, a wife cannot borrow without her husband's consent.

Nora (*tossing her head*). Oh, if it is a wife who has any head for business—a wife who has the wit to be a little bit clever—

Mrs. Linde. I don't understand it at all, Nora.

Nora. There is no need you should. I never said I had borrowed the money. I may have got it some other way. (*Lies back on the sofa.*) Perhaps I got it from some other admirer. When anyone is as attractive as I am—

Mrs. Linde. You are a mad creature.

Nora. Now, you know you're full of curiosity, Christine.

Mrs. Linde. Listen to me, Nora dear. Haven't you been a little bit imprudent?

Nora (*sits up straight*). Is it imprudent to save your husband's life?

Mrs. Linde. It seems to me imprudent, without his knowledge, to—

Nora. But it was absolutely necessary that he should not know! My goodness, can't you understand that? It was necessary he should have no idea what a dangerous condition he was in. It was to me that the doctors came and said that his life was in danger, and that the only thing to save him was to live in the south. Do you suppose I didn't try, first of all, to get what I wanted as if it were for myself? I told him how much I should love to travel abroad like other young wives; I tried tears and entreaties with him; I told him that he ought to remember the condition I was in, and that he ought to be kind and indulgent to me; I even hinted that he might raise a loan. That nearly made him angry, Christine. He said I was thoughtless and that it was his duty as my husband not to indulge me in my whims and caprices—as I believe he called them. Very well, I thought, you must be saved—and that was how I came to devise a way out of the difficulty.

Mrs. Linde. And did your husband never get to know from your father that the money had not come from him?

Nora. No, never. Papa died just at that time. I had meant to let him into the secret and beg him never to reveal it. But he was so ill then—alas, there never was any need to tell him.

Mrs. Linde. And since then have you never told your secret to your husband?

Nora. Good Heavens, no! How could you think so? A man who has such strong opinions about these things! And besides, how painful and humiliating it would be for Torvald, with his manly independence, to know that he owed me anything! It would upset our mutual relations altogether; our beautiful happy home would no longer be what it is now.

Mrs. Linde. Do you mean never to tell him about it?

Nora (*meditatively, and with a half-smile*). Yes—some day, perhaps, after many years, when I am no longer as nice-looking as I am now. Don't laugh at me! I mean, of course, when Torvald is no longer as devoted to me as he is now; when my dancing and dressing-up and reciting have palled on him; then it may be a good thing to have something in reserve—(*Breaking off,*) What nonsense! That time will never come. Now, what do you think of my great secret, Christine? Do you still think I am of no use? I can tell you, too, that this affair has caused me a lot of worry. It has been by no means easy for me to meet my engagements punctually. I may tell you that there is something that is called, in business, quarterly interest, and another thing called payment in instalments, and it is always so dreadfully difficult to manage them. I have had to save a little here and there, where I could, you understand. I have not been able to put aside much from my housekeeping money, for Torvald must have a good table. I couldn't let my children be shabbily dressed; I have felt obliged to use up all he gave me for them, the sweet little darlings!

Mrs. Linde. So it has all had to come out of your own necessaries of life, poor Nora?

Nora. Of course. Besides, I was the one responsible for it. Whenever Torvald has given me money for new dresses and such things, I have never spent more than half of it; I have always bought the simplest and cheapest things. Thank Heaven, any clothes look well on me, and so Torvald has never noticed it. But it was often very hard on me, Christine—because it is delightful to be really well dressed, isn't it?

Mrs. Linde. Quite so.

Nora. Well, then I have found other ways of earning money. Last winter I was lucky enough to get a lot of copying to do, so I locked myself up and sat writing every evening until quite late at night. Many a time I was desperately tired, but all the same it was a tremendous pleasure to sit there working and earning money. It was like being a man.

Mrs. Linde. How much have you been able to pay off in that way?

Nora. I can't tell you exactly. You see, it is very difficult to keep an account of a business matter of that kind. I only know that I have paid every penny that I could scrape together. Many a time I was at my wits' end. (*Smiles.*) Then I used to sit here and imagine that a rich old gentleman had fallen in love with me—

Mrs. Linde. What! Who was it?

Nora. Be quiet!—That he had died; and that when his will was opened it contained, written in big letters, the instruction: "The lovely Mrs. Nora Helmer is to have all I possess paid over to her at once in cash."

Mrs. Linde. But, my dear Nora—who could the man be?

Nora. Good gracious, can't you understand? There was no old gentleman at all; it was only something that I used to sit here and imagine, when I couldn't think of any way of procuring money. But it's all the same now; the tiresome old person can stay where he is, as far as I am concerned; I don't care about him or his will either, for I am free from care now. (*Jumps up.*) My goodness, it's delightful to think of, Christine! Free from care! To be able to be free from care, quite free from care; to be able to play and romp with the children; to be able to keep the house beautifully and have everything just as Torvald likes it! And, think of it, soon the spring will come and the big blue sky! Perhaps we shall be able to take a little trip—perhaps I shall see the sea again! Oh, it's a wonderful thing to be alive and be happy. (*A bell is heard in the hall.*)

Mrs. Linde (*rising*). There is the bell; perhaps I had better go.

Nora. No, don't go; no one will come in here; it is sure to be for Torvald.

Servant (*at the hall door*). Excuse me, ma'am—there is a gentleman to see the master, and as the doctor is with him—

Nora. Who is it?

Krogstad (*at the door*). It is I, Mrs. Helmer. (*Mrs. Linde starts, trembles, and turns to the window.*)

Nora (*takes a step towards him, and speaks in a strained low voice*). You? What is it? What do you want to see my husband about?

Krogstad. Bank business—in a way. I have a small post in the Bank, and I hear your husband is to be our chief now.

Nora. Then it is—

Krogstad. Nothing but dry business matters, Mrs. Helmers; absolutely nothing else.

Nora. Be so good as to go into the study then. (*She bows indifferently to him and shuts the door into the hall; then comes back and makes up the fire in the stove.*)

Mrs. Linde. Nora—who was that man?

Nora. A lawyer of the name of Krogstad.

Mrs. Linde. Then it really was him.

Nora. Do you know the man?

Mrs. Linde. I used to—many years ago. At one time he was a solicitor's clerk in our town.

Nora. Yes, he was.

Mrs. Linde. He is greatly altered.

Nora. He made a very unhappy marriage.

Mrs. Linde. He is a widower now, isn't he?

Nora. With several children. There now, it is burning up. (*Shuts the door of the stove and moves the rocking-chair aside.*)

Mrs. Linde. They say he carries on various kinds of business.

Nora. Really! Perhaps he does; I don't know anything about it. But don't let us think of business; it is so tiresome.

Doctor Rank (*comes out of Helmer's study. Before he shuts the door he calls to him*). No, my dear fellow, I won't disturb you; I would rather go in to your wife for a little while. (*Shuts the door and sees Mrs. Linde.*) I beg your pardon; I am afraid I am disturbing you too.

Nora. No, not at all. (*Introducing him.*) Doctor Rank, Mrs. Linde.

Rank. I have often heard Mrs. Linde's name mentioned here. I think I passed you on the stairs when I arrived, Mrs. Linde?

Mrs. Linde. Yes, I go up very slowly; I can't manage stairs well.

Rank. Ah! Some slight internal weakness?

Mrs. Linde. No, the fact is I have been overworking myself.

Rank. Nothing more than that? Then I suppose you have come to town to amuse yourself with our entertainments?

Mrs. Linde. I have come to look for work.

Rank. Is that a good cure for overwork?

Mrs. Linde. One must live, Doctor Rank.

Rank. Yes, the general opinion seems to be that it is necessary.

Nora. Look here, Doctor Rank—you know you want to live.

Rank. Certainly. However wretched I may feel, I want to prolong the agony as long as possible. All my patients are like that. And so are those who are morally diseased; one of them, and a bad case, too, is at this very moment with Helmer—

Mrs. Linde (*sadly*). Ah!

Nora. Whom do you mean?

Rank. A lawyer of the name of Krogstad, a fellow you don't know at all. He suffers from a diseased moral character, Mrs. Helmer; but even he began talking of its being highly important that he should live.

Nora. Did he? What did he want to speak to Torvald about?

Rank. I have no idea; I only heard that it was something about the bank.

Nora. I didn't know this—what's his name—Krogstad had anything to do with the Bank.

Rank. Yes, he has some sort of appointment there. (*To Mrs. Linde.*) I don't know whether you find also in your part of the world that there are certain people who go zealously snuffing about to smell out moral corruption, and, as soon as they have found some, put the person concerned into some lucrative position where they can keep their eye on him. Healthy natures are left out in the cold.

Mrs. Linde. Still I think the sick are those who most need taking care of.

Rank (*shrugging his shoulders*). Yes, there you are. That is the sentiment that is turning Society into a sick-house.

(*Nora, who has been absorbed in her thoughts, breaks out into smothered laughter and claps her hands.*)

Rank. Why do you laugh at that? Have you any notion what society really is?

Nora. What do I care about tiresome society? I am laughing at something quite different, something extremely amusing. Tell me, Doctor Rank, are all the people who are employed in the bank dependent on Torvald now?

Rank. Is that what you find so extremely amusing?

Nora (*smiling and humming*). That's my affair! (*Walking about the room.*) It's perfectly glorious to think that we have—that Torvald has so much power over so many people. (*Takes the packet from her pocket.*) Doctor Rank, what do you say to a macaroon?

Rank. What, macaroons? I thought they were forbidden here.

Nora. Yes, but these are some Christine gave me.

Mrs. Linde. What! I?

Nora. Oh, well, don't be alarmed! You couldn't know that Torvald had forbidden them. I must tell you that he is afraid they will spoil my teeth. But, bah!—once in a way—That's so, isn't it, Doctor Rank? By your leave! (*Puts a macaroon into his mouth.*) You must have one too, Christine. And I shall have one, just a little one—or at most two. (*Walking about.*) I am tremendously happy. There is just one thing in the world now that I should dearly love to do.

Rank. Well, what is that?

Nora. It's something I should dearly love to say, if Torvald could hear me.

Rank. Well, why can't you say it?

Nora. No, I daren't; it's so shocking.

Mrs. Linde. Shocking?

Rank. Well, I should not advise you to say it. Still, with us you might. What is it you would so much like to say if Torvald could hear you?

Nora. I should just love to say—Well, I'm damned!

Rank. Are you mad?

Mrs. Linde. Nora, dear!

Rank. Say it, here he is!

Nora. (*hiding the packet*). Hush! Hush! Hush!

(*Helmer comes out of his room, with his coat over his arm and his hat in his hand.*)

Nora. Well, Torvald dear, have you got rid of him?

Helmer. Yes, he has just gone.

Nora. Let me introduce you—this is Christine, who has come to town.

Helmer. Christine? Excuse me, but I don't know—

Nora. Mrs. Linde, dear; Christine Linde.

Helmer. Of course. A school friend of my wife's, I presume?

Mrs. Linde. Yes, we have known each other since then.

Nora. And just think, she has taken a long journey in order to see you.

Helmer. What do you mean?

Mrs. Linde. No, really, I—

Nora. Christine is tremendously clever at bookkeeping, and she is frightfully anxious to work under some clever man, so as to perfect herself—

Helmer. Very sensible, Mrs. Linde.

Nora. And when she heard you had been appointed manager of the bank—the news was telegraphed, you know—she traveled here as quick as she could, Torvald, I am sure you will be able to do something for Christine, for my sake, won't you?

Helmer. Well, it is not altogether impossible. I presume you are a widow, Mrs. Linde?

Mrs. Linde. Yes.

Helmer. And have had some experience of bookkeeping?

Mrs. Linde. Yes, a fair amount.

Helmer. Ah well, it's very likely I may be able to find something for you—

Nora (*clapping her hands*). What did I tell you?

Helmer. You have just come at a fortunate moment, Mrs. Linde.

Mrs. Linde. How am I to thank you?

Helmer. There is no need. (*Puts on his coat.*) But today you must excuse me—

Rank. Wait a minute; I will come with you. (*Brings his fur coat from the hall and warms it at the fire.*)

Nora. Don't be long away, Torvald dear.

Helmer. About an hour, not more.

Nora. Are you going too, Christine?

Mrs. Linde (*putting on her cloak*). Yes, I must go and look for a room.

Helmer. Oh, well then, we can walk down the street together.

Nora (*helping her*). What a pity it is we are so short of space here; I am afraid it is impossible for us—

Mrs. Linde. Please don't think of it! Good-bye, Nora dear, and many thanks.

Nora. Good-bye for the present. Of course you will come back this evening. And you too, Doctor. Rank. What do you say? If you are well enough? Oh, you must be! Wrap yourself up well. (*They go to the door all talking together. Children's voices are heard on the staircase.*)

Nora. There they are. There they are! (*She runs to open the door.*

The Nurse comes in with the children.) Come in! Come in! (*Stoops and kisses them.*) Oh, you sweet blessings! Look at them, Christine! Aren't they darlings?

Rank. Don't let us stand here in the draught.

Helmer. Come along, Mrs. Linde; the place will only be bearable for a mother now!

(*Rank, Helmer, and Mrs. Linde go downstairs. The Nurse comes forward with the children; Nora shuts the hall door.*)

Nora. How fresh and well you look! Such red cheeks!—like apples and roses. (*The children all talk at once while she speaks to them.*) Have you had great fun? That's splendid! What, you pulled both Emmy and Bob along on the sledge? —Both at once? That was good. You are a clever boy, Ivar. Let me take her for a little, Anne. My sweet little baby doll! (*Takes the baby from the Maid and dances it up and down.*) Yes, yes, mother will dance with Bob too. What! Have you been snowballing? I wish I had been there too! No, no, I will take their things off, Anne; please let me do it, it is such fun. Go in now, you look half frozen. There is some hot coffee for you on the stove.

(*The Nurse goes into the room on the left. Nora takes off the children's things and throws them about, while they all talk to her at once.*)

Nora. Really! Did a big dog run after you? But it didn't bite you? No, dogs don't bite nice little dolly children. You mustn't look at the parcels, Ivar. What are they? Ah, I dare say you would like to know. No, no—it's something nasty! Come, let us have a game. What shall we play at? Hide and seek? Yes, we'll play hide and seek. Bob shall hide first. Must I hide? Very well, I'll hide first. (*She and the children laugh and shout and romp in and out of the room; at last Nora hides under the table; the children rush in and look for her but do not see her; they hear her smothered laughter, run to the table, lift up the cloth and find her. Shouts of laughter. She crawls forward and pretends to frighten them. Fresh laughter. Meanwhile there has been a knock at the hall door but none of them has noticed it. The door is half opened, and Krogstad appears. He waits a little; the game goes on.*)

Krogstad. Excuse me, Mrs. Helmer.

Nora (*with a stifled cry turns round and gets up on to her knees*). Ah! What do you want?

Krogstad. Excuse me, the outer door was ajar; I suppose someone forgot to shut it.

Nora (*rising*). My husband is out, Mr. Krogstad.

Krogstad. I know that.

Nora. What do you want here, then?

Krogstad. A word with you.

Nora. With me? (*To the children, gently.*) Go in to Nurse. What? No, the strange man won't do Mother any harm. When he has gone we will have another game. (*She takes the children into the room on the left and shuts the door after them.*) You want to speak to me?

Krogstad. Yes, I do.

Nora. Today? It is not the first of the month yet.

Krogstad. No, it is Christmas Eve, and it will depend on yourself what sort of a Christmas you will spend.

Nora. What do you want? Today it is absolutely impossible for me—

Krogstad. We won't talk about that till later on. This is something different. I presume you can give me a moment?

Nora. Yes—yes, I can—although—

Krogstad. Good. I was in Olsen's Restaurant and saw your husband going down the street—

Nora. Yes?

Krogstad. With a lady.

Nora. What then?

Krogstad. May I make so bold as to ask if it was a Mrs. Linde?

Nora. It was.

Krogstad. Just arrived in town?

Nora. Yes, today.

Krogstad. She is a great friend of yours, isn't she?

Nora: She is. But I don't see—

Krogstad. I knew her too, once upon a time.

Nora. I am aware of that.

Krogstad. Are you? So you know all about it; I thought as much. Then I can ask you, without beating about the bush—is Mrs. Linde to have an appointment in the Bank?

Nora. What right have you to question me, Mr. Krogstad? You, one of my husband's subordinates! But since you ask, you shall know. Yes, Mrs. Linde is to have an appointment. And it was I who pleaded her cause, Mr. Krogstad, let me tell you that.

Krogstad. I was right in what I thought, then.

Nora (*walking up and down the stage*). Sometimes one has a tiny little bit of influence, I should hope. Because one is a woman it does not necessarily follow that—When anyone is in a subordinate position, Mr. Krogstad, they should really be careful to avoid offending anyone who—who—

Krogstad. Who has influence?

Nora. Exactly.

Krogstad (*changing his tone*). Mrs. Helmer, you will be so good as to use your influence on my behalf.

Nora. What? What do you mean?

Krogstad. You will be so kind as to see that I am allowed to keep my subordinate position in the bank.

Nora. What do you mean by that? Who proposes to take your post away from you?

Krogstad. Oh, there is no necessity to keep up the pretence of ignorance. I can quite understand that your friend is not very anxious to expose herself to the chance of rubbing shoulders with me, and I quite understand, too, whom I have to thank for being turned off.

Nora. But I assure you—

Krogstad. Very likely; but, to come to the point, the time has come when I should advise you to use your influence to prevent that.

Nora. But, Mr. Krogstad, I have no influence.

Krogstad. Haven't you? I thought you said yourself just now—

Nora. Naturally I did not mean you to put that construction on it. I! What should make you think I have any influence of that kind with my husband?

Krogstad. Oh, I have known your husband from our student days. I don't suppose he is anymore unassailable than other husbands.

Nora. If you speak slightly of my husband, I shall turn you out of the house.

Krogstad. You are bold, Mrs. Helmer.

Nora. I am not afraid of you any longer, As soon as the New Year comes, I shall in a very short time be free of the whole thing.

Krogstad (*controlling himself*). Listen to me, Mrs. Helmer. If necessary, I am prepared to fight for my small post in the Bank as if I were fighting for my life.

Nora. So it seems.

Krogstad. It is not only for the sake of the money; indeed, that weighs least with me in the matter. There is another reason—well, I may as well tell you. My position is this. I daresay you know, like everybody else, that once, many years ago, I was guilty of an indiscretion.

Nora. I think I have heard something of the kind.

Krogstad. The matter never came into court, but every way seemed to be closed to me after that. So I took to the business that you know of. I had to do something; and, honestly, don't think I've been one of the worst. But now I must cut myself free from all that. My sons are growing up; for their sake I must try and win back as much respect as I can in the town. This post in the Bank was like the first step up for me, and now your husband is going to kick me downstairs again into the mud.

Nora. But you must believe me, Mr. Krogstad; it is not in my power to help you at all.

Krogstad. Then it is because you haven't the will, but I have means to compel you.

Nora. You don't mean that you will tell my husband that I owe you money?

Krogstad. Hm!—Suppose I were to tell him?

Nora. It would be perfectly infamous of you. (*Sobbing.*) To think of his learning my secret, which has been my joy and pride, in such an ugly, clumsy way—that he should learn it from you! And it would put me in a horribly disagreeable position.

Krogstad. Only disagreeable?

Nora (*impetuously*). Well, do it then!—and it will be the worse for you. My husband will see for himself what a blackguard you are, and you certainly won't keep your post then.

Krogstad. I asked you if it was only a disagreeable scene at home that you were afraid of?

Nora. If my husband does get to know of it, of course he will at once pay you what is still owing, and we shall have nothing more to do with you.

Krogstad (*coming a step nearer*). Listen to me, Mrs. Helmer. Either you have a very bad memory or you know very little of business. I shall be obliged to remind you of a few details.

Nora. What do you mean?

Krogstad. When your husband was ill you came to me to borrow two hundred and fifty pounds.

Nora. I didn't know anyone else to go to.

Krogstad. I promised to get you that amount—

Nora. Yes, and you did so.

Krogstad. I promised to get you that amount on certain conditions. Your mind was so taken up with your husband's illness and you were so anxious to get the money for your journey that you seem to have paid no attention to the conditions of our bargain. Therefore it will not be amiss if I remind you of them. Now, I promised to get the money on the security of a bond which I drew up.

Nora. Yes, and which I signed.

Krogstad. Good. But below your signature there were a few lines constituting your father a surety for the money; those lines your father should have signed.

Nora. Should? He did sign them.

Krogstad. I had left the date blank; that is to say your father should himself have inserted the date on which he signed the paper. Do you remember that?

Nora. Yes, I think I remember.

Krogstad. Then I gave you the bond to send by post to your father. Is that not so?

Nora. Yes.

Krogstad. And you naturally did so at once, because five or six days afterwards you brought me the bond with your father's signature. And then I gave you the money.

Nora. Well, haven't I been paying it off regularly?

Krogstad. Fairly so, yes. But—to come back to the matter in hand—that must have been a very trying time for you, Mrs. Helmer?

Nora. It was, indeed.

Krogstad. Your father was very ill, wasn't he?

Nora. He was very near his end.

Krogstad. And died soon afterwards?

Nora. Yes.

Krogstad. Tell me, Mrs. Helmer, can you by any chance remember what day your father died?—on what day of the month, I mean.

Nora. Papa died on the twenty-ninth of September.

Krogstad. That is correct; I have ascertained it for myself. And, as that is so, there is a discrepancy (*taking a paper from his pocket*) which I cannot account for.

Nora. What discrepancy? I don't know—

Krogstad. The discrepancy consists, Mrs. Helmer, in the fact that your father signed this bond three days after his death.

Nora. What do you mean? I don't understand—

Krogstad. Your father died on the twenty-ninth of September. But, look here; your father dated his signature the second of October. It is a discrepancy, isn't it? (*Nora is silent.*) Can you explain it to me? (*Nora is still silent.*) It is a remarkable thing, too, that the words "second of October," as well as the year, are not written in your father's handwriting but in one that I think I know. Well, of course it can be explained; your father may have forgotten to date his signature, and someone else may have dated it haphazard before they knew of his death. There is no harm in that. It all depends on the signature of the name; and that is genuine, I suppose, Mrs. Helmer? It was your father himself who signed his name here?

Nora (*after a short pause, throws her head up and looks defiantly at him*). No, it was not. It was I that wrote Papa's name.

Krogstad. Are you aware that is a dangerous confession?

Nora. In what way? You shall have your money soon.

Krogstad. Let me ask you a question; why did you not send the paper to your father?

Nora. It was impossible; Papa was so ill. If I had asked him for his signature, I should have had to tell him what the money was to be used for; and when he was so ill himself I couldn't tell him that my husband's life was in danger—it was impossible.

Krogstad. It would have been better for you if you had given up your trip abroad.

Nora. No, that was impossible. That trip was to save my husband's life; I couldn't give that up.

Krogstad. But did it never occur to you that you were committing a fraud on me?

Nora. I couldn't take that into account; I didn't trouble myself about you at all. I couldn't bear you because you put so many heartless difficulties in my way although you knew what a dangerous condition my husband was in.

Krogstad. Mrs. Helmer, you evidently do not realise clearly what it is that you have been guilty of. But I can assure you that my one false step, which lost me all my reputation, was nothing more or nothing worse than what you have done.

Nora. You? Do you ask me to believe that you were brave enough to run a risk to save your wife's life?

Krogstad. The law cares nothing about motives.

Nora. Then it must be a very foolish law.

Krogstad. Foolish or not, it is the law by which you will be judged if I produce this paper in court.

Nora. I don't believe it. Is a daughter not to be allowed to spare her dying father anxiety and care? Is a wife not to be allowed to save her husband's life? I don't know much about law, but I am certain that there must be laws permitting such things as that. Have you no knowledge of such laws—you who are a lawyer? You must be a very poor lawyer, Mr. Krogstad.

Krogstad. Maybe. But matters of business—such business as you and I have had together—do you think I don't understand that? Very well. Do as you please. But let me tell you this—if I lose my position a second time, you shall lose yours with me. (*He bows, and goes out through the hall.*)

Nora (*appears buried in thought for a short time, then tosses her head*). Nonsense! Trying to frighten me like that! I am not so silly as he thinks. (*Begins to busy herself putting the children's things in order.*) And yet— No, it's impossible! I did it for love's sake.

The Children (*in the doorway on the left*). Mother, the stranger man has gone out through the gate.

Nora. Yes, dears, I know. But, don't tell anyone about the stranger man. Do you hear? Not even Papa.

Children. No, mother; but will you come and play again?

Nora. No no—not now.

Children. But, mother, you promised us.

Nora. Yes, but I can't now. Run away in; I have such a lot to do. Run away in, sweet little darlings. (*She gets them into the room by degrees and shuts the door on them; then sits down on the sofa, takes up a piece of needlework and sews a few stitches but soon stops.*) No! (*Throws down the work, gets up, goes to the hall door and calls out.*) Helen! Bring the Tree in. (*Goes to the table on the left, opens a drawer, and stops again.*) No, no! it is quite impossible!

Maid (*coming in with the Tree*). Where shall I put it, ma'am?

Nora. Here, in the middle of the floor.

Maid. Shall I get you anything else?

Nora. No, thank you. I have all I want.

(*Exit Maid.*)

Nora (*begins dressing the tree*). A candle here—and flowers here— The horrible man! It's all nonsense—there's nothing wrong. The Tree shall be splendid! I will do everything I can think of to please you, Torvald! I will sing for you, dance for you— (*Helmer comes in with some papers under his arm.*) Oh, are you back already?

Helmer. Yes. Has anyone been here?

Nora. Here? No.

Helmer. That is strange. I saw Krogstad going out of the gate.

Nora. Did you? Oh yes, I forgot, Krogstad was here for a moment.

Helmer. Nora, I can see from your manner that he has been here begging you to say a good word for him.

Nora. Yes.

Helmer. And you were to appear to do it of your own accord; you were to conceal from me the fact of his having been here; didn't he beg that of you too?

Nora. Yes, Torvald, but—

Helmer. Nora, Nora, and you would be a party to that sort of thing? To have any talk with a man like that and give him any sort of promise? And to tell me a lie into the bargain?

Nora. A lie?

Helmer. Didn't you tell me no one had been here? (*Shakes his* *finger at her.*) My little songbird must never do that again. A songbird must have a clean beak to chirp with—no false notes! (*Puts his arm round her waist.*) That is so, isn't it? Yes, I am sure it is. (*Lets her go.*) *We will say no more about it.* (*Sits down by the stove.*) How warm and snug it is here! (*Turns over his papers.*)

Nora (*after a short pause, during which she busies herself with the Christmas Tree*). Torvald!

Helmer. Yes.

Nora: I am looking forward tremendously to the fancy-dress ball at the Stensborgs' the day after tomorrow.

Helmer. And I am tremendously curious to see what you are going to surprise me with.

Nora. It was very silly of me to want to do that.

Helmer. What do you mean?

Nora. I can't hit upon anything that will do; everything I think of seems so silly and insignificant.

Helmer. Does my little Nora acknowledge that at last?

Nora (*standing behind his chair with her arms on the back of it*). Are you very busy, Torvald?

Helmer. Well—

Nora. What are all those papers?

Helmer. Bank business.

Nora. Already?

Helmer. I have got authority from the retiring manager to undertake the necessary changes in the staff and in the rearrangement of the work, and I must make use of the

Christmas week for that, so as to have everything in order for the new year.

Nora. Then that was why this poor Krogstad—

Helmer. Hm!

Nora (*leans against the back of his chair and strokes his hair*). If you hadn't been so busy I should have asked you a tremendously big favor, Torvald.

Helmer. What is that? Tell me.

Nora. There is no one has such good taste as you. And I do so want to look nice at the fancy-dress ball. Torvald, couldn't you take me in hand and decide what I shall go as and what sort of a dress I shall wear?

Helmer. Aha! So my obstinate little woman is obliged to get someone to come to her rescue?

Nora. Yes, Torvald, I can't get along a bit without your help.

Helmer. Very well, I will think it over; we shall manage to hit upon something.

Nora. That is nice of you. (*Goes to the Christmas Tree. A short pause.*) How pretty the red flowers look! But tell me, was it really something very bad that this Krogstad was guilty of?

Helmer. He forged someone's name. Have you any idea what that means?

Nora. Isn't it possible that he was driven to do it by necessity?

Helmer. Yes; or, as in so many cases, by imprudence. I am not so heartless as to condemn a man altogether because of a single false step of that kind.

Nora. No you wouldn't, would you, Torvald?

Helmer. Many a man has been able to retrieve his character if he has openly confessed his fault and taken his punishment.

Nora. Punishment?

Helmer. But Krogstad did nothing of that sort; he got himself out of it by a cunning trick, and that is why he has gone under altogether.

Nora. But do you think it would—

Helmer. Just think how a guilty man like that has to lie and play the hypocrite with everyone, how he has to wear a mask in the presence of those near and dear to him, even before his own wife and children. And about the children—that is the most terrible part of it all, Nora.

Nora. How?

Helmer. Because such an atmosphere of lies infects and poisons the whole life of a home. Each breath the children take in such a house is full of the germs of evil.

Nora (*coming nearer him*). Are you sure of that?

Helmer. My dear, I have often seen it in the course of my life as a lawyer. Almost everyone who has gone to the bad early in life has had a deceitful mother.

Nora. Why do you only say—mother?

Helmer. It seems most commonly to be the mother's influence, though naturally a bad father's would have the same result. Every lawyer is familiar with the fact. This Krogstad, now, has been persistently poisoning his own children with lies and dissimulation; that is why I say he has lost all moral character. (*Holds out his hands to her.*) That is why my sweet little Nora must promise me not to plead his cause. Give me your hand on it. Come, come, what is this? Give me your hand. There now, that's settled. I assure you it would be quite impossible for me to work with him; I literally feel physically ill when I am in the company of such people.

Nora (*takes her hand out of his and goes to the opposite side of the Christmas Tree*). How hot it is in here, and I have such a lot to do.

Helmer (*getting up and putting his papers in order*). Yes, and I must try and read through some of these before dinner, and I must think about your costume, too. And it is just possible I may have something ready in gold paper to hang up on the Tree. (*Puts his hand on her head.*) My precious little singing bird! (*He goes into his room and shuts the door after him.*)

Nora (*after a pause, whispers*). No, no—it isn't true. It's impossible; it must be impossible.

(*The Nurse opens the door on the left.*)

Nurse. The little ones are begging so hard to be allowed to come in to Mamma.

Nora. No, no, no! Don't let them come in to me! You stay with them, Anne.

Nurse. Very well, ma'am. (*Shuts the door.*)

Nora (*pale with terror*). Deprave my little children? Poison my home? (*A short pause. Then she tosses her head.*) It's not true. It can't possibly be true.

ACT II

The same scene—The Christmas Tree is in the corner by the piano, stripped of its ornaments and with burnt-down candle ends on its dishevelled branches. Nora's cloak and hat are lying on the sofa. She is alone in the room, walking about uneasily. She stops by the sofa and takes up her cloak.

Nora (*drops the cloak*). Someone is coming now! (*Goes to the door and listens.*) No—it is no one. Of course, no one will come today, Christmas Day—nor tomorrow either. But perhaps— (*Opens the door and looks out.*) No, nothing in the letter box; it is quite empty. (*Comes forward.*) What rubbish! Of course he can't be in earnest about it. Such a thing couldn't happen; it is impossible—I have three little children.

(*Enter the Nurse from the room on the left, carrying a big cardboard box.*)

Nurse. At last I have found the box with the fancy dress.

Nora. Thanks; put it on the table.

Nurse (*in doing so*). But it is very much in want of mending.

Nora. I should like to tear it into a hundred thousand pieces.

Nurse. What an idea! It can easily be put in order—just a little patience.

Nora. Yes, I will go and get Mrs. Linde to come and help me with it.

Nurse. What, out again? In this horrible weather? You will catch cold, ma'am, and make yourself ill.

Nora. Well, worse than that might happen. How are the children?

Nurse. The poor little souls are playing with their Christmas presents, but—

Nora. Do they ask much for me?

Nurse. You see, they are so accustomed to have their mamma with them.

Nora. Yes—but, Nurse, I shall not be able to be so much with them now as I was before.

Nurse. Oh well, young children easily get accustomed to anything.

Nora. Do you think so? Do you think they would forget their mother if she went away altogether?

Nurse. Good heavens!—Went away altogether?

Nora. Nurse, I want you to tell me something I have often wondered about—how could you have the heart to put your own child out among strangers?

Nurse. I was obliged to if I wanted to be little Nora's nurse.

Nora. Yes, but how could you be willing to do it?

Nurse. What, when I was going to get such a good place by it? A poor girl who has got into trouble should be glad to. Besides, that wicked man didn't do a single thing for me.

Nora. But I suppose your daughter has quite forgotten you.

Nurse. No, indeed she hasn't. She wrote to me when she was confirmed, and when she was married.

Nora (*putting her arms round her neck*). Dear old Anne, you were a good mother to me when I was little.

Nurse. Little Nora, poor dear, had no other mother but me.

Nora. And if my little ones had no other mother, I am sure you would—What nonsense I am talking! (*Opens the box.*) Go in to them. Now I must—You will see tomorrow how charming I shall look.

Nurse. I am sure there will be no one at the ball so charming as you, ma'am. (*Goes into the room on the left.*)

Nora (*begins to unpack the box but soon pushes it away from her*). If only I dared go out. If only no one would come. If only I could be sure nothing would happen here in the meantime. Stuff and nonsense! No one will come. Only I mustn't think about it. I will brush my muff. What lovely, lovely gloves! Out of my thoughts, out of my thoughts! One, two, three, four, five, six— (*Screams.*) Ah! there is someone coming—. (*Makes a movement towards the door but stands irresolute.*)

(*Enter Mrs. Linde from the hall, where she has taken off her cloak and hat.*)

Nora. Oh, it's you, Christine. There is no one else out there, is there? How good of you to come!

Mrs. Linde. I heard you were up asking for me.

Nora. Yes, I was passing by. As a matter of fact, it is something you could help me with. Let us sit down here on the sofa. Look here. Tomorrow evening there is to be a fancy-dress ball at the Stenborgs', who live above us; and Torvald wants me to go as a Neapolitan fishergirl, and dance the tarantella that I learnt at Capri.

Mrs. Linde. I see; you are going to keep up the character.

Nora. Yes, Torvald wants me to. Look, here is the dress; Torvald had it made for me there, but now it is all so torn, and I haven't any idea—

Mrs. Linde. We will easily put that right. It is only some of the trimming come unsewn here and there. Needle and thread? Now then, that's all we want.

Nora. It is nice of you.

Mrs. Linde (*sewing*). So you are going to be dressed up tomorrow, Nora. I will tell you what—I shall come in for a moment and see you in your fine feathers. But I have completely forgotten to thank you for a delightful evening yesterday.

Nora (*gets up, and crosses the stage*). Well I don't think yesterday was as pleasant as usual. You ought to have come to town a little earlier, Christine. Certainly Torvald does understand how to make a house dainty and attractive.

Mrs. Linde. And so do you, it seems to me; you are not your father's daughter for nothing. But tell me, is Doctor Rank always as depressed as he was yesterday?

Nora. No; yesterday it was very noticeable. I must tell you that he suffers from a very dangerous disease. He has consumption of the spine, poor creature. His father was a horrible man who committed all sorts of excesses, and that is why his son was sickly from childhood, do you understand?

Mrs. Linde (*dropping her sewing*). But, my dearest Nora, how do you know anything about such things?

Nora (*walking about*). Pooh! When you have three children you get visits now and then from—from married women who know something of medical matters, and they talk about one thing and another.

Mrs. Linde (*goes on sewing. A short silence*). Does Doctor Rank come here every day?

Nora. Every day regularly. He is Torvald's most intimate friend and a great friend of mine too. He is just like one of the family.

Mrs. Linde. But tell me this—is he perfectly sincere? I mean, isn't he the kind of a man that is very anxious to make himself agreeable?

Nora. Not in the least. What makes you think that?

Mrs. Linde. When you introduced him to me yesterday he declared he had often heard my name mentioned in this house; but afterward I noticed that your husband hadn't the slightest idea who I was. So how could Doctor Rank—

Nora. That is quite right, Christine. Torvald is so absurdly fond of me that he wants me absolutely to himself, as he says. At first he used to seem almost jealous if I mentioned any of the dear folk at home, so naturally I gave up doing so. But I often talk about such things with Doctor Rank because he likes hearing about them.

Mrs. Linde. Listen to me, Nora. You are still very like a child in many ways, and I am older than you in many ways and have a little more experience. Let me tell you this—you ought to make an end of it with Doctor Rank.

Nora. What ought I to make an end of?

Mrs. Linde. Of two things, I think. Yesterday you talked some nonsense about a rich admirer who was to leave you money—

Nora. An admirer who doesn't exist, unfortunately! But what then?

Mrs. Linde. Is Doctor Rank a man of means?

Nora. Yes, he is.

Mrs. Linde. And has no one to provide for?

Nora. No, no one; but—

Mrs. Linde. And comes here every day?

Nora. Yes, I told you so.

Mrs. Linde. But how can this well-bred man be so tactless?

Nora. I don't understand you at all.

Mrs. Linde. Don't prevaricate, Nora. Do you suppose I don't guess who lent you the two hundred and fifty pounds.

Nora. Are you out of your senses? How can you think of such a thing! A friend of ours, who comes here every day! Do you realise what a horribly painful position that would be?

Mrs. Linde. Then it really isn't he?

Nora. No, certainly not. It would never have entered into my head for a moment. Besides, he had no money to lend then; he came into his money afterwards.

Mrs. Linde. Well, I think that was lucky for you, my dear Nora.

Nora. No, it would never have come into my head to ask Doctor Rank. Although I am quite sure that if I had asked him—

Mrs. Linde. But of course you won't.

Nora. Of course not. I have no reason to think it could possibly be necessary. But I am quite sure that if I told Doctor Rank—

Mrs. Linde. Behind your husband's back?

Nora. I must make an end of it with the other one, and that will be behind his back too. I must make an end of it with him.

Mrs. Linde. Yes, that is what I told you yesterday, but—

Nora (*walking up and down*). A man can put a thing like that straight much easier than a woman—

Mrs. Linde. One's husband, yes.

Nora. Nonsense! (*Standing still.*) When you pay off a debt you get your bond back, don't you?

Mrs. Linde. Yes, as a matter of course.

Nora. And can tear it into a hundred thousand pieces, and burn it up—the nasty, dirty paper!

Mrs. Linde (*looks hard at her, lays down her sewing and gets up slowly*). Nora, you are concealing something from me.

Nora. Do I look as if I were?

Mrs. Linde. Something has happened to you since yesterday morning. Nora, what is it?

Nora (*going nearer to her*). Christine! (*Listens.*) Hush! There's Torvald come home. Do you mind going in to the children for the present? Torvald can't bear to see dressmaking going on. Let Anne help you.

Mrs. Linde (*gathering some of the things together*). Certainly—but I am not going away from here till we have had it out with one another. (*She goes into the room, on the left, as Helmer comes in from the hall.*)

Nora (*going up to Helmar*). I have wanted you so much, Torvald dear.

Helmer. Was that the dressmaker?

Nora. No, it was Christine; she is helping me to put my dress in order. You will see I shall look quite smart.

Helmer. Wasn't that a happy thought of mine, now?

Nora. Splendid! But don't you think it is nice of me, too, to do as you wish?

Helmer. Nice?—because you do as your husband wishes? Well, well, you little rogue, I am sure you did not mean it in that way. But I am not going to disturb you; you will want to be trying on your dress, I expect.

Nora. I suppose you are going to work.

Helmer. Yes. (*Shows her a bundle of papers.*) Look at that. I have just been into the bank. (*Turns to go into his room.*)

Nora. Torvald.

Helmer. Yes.

Nora. If your little squirrel were to ask you for something very, very prettily—?

Helmer. What then?

Nora. Would you do it?

Helmer. I should like to hear what it is, first.

Nora. Your squirrel would run about and do all her tricks if you would be nice and do what she wants.

Helmer. Speak plainly.

Nora. Your skylark would chirp, chirp about in every room, with her song rising and falling—

Helmer. Well, my skylark does that anyhow.

Nora. I would play the fairy and dance for you in the moonlight, Torvald.

Helmer. Nora—you surely don't mean that request you made of me this morning?

Nora (*going near him*). Yes, Torvald, I beg you so earnestly—

Helmer. Have you really the courage to open up that question again?

Nora. Yes, dear, you must do as I ask; you must let Krogstad keep his post in the bank.

Helmer. My dear Nora, it is his post that I have arranged Mrs. Linde shall have.

Nora. Yes, you have been awfully kind about that, but you could just as well dismiss some other clerk instead of Krogstad.

Helmer. This is simply incredible obstinacy! Because you chose to give him a thoughtless promise that you would speak for him I am expected to—

Nora. That isn't the reason, Torvald. It is for your own sake. This fellow writes in the most scurrilous newspapers; you have told me so yourself. He can do you an unspeakable amount of harm. I am frightened to death of him—

Helmer. Ah, I understand; it is recollections of the past that scare you.

Nora. What do you mean?

Helmer. Naturally you are thinking of your father.

Nora. Yes—yes, of course. Just recall to your mind what these malicious creatures wrote in the papers about Papa, and how horribly they slandered him. I believe they would have procured his dismissal if the Department had not sent you over to inquire into it, and if you had not been so kindly disposed and helpful to him.

Helmer. My little Nora, there is an important difference between your father and me. Your father's reputation as a public official was not above suspicion. Mine is, and I hope it will continue to be so, as long as I hold my office.

Nora. You never can tell what mischief these men may contrive. We ought to be so well off, so snug and happy here in our peaceful home, and have no cares—you and I and the children, Torvald! That is why I beg you so earnestly—

Helmer. And it is just by interceding for him that you make it impossible for me to keep him. It is already known at the bank that I mean to dismiss Krogstad. Is it to get about now that the new manager has changed his mind at his wife's bidding?

Nora. And what if it did?

Helmer. Of course!—if only this obstinate little person can get her way! Do you suppose I am going to make myself ridiculous before my whole staff, to let people think I am a man to be swayed by all sorts of outside influence? I should very soon feel the consequences of it, I can tell you! And besides, there is one thing that makes it quite impossible for me to have Krogstad in the bank as long as I am manager.

Nora. Whatever is that?

Helmer. His moral failings I might perhaps have overlooked if necessary—

Nora. Yes, you could—couldn't you?

Helmer. And I hear he is a good worker too. But I knew him when we were boys. It was one of those rash friendships that so often prove an incubus in afterlife. I may as well tell you plainly, we were once on very intimate terms with one another. But this tactless fellow lays no restraint on himself when other people are present. On the contrary, he thinks it gives him the right to adopt a familiar tone with me, and every minute it is "I say, Helmer, old fellow!" and that sort of thing. I assure you it is extremely painful for me. He would make my position in the bank intolerable.

Nora. Torvald, I don't believe you mean that.

Helmer. Don't you? Why not?

Nora. Because it is such a narrow-minded way of looking at things.

Helmer. What are you saying? Narrow-minded? Do you think I am narrow-minded?

Nora. No, just the opposite, dear—and it is exactly for that reason—

Helmer. It's the same thing. You say my point of view is narrow-minded, so I must be so too. Narrow-minded! Very well—I must put an end to this. (*Goes to the hall door and calls.*) Helen!

Nora. What are you going to do?

Helmer (*looking among his papers*). Settle it. (*Enter Maid.*) Look here; take this letter and go downstairs with it at once. Find a messenger and tell him to deliver it and be quick. The address is on it, and here is the money.

Maid. Very well, sir. (*Exit with the letter.*)

Helmer (*putting his papers together*). Now, then, little Miss

Obstinate.

Nora (*breathlessly*). Torvald—what was that letter?

Helmer. Krogstad's dismissal.

Nora. Call her back, Torvald! There is still time. Oh Torvald, call her back! Do it for my sake—for your own sake—for the children's sake! Do you hear me, Torvald? Call her back! You don't know what that letter can bring upon us.

Helmer. It's too late.

Nora. Yes, it's too late.

Helmer. My dear Nora, I can forgive the anxiety you are in, although really it is an insult to me. It is, indeed. Isn't it an insult to think that I should be afraid of a starving quill driver's vengeance? But I forgive you nevertheless, because it is such eloquent witness to your great love for me. (*Takes her in his arms.*) And that is as it should be, my own darling Nora. Come what will, you may be sure I shall have both courage and strength if they be needed. You will see I am man enough to take everything upon myself.

Nora (*in a horror-stricken voice*). What do you mean by that?

Helmer. Everything I say.

Nora (*recovering herself*). You will never have to do that.

Helmer. That's right. Well, we will share it, Nora, as man and wife should. That is how it shall be. (*Caressing her.*) Are you content now? There! There!—not these frightened dove's eyes! The whole thing is only the wildest fancy! Now, you must go and play through the tarantella and practice with your tambourine. I shall go into the inner office and shut the door, and I shall hear nothing; you can make as much noise as you please. (*Turns back at the door.*) And when Rank comes tell him where he will find me. (*Nods to her, takes his papers and goes into his room and shuts the door after him.*)

Nora (*bewildered with anxiety, stands as if rooted to the spot and whispers*). He was capable of doing it. He will do it. He will do it in spite of everything. No, not that! Never, never! Anything rather than that! Oh, for some help, some way out of it! (*The doorbell rings.*) Doctor Rank! Anything rather than that— anything, whatever it is! (*She puts her hands over her face, pulls herself together, goes to the door and opens it. Rank is standing without, hanging up his coat. During the following dialogue it begins to grow dark.*)

Nora. Good day, Doctor Rank. I knew your ring. But you mustn't go into Torvald now; I think he is busy with something.

Rank. And you?

Nora (*brings him in and shuts the door after him*). Oh, you know very well I always have time for you.

Rank. Thank you. I shall make use of as much of it as I can.

Nora. What do you mean by that? As much of it as you can?

Rank. Well, does that alarm you?

Nora. It was such a strange way of putting it. Is anything likely to happen?

Rank. Nothing but what I have long been prepared for. But I certainly didn't expect it to happen so soon.

Nora (*gripping him by the arm*). What have you found out? Doctor Rank, you must tell me.

Rank (*sitting down by the stove*). It is all up with me. And it can't be helped.

Nora (*with a sigh of relief*). Is it about yourself?

Rank. Who else? It is no use lying to one's self. I am the most wretched of all my patients, Mrs. Helmer. Lately I have been taking stock of my internal economy. Bankrupt! Probably within a month I shall lie rotting in the churchyard.

Nora. What an ugly thing to say!

Rank. The thing itself is cursedly ugly, and the worst of it is that I shall have to face so much more that is ugly before that. I shall only make one more examination of myself; when I have done that I shall know pretty certainly when it will be that the horrors of dissolution will begin. There is something I want to tell you. Helmer's refined nature gives him an unconquerable disgust of everything that is ugly; I won't have him in my sickroom.

Nora. Oh, but, Doctor Rank—

Rank. I won't have him there. Not on any account. I bar my door to him. As soon as I am quite certain that the worst has come I shall send you my card with a black cross on it, and then you will know that the loathsome end has begun.

Nora. You are quite absurd today. And I wanted you so much to be in a really good humour.

Rank. With death stalking beside me? To have to pay this penalty for another man's sin! Is there any justice in that? And in every single family, in one way or another, some such inexorable retribution is being exacted.

Nora (*putting her hands over her ears*). Rubbish! Do talk of something cheerful.

Rank. Oh, it's a mere laughing matter, the whole thing. My poor innocent spine has to suffer for my father's youthful amusements.

Nora (*sitting at the table on the left*). I suppose you mean that he was too partial to asparagus and pâté de foie gras, don't you?

Rank. Yes, and to truffles.

Nora. Truffles, yes. And oysters too, I suppose?

Rank. Oysters, of course; that goes without saying.

Nora. And heaps of port and champagne. It is sad that all these nice things should take their revenge on our bones.

Rank. Especially that they should revenge themselves on the unlucky bones of those who have not had the satisfaction of enjoying them.

Nora. Yes, that's the saddest part of it all.

Rank (*with a searching look at her*). Hm!

Nora (*after a short pause*). Why did you smile?

Rank. No, it was you that laughed.

Nora. No, it was you that smiled, Doctor Rank!

Rank (*rising*). You are a greater rascal than I thought.

Nora. I am in a silly mood today.

Rank. So it seems.

Nora (*putting her hands on his shoulders*). Dear, dear Doctor Rank, death mustn't take you away from Torvald and me.

Rank. It is a loss you would easily recover from. Those who are gone are soon forgotten.

Nora (*looking at him anxiously*). Do you believe that?

Rank. People form new ties, and then—

Nora. Who will form new ties?

Rank. Both you and Helmer, when I am gone. You yourself are already on the highroad to it, I think. What did that Mrs. Linde want here last night?

Nora. Oho! You don't mean to say that you are jealous of poor Christine?

Rank. Yes, I am. She will be my successor in this house. When I am done for, this woman will—

Nora. Hush! don't speak so loud. She is in that room.

Rank. Today again. There, you see.

Nora. She has only come to sew my dress for me. Bless my soul, how unreasonable you are! (*Sits down on the sofa.*) Be nice now, Doctor Rank, and tomorrow you will see how beautifully I shall dance, and you can imagine I am doing it all for you—and for Torvald too, of course. (*Takes various things out of the box.*) Doctor Rank, come and sit down here, and I will show you something.

Rank (*sitting down*). What is it?

Nora. Just look at those.

Rank. Silk stockings.

Nora. Flesh coloured. Aren't they lovely? It is so dark here now, but to-morrow—No, no, no! You must only look at the feet. Oh well, you may have leave to look at the legs too.

Rank. Hm!

Nora. Why are you looking so critical? Don't you think they will fit me?

Rank. I have no means of forming an opinion about that.

Nora (*looks at him for a moment*). For shame! (*Hits him lightly on the ear with the stockings.*) That's to punish you. (*Folds them up again.*)

Rank. And what other nice things am I to be allowed to see?

Nora. Not a single thing more, for being so naughty. (*She looks among the things, humming to herself.*)

Rank (*after a short silence*). When I am sitting here, talking to you as intimately as this I cannot imagine for a moment what would have become of me if I had never come into this house.

Nora (*smiling*). I believe you do feel thoroughly at home with us.

Rank (*in a lower voice, looking straight in front of him*). And to be obliged to leave it all—

Nora. Nonsense, you are not going to leave it.

Rank (*as before*). And not be able to leave behind one the slightest token of one's gratitude, scarcely even a fleeting regret—nothing but an empty place which the firstcomer can fill as well as any other.

Nora. And if I asked you now for a—? No!

Rank. For what?

Nora. For a big proof of your friendship—

Rank. Yes, yes!

Nora. I mean a tremendously big favour—

Rank. Would you really make me so happy for once?

Nora. Ah, but you don't know what it is yet.

Rank. No—but tell me.

Nora. I really can't, Doctor Rank. It is something out of all reason; it means advice and help, and a favour—

Rank. The bigger a thing it is, the better. I can't conceive what it is you mean. Do tell me. Haven't I your confidence?

Nora. More than anyone else. I know you are my truest and best friend, and so I will tell you what it is. Well, Doctor Rank, it is something you must help me to prevent. You know how devotedly, how inexpressibly deeply Torvald loves me; he would never for a moment hesitate to give his life for me.

Rank (*leaning toward her*). Nora—do you think he is the only one—?

Nora (*with a slight start*). The only one—?

Rank. The only one who would gladly give his life for your sake.

Nora (*sadly*). Is that it?

Rank. I was determined you should know it before I went away, and there will never be a better opportunity than this. Now you know it, Nora. And now you know, too, that you can trust me as you would trust no one else.

Nora (*rises deliberately and quietly*). Let me pass.

Rank (*makes room for her to pass him, but sits still*). Nora!

Nora (*at the hall door*). Helen, bring in the lamp. (*Goes over to the stove.*) Dear Doctor Rank, that was really horrid of you.

Rank. To have loved you as much as anyone else does? Was that horrid?

Nora. No, but to go and tell me so. There was really no need—

Rank. What do you mean? Did you know—? (*Maid enters with lamp, puts it down on the table and goes out.*) Nora—Mrs. Helmer—tell me, had you any idea of this?

Nora. Oh, how do I know whether I had or whether I hadn't? I really can't tell you. To think you could be so clumsy, Doctor Rank! We were getting on so nicely.

Bank. Well, at all events you know that you can command me body and soul. So won't you speak out?

Nora (*looking at him*). After what happened?

Rank. I beg you to let me know what it is.

Nora. I can't tell you anything now.

Rank. Yes, yes. You mustn't punish me in that way. Let me have permission to do for you whatever a man may do.

Nora. You can do nothing for me now. Besides, I really don't need any help at all. You will find that the whole thing is merely fancy on my part. It really is so—of course it is! (*Sits down in the rocking-chair, and looks at him with a smile.*) You are a nice sort of man, Doctor Rank! Don't you feel ashamed of yourself now the lamp has come?

Rank. Not a bit. But perhaps I had better go—forever?

Nora. No, indeed, you shall not. Of course you must come here just as before. You know very well Torvald can't do without you.

Rank. Yes, but you?

Nora. Oh, I am always tremendously pleased when you come.

Rank. It is just that that put me on the wrong track. You are a riddle to me. I have often thought that you would almost as soon be in my company as in Helmer's.

Nora. Yes—you see, there are some people one loves best and others whom one would almost always rather have as companions.

Rank. Yes, there is something in that.

Nora. When I was at home of course I loved Papa best. But I always thought it tremendous fun if I could steal down into the maids' room, because they never moralized at all and talked to each other about such entertaining things.

Rank. I see—it is their place I have taken.

Nora (*jumping up and going to him*). Oh, dear, nice Doctor Rank, I never meant that at all. But surely you can understand that being with Torvald is a little like being with Papa—

(*Enter Maid from the hall.*)

Maid. If you please, ma'am. (*Whispers and hands her a card.*)

Nora (*glancing at the card*). Oh! (*Puts it in her pocket.*)

Rank. Is there anything wrong?

Nora. No, no, not in the least. It is only something—It is my new dress—

Rank. What? Your dress is lying there.

Nora. Oh, yes, that one; but this is another. I ordered it. Torvald mustn't know about it.

Rank. Oho! Then that was the great secret.

Nora. Of course. Just go in to him; he is sitting in the inner room. Keep him as long as—

Rank. Make your mind easy; I won't let him escape. (*Goes into Helmer's room.*)

Nora (*to the Maid*). And he is standing waiting in the kitchen?

Maid. Yes; he came up the back stairs.

Nora. But didn't you tell him no one was in?

Maid. Yes, but it was no good.

Nora. He won't go away?

Maid. No; he says he won't until he has seen you, ma'am.

Nora. Well, let him come in—but quietly. Helen, you mustn't say anything about it to anyone. It is a surprise for my husband.

Maid. Yes, ma'am, I quite understand. (*Exit.*)

Nora. This dreadful thing is going to happen! It will happen in spite of me! No, no, no, it can't happen—it shan't happen! (*She bolts the door of Helmer's room. The Maid opens the hall door for Krogstad and shuts it after him. He is wearing a fur coat, high* *boots and a fur cap.*)

Nora (*advancing towards him*). Speak low—my husband is at home.

Krogstad. No matter about that.

Nora. What do you want of me?

Krogstad. An explanation of something.

Nora. Make haste then. What is it?

Krogstad. You know, I suppose, that I have got my dismissal.

Nora. I couldn't prevent it, Mr. Krogstad. I fought as hard as I could on your side, but it was no good.

Krogstad. Does your husband love you so little then? He knows what I can expose you to, and yet he ventures—

Nora. How can you suppose that he has any knowledge of the sort?

Krogstad. I didn't suppose so at all. It would not be the least like our dear Torvald Helmer to show so much courage—

Nora. Mr. Krogstad, a little respect for my husband, please.

Krogstad. Certainly—all the respect he deserves. But since you have kept the matter so carefully to yourself, I make bold to suppose that you have a little clearer idea than you had yesterday of what it actually is that you have done?

Nora. More than you could ever teach me.

Krogstad. Yes, such a bad lawyer as I am.

Nora. What is it you want of me?

Krogstad. Only to see how you were, Mrs. Helmer. I have been thinking about you all day long. A mere cashier, a quill driver, a—well, a man like me—even he has a little of what is called feeling, you know.

Nora. Show it then; think of my little children.

Krogstad. Have you and your husband thought of mine? But never mind about that. I only wanted to tell you that you need not take this matter too seriously. In the first place there will be no accusation made on my part.

Nora. No, of course not; I was sure of that.

Krogstad. The whole thing can be arranged amicably; there is no reason why anyone should know anything about it. It will remain a secret between us three.

Nora. My husband must never get to know anything about it.

Krogstad. How will you be able to prevent it? Am I to understand that you can pay the balance that is owing?

Nora. No, not just at present.

Krogstad. Or perhaps that you have some expedient for raising the money soon?

Nora. No expedient that I mean to make use of.

Krogstad. Well, in any case, it would have been of no use to you now. If you stood there with ever so much money in your hand, I would never part with your bond.

Nora. Tell me what purpose you mean to put it to.

Krogstad. I shall only preserve it—keep it in my possession. No one who is not concerned in the matter shall have the slightest hint of it. So that if the thought of it has driven you to any desperate resolution—

Nora. It has.

Krogstad. If you had it in your mind to run away from your home—

Nora. I had.

Krogstad. Or even something worse—

Nora. How could you know that?

Krogstad. Give up the idea.

Nora. How did you know I had thought of that?

Krogstad. Most of us think of that at first. I did, too—but I hadn't the courage.

Nora (*faintly*). No more than I.

Krogstad (*in a tone of relief*). No, that's it, isn't it—you hadn't the courage either?

Nora. No, I haven't—I haven't.

Krogstad. Besides, it would have been a great piece of folly. Once the first storm at home is over—I have a letter for your husband in my pocket.

Nora. Telling him everything?

Krogstad. In as lenient a manner as I possibly could.

Nora (*quickly*). He mustn't get the letter. Tear it up. I will find some means of getting money.

Krogstad. Excuse me, Mrs. Helmer, but I think I told you just how—

Nora. I am not speaking of what I owe you. Tell me what sum you are asking my husband for, and I will get the money.

Krogstad. I am not asking your husband for a penny.

Nora. What do you want then?

Krogstad. I will tell you. I want to rehabilitate myself, Mrs. Helmer; I want to get on, and in that your husband must help me. For the last year and a half I have not had a hand in anything dishonourable, and all that time I have been struggling in most restricted circumstances. I was content to work my way up step by step. Now I am turned out, and I am not going to be satisfied with merely being taken into favor again. I want to get on, I tell you. I want to get into the bank again, in a higher position. Your husband must make a place for me—

Nora. That he will never do!

Krogstad. He will; I know him; he dare not protest. And as soon as I am in there again with him then you will see! Within a year I shall be the manager's right hand. It will be Nils Krogstad and not Torvald Helmer who manages the bank.

Nora. That's a thing you will never see!

Krogstad. Do you mean that you will—

Nora. I have courage enough for it now.

Krogstad. Oh, you can't frighten me. A fine, spoilt lady like you—

Nora. You will see, you will see.

Krogstad. Under the ice, perhaps? Down into the cold, coal-black water? And then, in the spring, to float up to the surface, all horrible and unrecognizable, with your hair fallen out—

Nora. You can't frighten me.

Krogstad. Nor you me. People don't do such things, Mrs. Helmer. Besides, what use would it be? I should have him completely in my power all the same.

Nora. Afterwards? When I am no longer—

Krogstad. Have you forgotten that it is I who have the keeping of your reputation? (*Nora stands speechlessly looking at him.*) Well, now, I have warned you. Do not do anything foolish. When Helmer has had my letter I shall expect a message from him. And be sure you remember that it is your husband himself who has forced me into such ways as this again. I will never forgive him for that. Good-bye, Mrs. Helmer. (*Exit through the hall.*)

Nora (*goes to the hall door, opens it slightly and listens*). He is going. He is not putting the letter in the box. Oh, no, no! that's impossible! (*Opens the door by degrees.*) What is that? He is standing outside. He is not going downstairs. Is he hesitating? Can he— (*A letter drops into the box; then Krogstad's footsteps are heard, till they die away as he goes downstairs. Nora utters a stifled cry, and runs across the room to the table by the sofa. A short pause.*) In the letter box. (*Steals across to the hall door.*) There it lies—Torvald, Torvald, there is no hope for us now!

(*Mrs. Linde comes in from the room on the left, carrying the dress.*)

Mrs. Linde. There, I can't see anything more to mend now.

Would you like to try it on?

Nora (*in a hoarse whisper*). Christine, come here.

Mrs. Linde (*throwing the dress down on the sofa*). What is the matter with you? You look so agitated!

Nora. Come here. Do you see that letter? There, look—you can see it through the glass in the letter box.

Mrs. Linde. Yes, I see it.

Nora. That letter is from Krogstad.

Mrs. Linde. Nora—it was Krogstad who lent you the money!

Nora. Yes, and now Torvald will know all about it.

Mrs. Linde. Believe me, Nora, that's the best thing for both of you.

Nora. You don't know all. I forged a name.

Mrs. Linde. Good heavens—!

Nora. I only want to say this to you, Christine—you must be my witness.

Mrs. Linde. Your witness! What do you mean? What am I to—

Nora. If I should go out of my mind—and it might easily happen—

Mrs. Linde. Nora!

Nora. Or if anything else should happen to me—anything, for instance, that might prevent my being here—

Mrs. Linde. Nora! Nora! you are quite out of your mind.

Nora. And if it should happen that there were someone who wanted to take all the responsibility, all the blame, you understand—

Mrs. Linde. Yes, yes—but how can you suppose—?

Nora. Then you must be my witness, that it is not true, Christine. I am not out of my mind at all; I am in my right senses now, and I tell you no one else has known anything about it; I, and I alone, did the whole thing. Remember that.

Mrs. Linde. I will, indeed. But I don't understand all this.

Nora. How should you understand it? A wonderful thing is going to happen.

Mrs. Linde. A wonderful thing?

Nora. Yes, a wonderful thing! But it is so terrible. Christine, it *mustn't* happen, not for all the world.

Mrs. Linde. I will go at once and see Krogstad.

Nora. Don't go to him; he will do you some harm.

Mrs. Linde. There was a time when he would gladly do anything for my sake.

Nora. He?

Mrs. Linde. Where does he live?

Nora. How should I know? Yes—(*feeling in her pocket*)—here is his card. But the letter, the letter!

Helmer. (*calls from his room, knocking at the door*). Nora!

Nora. (*cries out anxiously*). Oh, what's that? What do you want?

Helmer. Don't be so frightened. We are not coming in; you have locked the door. Are you trying on your dress?

Nora. Yes, that's it. I look so nice, Torvald.

Mrs. Linde (*who has read the card*). I see he lives at the corner here.

Nora. Yes, but it's no use. It is hopeless. The letter is lying there in the box.

Mrs. Linde. And your husband keeps the key?

Nora. Yes, always.

Mrs. Linde. Krogstad must ask for his letter back unread, he must find some pretense—

Nora. But it is just at this time that Torvald generally—

Mrs. Linde. You must delay him. Go in to him in the meantime. I will come back as soon as I can. (*She goes out hurriedly through the hall door.*)

Nora (*goes to Helmer's door, opens it and peeps in*). Torvald!

Helmer (*from the inner room*). Well? May I venture at last to come into my own room again? Come along, Rank, now you will see— (*Halting in the doorway.*) But what is this?

Nora. What is what, dear?

Helmer. Rank led me to expect a splendid transformation.

Rank (*in the doorway*). I understood so, but evidently I was mistaken.

Nora. Yes, nobody is to have the chance of admiring me in my dress until tomorrow.

Helmer. But, my dear Nora, you look so worn out. Have you been practising too much?

Nora. No, I have not practised at all.

Helmer. But you will need to—

Nora. Yes, indeed I shall, Torvald. But I can't get on a bit without you to help me; I have absolutely forgotten the whole thing.

Helmer. Oh, we will soon work it up again.

Nora. Yes, help me, Torvald. Promise that you will! I am so nervous about it—all the people—. You must give yourself up to me entirely this evening. Not the tiniest bit of business—you mustn't even take a pen in your hand. Will you promise, Torvald dear?

Helmer. I promise. This evening I will be wholly and absolutely at your service, you helpless little mortal. Ah, by the way, first of all I will just— (*Goes toward the hall door.*)

Nora. What are you going to do there?

Helmer. Only see if any letters have come.

Nora. No, no! Don't do that, Torvald!

Helmer. Why not?

Nora. Torvald, please don't. There is nothing there.

Helmer. Well, let me look. (*Turns to go to the letter box. Nora, at the piano, plays the first bars of the tarantella. Helmer stops in the doorway.*) Aha!

Nora. I can't dance tomorrow if I don't practice with you.

Helmer (*going up to her*). Are you really so afraid of it, dear?

Nora. Yes, so dreadfully afraid of it. Let me practise at once; there is time now, before we go to dinner. Sit down and play for me, Torvald dear; criticise me and correct me as you play.

Helmer. With great pleasure, if you wish me to. (*Sits down at the* *piano.*)

Nora (*takes out of the box a tambourine and a long variegated shawl. She hastily drapes the shawl round her. Then she springs to the front of the stage and calls out*). Now play for me! I am going to dance!

(*Helmer plays and Nora dances. Rank stands by the piano behind Helmer and looks on.*)

Helmer (*as he plays*). Slower, slower!

Nora. I can't do it any other way.

Helmer. Not so violently, Nora!

Nora. This is the way.

Helmer (*stops playing*). No, no—that is not a bit right.

Nora (*laughing and swinging the tambourine*). Didn't I tell you so?

Rank. Let me play for her.

Helmer (*getting up*). Yes, do. I can correct her better then.

(*Rank sits down at the piano and plays. Nora dances more and more wildly. Helmer has taken up a position by the stove and during her dance gives her frequent instructions. She does not seem to hear him; her hair comes down and falls over her shoulders; she pays no attention to it but goes on dancing. Enter Mrs. Linde.*)

Mrs. Linde (*standing as if spellbound in the doorway*). Oh!

Nora (*as she dances*). Such fun, Christine!

Helmer. My dear darling Nora, you are dancing as if your life depended on it.

Nora. So it does.

Helmer. Stop, Rank; this is sheer madness. Stop, I tell you. (*Rank* *stops playing, and, Nora suddenly stands still. Helmer goes up to her.*) I could never have believed it. You have forgotten everything I taught you.

Nora (*throwing away the tambourine*). There, you see.

Helmer. You will want a lot of coaching.

Nora. Yes, you see how much I need it. You must coach me up to the last minute. Promise me that, Torvald!

Helmer. You can depend on me.

Nora. You must not think of anything but me, either today or tomorrow; you mustn't open a single letter—not even open the letter box—

Helmer. Ah, you are still afraid of that fellow——

Nora. Yes, indeed I am.

Helmer. Nora, I can tell from your looks that there is a letter from him lying there.

Nora. I don't know; I think there is; but you must not read anything of that kind now. Nothing horrid must come between us till this is all over.

Rank (*whispers to Helmer*). You mustn't contradict her.

Helmer (*taking her in his arms*). The child shall have her way. But to-morrow night, after you have danced—

Nora. Then you will be free. (*The Maid appears in the doorway to the right.*)

Maid. Dinner is served, ma'am.

Nora. We will have champagne, Helen.

Maid. Very good, ma'am. (*Exit.*)

Helmer. Hullo!—are we going to have a banquet?

Nora. Yes, a champagne banquet till the small hours. (*Calls out.*) And a few macaroons, Helen—lots, just for once!

Helmer. Come, come, don't be so wild and nervous. Be my own little skylark, as you used.

Nora. Yes, dear, I will. But go in now, and you too, Doctor Rank. Christine, you must, help me to do up my hair.

Rank (*whispers to Helmer as they go out*). I suppose there is nothing—she is not expecting anything?

Helmer. Far from it, my dear fellow; it is simply nothing more than this childish nervousness I was telling you of. (*They go into the right-hand room.*)

Nora. Well!

Mrs. Linde. Gone out of town.

Nora. I could tell from your face.

Mrs. Linde. He is coming home tomorrow evening. I wrote a note for him.

Nora. You should have let it alone; you must prevent nothing. After all, it is splendid to be waiting for a wonderful thing to happen.

Mrs. Linde. What is it that you are waiting for?

Nora. Oh, you wouldn't understand. Go in to them. I will come in a moment. (*Mrs. Linde goes into the dining-room. Nora stands still for a little while, as if to compose herself. Then she looks at her watch.*) Five o'clock. Seven hours till midnight; and then four-and-twenty hours till the next midnight. Then the tarantella will be over. Twenty-four and seven? Thirty-one hours to live.

Helmer (*from the doorway on the right*). Where's my little skylark?

Nora (*going to him with her arms outstretched*). Here she is!

ACT III

The same scene—The table has been placed in the middle of the stage, with chairs round it. A lamp is burning on the table. The door into the hall stands open. Dance music is heard in the room above. Mrs. Linde is sitting at the table idly turning over the leaves of a book; she tries to read but does not seem able to collect her thoughts. Every now and then she listens intently for a sound at the outer door.

Mrs. Linde (*looking at her watch*). Not yet—and the time is nearly up. If only he does not— (*Listens again.*) Ah, there he is. (*Goes into the hall and opens the outer door carefully. Light footsteps are heard on the stairs. She whispers.*) Come in. There is no one here.

Krogstad (*in the doorway*). I found a note from you at home. What does this mean?

Mrs. Linde. It is absolutely necessary that I should have a talk with you.

Krogstad. Really? And it is absolutely necessary that it should be here?

Mrs. Linde. It is impossible where I live; there is no private entrance to my rooms. Come in; we are quite alone. The maid is asleep, and the Helmers are at the dance upstairs.

Krogstad (*coming into the room*). Are the Helmers really at a dance tonight?

Mrs. Linde. Yes, why not?

Krogstad. Certainly—why not?

Mrs. Linde. Now, Nils, let us have a talk.

Krogstad. Can we two have anything to talk about?

Mrs. Linde. We have a great deal to talk about.

Krogstad. I shouldn't have thought so.

Mrs. Linde. No, you have never properly understood me.

Krogstad. Was there anything else to understand except what was obvious to all the world—a heartless woman jilts a man when a more lucrative chance turns up?

Mrs. Linde. Do you believe I am as absolutely heartless as all that? And do you believe that I did it with a light heart?

Krogstad. Didn't you?

Mrs. Linde. Nils, did you really think that?

Krogstad. If it were as you say, why did you write to me as you did at the time?

Mrs. Linde. I could do nothing else. As I had to break with you, it was my duty also to put an end to all that you felt for me.

Krogstad (*wringing his hands*). So that was it. And all this—only for the sake of money!

Mrs. Linde. You must not forget that I had a helpless mother and two little brothers. We couldn't wait for you, Nils; your prospects seemed hopeless then.

Krogstad. That may be so, but you had no right to throw me over for any-one else's sake.

Mrs. Linde. Indeed I don't know. Many a time did I ask myself if I had the right to do it.

Krogstad (*more gently*). When I lost you it was as if all the solid ground went from under my feet. Look at me now—I am a shipwrecked man clinging to a bit of wreckage.

Mrs. Linde. But help may be near.

Krogstad. It was near, but then you came and stood in my way.

Mrs. Linde. Unintentionally, Nils. It was only today that I learned it was your place I was going to take in the bank.

Krogstad. I believe you, if you say so. But now that you know it, are you not going to give it up to me?

Mrs. Linde. No, because that would not benefit you in the least.

Krogstad. Oh, benefit, benefit—I would have done it whether or no.

Mrs. Linde. I have learned to act prudently. Life, and hard, bitter necessity have taught me that.

Krogstad. And life has taught me not to believe in fine speeches.

Mrs. Linde. Then life has taught you something very reasonable. But deeds you must believe in.

Krogstad. What do you mean by that?

Mrs. Linde. You said you were like a shipwrecked man clinging to some wreckage.

Krogstad. I had good reason to say so.

Mrs. Linde. Well, I am like a shipwrecked woman clinging to some wreckage—no one to mourn for, no one to care for.

Krogstad. It was your own choice.

Mrs. Linde. There was no other choice, then.

Krogstad. Well, what now?

Mrs. Linde. Nils, how would it be if we two shipwrecked people could join forces?

Krogstad. What are you saying?

Mrs. Linde. Two on the same piece of wreckage would stand a better chance than each on their own.

Krogstad. Christine!

Mrs. Linde. What do you suppose brought me to town?

Krogstad. Do you mean that you gave me a thought?

Mrs. Linde. I could not endure life without work. All my life, as long as I can remember, I have worked, and it has been my greatest and only pleasure. But now I am quite alone in the world—my life is so dreadfully empty and I feel so forsaken. There is not the least pleasure in working for one's self. Nils, give me someone and something to work for.

Krogstad. I don't trust that. It is nothing but a woman's overstrained sense of generosity that prompts you to make such an offer of yourself.

Mrs. Linde. Have you ever noticed anything of the sort in me?

Krogstad. Could you really do it? Tell me—do you know all about my past life?

Mrs. Linde. Yes.

Krogstad. And do you know what they think of me here?

Mrs. Linde. You seemed to me to imply that with me you might have been quite another man.

Krogstad. I am certain of it.

Mrs. Linde. Is it too late now?

Krogstad. Christine, are you saying this deliberately? Yes, I am sure you are. I see it in your face. Have you really the courage, then—?

Mrs. Linde. I want to be a mother to someone, and your children need a mother. We two need each other. Nils, I have faith in your real character—I can dare anything with you.

Krogstad (*grasps her hands*). Thanks, thanks, Christine! Now I shall find a way to clear myself in the eyes of the world. Ah, but I forgot—

Mrs. Linde (*listening*). Hush! The Tarantella! Go, go!

Krogstad. Why? What is it?

Mrs. Linde. Do you hear them up there? When that is over we may expect them back.

Krogstad. Yes, yes—I will go. But it is all no use. Of course you are not aware what steps I have taken in the matter of the Helmers.

Mrs. Linde. Yes, I know all about that.

Krogstad. And in spite of that have you the courage to——?

Mrs. Linde. I understand very well to what lengths a man like you might be driven by despair.

Krogstad. If I could only undo what I have done!

Mrs. Linde. You cannot. Your letter is lying in the letter box now.

Krogstad. Are you sure of that?

Mrs. Linde. Quite sure, but——

Krogstad (*with a searching look at her*). Is that what it all means?—that you want to save your friend at any cost? Tell me frankly. Is that it?

Mrs. Linde. Nils, a woman who has once sold herself for another's sake, doesn't do it a second time.

Krogstad. I will ask for my letter back.

Mrs. Linde. No, no.

Krogstad. Yes, of course I will. I will wait here till Helmer comes; I will tell him he must give me my letter back—that it only concerns my dismissal—that he is not to read it—

Mrs. Linde. No, Nils, you must not recall your letter.

Krogstad. But, tell me, wasn't it for that very purpose that you asked me to meet you here?

Mrs. Linde. In my first moment of fright it was. But twenty-four hours have elapsed since then, and in that time I have witnessed incredible things in this house. Helmer must know all about it. This unhappy secret must be disclosed; they must have a complete understanding between them, which is impossible with all this concealment and falsehood going on.

Krogstad. Very well, if you will take the responsibility. But there is one thing I can do in any case, and I shall do it at once.

Mrs. Linde (*listening*). You must be quick and go! The dance is over; we are not safe a moment longer.

Krogstad. I will wait for you below.

Mrs. Linde. Yes, do. You must see me back to my door.

Krogstad. I have never had such an amazing piece of good fortune in my life! (*Goes out through the outer door. The door between the room and the hall remains open.*)

Mrs. Linde (*tidying up the room and laying her hat and cloak ready*). What a difference! What a difference! Someone to work for and live for—a home to bring comfort into. That I will do, indeed. I wish they would be quick and come. (*Listens.*) Ah, there they are now. I must put on my things. (*Takes up her hat and cloak. Helmer's and Nora's voices are heard outside; a key is turned, and Helmer brings Nora almost by force into the hall. She is in an Italian costume with a large black shawl round her; he is in evening dress, and a black domino which is flying open.*)

Nora (*hanging back in the doorway, and struggling with him*). No, no, no!—Don't take me in. I want to go upstairs again; I don't want to leave so early.

Helmer. But, my dearest Nora—

Nora. Please, Torvald dear—please, please—only an hour more.

Helmer. Not a single minute, my sweet Nora. You know that was our agreement. Come along into the room; you are catching cold standing there. (*He brings her gently into the room in spite of her resistance.*)

Mrs. Linde. Good evening.

Nora. Christine!

Helmer. You here so late, Mrs. Linde?

Mrs. Linde. Yes, you must excuse me; I was so anxious to see Nora in her dress.

Nora. Have you been sitting here waiting for me?

Mrs. Linde. Yes, unfortunately I came too late—you had already gone upstairs—and I thought I couldn't go away again without having seen you.

Helmer (*taking off Nora's shawl*). Yes, take a good look at her. I think she is worth looking at. Isn't she charming, Mrs. Linde?

Mrs. Linde. Yes, indeed she is.

Helmer. Doesn't she look remarkably pretty? Everyone thought so at the dance. But she is terribly self-willed, this sweet little person. What are we to do with her? You will hardly believe that I had almost to bring her away by force.

Nora. Torvald, you will repent not having let me stay, even if it were only for half an hour.

Helmer. Listen to her, Mrs. Linde! She had danced her Tarantella, and it had been a tremendous success, as it deserved—although possibly the performance was a trifle too realistic—a little more so, I mean, than was strictly compatible with the limitations of art. But never mind about that! The chief thing is, she had made a success—she had made a tremendous success. Do you think I was going to let her remain there after that and spoil the effect? No indeed! I took my charming little Capri maiden—my capricious little Capri maiden, I should say—on my arm, took one quick turn round the room, a curtsey on either side, and, as they say in novels, the beautiful apparition disappeared. An exit ought always to be effective, Mrs. Linde; but that is what I cannot make Nora understand. Pooh! this room is hot. (*Throws his domino on a chair and opens the door of his room.*) Hullo! it's all dark in here. Oh, of course—excuse me. (*He goes in, and lights some candles.*)

Nora (*in a hurried and breathless whisper*). Well?

Mrs. Linde. (*in a low voice*). I have had a talk with him.

Nora. Yes, and—

Mrs. Linde. Nora, you must tell your husband all about it.

Nora (*in an expressionless voice*). I knew it.

Mrs. Linde. You have nothing to be afraid of as far as Krogstad is concerned, but you must tell him.

Nora. I won't tell him.

Mrs. Linde. Then the letter will.

Nora. Thank you, Christine. Now I know what I must do. Hush!

Helmer (*coming in again*). Well, Mrs. Linde, have you admired her?

Mrs. Linde. Yes, and now I will say good night.

Helmer. What, already? Is this yours, this knitting?

Mrs. Linde (*taking it*). Yes, thank you. I had very nearly forgotten it.

Helmer. So you knit?

Mrs. Linde. Of course.

Helmer. Do you know, you ought to embroider.

Mrs. Linde. Really? Why?

Helmer. Yes, it's far more becoming. Let me show you. You hold the embroidery thus in your left hand and use the needle with the right—like this—with a long easy sweep. Do you see?

Mrs. Linde. Yes, perhaps—

Helmer. But in the case of knitting—that can never be anything but ungraceful; look here—the arms close together, the knitting needles going up and down—it has a sort of Chinese effect....That was really excellent champagne they gave us.

Mrs. Linde. Well—good night, Nora, and don't be self-willed anymore.

Helmer. That's right, Mrs. Linde.

Mrs. Linde. Good night, Mr. Helmer.

Helmer (*accompanying her to the door*). Good night, good night. I hope you will get home all right. I should be very happy to—but you haven't any great distance to go. Good night, good night. (*She goes out; he shuts the door after her and comes in again.*) Ah!—At last we have got rid of her. She is a frightful bore, that woman.

Nora. Aren't you very tired, Torvald?

Helmer. No, not in the least.

Nora. Nor sleepy?

Helmer. Not a bit. On the contrary I feel extraordinarily lively. And you?—You really look both tired and sleepy.

Nora. Yes, I am very tired. I want to go to sleep at once.

Helmer. There, you see it was quite right of me not to let you stay there any longer.

Nora. Everything you do is quite right, Torvald.

Helmer (*kissing her on the forehead*). Now my little skylark is speaking reasonably. Did you notice what good spirits Rank was in this evening?

Nora. Really? Was he? I didn't speak to him at all.

Helmer. And I very little, but I have not for a long time seen him in such good form. (*Looks for a while at her and then goes nearer to her.*) It is delightful to be at home by ourselves again, to be all alone with you—you fascinating, charming little darling!

Nora. Don't look at me like that, Torvald.

Helmer. Why shouldn't I look at my dearest treasure?—at all the beauty that is mine, all my very own?

Nora (*going to the other side of the table*). You mustn't say things like that to me tonight.

Helmer (*following her*). You have still got the Tarantella in your blood, I see. And it makes you more captivating than ever. Listen—the guests are beginning to go now. (*In a lower voice.*) Nora—soon the whole house will be quiet.

Nora. Yes, I hope so.

Helmer. Yes, my own darling Nora. Do you know, when I am out at a party with you like this, why I speak so little to you, keep away from you and only send a stolen glance in your direction now and then?—Do you know why I do that? It is because I make believe to myself that we are secretly in love and you are my secretly promised bride and that no one suspects there is anything between us.

Nora. Yes, yes—I know very well your thoughts are with me all the time.

Helmer. And when we are leaving and I am putting the shawl over your beautiful young shoulders—on your lovely neck—then I imagine that you are my young bride and that we have just come from our wedding and I am bringing you, for the first time, into our home—to be alone with you for the first time—quite alone with my shy little darling! All this evening I have longed for nothing but you. When I watched the seductive figures of the tarantella my blood was on fire; I could endure it no longer, and that was why I brought you down so early—

Nora. Go away, Torvald! You must let me go. I won't—

Helmer. What's that? You're joking, my little Nora! You won't—you won't? Am I not your husband—? (*A knock is heard at the outer door.*)

Nora (*starting*). Did you hear—?

Helmer (*going into the hall*). Who is it?

Rank (*outside*). It is me. May I come in for a moment?

Helmer (*in a fretful whisper*). Oh, what does he want now? (*Aloud.*) Wait a minute? (*Unlocks the door.*) Come, that's kind of you not to pass by our door.

Rank. I thought I heard your voice, and felt as if I should like to look in. (*With a swift glance round.*) Ah yes!—These dear familiar rooms. You are very happy and cosy in here, you two.

Helmer. It seems to me that you looked after yourself pretty well upstairs too.

Rank. Excellently. Why shouldn't I? Why shouldn't one enjoy everything in this world?—At any rate as much as one can, and as long as one can. The wine was capital—

Helmer. Especially the champagne.

Rank. So you noticed that too? It is almost incredible how much I managed to put away!

Nora. Torvald drank a great deal of champagne tonight, too.

Rank. Did he?

Nora. Yes, and he is always in such good spirits afterwards.

Rank. Well, why should one not enjoy a merry evening after a well-spent day?

Helmer. Well spent? I am afraid I can't take credit for that.

Rank (*clapping him on the back*). But I can, you know!

Nora. Doctor Rank, you must have been occupied with some scientific investigation today.

Rank. Exactly.

Helmer. Just listen!—Little Nora talking about scientific investigations!

Nora. And may I congratulate you on the result?

Rank. Indeed you may.

Nora. Was it favourable, then.

Rank. The best possible, for both doctor and patient—certainty.

Nora (*quickly and searchingly*). Certainty?

Rank. Absolute certainty. So wasn't I entitled to make a merry evening of it after that?

Nora. Yes, you certainly were, Doctor Rank.

Helmer. I think so too, so long as you don't have to pay for it in the morning.

Rank. Oh well, one can't have anything in this life without paying for it.

Nora. Doctor Rank—are you fond of fancy-dress balls?

Rank. Yes, if there is a fine lot of pretty costumes.

Nora. Tell me—what shall we two wear at the next?

Helmer. Little featherbrain!—are you thinking of the next already?

Rank. We two? Yes, I can tell you. You shall go as a good fairy—

Helmer. Yes, but what do you suggest as an appropriate costume for that?

Rank. Let your wife go dressed just as she is in everyday life.

Helmer. That was really very prettily turned. But can't you tell us what you will be?

Rank. Yes, my dear friend, I have quite made up my mind about that.

Helmer. Well?

Rank. At the next fancy-dress ball I shall be invisible.

Helmer. That's a good joke!

Rank. There is a big black hat—have you never heard of hats that make you invisible? If you put one on, no one can see you.

Helmer (*suppressing a smile*). Yes, you are quite right.

Rank. But I am clean forgetting what I came for. Helmer, give me a cigar—one of the dark Havanas.

Helmer. With the greatest pleasure. (*Offers him his case.*)

Rank (*takes a cigar and cuts off the end*). Thanks.

Nora (*striking a match*). Let me give you a light.

Rank. Thank you. (*She holds the match for him to light his cigar.*) And now good-bye!

Helmer. Good-bye, good-bye, dear old man!

Nora. Sleep well, Doctor Rank.

Rank. Thank you for that wish.

Nora. Wish me the same.

Rank. You? Well, if you want me to sleep well! And thanks for the light. (*He nods to them both and goes out.*)

Helmer (*in a subdued voice*). He has drunk more than he ought.

Nora (*absently*). Maybe. (*Helmer takes a bunch of keys out of his pocket and goes into the hall.*) Torvald! What are you going to do there?

Helmer. Empty the letter box; it is quite full; there will be no room to put the newspaper in tomorrow morning.

Nora. Are you going to work tonight?

Helmer. You know quite well I'm not. What is this? Someone has been at the lock.

Nora. At the lock?

Helmer. Yes, someone has. What can it mean? I should never have thought the maid.—Here is a broken hairpin. Nora, it is one of yours.

Nora (*quickly*). Then it must have been the children—

Helmer. Then you must get them out of those ways. There, at last I have got it open. (*Takes out the contents of the letter box, and calls to the kitchen.*) Helen! Helen, put out the light over the front door. (*Goes back into the room and shuts the door into the hall. He holds out his hand full of letters.*) Look at that—look what a heap of them there are. (*Turning them over.*) What on earth is that?

Nora (*at the window*). The letter—No! Torvald, no!

Helmer. Two cards—of Rank's.

Nora. Of Doctor Rank's?

Helmer (*looking at them*). Doctor Rank. They were on the top. He must have put them in when he went out.

Nora. Is there anything written on them?

Helmer. There is a black cross over the name. Look there— what an un-comfortable idea! It looks as if he were announcing his own death.

Nora. It is just what he is doing.

Helmer. What? Do you know anything about it? Has he said anything to you?

Nora. Yes. He told me that when the cards came it would be his leave-taking from us. He means to shut himself up and die.

Helmer. My poor old friend. Certainly I knew we should not have him very long with us. But so soon! And so he hides himself away like a wounded animal.

Nora. If it has to happen, it is best it should be without a word—don't you think so, Torvald?

Helmer (*walking up and down*). He has so grown into our lives. I can't think of him as having gone out of them. He, with his sufferings and his loneliness, was like a cloudy background to our sunlit happiness. Well, perhaps it is best so. For him, anyway. (*Standing still.*) And perhaps for us too, Nora. We two are thrown quite upon each other now. (*Puts his arms around her.*) My darling wife, I don't feel as if

I could hold you tight enough. Do you know, Nora, I have often wished that you might be threatened by some great danger, so that I might risk my life's blood, and everything, for your sake.

Nora (*disengages herself, and says firmly and decidedly*). Now you must read your letters, Torvald.

Helmer. No, no; not tonight. I want to be with you, my darling wife.

Nora. With the thought of your friend's death—

Helmer. You are right, it has affected us both. Something ugly has come between us—the thought of the horrors of death. We must try and rid our minds of that. Until then—we will each go to our own room.

Nora (*hanging on his neck*). Good night, Torvald—Good night!

Helmer (*kissing her on the forehead*). Good night, my little singing-bird. Sleep sound, Nora. Now I will read my letters through. (*He takes his letters and goes into his room, shutting the door after him.*)

Nora (*gropes distractedly about, seizes Helmer's domino, throws it round her, while she says in quick, hoarse, spasmodic whispers*). Never to see him again. Never! Never! (*Puts her shawl over her head.*) Never to see my children again either—never again. Never! Never!—Ah! the icy, black water—the unfathomable depths—If only it were over! He has got it now—now he is reading it. Good-bye, Torvald and my children! (*She is about to rush out through the hall, when Helmer opens his door* *hurriedly and stands with an open letter in his hand.*)

Helmer. Nora!

Nora. Ah!

Helmer. What is this? Do you know what is in this letter?

Nora. Yes, I know. Let me go! Let me get out!

Helmer (*holding her back*). Where are you going?

Nora (*trying to get free*). You shan't save me, Torvald!

Helmer (*reeling*). True? Is this true, that I read here? Horrible! No, no—it is impossible that it is true.

Nora. It is true. I have loved you above everything else in the world.

Helmer. Oh, don't let us have any silly excuses.

Nora (*taking a step towards him*). Torvald!

Helmer. Miserable creature—what have you done?

Nora. Let me go. You shall not suffer for my sake. You shall not take it upon yourself.

Helmer. No tragedy airs, please. (*Locks the hall door.*) Here you shall stay and give me an explanation. Do you understand what you have done? Answer me? Do you understand what you have done?

Nora (*looks steadily at him and says with a growing look of coldness in her face*). Yes, now I am beginning to understand thoroughly.

Helmer (*walking about the room*). What a horrible awakening! All these eight years—she who was my joy and pride—a hypocrite, a liar—worse, worse—a criminal! The unutterable ugliness of it all!—For shame! For shame!

(*Nora is silent and looks steadily at him. He stops in front of her.*) I ought to have suspected that something of the sort would happen. I ought to have foreseen it. All your father's want of principle—be silent!—all your father's want of principle has come out in you. No religion, no morality, no sense of duty—How I am punished for having winked at what he did! I did it for your sake, and this is how you repay me.

Nora. Yes, that's just it.

Helmer. Now you have destroyed all my happiness. You have ruined all my future. It is horrible to think of! I am in the power of an unscrupulous man; he can do what he likes with me, ask anything he likes of me, give me any orders he pleases—I dare not refuse. And I must sink to such miserable depths because of a thoughtless woman!

Nora. When I am out of the way, you will be free.

Helmer. No fine speeches, please. Your father had always plenty of those ready, too. What good would it be to me if you were out of the way, as you say? Not the slightest. He can make the affair known everywhere; and if he does, I may be falsely suspected of having been a party to your criminal action. Very likely people will think I was behind it all—that it was I who prompted you! And I have to thank you for all this—you whom I have cherished during the whole of our married life. Do you understand now what it is you have done for me?

Nora (*coldly and quietly*). Yes.

Helmer. It is so incredible that I can't take it in. But we must come to some understanding. Take off that shawl. Take it off, I tell you. I must try and appease him in some way or another. The matter must be hushed up at any cost. And as for you and me, it must appear as if everything between us were as before—but naturally only in the eyes of the world. You will still remain in my house, that is a matter of course. But I shall not allow you to bring up the children; I dare not trust them to you. To think that I should be obliged to say so to one whom I have loved so dearly, and whom I still——. No, that is all over. From this moment happiness is not the question; all that concerns us is to save the remains, the fragments, the appearance—

(*A ring is heard at the front-door bell.*)

Helmer (*with a start*). What is that? So late! Can the worst——? Can he——? Hide yourself, Nora. Say you are ill.

(*Nora stands motionless. Helmer goes and unlocks the hall door.*)

Maid (*half-dressed, comes to the door*). A letter for the mistress.

Helmer. Give it to me. (*Takes the letter, and shuts the door.*) Yes, it is from him. You shall not have it; I will read it myself.

Nora. Yes, read it.

Helmer (*standing by the lamp*). I scarcely have the courage to do it. It may mean ruin for both of us. No, I must know. (*Tears open the letter, runs his eye over a few lines, looks at a paper enclosed, and gives a shout of joy.*) Nora! (*She looks at him, questioningly.*) Nora! No, I must read it once again——. Yes, it is true! I am saved! Nora, I am saved!

Nora. And I?

Helmer. You too, of course; we are both saved, both saved, both you and I. Look, he sends you your bond back. He says he regrets and repents—that a happy change in his life—never mind what he says! We are saved, Nora! No one can do anything to you. Oh, Nora, Nora!—No, first I must destroy these hateful things. Let me see—. (*Takes a look at the bond.*) No, no, I won't look at it. The whole thing shall be nothing but a bad dream to me. (*Tears up the bond and both letters, throws them all into the stove, and watches them burn.*) There—now it doesn't exist any longer. He says that since Christmas Eve you—. These must have been three dreadful days for you, Nora.

Nora. I have fought a hard fight these three days.

Helmer. And suffered agonies, and seen no way out but—. No, we won't call any of the horrors to mind. We will only shout with joy and keep saying, "It's all over! It's all over!" Listen to me, Nora. You don't seem to realise that it is all over. What is this?—Such a cold, set face! My poor little Nora, I quite understand; you don't feel as if you could believe that I have forgiven you. But it is true, Nora, I swear it; I have forgiven you everything. I know that what you did you did out of love for me.

Nora. That is true.

Helmer. You have loved me as a wife ought to love her

husband. Only you had not sufficient knowledge to judge of the means you used. But do you suppose you are any the less dear to me because you don't understand how to act on your own responsibility? No, no; only lean on me; I will advise you and direct you. I should not be a man if this womanly helplessness did not just give you a double attractiveness in my eyes. You must not think anymore about the hard things I said in my first moment of consternation, when I thought everything was going to overwhelm me. I have forgiven you, Nora; I swear to you I have forgiven you.

Nora. Thank you for your forgiveness. (*She goes out through the door to the right.*)

Helmer. No, don't go——. (*Looks in.*) What are you doing in there?

Nora (*from within*). Taking off my fancy dress.

Helmer (*standing at the open door*). Yes, do. Try and calm yourself and make your mind easy again, my frightened little singing bird. Be at rest, and feel secure; I have broad wings to shelter you under. (*Walks up and down by the door.*) How warm and cosy our home is, Nora. Here is shelter for you; here I will protect you like a hunted dove that I have saved from a hawk's claws; I will bring peace to your poor beating heart. It will come, little by little, Nora, believe me. To-morrow morning you will look upon it all quite differently; soon everything will be just as it was before.

Very soon you won't need me to assure you that I have forgiven you; you will yourself feel the certainty that I have done so. Can you suppose I should ever think of such a thing as repudiating you or even reproaching you? You have no idea what a true man's heart is like, Nora. There is something so indescribably sweet and satisfying, to a man, in the knowledge that he has forgiven his wife—forgiven her freely, and with all his heart. It seems as if that had made her, as it were, doubly his own; he has given her a new life, so to speak; and she has in a way become both wife and child to him. So you shall be for me after this, my little scared, helpless darling. Have no anxiety about anything, Nora; only be frank and open with me, and I will serve as will and conscience both to you——. What is this? Not gone to bed? Have you changed your things?

Nora (*in everyday dress*). Yes, Torvald, I have changed my things now.

Helmer. But what for?—So late as this.

Nora. I shall not sleep tonight.

Helmer. But, my dear Nora—

Nora (*looking at her watch*). It is not so very late. Sit down here, Torvald. You and I have much to say to one another. (*She sits down at one side of the table.*)

Helmer. Nora—what is this?—This cold, set face?

Nora. Sit down. It will take some time; I have a lot to talk over with you.

Helmer (*sits down at the opposite side of the table*). You alarm me, Nora!—And I don't understand you.

Nora. No, that is just it. You don't understand me, and I have never understood you either—before tonight. No, you mustn't interrupt me. You must simply listen to what I say. Torvald, this is a settling of accounts.

Helmer. What do you mean by that?

Nora (*after a short silence*). Isn't there one thing that strikes you as strange in our sitting here like this?

Helmer. What is that?

Nora. We have been married now eight years. Does it not occur to you that this is the first time we two, you and I, husband and wife, have had a serious conversation?

Helmer. What do you mean, serious?

Nora. In all these eight years—longer than that—from the very beginning of our acquaintance, we have never exchanged a word on any serious subject.

Helmer. Was it likely that I would be continually and forever telling you about worries that you could not help me to bear?

Nora. I am not speaking about business matters. I say that we have never sat down in earnest together to try and get at the bottom of anything.

Helmer. But, dearest Nora, would it have been any good to you?

Nora. That is just it; you have never understood me. I have been greatly wronged, Torvald—first by Papa and then by you.

Helmer. What! By us two—by us two, who have loved you better than anyone else in in the world?

Nora (*shaking her head*). You have never loved me. You have only thought it pleasant to be in love with me.

Helmer. Nora, what do I hear you saying?

Nora. It is perfectly true, Torvald. When I was at home with Papa, he told me his opinion about everything, and so I had the same opinions; and if I differed from him I concealed the fact, because he would not have liked it. He called me his doll-child, and he played with me just as I used to play with my dolls. And when I came to live with you—

Helmer. What sort of an expression is that to use about our marriage?

Nora (*undisturbed*). I mean that I was simply transferred from Papa's hands into yours. You arranged everything according to your own taste and so I got the same tastes as you—or else I pretended to. I am really not quite sure which—I think sometimes the one and sometimes the other. When I look back on it, it seems to me as if I had been living here like a poor woman—just from hand to mouth. I have existed merely to perform tricks for you, Torvald. But you would have it so. You and Papa have committed a great sin against me. It is your fault that I have made nothing of my life.

Helmer. How unreasonable and how ungrateful you are, Nora! Have you not been happy here?

Nora. No, I have never been happy. I thought I was, but it has never really been so.

Helmer. Not—not happy!

Nora. No, only merry. And you have always been so kind to me. But our home has been nothing but a playroom. I have been your doll-wife, just as at home I was papa's doll-child; and here the children have been my dolls. I thought it great fun when you played with me, just as they thought it great fun when I played with them. That is what our marriage has been, Torvald.

Helmer. There is some truth in what you say—exaggerated and strained as your view of it is. But for the future it shall be different. Playtime shall be over, and lesson time shall begin.

Nora. Whose lessons? Mine, or the children's?

Helmer. Both yours and the children's, my darling Nora.

Nora. Alas, Torvald, you are not the man to educate me into being a proper wife for you.

Helmer. And you can say that!

Nora. And I—how am I fitted to bring up the children?

Helmer. Nora!

Nora. Didn't you say so yourself a little while ago—that you dare not trust me to bring them up?

Helmer. In a moment of anger! Why do you pay any heed to that?

Nora. Indeed, you were perfectly right. I am not fit for the task. There is another task I must undertake first. I must try and educate myself—you are not the man to help me in that. I must do that for myself. And that is why I am going to leave you now.

Helmer (*springing up*). What do you say?

Nora. I must stand quite alone if I am to understand myself and everything about me. It is for that reason that I cannot remain with you any longer.

Helmer. Nora, Nora!

Nora. I am going away from here now, at once. I am sure Christine will take me in for the night.

Helmer. You are out of your mind! I won't allow it! I forbid you!

Nora. It is no use forbidding me anything any longer. I will take with me what belongs to myself. I will take nothing from you, either now or later.

Helmer. What sort of madness is this!

Nora. Tomorrow I shall go home—I mean to my old home. It will be easiest for me to find something to do there.

Helmer. You blind, foolish woman!

Nora. I must try and get some sense, Torvald.

Helmer. To desert your home, your husband and your children! And you don't consider what people will say!

Nora. I cannot consider that at all. I only know that it is necessary for me.

Helmer. It's shocking. This is how you would neglect your most sacred duties.

Nora. What do you consider my most sacred duties?

Helmer. Do I need to tell you that? Are they not your duties to your husband and your children?

Nora. I have other duties just as sacred.

Helmer. That you have not. What duties could those be?

Nora. Duties to myself.

Helmer. Before all else, you are a wife and mother.

Nora. I don't believe that any longer. I believe that before all else I am a reasonable human being, just as you are—or, at all events, that I must try and become one. I know quite well, Torvald, that most people would think you right, and that views of that kind are to be found in books; but I can no longer content myself with what most people say, or with what is found in books. I must think over things for myself and get to understand them.

Helmer. Can you not understand your place in your own home? Have you not a reliable guide in such matters as that?—Have you no religion?

Nora. I am afraid, Torvald, I do not exactly know what religion is.

Helmer. What are you saying?

Nora. I know nothing but what the clergyman said when I

went to be confirmed. He told us that religion was this and that and the other. When I am away from all this and am alone, I will look into that matter too. I will see if what the clergyman said is true, or at all events if it is true for me.

Helmer. This is unheard of in a girl of your age! But if religion cannot lead you aright, let me try and awaken your conscience. I suppose you have some moral sense? Or—answer me—am I to think you have none?

Nora. I assure you, Torvald, that is not an easy question to answer. I really don't know. The thing perplexes me altogether. I only know that you and I look at it in quite a different light. I am learning, too, that the law is quite another thing from what I supposed; but I find it impossible to convince myself that the law is right. According to it a woman has no right to spare her old dying father, or to save her husband's life. I can't believe that.

Helmer. You talk like a child. You don't understand the conditions of the world in which you live.

Nora. No, I don't. But now I am going to try. I am going to see if I can make out who is right, the world or I.

Helmer. You are ill, Nora; you are delirious; I almost think you are out of your mind.

Nora. I have never felt my mind so clear and certain as tonight.

Helmer. And is it with a clear and certain mind that you forsake your husband and your children?

Nora. Yes, it is.

Helmer. Then there is only one possible explanation.

Nora. What is that?

Helmer. You do not love me anymore.

Nora. No, that is just it.

Helmer. Nora!—And you can say that?

Nora. It gives me great pain, Torvald, for you have always been so kind to me, but I cannot help it. I do not love you anymore.

Helmer (*regaining his composure*). Is that a clear and certain conviction too?

Nora. Yes, absolutely clear and certain. That is the reason why I will not stay here any longer.

Helmer. And can you tell me what I have done to forfeit your love?

Nora. Yes, indeed I can. It was tonight, when the wonderful thing did not happen; then I saw you were not the man I had thought you.

Helmer. Explain yourself better—I don't understand you.

Nora. I have waited so patiently for eight years; for, goodness knows, I knew very well that wonderful things don't happen every day. Then this horrible misfortune came upon me, and then I felt quite certain that the wonderful thing was going to happen at last. When Krogstad's letter was lying out there never for a moment did I imagine that you would consent to accept this man's conditions. I was so absolutely certain that you would say to him: Publish the thing to the whole world. And when that was done—

Helmer. Yes, what then?—When I had exposed my wife to shame and disgrace?

Nora. When that was done, I was so absolutely certain, you would come forward and take everything upon yourself, and say: I am the guilty one.

Helmer. Nora—!

Nora. You mean that I would never have accepted such a sacrifice on your part? No, of course not. But what would my assurances have been worth against yours? That was the wonderful thing which I hoped for and feared; and it was to prevent that that I wanted to kill myself.

Helmer. I would gladly work night and day for you, Nora—bear sorrow and want for your sake. But no man would sacrifice his honor for the one he loves.

Nora. It is a thing hundreds of thousands of women have done.

Helmer. Oh, you think and talk like a heedless child.

Nora. Maybe. But you neither think nor talk like the man I could bind myself to. As soon as your fear was over—and it was not fear for what threatened me, but for what might happen to you—when the whole thing was past, as far as you were concerned it was exactly as if nothing at all had happened. Exactly as before, I was your little skylark, your doll, which you would in future treat with doubly gentle care, because it was so brittle and fragile. (*Getting up.*) Torvald—it was then it dawned upon me that for eight years I had been living here with a strange man and had borne him three children. Oh! I can't bear to think of it! I could tear myself into little bits!

Helmer (*sadly*). I see, I see. An abyss has opened between us—there is no denying it. But, Nora, would it not be possible to fill it up?

Nora. As I am now, I am no wife for you.

Helmer. I have it in me to become a different man.

Nora. Perhaps—if your doll is taken away from you.

Helmer. But to part! To part from you! No, no, Nora, I can't understand that idea.

Nora (*going out to the right*). That makes it all the more certain that it must be done. (*She comes back with her cloak and hat and a small bag which she puts on a chair by the table.*)

Helmer. Nora, Nora, not now! Wait till tomorrow.

Nora (*putting on her cloak*). I cannot spend the night in a strange man's room.

Helmer. But can't we live here like brother and sister—?

Nora (*putting on her hat*). You know very well that would not last long. (*Puts the shawl round her.*) Good-bye, Torvald. I won't see the little ones. I know they are in better hands than mine. As I am now, I can be of no use to them.

Helmer. But someday, Nora—someday?

Nora. How can I tell? I have no idea what is going to become of me.

Helmer. But you are my wife, whatever becomes of you.

Nora. Listen, Torvald. I have heard that when a wife deserts her husband's house, as I am doing now, he is legally freed from all obligations towards her. In any case I set you free from all your obligations. You are not to feel yourself bound in the slightest way, anymore than I shall. There must be perfect freedom on both sides. See, here is your ring back. Give me mine.

Helmer. That too?

Nora. That too.

Helmer. Here it is.

Nora. That's right. Now it is all over. I have put the keys here. The maids know all about everything in the house—better than I do. Tomorrow, after I have left her, Christine will come here and pack up my own things that I brought with me from home. I will have them sent after me.

Helmer. All over! All over! Nora, shall you never think of me again?

Nora. I know I shall often think of you and the children and this house.

Helmer. May I write to you, Nora?

Nora. No—never. You must not do that.

Helmer. But at least let me send you—

Nora. Nothing—nothing.

Helmer. Let me help you if you are in want.

Nora. No. I can receive nothing from a stranger.

Helmer. Nora—can I never be anything more than a stranger to you?

Nora (*taking her bag*). Ah, Torvald, the most wonderful thing of all would have to happen.

Helmer. Tell me what that would be!

Nora. Both you and I would have to be so changed that—. Oh, Torvald, I don't believe any longer in wonderful things happening.

Helmer. But I will believe in it. Tell me. So changed that—?

Nora. That our life together would be a real wedlock. Goodbye. (*She goes out through the hall.*)

Helmer (*sinks down on a chair at the door and buries his face in his hands*). Nora! Nora! (*Looks round and rises.*) Empty. She is gone. (*A hope flashes across his mind.*) The most wonderful thing of all—?

(*The sound of a door shutting is heard from below.*)

The End

AN ENEMY OF THE PEOPLE

The Characters

Dr. Thomas Stockmann, Medical Officer of the Municipal Baths

Mrs. Stockmann, his wife

Petra, their daughter, a teacher

Ejlif & Morten, their sons, aged 13 and 10 respectively

Peter Stockmann, the Doctor's elder brother, Mayor of the Town and Chief Constable, Chairman of the Baths' Committee, etc.

Morten Kiil, a tanner, Mrs. Stockmann's adoptive father

Hovstad, editor of the "People's Messenger."

Billing, sub-editor

Captain Horster

Aslaksen, a printer

Men of various conditions and occupations, a few women, and a troop of schoolboys—the audience at a public meeting

(*The action takes place in a coastal town in southern Norway.*)

ACT I

Scene.—Dr. Stockmann's sitting-room. It is evening. The room is plainly but neatly appointed and furnished. In the right-hand wall are two doors; the farther leads out to the hall, the nearer to the doctor's study. In the left-hand wall, opposite the door leading to the hall, is a door leading to the other rooms occupied by the family. In the middle of the same wall stands the stove, and, further forward, a couch with a looking-glass hanging over it and an oval table in front of it. On the table, a lighted lamp, with a lampshade. At the back of the room, an open door leads to the dining-room. Billing is seen sitting at the dining table, on which a lamp is burning. He has a napkin tucked under his chin, and Mrs. Stockmann is standing by the table handing him a large plate full of roast beef. The other places at the table are empty, and the table somewhat in disorder, evidently a meal having recently been finished.

Mrs. Stockmann. You see, if you come an hour late, Mr. Billing, you have to put up with cold meat.

Billing (*as he eats*). It is uncommonly good, thank you—

remarkably good.

Mrs. Stockmann. My husband makes such a point of having his meals punctually, you know.

Billing. That doesn't affect me a bit. Indeed, I almost think I enjoy a meal all the better when I can sit down and eat all by myself, and undisturbed.

Mrs. Stockmann. Oh well, as long as you are enjoying it——. (*Turns to the hall door, listening.*) I expect that is Mr. Hovstad coming too.

Billing. Very likely.

(*Peter Stockmann comes in. He wears an overcoat and his official hat, and carries a stick.*)

Peter Stockmann. Good evening, Katherine.

Mrs. Stockmann (*coming forward into the sitting-room*). Ah, good evening—is it you? How good of you to come up and see us!

Peter Stockmann. I happened to be passing, and so—— (*looks into the dining-room*). But you have company with you, I see.

Mrs. Stockmann (*a little embarrassed*). Oh, no—it was quite by chance he came in. (*Hurriedly.*) Won't you come in and have something, too?

Peter Stockmann. I! No, thank you. Good gracious—hot meat at night! Not with my digestion.

Mrs. Stockmann. Oh, but just once in a way—

Peter Stockmann. No, no, my dear lady; I stick to my tea and bread and butter. It is much more wholesome in the long run—and a little more economical, too.

Mrs. Stockmann (*smiling*). Now you mustn't think that Thomas and I are spendthrifts.

Peter Stockmann. Not you, my dear; I would never think that of you. (*Points to the Doctor's study.*) Is he not at home?

Mrs. Stockmann. No, he went out for a little turn after supper—he and the boys.

Peter Stockmann. I doubt if that is a wise thing to do. (*Listens.*) I fancy I hear him coming now.

Mrs. Stockmann. No, I don't think it is he. (*A knock is heard at the door.*) Come in! (*Hovstad comes in from the hall.*) Oh, it is you, Mr. Hovstad!

Hovstad. Yes, I hope you will forgive me, but I was delayed at the printers. Good evening, Mr. Mayor.

Peter Stockmann (*bowing a little distantly*). Good evening. You have come on business, no doubt.

Hovstad. Partly. It's about an article for the paper.

Peter Stockmann. So I imagined. I hear my brother has become a prolific contributor to the "People's Messenger."

Hovstad. Yes, he is good enough to write in the "People's Messenger" when he has any home truths to tell.

Mrs. Stockmann (*to Hovstad*). But won't you—? (*Points to the dining-room.*)

Peter Stockmann. Quite so, quite so. I don't blame him in the least, as a writer, for addressing himself to the quarters where he will find the readiest sympathy. And, besides that, I personally have no reason to bear any ill will to your paper, Mr. Hovstad.

Hovstad. I quite agree with you.

Peter Stockmann. Taking one thing with another, there is an excellent spirit of toleration in the town—an admirable municipal spirit. And it all springs from the fact of our having a great common interest to unite us—an interest that is in an equally high degree the concern of every right-minded citizen—

Hovstad. The Baths, yes.

Peter Stockmann. Exactly—our fine, new, handsome Baths. Mark my words, Mr. Hovstad—the Baths will become the focus of our municipal life! Not a doubt of it!

Mrs. Stockmann. That is just what Thomas says.

Peter Stockmann. Think how extraordinarily the place has developed within the last year or two! Money has been flowing in, and there is some life and some business doing in the town. Houses and landed property are rising in value every day.

Hovstad. And unemployment is diminishing,

Peter Stockmann. Yes, that is another thing. The burden on the poor rates has been lightened, to the great relief of the propertied classes; and that relief will be even greater if only we get a really good summer this year, and lots of visitors—plenty of invalids, who will make the Baths talked about.

Hovstad. And there is a good prospect of that, I hear.

Peter Stockmann. It looks very promising. Inquiries about apartments and that sort of thing are reaching us, every day.

Hovstad. Well, the doctor's article will come in very suitably.

Peter Stockmann. Has he been writing something just lately?

Hovstad. This is something he wrote in the winter; a recommendation of the Baths—an account of the excellent sanitary conditions here. But I held the article over, temporarily.

Peter Stockmann. Ah,—some little difficulty about it, I suppose?

Hovstad. No, not at all; I thought it would be better to wait until the spring, because it is just at this time that people begin to think seriously about their summer quarters.

Peter Stockmann. Quite right; you were perfectly right, Mr. Hovstad.

Hovstad. Yes, Thomas is really indefatigable when it is a question of the Baths.

Peter Stockmann. Well remember, he is the Medical Officer to the Baths.

Hovstad. Yes, and what is more, they owe their existence to him.

Peter Stockmann. To him? Indeed! It is true I have heard from time to time that some people are of that opinion. At the same time I must say I imagined that I took a modest part in the enterprise.

Mrs. Stockmann. Yes, that is what Thomas is always saying.

Hovstad. But who denies it, Mr. Stockmann? You set the thing going and made a practical concern of it; we all know that. I only meant that the idea of it came first from the doctor.

Peter Stockmann. Oh, ideas yes! My brother has had plenty of them in his time—unfortunately. But when it is a question of putting an idea into practical shape, you have to apply to a man of different mettle, Mr. Hovstad. And I certainly should have thought that in this house at least—

Mrs. Stockmann. My dear Peter—

Hovstad. How can you think that—?

Mrs. Stockmann. Won't you go in and have something, Mr. Hovstad? My husband is sure to be back directly.

Hovstad. Thank you, perhaps just a morsel. (*Goes into the dining-room.*)

Peter Stockmann (*lowering his voice a little*). It is a curious thing that these farmers' sons never seem to lose their want of tact.

Mrs. Stockmann. Surely it is not worth bothering about! Cannot you and Thomas share the credit as brothers?

Peter Stockmann. I should have thought so; but apparently some people are not satisfied with a share.

Mrs. Stockmann. What nonsense! You and Thomas get on so capitally together. (*Listens.*) There he is at last, I think. (*Goes out and opens the door leading to the hall.*)

Dr. Stockmann (*laughing and talking outside*). Look here—here is another guest for you, Katherine. Isn't that jolly! Come in, Captain Horster; hang your coat up on this peg. Ah, you don't wear an overcoat. Just think, Katherine; I met him in the street and could hardly persuade him to come up! (*Captain Horster comes into the room and greets Mrs. Stockmann. He is followed by Dr. Stockmann.*) Come along in, boys. They are ravenously hungry again, you know. Come along, Captain Horster; you must have a slice of beef. (*Pushes Horster into the dining-room. Ejlif and Morten go in after them.*)

Mrs. Stockmann. But, Thomas, don't you see—?

Dr. Stockmann (*turning in the doorway*). Oh, is it you, Peter? (*Shakes hands with him.*) Now that is very delightful.

Peter Stockmann. Unfortunately I must go in a moment—

Dr. Stockmann. Rubbish! There is some toddy just coming in. You haven't forgotten the toddy, Katherine?

Mrs. Stockmann. Of course not; the water is boiling now. (*Goes into the dining-room.*)

Peter Stockmann. Toddy too!

Dr. Stockmann. Yes, sit down and we will have it comfortably.

Peter Stockmann. Thanks, I never care about an evening's drinking.

Dr. Stockmann. But this isn't an evening's drinking.

Peter Stockmann. It seems to me—. (*Looks towards the dining-room.*) It is extraordinary how they can put away all that food.

Dr. Stockmann (*rubbing his hands*). Yes, isn't it splendid to see young people eat? They have always got an appetite, you know! That's as it should be. Lots of food—to build up their strength! They are the people who are going to stir up the fermenting forces of the future, Peter.

Peter Stockmann. May I ask what they will find here to "stir up," as you put it?

Dr. Stockmann. Ah, you must ask the young people that—when the times comes. We shan't be able to see it, of course. That stands to reason—two old fogies, like us.

Peter Stockmann. Really, really! I must say that is an extremely odd expression to—

Dr. Stockmann. Oh, you mustn't take me too literally, Peter. I am so heartily happy and contented, you know. I think it is such an extraordinary piece of good fortune to be in the middle of all this growing, germinating life. It is a splendid time to live in! It is as if a whole new world were being created around one.

Peter Stockmann. Do you really think so?

Dr. Stockmann. Ah, naturally you can't appreciate it as keenly as I. You have lived all your life in these surroundings, and your impressions have been blunted. But I, who have been buried all these years in my little corner up north, almost without ever seeing a stranger who might bring new ideas with him—well, in my case it has just the same effect as if I had been transported into the middle of a crowded city.

Peter Stockmann. Oh, a city—!

Dr. Stockmann. I know, I know; it is all cramped enough here, compared with many other places. But there is life here—there is promise—there are innumerable things to work for and fight for; and that is the main thing. (*Calls.*) Katherine, hasn't the postman been here?

Mrs. Stockmann (*from the dining-room*). No.

Dr. Stockmann. And then to be comfortably off, Peter! That is something one learns to value, when one has been on the brink of starvation, as we have.

Peter Stockmann. Oh, surely—

Dr. Stockmann. Indeed I can assure you we have often been very hard put to it, up there. And now to be able to live like a lord! Today, for instance, we had roast beef for dinner—and, what is more, for supper too. Won't you come and have a little bit? Or let me show it you, at any rate? Come here—

Peter Stockmann. No, no—not for worlds!

Dr. Stockmann. Well, but just come here then. Do you see, we have got a table-cover?

Peter Stockmann. Yes, I noticed it.

Dr. Stockmann. And we have got a lamp-shade too. Do you see? All out of Katherine's savings! It makes the room so cosy. Don't you think so? Just stand here for a moment—no, no, not there—just here, that's it! Look now, when you get the light on it altogether. I really think it looks very nice, doesn't it?

Peter Stockmann. Oh, if you can afford luxuries of this kind—

Dr. Stockmann. Yes, I can afford it now. Katherine tells me I earn almost as much as we spend.

Peter Stockmann. Almost—yes!

Dr. Stockmann. But a scientific man must live in a little bit of style. I am quite sure an ordinary civil servant spends more in a year than I do.

Peter Stockmann. I daresay. A civil servant—a man in a well-paid position—

Dr. Stockmann. Well, any ordinary merchant, then! A man in that position spends two or three times as much as—

Peter Stockmann. It just depends on circumstances.

Dr. Stockmann. At all events I assure you I don't waste money unprofitably. But I can't find it in my heart to deny myself the pleasure of entertaining my friends. I need that sort of thing, you know. I have lived for so long shut out of it all, that it is a necessity of life to me to mix with young, eager, ambitious men, men of liberal and active minds; and that describes every one of those fellows who are enjoying their supper in there. I wish you knew more of Hovstad—

Peter Stockmann. By the way, Hovstad was telling me he was going to print another article of yours.

Dr. Stockmann. An article of mine?

Peter Stockmann. Yes, about the Baths. An article you wrote in the winter.

Dr. Stockmann. Oh, that one! No, I don't intend that to appear just for the present.

Peter Stockmann. Why not? It seems to me that this would be the most opportune moment.

Dr. Stockmann. Yes, very likely—under normal conditions. (*Crosses the room.*)

Peter Stockmann (*following him with his eyes*). Is there anything abnormal about the present conditions?

Dr. Stockmann (*standing still*). To tell you the truth, Peter, I can't say just at this moment—at all events not tonight. There may be much that is very abnormal about the present conditions—and it is possible there may be nothing abnormal about them at all. It is quite possible it may be merely my imagination.

Peter Stockmann. I must say it all sounds most mysterious. Is there something going on that I am to be kept in ignorance of? I should have imagined that I, as Chairman of the governing body of the Baths—

Dr. Stockmann. And I should have imagined that I—. Oh, come, don't let us fly out at one another, Peter.

Peter Stockmann. Heaven forbid! I am not in the habit of flying out at people, as you call it. But I am entitled to request most emphatically that all arrangements shall be made in a businesslike manner, through the proper channels, and shall be dealt with by the legally constituted authorities. I can allow no going behind our backs by any roundabout means.

Dr. Stockmann. Have I ever at any time tried to go behind your backs?

Peter Stockmann. You have an ingrained tendency to take your own way, at all events; and, that is almost equally inadmissible in a well ordered community. The individual ought undoubtedly to acquiesce in subordinating himself to the community—or, to speak more accurately, to the authorities who have the care of the community's welfare.

Dr. Stockmann. Very likely. But what the deuce has all this got to do with me?

Peter Stockmann. That is exactly what you never appear to be willing to learn, my dear Thomas. But, mark my words, some day you will have to suffer for it—sooner or later. Now I have told you. Good-bye.

Dr. Stockmann. Have you taken leave of your senses? You are on the wrong scent altogether.

Peter Stockmann. I am not usually that. You must excuse me now if I— (*calls into the dining-room*). Good night, Katherine. Good night, gentlemen. (*Goes out.*)

Mrs. Stockmann (*coming from the dining-room*). Has he gone?

Dr. Stockmann. Yes, and in such a bad temper.

Mrs. Stockmann. But, dear Thomas, what have you been doing to him again?

Dr. Stockmann. Nothing at all. And, anyhow, he can't oblige me to make my report before the proper time.

Mrs. Stockmann. What have you got to make a report to him about?

Dr. Stockmann. Hm! Leave that to me, Katherine. It is an extraordinary thing that the postman doesn't come.

(*Hovstad, Billing and Horster have got up from the table and come into the sitting-room. Ejlif and Morten come in after them.*)

Billing (*stretching himself*). Ah!—one feels a new man after a meal like that.

Hovstad. The mayor wasn't in a very sweet temper tonight, then.

Dr. Stockmann. It is his stomach; he has wretched digestion.

Hovstad. I rather think it was us two of the "People's Messenger" that he couldn't digest.

Mrs. Stockmann. I thought you came out of it pretty well with him.

Hovstad. Oh yes; but it isn't anything more than a sort of truce.

Billing. That is just what it is! That word sums up the situation.

Dr. Stockmann. We must remember that Peter is a lonely man, poor chap. He has no home comforts of any kind; nothing but everlasting business. And all that infernal weak tea wash that he pours into himself! Now then, my boys, bring chairs up to the table. Aren't we going to have that today, Katherine?

Mrs. Stockmann (*going into the dining-room*). I am just getting it.

Dr. Stockmann. Sit down here on the couch beside me, Captain Horster. We so seldom see you. Please sit down, my friends. (*They sit down at the table. Mrs. Stockmann brings a* *tray, with a spirit-lamp, glasses, bottles, etc., upon it.*)

Mrs. Stockmann. There you are! This is arrack, and this is rum, and this one is the brandy. Now everyone must help themselves.

Dr. Stockmann (*taking a glass*). We will. (*They all mix themselves some toddy.*) And let us have the cigars. Ejlif, you know where the box is. And you, Morten, can fetch my pipe. (*The two boys go into the room on the right.*) I have a suspicion that Ejlif pockets a cigar now and then!—but I take no notice of it. (*Calls out.*) And my smoking-cap too, Morten. Katherine, you can tell him where I left it. Ah, he has got it. (*The boys bring the various things.*) Now, my friends. I stick to my pipe, you know. This one has seen plenty of bad weather with me up north. (*Touches glasses with them.*) Your good health! Ah, it is good to be sitting snug and warm here.

Mrs. Stockmann (*who sits knitting*). Do you sail soon, Captain Horster?

Horster. I expect to be ready to sail next week.

Mrs. Stockmann. I suppose you are going to America?

Horster. Yes, that is the plan.

Mrs. Stockmann. Then000 you won't be able to take part in the coming election?

Horster. Is there going to be an election?

Billing. Didn't you know?

Horster. No, I don't mix myself up with those things.

Billing. But do you not take an interest in public affairs?

Horster. No, I don't know anything about politics.

Billing. All the same, one ought to vote, at any rate.

Horster. Even if one doesn't know anything about what is going on?

Billing. Doesn't know! What do you mean by that? A community is like a ship; everyone ought to be prepared to take the helm.

Horster. Maybe that is all very well on shore; but on board ship it wouldn't work.

Hovstad. It is astonishing how little most sailors care about what goes on on shore.

Billing. Very extraordinary.

Dr. Stockmann. Sailors are like birds of passage; they feel equally at home in any latitude. And that is only an additional reason for our being all the more keen, Hovstad. Is there to be anything of public interest in tomorrow's "Messenger"?

Hovstad. Nothing about municipal affairs. But the day after tomorrow I was thinking of printing your article—

Dr. Stockmann. Ah, devil take it—my article! Look here, that must wait a bit.

Hovstad. Really? We had just got convenient space for it, and I thought it was just the opportune moment—

Dr. Stockmann. Yes, yes, very likely you are right; but it must wait all the same. I will explain to you later. (*Petra comes in from the hall, in hat and cloak and with a bundle of exercise books* *under her arm.*)

Petra. Good evening.

Dr. Stockmann. Good evening, Petra; come along.

(*Mutual greetings; Petra takes off her things and puts them down on a chair by the door.*)

Petra. And you have all been sitting here enjoying yourselves, while I have been out slaving!

Dr. Stockmann. Well, come and enjoy yourself too!

Billing. May I mix a glass for you?

Petra (*coming to the table*). Thanks, I would rather do it; you always mix it too strong. But I forgot, father—I have a letter for you. (*Goes to the chair where she has laid her things.*)

Dr. Stockmann. A letter? From whom?

Petra (*looking in her coat pocket*). The postman gave it to me just as I was going out.

Dr. Stockmann (*getting up and going to her*). And you only give to me now!

Petra. I really had not time to run up again. There it is!

Dr. Stockmann (*seizing the letter*). Let's see, let's see, child! (*Looks at the address.*) Yes, that's all right!

Mrs. Stockmann. Is it the one you have been expecting go anxiously, Thomas?

Dr. Stockmann. Yes, it is. I must go to my room now and— Where shall I get a light, Katherine? Is there no lamp in my room again?

Mrs. Stockmann. Yes, your lamp is already lit on your desk.

Dr. Stockmann. Good, good. Excuse me for a moment—. (*Goes into his study.*)

Petra. What do you suppose it is, mother?

Mrs. Stockmann. I don't know; for the last day or two he has always been asking if the postman has not been.

Billing. Probably some country patient.

Petra. Poor old dad!—He will overwork himself soon. (*Mixes a glass for herself.*) There, that will taste good!

Hovstad. Have you been teaching in the evening school again today?

Petra (*sipping from her glass*). Two hours.

Billing. And four hours of school in the morning?

Petra. Five hours.

Mrs. Stockmann. And you have still got exercises to correct, I see.

Petra. A whole heap, yes.

Horster. You are pretty full up with work too, it seems to me.

Petra. Yes—but that is good. One is so delightfully tired after it.

Billing. Do you like that?

Petra. Yes, because one sleeps so well then.

Morten. You must be dreadfully wicked, Petra.

Petra. Wicked?

Morten. Yes, because you work so much. Mr. Rörlund says work is a punishment for our sins.

Ejlif. Pooh, what a duffer, you are, to believe a thing like that!

Mrs. Stockmann. Come, come, Ejlif!

Billing (*laughing*). That's capital!

Hovstad. Don't you want to work as hard as that, Morten?

Morten. No, indeed I don't.

Hovstad. What do you want to be, then?

Morten. I should like best to be a Viking.

Ejlif. You would have to be a pagan then.

Morten. Well, I could become a pagan, couldn't I?

Billing. I agree with you, Morten! My sentiments, exactly.

Mrs. Stockmann (*signalling to him*). I am sure that is not true, Mr. Billing.

Billing. Yes, I swear it is! I am a pagan, and I am proud of it. Believe me, before long we shall all be pagans.

Morten. And then shall be allowed to do anything we like?

Billing. Well, you'll see, Morten.

Mrs. Stockmann. You must go to your room now, boys; I am sure you have some lessons to learn for tomorrow.

Ejlif. I should like so much to stay a little longer—

Mrs. Stockmann. No, no; away you go, both of you, (*The boys say good night and go into the room on the left.*)

Hovstad. Do you really think it can do the boys any harm to hear such things?

Mrs. Stockmann. I don't know; but I don't like it.

Petra. But you know, mother, I think you really are wrong about it.

Mrs. Stockmann. Maybe, but I don't like it—not in our own home.

Petra. There is so much falsehood both at home and at school.

At home one must not speak, and at school we have to stand and tell lies to the children.

Horster. Tell lies?

Petra. Yes, don't you suppose we have to teach them all sorts of things that we don't believe?

Billing. That is perfectly true.

Petra. If only I had the means, I would start a school of my own; and it would be conducted on very different lines.

Billing. Oh, bother the means—!

Horster. Well if you are thinking of that, Miss Stockmann, I shall be delighted to provide you with a schoolroom. The great big old house my father left me is standing almost empty; there is an immense dining-room downstairs—

Petra (*laughing*). Thank you very much; but I am afraid nothing will come of it.

Hovstad. No, Miss Petra is much more likely to take to journalism, I expect. By the way, have you had time to do anything with that English story you promised to translate for us?

Petra. No, not yet, but you shall have it in good time.

(*Dr. Stockmann comes in from his room with an open letter in his hand.*)

Dr. Stockmann (*waving the letter*). Well, now the town will have something new to talk about, I can tell you!

Billing. Something new?

Mrs. Stockmann. What is this?

Dr. Stockmann. A great discovery, Katherine.

Hovstad. Really?

Mrs. Stockmann. A discovery of yours?

Dr. Stockmann. A discovery of mine. (*Walks up and down.*) Just let them come saying, as usual, that it is all fancy and a crazy man's imagination! But they will be careful what they say this time, I can tell you!

Petra. But, father, tell us what it is.

Dr. Stockmann. Yes, yes—only give me time, and you shall know all about it. If only I had Peter here now! It just shows how we men can go about forming our judgments, when in reality we are as blind as any moles—

Hovstad. What are you driving at, Doctor?

Dr. Stockmann (*standing still by the table*). Isn't it the universal opinion that our town is a healthy spot?

Hovstad. Certainly.

Dr. Stockmann. Quite an unusually healthy spot, in fact—a place that deserves to be recommended in the warmest possible manner either for invalids or for people who are well—

Mrs. Stockmann. Yes, but my dear Thomas—

Dr. Stockmann. And we have been recommending it and praising it—I have written and written, both in the "Messenger" and in pamphlets—

Hovstad. Well, what then?

Dr. Stockmann. And the Baths—we have called them the "main artery of the town's life-blood," the "nerve-centre of our town," and the devil knows what else—

Billing. "The town's pulsating heart" was the expression I once used on an important occasion.

Dr. Stockmann. Quite so. Well, do you know what they really are, these great, splendid, much praised Baths, that have cost so much money—do you know what they are?

Hovstad. No, what are they?

Mrs. Stockmann. Yes, what are they?

Dr. Stockmann. The whole place is a pest-house!

Petra. The Baths, father?

Mrs. Stockmann (*at the same time*). Our Baths?

Hovstad. But, Doctor—

Billing. Absolutely incredible!

Dr. Stockmann. The whole Bath establishment is a whited, poisoned sepulchre, I tell you—the gravest possible danger to the public health! All the nastiness up at Mölledal, all that stinking filth, is infecting the water in the conduit-pipes leading to the reservoir; and the same cursed, filthy poison oozes out on the shore too—

Horster. Where the bathing-place is?

Dr. Stockmann. Just there.

Hovstad. How do you come to be so certain of all this, Doctor?

Dr. Stockmann. I have investigated the matter most conscientiously. For a long time past I have suspected something of the kind. Last year we had some very strange cases of illness among the visitors—typhoid cases, and cases of gastric fever—

Mrs. Stockmann. Yes, that is quite true.

Dr. Stockmann. At the time, we supposed the visitors had been infected before they came; but later on, in the winter, I began to have a different opinion; and so I set myself to examine the water, as well as I could.

Mrs. Stockmann. Then that is what you have been so busy with?

Dr. Stockmann. Indeed I have been busy, Katherine. But here I had none of the necessary scientific apparatus; so I sent samples, both of the drinking-water and of the sea-water, up to the University, to have an accurate analysis made by a chemist.

Hovstad. And have you got that?

Dr. Stockmann (*showing him the letter*). Here it is! It proves the presence of decomposing organic matter in the water—it is full of infusoria. The water is absolutely dangerous to use, either internally or externally.

Mrs. Stockmann. What a mercy you discovered it in time.

Dr. Stockmann. You may well say so.

Hovstad. And what do you propose to do now, Doctor?

Dr. Stockmann. To see the matter put right, naturally.

Hovstad. Can that be done?

Dr. Stockmann. It must be done. Otherwise the Baths will be absolutely useless and wasted. But we need not anticipate that; I have a very clear idea what we shall have to do.

Mrs. Stockmann. But why have you kept this all so secret, dear?

Dr. Stockmann. Do you suppose I was going to run about the town gossiping about it, before I had absolute proof? No, thank you. I am not such a fool.

Petra. Still, you might have told us—

Dr. Stockmann. Not a living soul. But tomorrow you may run around to the old Badger—

Mrs. Stockmann. Oh, Thomas! Thomas!

Dr. Stockmann. Well, to your grandfather, then. The old boy will have something to be astonished at! I know he thinks I am cracked—and there are lots of other people who think so too, I have noticed. But now these good folks shall see—they shall just see! (*Walks about, rubbing his hands.*) There will be a nice upset in the town, Katherine; you can't imagine what it will be. All the conduit-pipes will have to be relaid.

Hovstad (*getting up*). All the conduit-pipes—?

Dr. Stockmann. Yes, of course. The intake is too low down; it will have to be lifted to a position much higher up.

Petra. Then you were right after all.

Dr. Stockmann. Ah, you remember, Petra—I wrote opposing the plans before the work was begun. But at that time no one would listen to me. Well, I am going to let them have it now. Of course I have prepared a report for the Baths Committee; I have had it ready for a week, and was only waiting for this to come. (*Shows the letter.*) Now it shall go off at once. (*Goes into his room and comes back with some papers.*) Look at that! Four closely written sheets!—and the letter shall go with them. Give me a bit of paper, Katherine—something to wrap them up in. That will do! Now give it to-to- (*stamps his foot*)—what the deuce is her name?—give it to the maid, and tell her to take it at once to the Mayor.

(*Mrs. Stockmann takes the packet and goes out through the dining-room.*)

Petra. What do you think Uncle Peter will say, father?

Dr. Stockmann. What is there for him to say? I should think he would be very glad that such an important truth has been brought to light.

Hovstad. Will you let me print a short note about your discovery in the "Messenger?"

Dr. Stockmann. I shall be very much obliged if you will.

Hovstad. It is very desirable that the public should be informed of it without delay.

Dr. Stockmann. Certainly.

Mrs. Stockmann (*coming back*). She has just gone with it.

Billing. Upon my soul, Doctor, you are going to be the foremost man in the town!

Dr. Stockmann (*walking about happily*). Nonsense! As a matter of fact I have done nothing more than my duty. I have only made a lucky find—that's all. Still, all the same—

Billing. Hovstad, don't you think the town ought to give Dr. Stockmann some sort of testimonial?

Hovstad. I will suggest it, anyway.

Billing. And I will speak to Aslaksen about it.

Dr. Stockmann. No, my good friends, don't let us have any of that nonsense. I won't hear anything of the kind. And if the Baths Committee should think of voting me an increase of salary, I will not accept it. Do you hear, Katherine?—I won't accept it.

Mrs. Stockmann. You are quite right, Thomas.

Petra (*lifting her glass*). Your health, father!

Hovstad and Billing. Your health, Doctor! Good health!

Horster (*touches glasses with Dr. Stockmann*). I hope it will bring you nothing but good luck.

Dr. Stockmann. Thank you, thank you, my dear fellows! I feel tremendously happy! It is a splendid thing for a man to be able to feel that he has done a service to his native town and to his fellow-citizens. Hurrah, Katherine! (*He puts his arms round her and whirls her round and round, while she protests with laughing cries. They all laugh, clap their hands, and cheer the Doctor. The boys put their heads in at the door to see what is going on.*)

ACT II

Scene.—The same. The door into the dining-room is shut. It is morning. Mrs. Stockmann, with a sealed letter in her hand, comes in from the dining-room, goes to the door of the Doctor's study, and peeps in.

Mrs. Stockmann. Are you in, Thomas?

Dr. Stockmann (*from within his room*). Yes, I have just come in. (*Comes into the room.*) What is it?

Mrs. Stockmann. A letter from your brother.

Dr. Stockmann. Aha, let us see! (*Opens the letter and reads:*) "I return herewith the manuscript you sent me" (*reads on in a low murmur*) H'm!—

Mrs. Stockmann. What does he say?

Dr. Stockmann (*putting the papers in his pocket*). Oh, he only writes that he will come up here himself about midday.

Mrs. Stockmann. Well, try and remember to be at home this time.

Dr. Stockmann. That will be all right; I have got through all my morning visits.

Mrs. Stockmann. I am extremely curious to know how he takes it.

Dr. Stockmann. You will see he won't like it's having been I, and not he, that made the discovery.

Mrs. Stockmann. Aren't you a little nervous about that?

Dr. Stockmann. Oh, he really will be pleased enough, you know. But, at the same time, Peter is so confoundedly afraid of anyone's doing any service to the town except himself.

Mrs. Stockmann. I will tell you what, Thomas—you should be good natured, and share the credit of this with him. Couldn't you make out that it was he who set you on the scent of this discovery?

Dr. Stockmann. I am quite willing. If only I can get the thing set right. I—

(*Morten Kiil puts his head in through the door leading from the hall, looks around in an enquiring manner, and chuckles.*)

Morten Kiil (*slyly*). Is it—is it true?

Mrs. Stockmann (*going to the door*). Father!—Is it you?

Dr. Stockmann. Ah, Mr. Kiil—good morning, good morning!

Mrs. Stockmann. But come along in.

Morten Kiil. If it is true, I will; if not, I am off.

Dr. Stockmann. If what is true?

Morten Kiil. This tale about the water supply, is it true?

Dr. Stockmann. Certainly it is true, but how did you come to hear it?

Morten Kiil (*coming in*). Petra ran in on her way to the school—

Dr. Stockmann. Did she?

Morten Kiil. Yes; and she declares that—I thought she was only making a fool of me—but it isn't like Petra to do that.

Dr. Stockmann. Of course not. How could you imagine such a thing!

Morten Kiil. Oh well, it is better never to trust anybody; you may find you have been made a fool of before you know where you are. But it is really true, all the same?

Dr. Stockmann. You can depend upon it that it is true. Won't you sit down? (*Settles him on the couch.*) Isn't it a real bit of luck for the town—

Morten Kiil (*suppressing his laughter*). A bit of luck for the town?

Dr. Stockmann. Yes, that I made the discovery in good time.

Morten Kiil (*as before*). Yes, yes. Yes!—But I should never have thought you the sort of man to pull your own brother's leg like this!

Dr. Stockmann. Pull his leg!

Mrs. Stockmann. Really, father dear—

Morten Kiil (*resting his hands and his chin on the handle of his stick and winking slyly at the Doctor*). Let me see, what was the story? Some kind of beast that had got into the water-pipes, wasn't it?

Dr. Stockmann. Infusoria—yes.

Morten Kiil. And a lot of these beasts had got in, according to Petra—a tremendous lot.

Dr. Stockmann. Certainly; hundreds of thousands of them, probably.

Morten Kiil. But no one can see them—isn't that so?

Dr. Stockmann. Yes, you can't see them.

Morten Kiil (*with a quiet chuckle*). Damn—it's the finest story I have ever heard!

Dr. Stockmann. What do you mean?

Morten Kiil. But you will never get the Mayor to believe a thing like that.

Dr. Stockmann. We shall see.

Morten Kiil. Do you think he will be fool enough to——?

Dr. Stockmann. I hope the whole town will be fools enough.

Morten Kiil. The whole town! Well, it wouldn't be a bad thing. It would just serve them right, and teach them a lesson. They think themselves so much cleverer than we old fellows. They hounded me out of the council; they did, I tell you—they hounded me out. Now they shall pay for it. You pull their legs too, Thomas!

Dr. Stockmann. Really, I——

Morten Kiil. You pull their legs! (*Gets up.*) If you can work it so that the Mayor and his friends all swallow the same bait, I will give ten pounds to a charity—like a shot!

Dr. Stockmann. That is very kind of you.

Morten Kiil. Yes, I haven't got much money to throw away,

I can tell you; but, if you can work this, I will give five pounds to a charity at Christmas.

(*Hovstad comes in by the hall door.*)

Hovstad. Good morning! (*Stops.*) Oh, I beg your pardon—

Dr. Stockmann. Not at all; come in.

Morten Kiil (*with another chuckle*). Oho!—Is he in this too?

Hovstad. What do you mean?

Dr. Stockmann. Certainly he is.

Morten Kiil. I might have known it! It must get into the papers. You know how to do it, Thomas! Set your wits to work. Now I must go.

Dr. Stockmann. Won't you stay a little while?

Morten Kiil. No, I must be off now. You keep up this game for all it is worth; you won't repent it, I'm damned if you will!

(*He goes out; Mrs. Stockmann follows him into the hall.*)

Dr. Stockmann (*laughing*). Just imagine—the old chap doesn't believe a word of all this about the water supply.

Hovstad. Oh that was it, then?

Dr. Stockmann. Yes, that was what we were talking about. Perhaps it is the same thing that brings you here?

Hovstad. Yes, it is, Can you spare me a few minutes, Doctor?

Dr. Stockmann. As long as you like, my dear fellow.

Hovstad. Have you heard from the Mayor yet?

Dr. Stockmann. Not yet. He is coming here later.

Hovstad. I have given the matter a great deal of thought since last night.

Dr. Stockmann. Well?

Hovstad. From your point of view, as a doctor and a man of science, this affair of the water supply is an isolated matter. I mean, you do not realise that it involves a great many other things.

Dr. Stockmann. How do you mean?—Let us sit down, my dear fellow. No, sit here on the couch. (*Hovstad Sits down on the couch, Dr. Stockmann on a chair on the other side of the table.*) Now then. You mean that—?

Hovstad. You said yesterday that the pollution of the water was due to impurities in the soil.

Dr. Stockmann. Yes, unquestionably it is due to that poisonous morass up at Mölledal.

Hovstad. Begging your pardon, Doctor, I fancy it is due to quite another morass altogether.

Dr. Stockmann. What morass?

Hovstad. The morass that the whole life of our town is built on and is rotting in.

Dr. Stockmann. What the deuce are you driving at, Hovstad?

Hovstad. The whole of the town's interests have, little by little, got into the hands of a pack of officials.

Dr. Stockmann. Oh, come!—They are not all officials.

Hovstad. No, but those that are not officials are at any rate the officials' friends and adherents; it is the wealthy folk, the old families in the town, that have got us entirely in their hands.

Dr. Stockmann. Yes, but after all they are men of ability and knowledge.

Hovstad. Did they show any ability or knowledge when they laid the conduit pipes where they are now?

Dr. Stockmann. No, of course that was a great piece of stupidity on their part. But that is going to be set right now.

Hovstad. Do you think that will be all such plain sailing?

Dr. Stockmann. Plain sailing or no, it has got to be done, anyway.

Hovstad. Yes, provided the press takes up the question.

Dr. Stockmann. I don't think that will be necessary, my dear fellow, I am certain my brother—

Hovstad. Excuse me, doctor; I feel bound to tell you I am inclined to take the matter up.

Dr. Stockmann. In the paper?

Hovstad. Yes. When I took over the "People's Messenger" my idea was to break up this ring of self-opinionated old fossils who had got hold of all the influence.

Dr. Stockmann. But you know you told me yourself what the result had been; you nearly ruined your paper.

Hovstad. Yes, at the time we were obliged to climb down a peg or two, it is quite true—because there was a danger of the whole project of the Baths coming to nothing if they failed us. But now the scheme has been carried through, and we can dispense with these grand gentlemen.

Dr. Stockmann. Dispense with them, yes; but, we owe them a great debt of gratitude.

Hovstad. That shall be recognised ungrudgingly, But a journalist of my democratic tendencies cannot let such an opportunity as this slip. The bubble of official infallibility must be pricked. This superstition must be destroyed, like any other.

Dr. Stockmann. I am whole-heartedly with you in that, Mr. Hovstad; if it is a superstition, away with it!

Hovstad. I should be very reluctant to bring the Mayor into it, because he is your brother. But I am sure you will agree with me that truth should be the first consideration.

Dr. Stockmann. That goes without saying. (*With sudden emphasis.*) Yes, but—but—

Hovstad. You must not misjudge me. I am neither more self-interested nor more ambitious than most men.

Dr. Stockmann. My dear fellow—who suggests anything of the kind?

Hovstad. I am of humble origin, as you know; and that has given me opportunities of knowing what is the most crying need in the humbler ranks of life. It is that they should be allowed some part in the direction of public affairs, Doctor. That is what will develop their faculties and intelligence and self-respect—

Dr. Stockmann. I quite appreciate that.

Hovstad. Yes—and in my opinion a journalist incurs a heavy responsibility if he neglects a favourable opportunity of emancipating the masses—the humble and oppressed. I know well enough that in exalted circles I shall be called an agitator, and all that sort of thing; but they may call what they like. If only my conscience doesn't reproach me, then—

Dr. Stockmann. Quite right! Quite right, Mr. Hovstad. But all the same—devil take it! (*A knock is heard at the door.*) Come in!

(*Aslaksen appears at the door. He is poorly but decently dressed, in black, with a slightly crumpled white neck-cloth; he wears gloves and has a felt hat in his hand.*)

Aslaksen (*bowing*). Excuse my taking the liberty, Doctor—

Dr. Stockmann (*getting up*). Ah, it is you, Aslaksen!

Aslaksen. Yes, Doctor.

Hovstad (*standing up*). Is it me you want, Aslaksen?

Aslaksen. No; I didn't know I should find you here. No, it was the Doctor I—

Dr. Stockmann. I am quite at your service. What is it?

Aslaksen. Is what I heard from Mr. Billing true, sir—that you mean to improve our water supply?

Dr. Stockmann. Yes, for the Baths.

Aslaksen. Quite so, I understand. Well, I have come to say that I will back that up by every means in my power.

Hovstad (*to the Doctor*). You see!

Dr. Stockmann. I shall be very grateful to you, but—

Aslaksen. Because it may be no bad thing to have us small tradesmen at your back. We form, as it were, a compact majority in the town—if we choose. And it is always a good thing to have the majority with you, Doctor.

Dr. Stockmann. That is undeniably true; but I confess I don't see why such unusual precautions should be necessary in this case. It seems to me that such a plain, straightforward thing—

Aslaksen. Oh, it may be very desirable, all the same. I know our local authorities so well; officials are not generally very ready to act on proposals that come from other people. That is why I think it would not be at all amiss if we made a little demonstration.

Hovstad. That's right.

Dr. Stockmann. Demonstration, did you say? What on earth are you going to make a demonstration about?

Aslaksen. We shall proceed with the greatest moderation, Doctor. Moderation is always my aim; it is the greatest virtue in a citizen—at least, I think so.

Dr. Stockmann. It is well known to be a characteristic of yours, Mr. Aslaksen.

Aslaksen. Yes, I think I may pride myself on that. And this matter of the water supply is of the greatest importance to us small tradesmen. The Baths promise to be a regular gold-mine for the town. We shall all make our living out of them, especially those of us who are householders. That is why we will back up the project as strongly as possible. And as I am at present Chairman of the Householders'

Association.

Dr. Stockmann. Yes—?

Aslaksen. And, what is more, local secretary of the Temperance Society—you know, sir, I suppose, that I am a worker in the temperance cause?

Dr. Stockmann. Of course, of course.

Aslaksen. Well, you can understand that I come into contact with a great many people. And as I have the reputation of a temperate and law-abiding citizen—like yourself, Doctor—I have a certain influence in the town, a little bit of power, if I may be allowed to say so.

Dr. Stockmann. I know that quite well, Mr. Aslaksen.

Aslaksen. So you see it would be an easy matter for me to set on foot some testimonial, if necessary.

Dr. Stockmann. A testimonial?

Aslaksen. Yes, some kind of an address of thanks from the townsmen for your share in a matter of such importance to the community. I need scarcely say that it would have to be drawn up with the greatest regard to moderation, so as not to offend the authorities—who, after all, have the reins in their hands. If we pay strict attention to that, no one can take it amiss, I should think!

Hovstad. Well, and even supposing they didn't like it—

Aslaksen. No, no, no; there must be no discourtesy to the authorities, Mr. Hovstad. It is no use falling foul of those upon whom our welfare so closely depends. I have done that in my time, and no good ever comes of it. But no one can take exception to a reasonable and frank expression of a citizen's views.

Dr. Stockmann (*shaking him by the hand*). I can't tell you, dear Mr. Aslaksen, how extremely pleased I am to find such hearty support among my fellow-citizens. I am delighted—delighted! Now, you will take a small glass of sherry, eh?

Aslaksen. No, thank you; I never drink alcohol of that kind.

Dr. Stockmann. Well, what do you say to a glass of beer, then?

Aslaksen. Nor that either, thank you, Doctor. I never drink anything as early as this. I am going into town now to talk this over with one or two householders, and prepare the ground.

Dr. Stockmann. It is tremendously kind of you, Mr. Aslaksen; but I really cannot understand the necessity for all these precautions. It seems to me that the thing should go of itself.

Aslaksen. The authorities are somewhat slow to move, Doctor. Far be it from me to seem to blame them—

Hovstad. We are going to stir them up in the paper tomorrow, Aslaksen.

Aslaksen. But not violently, I trust, Mr. Hovstad. Proceed with moderation, or you will do nothing with them. You may take my advice; I have gathered my experience in the school of life. Well, I must say goodbye, Doctor. You know now that we small tradesmen are at your back at all events, like a solid wall. You have the compact majority on your side Doctor.

Dr. Stockmann. I am very much obliged, dear Mr. Aslaksen, (*Shakes hands with him.*) Goodbye, goodbye.

Aslaksen. Are you going my way, towards the printing-office. Mr. Hovstad?

Hovstad. I will come later; I have something to settle up first.

Aslaksen. Very well. (*Bows and goes out; Stockmann follows him into the hall.*)

Hovstad (*as Stockmann comes in again*). Well, what do you think of that, Doctor? Don't you think it is high time we stirred a little life into all this slackness and vacillation and cowardice?

Dr. Stockmann. Are you referring to Aslaksen?

Hovstad. Yes, I am. He is one of those who are floundering in a bog—decent enough fellow though he may be, otherwise. And most of the people here are in just the same case—see-sawing and edging first to one side and then to the other, so overcome with caution and scruple that they never dare to take any decided step.

Dr. Stockmann. Yes, but Aslaksen seemed to me so thoroughly well-intentioned.

Hovstad. There is one thing I esteem higher than that; and that is for a man to be self-reliant and sure of himself.

Dr. Stockmann. I think you are perfectly right there.

Hovstad. That is why I want to seize this opportunity, and try if I cannot manage to put a little virility into these well-intentioned people for once. The idol of Authority must be shattered in this town. This gross and inexcusable blunder about the water supply must be brought home to the mind of every municipal voter.

Dr. Stockmann. Very well; if you are of opinion that it is for the good of the community, so be it. But not until I have had a talk with my brother.

Hovstad. Anyway, I will get a leading article ready; and if the Mayor refuses to take the matter up—

Dr. Stockmann. How can you suppose such a thing possible!

Hovstad. It is conceivable. And in that case—

Dr. Stockmann. In that case I promise you—. Look here, in that case you may print my report—every word of it.

Hovstad. May I? Have I your word for it?

Dr. Stockmann (*giving him the MS.*). Here it is; take it with you. It can do no harm for you to read it through, and you can give it me back later on.

Hovstad. Good, good! That is what I will do. And now goodbye, Doctor.

Dr. Stockmann. Goodbye, goodbye. You will see everything will run quite smoothly, Mr. Hovstad—quite smoothly.

Hovstad. Hm!—We shall see. (*Bows and goes out.*)

Dr. Stockmann (*opens the dining-room door and looks in*). Katherine! Oh, you are back, Petra?

Petra (*coming in*). Yes, I have just come from the school.

Mrs. Stockmann (*coming in*). Has he not been here yet?

Dr. Stockmann. Peter? No, but I have had a long talk with Hovstad. He is quite excited about my discovery, I find it has a much wider bearing than I at first imagined. And he has put his paper at my disposal if necessity should arise.

Mrs. Stockmann. Do you think it will?

Dr. Stockmann. Not for a moment. But at all events it makes me feel proud to know that I have the liberal-minded independent press on my side. Yes, and just imagine—I have had a visit from the Chairman of the Householders' Association!

Mrs. Stockmann. Oh! What did he want?

Dr. Stockmann. To offer me his support too. They will support me in a body if it should be necessary. Katherine—do you know what I have got behind me?

Mrs. Stockmann. Behind you? No, what have you got behind you?

Dr. Stockmann. The compact majority.

Mrs. Stockmann. Really? Is that a good thing for you Thomas?

Dr. Stockmann. I should think it was a good thing. (*Walks up and down rubbing his hands.*) By Jove, it's a fine thing to feel this bond of brotherhood between oneself and one's fellow citizens!

Petra. And to be able to do so much that is good and useful, father!

Dr. Stockmann. And for one's own native town into the bargain, my child!

Mrs. Stockmann. That was a ring at the bell.

Dr. Stockmann. It must be he, then. (*A knock is heard at the door.*) Come in!

Peter Stockmann (*comes in from the hall*). Good morning.

Dr. Stockmann. Glad to see you, Peter!

Mrs. Stockmann. Good morning, Peter, How are you?

Peter Stockmann. So so, thank you. (*To Dr. Stockmann.*) I received from you yesterday, after office hours, a report dealing with the condition of the water at the Baths.

Dr. Stockmann. Yes. Have you read it?

Peter Stockmann. Yes, I have,

Dr. Stockmann. And what have you to say to it?

Peter Stockmann (*with a sidelong glance*). Hm!—

Mrs. Stockmann. Come along, Petra. (*She and Petra go into the room on the left.*)

Peter Stockmann (*after a pause*). Was it necessary to make all these investigations behind my back?

Dr. Stockmann. Yes, because until I was absolutely certain about it—

Peter Stockmann. Then you mean that you are absolutely certain now?

Dr. Stockmann. Surely you are convinced of that.

Peter Stockmann. Is it your intention to bring this document before the Baths Committee as a sort of official communication?

Dr. Stockmann. Certainly. Something must be done in the

matter—and that quickly.

Peter Stockmann. As usual, you employ violent expressions in your report. You say, amongst other things, that what we offer visitors in our Baths is a permanent supply of poison.

Dr. Stockmann. Well, can you describe it any other way, Peter? Just think—water that is poisonous, whether you drink it or bathe in it! And this we offer to the poor sick folk who come to us trustfully and pay us at an exorbitant rate to be made well again!

Peter Stockmann. And your reasoning leads you to this conclusion, that we must build a sewer to draw off the alleged impurities from Mölledal and must relay the water conduits.

Dr. Stockmann. Yes. Do you see any other way out of it? I don't.

Peter Stockmann. I made a pretext this morning to go and see the town engineer, and, as if only half seriously, broached the subject of these proposals as a thing we might perhaps have to take under consideration some time later on.

Dr. Stockmann. Some time later on!

Peter Stockmann. He smiled at what he considered to be my extravagance, naturally. Have you taken the trouble to consider what your proposed alterations would cost? According to the information I obtained, the expenses would probably mount up to fifteen or twenty thousand pounds.

Dr. Stockmann. Would it cost so much?

Peter Stockmann. Yes; and the worst part of it would be that the work would take at least two years.

Dr. Stockmann. Two years? Two whole years?

Peter Stockmann. At least. And what are we to do with the Baths in the meantime? Close them? Indeed we should be obliged to. And do you suppose anyone would come near the place after it had got out that the water was dangerous?

Dr. Stockmann. Yes but, Peter, that is what it is.

Peter Stockmann. And all this at this juncture—just as the Baths are beginning to be known. There are other towns in the neighbourhood with qualifications to attract visitors for bathing purposes. Don't you suppose they would immediately strain every nerve to divert the entire stream of strangers to themselves? Unquestionably they would; and then where should we be? We should probably have to abandon the whole thing, which has cost us so much money—and then you would have ruined your native town.

Dr. Stockmann. I—should have ruined—!

Peter Stockmann. It is simply and solely through the Baths that the town has before it any future worth mentioning. You know that just as well as I.

Dr. Stockmann. But what do you think ought to be done, then?

Peter Stockmann. Your report has not convinced me that the condition of the water at the Baths is as bad as you represent it to be.

Dr. Stockmann. I tell you it is even worse!—Or at all events it will be in summer, when the warm weather comes.

Peter Stockmann. As I said, I believe you exaggerate the matter considerably. A capable physician ought to know what measures to take—he ought to be capable of preventing injurious influences or of remedying them if they become obviously persistent.

Dr. Stockmann. Well? What more?

Peter Stockmann. The water supply for the Baths is now an established fact, and in consequence must be treated as such. But probably the Committee, at its discretion, will not be disinclined to consider the question of how far it might be possible to introduce certain improvements consistently with a reasonable expenditure.

Dr. Stockmann. And do you suppose that I will have anything to do with such a piece of trickery as that?

Peter Stockmann. Trickery!!

Dr. Stockmann. Yes, it would be a trick—a fraud, a lie, a downright crime towards the public, towards the whole community!

Peter Stockmann. I have not, as I remarked before, been able to convince myself that there is actually any imminent danger.

Dr. Stockmann. You have! It is impossible that you should not be convinced. I know I have represented the facts absolutely truthfully and fairly. And you know it very well, Peter, only you won't acknowledge it. It was owing to your action that both the Baths and the water conduits were built where they are; and that is what you won't acknowledge—that damnable blunder of yours. Pooh!—do you suppose I don't see through you?

Peter Stockmann. And even if that were true? If I perhaps guard my reputation somewhat anxiously, it is in the interests of the town. Without moral authority I am powerless to direct public affairs as seems, to my judgment, to be best for the common good. And on that account—and for various other reasons too—it appears to me to be a matter of importance that your report should not be delivered to the Committee. In the interests of the public, you must withhold it. Then, later on, I will raise the question and we will do our best, privately; but nothing of this unfortunate affair not a single word of it—must come to the ears of the public.

Dr. Stockmann. I am afraid you will not be able to prevent that now, my dear Peter.

Peter Stockmann. It must and shall be prevented.

Dr. Stockmann. It is no use, I tell you. There are too many people that know about it.

Peter Stockmann. That know about it? Who? Surely you don't mean those fellows on the "People's Messenger"?

Dr. Stockmann. Yes, they know. The liberal-minded independent press is going to see that you do your duty.

Peter Stockmann (*after a short pause*). You are an extraordinarily independent man, Thomas. Have you given no thought to the consequences this may have for yourself?

Dr. Stockmann. Consequences?—For me?

Peter Stockmann. For you and yours, yes.

Dr. Stockmann. What the deuce do you mean?

Peter Stockmann. I believe I have always behaved in a brotherly way to you—haven't I always been ready to oblige or to help you?

Dr. Stockmann. Yes, you have, and I am grateful to you for it.

Peter Stockmann. There is no need. Indeed, to some extent I was forced to do so—for my own sake. I always hoped that, if I helped to improve your financial position, I should be able to keep some check on you.

Dr. Stockmann. What! Then it was only for your own sake—!

Peter Stockmann. Up to a certain point, yes. It is painful for a man in an official position to have his nearest relative compromising himself time after time.

Dr. Stockmann. And do you consider that I do that?

Peter Stockmann. Yes, unfortunately, you do, without even being aware of it. You have a restless, pugnacious, rebellious disposition. And then there is that disastrous propensity of yours to want to write about every sort of possible and impossible thing. The moment an idea comes into your head, you must needs go and write a newspaper article or a whole pamphlet about it.

Dr. Stockmann. Well, but is it not the duty of a citizen to let the public share in any new ideas he may have?

Peter Stockmann. Oh, the public doesn't require any new ideas. The public is best served by the good, old established ideas it already has.

Dr. Stockmann. And that is your honest opinion?

Peter Stockmann. Yes, and for once I must talk frankly to you. Hitherto I have tried to avoid doing so, because I know how irritable you are; but now I must tell you the truth, Thomas. You have no conception what an amount of harm you do yourself by your impetuosity. You complain of the authorities, you even complain of the government—you are always pulling them to pieces; you insist that you have been neglected and persecuted. But what else can such a cantankerous man as you expect?

Dr. Stockmann. What next! Cantankerous, am I?

Peter Stockmann. Yes, Thomas, you are an extremely cantankerous man to work with—I know that to my cost. You disregard everything that you ought to have consideration for. You seem completely to forget that it is me you have to thank for your appointment here as medical officer to the Baths—

Dr. Stockmann. I was entitled to it as a matter of course!—I and nobody else! I was the first person to see that the town could be made into a flourishing watering-place, and I was the only one who saw it at that time. I had to fight single-handed in support of the idea for many years; and I wrote and wrote—

Peter Stockmann. Undoubtedly. But things were not ripe for the scheme then—though, of course, you could not judge of that in your out-of-the-way corner up north. But as soon as the opportune moment came I—and the others—took the matter into our hands—

Dr. Stockmann. Yes, and made this mess of all my beautiful plan. It is pretty obvious now what clever fellows you were!

Peter Stockmann. To my mind the whole thing only seems to mean that you are seeking another outlet for your combativeness. You want to pick a quarrel with your superiors—an old habit of yours. You cannot put up with any authority over you. You look askance at anyone who occupies a superior official position; you regard him as a personal enemy, and then any stick is good enough to beat him with. But now I have called your attention to the fact that the town's interests are at stake—and, incidentally, my own too. And therefore, I must tell you, Thomas, that you will find me inexorable with regard to what I am about to require you to do.

Dr. Stockmann. And what is that?

Peter Stockmann. As you have been so indiscreet as to speak of this delicate matter to outsiders, despite the fact that you ought to have treated it as entirely official and confidential, it is obviously impossible to hush it up now. All sorts of rumours will get about directly, and everybody who has a grudge against us will take care to embellish these rumours. So it will be necessary for you to refute them publicly.

Dr. Stockmann. I! How? I don't understand.

Peter Stockmann. What we shall expect is that, after making further investigations, you will come to the conclusion that the matter is not by any means as dangerous or as critical as you imagined in the first instance.

Dr. Stockmann. Oho!—So that is what you expect!

Peter Stockmann. And, what is more, we shall expect you to make public profession of your confidence in the Committee and in their readiness to consider fully and conscientiously what steps may be necessary to remedy any possible defects.

Dr. Stockmann. But you will never be able to do that by patching and tinkering at it—never! Take my word for it, Peter; I mean what I say, as deliberately and emphatically as possible.

Peter Stockmann. As an officer under the Committee, you have no right to any individual opinion.

Dr. Stockmann (*amazed*). No right?

Peter Stockmann. In your official capacity, no. As a private person, it is quite another matter. But as a subordinate member of the staff of the Baths, you have no right to express any opinion which runs contrary to that of your superiors.

Dr. Stockmann. This is too much! I, a doctor, a man of science, have no right to—!

Peter Stockmann. The matter in hand is not simply a scientific one. It is a complicated matter, and has its economic as well as its technical side.

Dr. Stockmann. I don't care what it is! I intend to be free to express my opinion on any subject under the sun.

Peter Stockmann. As you please—but not on any subject concerning the Baths. That we forbid.

Dr. Stockmann (*shouting*). You forbid—! You! A pack of—

Peter Stockmann. I forbid it—I, your chief; and if I forbid it, you have to obey.

Dr. Stockmann (*controlling himself*). Peter—if you were not my brother—

Petra (*throwing open the door*). Father, you shan't stand this!

Mrs. Stockmann (*coming in after her*). Petra, Petra!

Peter Stockmann. Oh, so you have been eavesdropping.

Mrs. Stockmann. You were talking so loud, we couldn't help it!

Petra. Yes, I was listening.

Peter Stockmann. Well, after all, I am very glad—

Dr. Stockmann (*going up to him*). You were saying something about forbidding and obeying?

Peter Stockmann. You obliged me to take that tone with you.

Dr. Stockmann. And so I am to give myself the lie, publicly?

Peter Stockmann. We consider it absolutely necessary that you should make some such public statement as I have asked for.

Dr. Stockmann. And if I do not—obey?

Peter Stockmann. Then we shall publish a statement ourselves to reassure the public.

Dr. Stockmann. Very well; but in that case I shall use my pen against you. I stick to what I have said; I will show that I am right and that you are wrong. And what will you do then?

Peter Stockmann. Then I shall not be able to prevent your being dismissed.

Dr. Stockmann. What—?

Petra. Father—dismissed!

Mrs. Stockmann. Dismissed!

Peter Stockmann. Dismissed from the staff of the Baths. I shall be obliged to propose that you shall immediately be given notice, and shall not be allowed any further participation in the Baths' affairs.

Dr. Stockmann. You would dare to do that!

Peter Stockmann. It is you that are playing the daring game.

Petra. Uncle, that is a shameful way to treat a man like father!

Mrs. Stockmann. Do hold your tongue, Petra!

Peter Stockmann (*looking at Petra*). Oh, so we volunteer our opinions already, do we? Of course. (*To Mrs. Stockmann.*) Katherine, I imagine you are the most sensible person in this house. Use any influence you may have over your husband, and make him see what this will entail for his family as well as—

Dr. Stockmann. My family is my own concern and nobody

else's!

Peter Stockmann.—For his own family, as I was saying, as well as for the town he lives in.

Dr. Stockmann. It is I who have the real good of the town at heart! I want to lay bare the defects that sooner or later must come to the light of day. I will show whether I love my native town.

Peter Stockmann. You, who in your blind obstinacy want to cut off the most important source of the town's welfare?

Dr. Stockmann. The source is poisoned, man! Are you mad? We are making our living by retailing filth and corruption! The whole of our flourishing municipal life derives its sustenance from a lie!

Peter Stockmann. All imagination—or something even worse. The man who can throw out such offensive insinuations about his native town must be an enemy to our community.

Dr. Stockmann (*going up to him*). Do you dare to—!

Mrs. Stockmann (*throwing herself between them*). Thomas!

Petra (*catching her father by the arm*). Don't lose your temper, father!

Peter Stockmann. I will not expose myself to violence. Now you have had a warning; so reflect on what you owe to yourself and your family. Goodbye. (*Goes out.*)

Dr. Stockmann (*walking up and down*). Am I to put up with such treatment as this? In my own house, Katherine! What do you think of that!

Mrs. Stockmann. Indeed it is both shameful and absurd, Thomas—

Petra. If only I could give uncle a piece of my mind—

Dr. Stockmann. It is my own fault. I ought to have flown out at him long ago!—Shown my teeth!—Bitten! To hear him call me an enemy to our community! Me! I shall not take that lying down, upon my soul!

Mrs. Stockmann. But, dear Thomas, your brother has power on his side.

Dr. Stockmann. Yes, but I have right on mine, I tell you.

Mrs. Stockmann. Oh yes, right—right. What is the use of having right on your side if you have not got might?

Petra. Oh, mother!—How can you say such a thing!

Dr. Stockmann. Do you imagine that in a free country it is no use having right on your side? You are absurd, Katherine. Besides, haven't I got the liberal-minded, independent press to lead the way, and the compact majority behind me? That is might enough, I should think!

Mrs. Stockmann. But, good heavens, Thomas, you don't mean to?

Dr. Stockmann. Don't mean to what?

Mrs. Stockmann. To set yourself up in opposition to your brother.

Dr. Stockmann. In God's name, what else do you suppose I should do but take my stand on right and truth?

Petra. Yes, I was just going to say that.

Mrs. Stockmann. But it won't do you any earthly good. If they won't do it, they won't.

Dr. Stockmann. Oho, Katherine! Just give me time, and you will see how I will carry the war into their camp.

Mrs. Stockmann. Yes, you carry the war into their camp, and you get your dismissal—that is what you will do.

Dr. Stockmann. In any case I shall have done my duty towards the public—towards the community, I, who am called its enemy!

Mrs. Stockmann. But towards your family, Thomas? Towards your own home! Do you think that is doing your duty towards those you have to provide for?

Petra. Ah, don't think always first of us, mother.

Mrs. Stockmann. Oh, it is easy for you to talk; you are able to shift for yourself, if need be. But remember the boys, Thomas; and think a little of yourself too, and of me—

Dr. Stockmann. I think you are out of your senses, Katherine! If I were to be such a miserable coward as to go on my knees to Peter and his damned crew, do you suppose I should ever know an hour's peace of mind all my life afterwards?

Mrs. Stockmann. I don't know anything about that; but God preserve us from the peace of mind we shall have, all the same, if you go on defying him! You will find yourself again without the means of subsistence, with no income to count upon. I should think we had had enough of that in the old days. Remember that, Thomas; think what that means.

Dr. Stockmann (*collecting himself with a struggle and clenching his fists*). And this is what this slavery can bring upon a free, honourable man! Isn't it horrible, Katherine?

Mrs. Stockmann. Yes, it is sinful to treat you so, it is perfectly true. But, good heavens, one has to put up with so much injustice in this world. There are the boys, Thomas! Look at them! What is to become of them? Oh, no, no, you can never have the heart—. (*Ejlif and Morten have come in, while she was speaking, with their school books in their hands.*)

Dr. Stockmann. The boys— I (*Recovers himself suddenly.*) No, even if the whole world goes to pieces, I will never bow my neck to this yokel (*Goes towards his room.*)

Mrs. Stockmann (*following him*). Thomas—what are you going to do!

Dr. Stockmann (*at his door*). I mean to have the right to look my sons in the face when they are grown men. (*Goes into his room.*)

Mrs. Stockmann (*bursting into tears*). God help us all!

Petra. Father is splendid! He will not give in.

(*The boys look on in amazement; Petra signs to them not to speak.*)

ACT III

SCENE.—The editorial office of the "People's Messenger." The entrance door is on the left-hand side of the back wall; on the right-hand side is another door with glass panels through which the printing room can be seen. Another door in the right-hand wall. In the middle of the room is a large table covered with papers, newspapers and books. In the foreground on the left a window, before which stands a desk and a high stool. There are a couple of easy chairs by the table, and other chairs standing along the wall. The room is dingy and uncomfortable; the furniture is old, the chairs stained and torn. In the printing room the compositors are seen at work, and a printer is working a hand-press. Hovstad is sitting at the desk, writing. Billing comes in from the right with Dr. Stockmann's manuscript in his hand.

Billing. Well, I must say!

Hovstad (*still writing*). Have you read it through?

Billing (*laying the MS. on the desk*). Yes, indeed I have.

Hovstad. Don't you think the Doctor hits them pretty hard?

Billing. Hard? Bless my soul, he's crushing! Every word falls like—how shall I put it?—like the blow of a sledgehammer.

Hovstad. Yes, but they are not the people to throw up the sponge at the first blow.

Billing. That is true; and for that reason we must strike blow upon blow until the whole of this aristocracy tumbles to pieces. As I sat in there reading this, I almost seemed to see a revolution in being.

Hovstad (*turning round*). Hush!—Speak so that Aslaksen cannot hear you.

Billing (*lowering his voice*). Aslaksen is a chicken-hearted chap, a coward; there is nothing of the man in him. But this time you will insist on your own way, won't you? You will put the Doctor's article in?

Hovstad. Yes, and if the Mayor doesn't like it—

Billing. That will be the devil of a nuisance.

Hovstad. Well, fortunately we can turn the situation to good account, whatever happens. If the Mayor will not fall in with the Doctor's project, he will have all the small tradesmen down on him—the whole of the Householders' Association and the rest of them. And if he does fall in with it, he will fall out with the whole crowd of large shareholders in the Baths, who up to now have been his most valuable supporters—

Billing. Yes, because they will certainly have to fork out a pretty penny—

Hovstad. Yes, you may be sure they will. And in this way the ring will be broken up, you see, and then in every issue of the paper we will enlighten the public on the Mayor's incapability on one point and another, and make it clear that all the positions of trust in the town, the whole control of municipal affairs, ought to be put in the hands of the Liberals.

Billing. That is perfectly true! I see it coming—I see it coming; we are on the threshold of a revolution!

(*A knock is heard at the door.*)

Hovstad. Hush! (*Calls out.*) Come in! (*Dr. Stockmann comes in by the street door. Hovstad goes to meet him.*) Ah, it is you, Doctor! Well?

Dr. Stockmann. You may set to work and print it, Mr. Hovstad!

Hovstad. Has it come to that, then?

Billing. Hurrah!

Dr. Stockmann. Yes, print away. Undoubtedly it has come to that. Now they must take what they get. There is going to be a fight in the town, Mr. Billing!

Billing. War to the knife, I hope! We will get our knives to their throats, Doctor!

Dr. Stockmann. This article is only a beginning. I have already got four or five more sketched out in my head. Where is Aslaksen?

Billing (*calls into the printing-room*). Aslaksen, just come here for a minute!

Hovstad. Four or five more articles, did you say? On the same subject?

Dr. Stockmann. No—far from it, my dear fellow. No, they are about quite another matter. But they all spring from the question of the water supply and the drainage. One thing leads to another, you know. It is like beginning to pull down an old house, exactly.

Billing. Upon my soul, it's true; you find you are not done till you have pulled all the old rubbish down.

Aslaksen (*coming in*). Pulled down? You are not thinking of pulling down the Baths surely, Doctor?

Hovstad. Far from it, don't be afraid.

Dr. Stockmann. No, we meant something quite different. Well, what do you think of my article, Mr. Hovstad?

Hovstad. I think it is simply a masterpiece.

Dr. Stockmann. Do you really think so? Well, I am very pleased, very pleased.

Hovstad. It is so clear and intelligible. One need have no special knowledge to understand the bearing of it. You will have every enlightened man on your side.

Aslaksen. And every prudent man too, I hope?

Billing. The prudent and the imprudent—almost the whole town.

Aslaksen. In that case we may venture to print it.

Dr. Stockmann. I should think so!

Hovstad. We will put it in tomorrow morning.

Dr. Stockmann. Of course—you must not lose a single day. What I wanted to ask you, Mr. Aslaksen, was if you would supervise the printing of it yourself.

Aslaksen. With pleasure.

Dr. Stockmann. Take care of it as if it were a treasure! No misprints—every word is important. I will look in again a little later; perhaps you will be able to let me see a proof. I can't tell you how eager I am to see it in print, and see it burst upon the public—

Billing. Burst upon them—yes, like a flash of lightning!

Dr. Stockmann.—And to have it submitted to the judgment of my intelligent fellow townsmen. You cannot imagine what I have gone through today. I have been threatened first with one thing and then with another; they have tried to rob me of my most elementary rights as a man—

Billing. What! Your rights as a man!

Dr. Stockmann.—They have tried to degrade me, to make a coward of me, to force me to put personal interests before my most sacred convictions.

Billing. That is too much—I'm damned if it isn't.

Hovstad. Oh, you mustn't be surprised at anything from that quarter.

Dr. Stockmann. Well, they will get the worst of it with me; they may assure themselves of that. I shall consider the "People's Messenger" my sheet-anchor now, and every single day I will bombard them with one article after another, like bombshells—

Aslaksen. Yes, but—

Billing. Hurrah!—It is war, it is war!

Dr. Stockmann. I shall smite them to the ground—I shall crush them—I shall break down all their defenses, before the eyes of the honest public! That is what I shall do!

Aslaksen, Yes, but in moderation, Doctor—proceed with moderation—

Billing. Not a bit of it, not a bit of it! Don't spare the dynamite!

Dr. Stockmann. Because it is not merely a question of water-supply and drains now, you know. No—it is the whole of our social life that we have got to purify and disinfect—

Billing. Spoken like a deliverer!

Dr. Stockmann. All the incapables must be turned out, you understand—and that in every walk of life! Endless vistas have opened themselves to my mind's eye today. I cannot see it all quite clearly yet, but I shall in time. Young and vigorous standard-bearers—those are what we need and must seek, my friends; we must have new men in command at all our outposts.

Billing. Hear hear!

Dr. Stockmann. We only need to stand by one another, and it will all be perfectly easy. The revolution will be launched like a ship that runs smoothly off the stocks. Don't you think so?

Hovstad. For my part I think we have now a prospect of

getting the municipal authority into the hands where it should lie.

Aslaksen. And if only we proceed with moderation, I cannot imagine that there will be any risk.

Dr. Stockmann. Who the devil cares whether there is any risk or not! What I am doing, I am doing in the name of truth and for the sake of my conscience.

Hovstad. You are a man who deserves to be supported, Doctor.

Aslaksen. Yes, there is no denying that the Doctor is a true friend to the town—a real friend to the community, that he is.

Billing. Take my word for it, Aslaksen, Dr. Stockmann is a friend of the people.

Aslaksen. I fancy the Householders' Association will make use of that expression before long.

Dr. Stockmann (*affected, grasps their hands*). Thank you, thank you, my dear staunch friends. It is very refreshing to me to hear you say that; my brother called me something quite different. By Jove, he shall have it back, with interest! But now I must be off to see a poor devil—I will come back, as I said. Keep a very careful eye on the manuscript, Aslaksen, and don't for worlds leave out any of my notes of exclamation! Rather put one or two more in! Capital, capital! Well, good-bye for the present—good-bye, good-bye!

(*They show him to the door, and bow him out.*)

Hovstad. He may prove an invaluably useful man to us.

Aslaksen. Yes, so long as he confines himself to this matter of the Baths. But if he goes farther afield, I don't think it would be advisable to follow him.

Hovstad. Hm!—That all depends—

Billing. You are so infernally timid, Aslaksen!

Aslaksen. Timid? Yes, when it is a question of the local authorities, I am timid, Mr. Billing; it is a lesson I have learned in the school of experience, let me tell you. But try me in higher politics, in matters that concern the government itself, and then see if I am timid.

Billing. No, you aren't, I admit. But this is simply contradicting yourself.

Aslaksen. I am a man with a conscience, and that is the whole matter. If you attack the government, you don't do the community any harm, anyway; those fellows pay no attention to attacks, you see—they go on just as they are, in spite of them. But local authorities are different; they can be turned out, and then perhaps you may get an ignorant lot into office who may do irreparable harm to the householders and everybody else.

Hovstad. But what of the education of citizens by self government—don't you attach any importance to that?

Aslaksen. When a man has interests of his own to protect, he cannot think of everything, Mr. Hovstad.

Hovstad. Then I hope I shall never have interests of my own to protect!

Billing. Hear, hear!

Aslaksen (*with a smile*). Hm! (*Points to the desk.*) Mr. Sheriff Stensgaard was your predecessor at that editorial desk.

Billing (*spitting*). Bah! That turncoat.

Hovstad. I am not a weathercock—and never will be.

Aslaksen. A politician should never be too certain of anything, Mr. Hovstad. And as for you, Mr. Billing, I should think it is time for you to be taking in a reef or two in your sails, seeing that you are applying for the post of secretary to the Bench.

Billing. I—!

Hovstad. Are you, Billing?

Billing. Well, yes—but you must clearly understand I am only doing it to annoy the bigwigs.

Aslaksen. Anyhow, it is no business of mine. But if I am to be accused of timidity and of inconsistency in my principles, this is what I want to point out: my political past is an open book. I have never changed, except perhaps to become a little more moderate, you see. My heart is still with the people; but I don't deny that my reason has a certain bias towards the authorities—the local ones, I mean. (*Goes into the printing room.*)

Billing. Oughtn't we to try and get rid of him, Hovstad?

Hovstad. Do you know anyone else who will advance the money for our paper and printing bill?

Billing. It is an infernal nuisance that we don't possess some capital to trade on.

Hovstad (*sitting down at his desk*). Yes, if we only had that, then—

Billing. Suppose you were to apply to Dr. Stockmann?

Hovstad (*turning over some papers*). What is the use? He has got nothing.

Billing. No, but he has got a warm man in the background, old Morten Kiil—"the Badger," as they call him.

Hovstad (*writing*). Are you so sure he has got anything?

Billing. Good Lord, of course he has! And some of it must come to the Stockmanns. Most probably he will do something for the children, at all events.

Hovstad (*turning half round*). Are you counting on that?

Billing. Counting on it? Of course I am not counting on anything.

Hovstad. That is right. And I should not count on the secretaryship to the Bench either, if I were you; for I can assure you—you won't get it.

Billing. Do you think I am not quite aware of that? My object is precisely not to get it. A slight of that kind stimulates a man's fighting power—it is like getting a supply of fresh bile—and I am sure one needs that badly enough in a hole-and-corner place like this, where it is so seldom anything happens to stir one up.

Hovstad (*writing*). Quite so, quite so.

Billing. Ah, I shall be heard of yet!—Now I shall go and write the appeal to the Householders' Association. (*Goes into the room on the right.*)

Hovstad (*sitting at his desk, biting his penholder, says slowly*). Hm!—that's it, is it. (*A knock is heard.*) Come in! (*Petra comes in by the outer door. Hovstad gets up.*) What, you!—here?

Petra. Yes, you must forgive me—

Hovstad (*pulling a chair forward*). Won't you sit down?

Petra. No, thank you; I must go again in a moment.

Hovstad. Have you come with a message from your father, by any chance?

Petra. No, I have come on my own account. (*Takes a book out of her coat pocket.*) Here is the English story.

Hovstad. Why have you brought it back?

Petra. Because I am not going to translate it.

Hovstad. But you promised me faithfully—

Petra. Yes, but then I had not read it, I don't suppose you have read it either?

Hovstad. No, you know quite well I don't understand English; but—

Petra. Quite so. That is why I wanted to tell you that you must find something else. (*Lays the book on the table.*) You can't use this for the "People's Messenger."

Hovstad. Why not?

Petra. Because it conflicts with all your opinions.

Hovstad. Oh, for that matter—

Petra. You don't understand me. The burden of this story is that there is a supernatural power that looks after the so-called good people in this world and makes everything happen for the best in their case—while all the so-called bad people are punished.

Hovstad. Well, but that is all right. That is just what our readers want.

Petra. And are you going to be the one to give it to them? For myself, I do not believe a word of it. You know quite well that things do not happen so in reality.

Hovstad. You are perfectly right; but an editor cannot always act as he would prefer. He is often obliged to bow to the wishes of the public in unimportant matters. Politics are the most important thing in life—for a newspaper, anyway; and if I want to carry my public with me on the path that leads to liberty and progress, I must not frighten them away. If they find a moral tale of this sort in the serial at the bottom of the page, they will be all the more ready to read what is printed above it; they feel more secure, as it were.

Petra. For shame! You would never go and set a snare like that for your readers; you are not a spider!

Hovstad (*smiling*). Thank you for having such a good opinion of me. No; as a matter of fact that is Billing's idea and not mine.

Petra. Billing's!

Hovstad. Yes; anyway, he propounded that theory here one day. And it is Billing who is so anxious to have that story in the paper; I don't know anything about the book.

Petra. But how can Billing, with his emancipated views—

Hovstad. Oh, Billing is a many-sided man. He is applying for the post of secretary to the Bench, too, I hear.

Petra. I don't believe it, Mr. Hovstad. How could he possibly bring himself to do such a thing?

Hovstad. Ah, you must ask him that.

Petra. I should never have thought it of him.

Hovstad (*looking more closely at her*). No? Does it really surprise you so much?

Petra. Yes. Or perhaps not altogether. Really, I don't quite know—

Hovstad. We journalists are not much worth, Miss Stockmann.

Petra. Do you really mean that?

Hovstad. I think so sometimes.

Petra. Yes, in the ordinary affairs of everyday life, perhaps; I can understand that. But now, when you have taken a weighty matter in hand—

Hovstad. This matter of your father's, you mean?

Petra. Exactly. It seems to me that now you must feel you are a man worth more than most.

Hovstad. Yes, today I do feel something of that sort.

Petra. Of course you do, don't you? It is a splendid vocation you have chosen—to smooth the way for the march of unappreciated truths, and new and courageous lines of thought. If it were nothing more than because you stand fearlessly in the open and take up the cause of an injured man—

Hovstad. Especially when that injured man is—ahem!—I don't rightly know how to—

Petra. When that man is so upright and so honest, you mean?

Hovstad (*more gently*). Especially when he is your father I meant.

Petra (*suddenly checked*). That?

Hovstad. Yes, Petra—Miss Petra.

Petra. Is it that, that is first and foremost with you? Not the matter itself? Not the truth?—Not my father's big generous heart?

Hovstad. Certainly—of course—that too.

Petra. No, thank you; you have betrayed yourself, Mr. Hovstad, and now I shall never trust you again in anything.

Hovstad. Can you really take it so amiss in me that it is mostly for your sake—?

Petra. What I am angry with you for, is for not having been honest with my father. You talked to him as if the truth and the good of the community were what lay nearest to your heart. You have made fools of both my father and me. You are not the man you made yourself out to be. And that I shall never forgive you—never!

Hovstad. You ought not to speak so bitterly, Miss Petra—least of all now.

Petra. Why not now, especially?

Hovstad. Because your father cannot do without my help.

Petra (*looking him up and down*). Are you that sort of man too? For shame!

Hovstad. No, no, I am not. This came upon me so unexpectedly—you must believe that.

Petra. I know what to believe. Goodbye.

Aslaksen (*coming from the printing room, hurriedly and with an air of mystery*). Damnation, Hovstad!— (*Sees Petra.*) Oh, this is awkward—

Petra. There is the book; you must give it to someone else. (*Goes towards the door.*)

Hovstad (*following her*). But, Miss Stockmann—

Petra. Goodbye. (*Goes out.*)

Aslaksen. I say—Mr. Hovstad—

Hovstad. Well, well!—what is it?

Aslaksen. The Mayor is outside in the printing room.

Hovstad. The Mayor, did you say?

Aslaksen. Yes he wants to speak to you. He came in by the back door—didn't want to be seen, you understand.

Hovstad. What can he want? Wait a bit—I will go myself. (*Goes to the door of the printing room, opens it, bows and invites Peter Stockmann in.*) Just see, Aslaksen, that no one—

Aslaksen. Quite so. (*Goes into the printing-room.*)

Peter Stockmann. You did not expect to see me here, Mr. Hovstad?

Hovstad. No, I confess I did not.

Peter Stockmann (*looking round*). You are very snug in here—very nice indeed.

Hovstad. Oh—

Peter Stockmann. And here I come, without any notice, to take up your time!

Hovstad. By all means, Mr. Mayor. I am at your service. But let me relieve you of your— (*takes Stockmann's hat and stick and puts them on a chair*). Won't you sit down?

Peter Stockmann (*sitting down by the table*). Thank you. (*Hovstad sits down.*) I have had an extremely annoying experience today, Mr. Hovstad.

Hovstad. Really? Ah well, I expect with all the various business you have to attend to—

Peter Stockmann. The Medical Officer of the Baths is responsible for what happened today.

Hovstad. Indeed? The Doctor?

Peter Stockmann. He has addressed a kind of report to the Baths Committee on the subject of certain supposed defects in the Baths.

Hovstad. Has he indeed?

Peter Stockmann. Yes—has he not told you? I thought he said—

Hovstad. Ah, yes—it is true he did mention something about—

Aslaksen (*coming from the printing-room*). I ought to have that copy.

Hovstad (*angrily*). Ahem!—There it is on the desk.

Aslaksen (*taking it*). Right.

Peter Stockmann. But look there—that is the thing I was speaking of!

Aslaksen. Yes, that is the Doctor's article, Mr. Mayor.

Hovstad. Oh, is *that* what you were speaking about?

Peter Stockmann. Yes, that is it. What do you think of it?

Hovstad. Oh, I am only a layman—and I have only taken a very cursory glance at it.

Peter Stockmann. But you are going to print it?

Hovstad. I cannot very well refuse a distinguished man.

Aslaksen. I have nothing to do with editing the paper, Mr. Mayor—

Peter Stockmann. I understand.

Aslaksen. I merely print what is put into my hands.

Peter Stockmann. Quite so.

Aslaksen. And so I must— (*moves off towards the printing-room*).

Peter Stockmann. No, but wait a moment, Mr. Aslaksen. You will allow me, Mr. Hovstad?

Hovstad. If you please, Mr. Mayor.

Peter Stockmann. You are a discreet and thoughtful man, Mr. Aslaksen.

Aslaksen. I am delighted to hear you think so, sir.

Peter Stockmann. And a man of very considerable influence.

Aslaksen. Chiefly among the small tradesmen, sir.

Peter Stockmann. The small tax-payers are the majority—here as everywhere else.

Aslaksen. That is true.

Peter Stockmann. And I have no doubt you know the general trend of opinion among them, don't you?

Aslaksen. Yes I think I may say I do, Mr. Mayor.

Peter Stockmann. Yes. Well, since there is such a praiseworthy spirit of self-sacrifice among the less wealthy citizens of our town—

Aslaksen. What?

Hovstad. Self-sacrifice?

Peter Stockmann. It is pleasing evidence of a public-spirited feeling, extremely pleasing evidence. I might almost say I hardly expected it. But you have a closer knowledge of public opinion than I.

Aslaksen. But, Mr. Mayor—

Peter Stockmann. And indeed it is no small sacrifice that the town is going to make.

Hovstad. The town?

Aslaksen. But I don't understand. Is it the Baths—?

Peter Stockmann. At a provisional estimate, the alterations that the Medical Officer asserts to be desirable will cost somewhere about twenty thousand pounds.

Aslaksen. That is a lot of money, but—

Peter Stockmann. Of course it will be necessary to raise a municipal loan.

Hovstad (*getting up*). Surely you never mean that the town must pay?

Aslaksen. Do you mean that it must come out of the municipal funds?—out of the ill-filled pockets of the small tradesmen?

Peter Stockmann. Well, my dear Mr. Aslaksen, where else is the money to come from?

Aslaksen. The gentlemen who own the Baths ought to provide that.

Peter Stockmann. The proprietors of the Baths are not in a position to incur any further expense.

Aslaksen. Is that absolutely certain, Mr. Mayor?

Peter Stockmann. I have satisfied myself that it is so. If the town wants these very extensive alterations, it will have to pay for them.

Aslaksen. But, damn it all—I beg your pardon—this is quite another matter, Mr. Hovstad!

Hovstad. It is, indeed.

Peter Stockmann. The most fatal part of it is that we shall be obliged to shut the Baths for a couple of years.

Hovstad. Shut them? Shut them altogether?

Aslaksen. For two years?

Peter Stockmann. Yes, the work will take as long as that—at least.

Aslaksen. I'm damned if we will stand that, Mr. Mayor! What are we householders to live upon in the meantime?

Peter Stockmann. Unfortunately, that is an extremely difficult question to answer, Mr. Aslaksen. But what would you have us do? Do you suppose we shall have a single visitor in the town, if we go about proclaiming that our water is polluted, that we are living over a plague spot, that the entire town—

Aslaksen. And the whole thing is merely imagination?

Peter Stockmann. With the best will in the world, I have not been able to come to any other conclusion.

Aslaksen. Well then I must say it is absolutely unjustifiable of Dr. Stockmann—I beg your pardon, Mr. Mayor.

Peter Stockmann. What you say is lamentably true, Mr. Aslaksen. My brother has unfortunately always been a headstrong man.

Aslaksen. After this, do you mean to give him your support, Mr. Hovstad?

Hovstad. Can you suppose for a moment that I—?

Peter Stockmann. I have drawn up a short resume of the situation as it appears from a reasonable man's point of view. In it I have indicated how certain possible defects might suitably be remedied without outrunning the resources of the Baths Committee.

Hovstad. Have you got it with you, Mr. Mayor?

Peter Stockmann (*fumbling in his pocket*). Yes, I brought it with me in case you should—

Aslaksen. Good Lord, there he is!

Peter Stockmann. Who? My brother?

Hovstad. Where? Where?

Aslaksen. He has just gone through the printing room.

Peter Stockmann. How unlucky! I don't want to meet him here, and I had still several things to speak to you about.

Hovstad (*pointing to the door on the right*). Go in there for the present.

Peter Stockmann. But—?

Hovstad. You will only find Billing in there.

Aslaksen. Quick, quick, Mr. Mayor—he is just coming.

Peter Stockmann. Yes, very well; but see that you get rid of him quickly. (*Goes out through the door on the right, which Aslaksen opens for him and shuts after him.*)

Hovstad. Pretend to be doing something, Aslaksen. (*Sits down and writes. Aslaksen begins foraging among a heap of newspapers that are lying on a chair.*)

Dr. Stockmann (*coming in from the printing room*). Here I am again. (*Puts down his hat and stick.*)

Hovstad (*writing*). Already, Doctor? Hurry up with what we were speaking about, Aslaksen. We are very pressed for time today.

Dr. Stockmann (*to Aslaksen*). No proof for me to see yet, I hear.

Aslaksen (*without turning round*). You couldn't expect it yet, Doctor.

Dr. Stockmann. No, no; but I am impatient, as you can understand. I shall not know a moment's peace of mind until I see it in print.

Hovstad. Hm!—It will take a good while yet, won't it, Aslaksen?

Aslaksen. Yes, I am almost afraid it will.

Dr. Stockmann. All right, my dear friends; I will come back. I do not mind coming back twice if necessary. A matter of such great importance—the welfare of the town at stake—it is no time to shirk trouble, (*is just going, but stops and comes back.*) Look here—there is one thing more I want to speak to you about.

Hovstad. Excuse me, but could it not wait till some other time?

Dr. Stockmann. I can tell you in half a dozen words. It is only this. When my article is read tomorrow and it is realised that I have been quietly working the whole winter for the welfare of the town—

Hovstad. Yes but, Doctor—

Dr. Stockmann. I know what you are going to say. You don't see how on earth it was anymore than my duty—my obvious duty as a citizen. Of course it wasn't; I know that as well as you. But my fellow citizens, you know—! Good Lord, think of all the good souls who think so highly of me—!

Aslaksen. Yes, our townsfolk have had a very high opinion of you so far, Doctor.

Dr. Stockmann. Yes, and that is just why I am afraid they—. Well, this is the point; when this reaches them, especially the poorer classes, and sounds in their ears like a summons to take the town's affairs into their own hands for the future—

Hovstad (*getting up*). Ahem! Doctor, I won't conceal from you the fact—

Dr. Stockmann. Ah I—I knew there was something in the wind! But I won't hear a word of it. If anything of that sort is being set on foot—

Hovstad. Of what sort?

Dr. Stockmann. Well, whatever it is—whether it is a demonstration in my honour, or a banquet, or a subscription list for some presentation to me—whatever it is, you most promise me solemnly and faithfully to put a stop to it. You too, Mr. Aslaksen; do you understand?

Hovstad. You must forgive me, Doctor, but sooner or later we must tell you the plain truth—

(*He is interrupted by the entrance Of Mrs. Stockmann, who comes in from the street door.*)

Mrs. Stockmann (*seeing her husband*). Just as I thought!

Hovstad (*going towards her*). You too, Mrs. Stockmann?

Dr. Stockmann. What on earth do you want here, Katherine?

Mrs. Stockmann. I should think you know very well what I want.

Hovstad. Won't you sit down? Or perhaps—

Mrs. Stockmann. No, thank you; don't trouble. And you must not be offended at my coming to fetch my husband; I am the mother of three children, you know.

Dr. Stockmann. Nonsense!—We know all about that.

Mrs. Stockmann. Well, one would not give you credit for much thought for your wife and children today; if you had

had that, you would not have gone and dragged us all into misfortune.

Dr. Stockmann. Are you out of your senses, Katherine! Because a man has a wife and children, is he not to be allowed to proclaim the truth—is he not to be allowed to be an actively useful citizen—is he not to be allowed to do a service to his native town!

Mrs. Stockmann. Yes, Thomas—in reason.

Aslaksen. Just what I say. Moderation in everything.

Mrs. Stockmann. And that is why you wrong us, Mr. Hovstad, in enticing my husband away from his home and making a dupe of him in all this.

Hovstad. I certainly am making a dupe of no one—

Dr. Stockmann. Making a dupe of me! Do you suppose I should allow myself to be duped!

Mrs. Stockmann. It is just what you do. I know quite well you have more brains than anyone in the town, but you are extremely easily duped, Thomas. (*To Hovstad.*) Please do realise that he loses his post at the Baths if you print what he has written.

Aslaksen. What!

Hovstad. Look here, Doctor!

Dr. Stockmann (*laughing*). Ha-ha!—Just let them try! No, no— they will take good care not to. I have got the compact majority behind me, let me tell you!

Mrs. Stockmann. Yes, that is just the worst of it—your having any such horrid thing behind you.

Dr. Stockmann. Rubbish, Katherine!—Go home and look after your house and leave me to look after the community. How can you be so afraid, when I am so confident and happy? (*Walks up and down, rubbing his hands.*) Truth and the People will win the fight, you may be certain! I see the whole of the broad-minded middle class marching like a victorious army—! (*Stops beside a chair.*) What the deuce is that lying there?

Aslaksen. Good Lord!

Hovstad. Ahem!

Dr. Stockmann. Here we have the topmost pinnacle of authority! (*Takes the Mayor's official hat carefully between his finger-tips and holds it up in the air.*)

Mrs. Stockmann. The Mayor's hat!

Dr. Stockmann. And here is the staff of office too. How in the name of all that's wonderful—?

Hovstad. Well, you see—

Dr. Stockmann. Oh, I understand. He has been here trying to talk you over. Ha-ha!—He made rather a mistake there! And as soon as he caught sight of me in the printing room. (*Bursts out laughing.*) Did he run away, Mr. Aslaksen?

Aslaksen (*hurriedly*). Yes, he ran away, Doctor.

Dr. Stockmann. Ran away without his stick or his—. Fiddlesticks! Peter doesn't run away and leave his belongings behind him. But what the deuce have you done with him? Ah!—in there, of course. Now you shall see, Katherine!

Mrs. Stockmann. Thomas—please don't—!

Aslaksen. Don't be rash, Doctor.

(*Dr. Stockmann has put on the Mayor's hat and taken his stick in his hand. He goes up to the door, opens it, and stands with his hand to his hat at the salute. Peter Stockmann comes in, red with anger. Billing follows him.*)

Peter Stockmann. What does this tomfoolery mean?

Dr. Stockmann. Be respectful, my good Peter. I am the chief authority in the town now. (*Walks up and down.*)

Mrs. Stockmann (*almost in tears*). Really, Thomas!

Peter Stockmann (*following him about*). Give me my hat and stick.

Dr. Stockmann (*in the same tone as before*). If you are chief constable, let me tell you that I am the Mayor—I am the master of the whole town, please understand!

Peter Stockmann. Take off my hat, I tell you. Remember it is part of an official uniform.

Dr. Stockmann. Pooh! Do you think the newly awakened lionhearted people are going to be frightened by an official hat? There is going to be a revolution in the town tomorrow, let me tell you. You thought you could turn me out; but now I shall turn you out—turn you out of all your various offices. Do you think I cannot? Listen to me. I have triumphant social forces behind me. Hovstad and Billing will thunder in the "People's Messenger," and Aslaksen will take the field at the head of the whole Householders'

Association—

Aslaksen. That I won't, Doctor.

Dr. Stockmann. Of course you will—

Peter Stockmann. Ah!—May I ask then if Mr. Hovstad intends to join this agitation?

Hovstad. No, Mr. Mayor.

Aslaksen. No, Mr. Hovstad is not such a fool as to go and ruin his paper and himself for the sake of an imaginary grievance.

Dr. Stockmann (*looking round him*). What does this mean?

Hovstad. You have represented your case in a false light, Doctor, and therefore I am unable to give you my support.

Billing. And after what the Mayor was so kind as to tell me just now, I—

Dr. Stockmann. A false light! Leave that part of it to me. Only print my article; I am quite capable of defending it.

Hovstad. I am not going to print it. I cannot and will not and dare not print it.

Dr. Stockmann. You dare not? What nonsense!—You are the editor; and an editor controls his paper, I suppose!

Aslaksen. No, it is the subscribers, Doctor.

Peter Stockmann. Fortunately, yes.

Aslaksen. It is public opinion—the enlightened public—householders and people of that kind; they control the newspapers.

Dr. Stockmann (*composedly*). And I have all these influences against me?

Aslaksen. Yes, you have. It would mean the absolute ruin of the community if your article were to appear.

Dr. Stockmann. Indeed.

Peter Stockmann. My hat and stick, if you please. (*Dr. Stockmann takes off the hat and lays it on the table with the stick. Peter Stockmann takes them up.*) Your authority as mayor has come to an untimely end.

Dr. Stockmann. We have not got to the end yet. (*To Hovstad.*) Then it is quite impossible for you to print my article in the "People's Messenger"?

Hovstad. Quite impossible—out of regard for your family as well.

Mrs. Stockmann. You need not concern yourself about his family, thank you, Mr. Hovstad.

Peter Stockmann (*taking a paper from his pocket*). It will be sufficient, for the guidance of the public, if this appears. It is an official statement. May I trouble you?

Hovstad (*taking the paper*). Certainly; I will see that it is printed.

Dr. Stockmann. But not mine. Do you imagine that you can silence me and stifle the truth! You will not find it so easy as you suppose. Mr. Aslaksen, kindly take my manuscript at once and print it as a pamphlet—at my expense. I will have four hundred copies—no, five or six hundred.

Aslaksen. If you offered me its weight in gold, I could not lend my press for any such purpose, Doctor. It would be flying in the face of public opinion. You will not get it printed anywhere in the town.

Dr. Stockmann. Then give it me back.

Hovstad (*giving him the MS.*). Here it is.

Dr. Stockmann (*taking his hat and stick*). It shall be made public all the same. I will read it out at a mass meeting of the townspeople. All my fellow-citizens shall hear the voice of truth!

Peter Stockmann. You will not find any public body in the town that will give you the use of their hall for such a purpose.

Aslaksen. Not a single one, I am certain.

Billing. No, I'm damned if you will find one.

Mrs. Stockmann. But this is too shameful! Why should everyone turn against you like that?

Dr. Stockmann (*angrily*). I will tell you why. It is because all the men in this town are old women—like you; they all think of nothing but their families, and never of the community.

Mrs. Stockmann (*putting her arm into his*). Then I will show them that an old woman can be a man for once. I am going to stand by you, Thomas!

Dr. Stockmann. Bravely said, Katherine! It shall be made public—as I am a living soul! If I can't hire a hall, I shall hire a drum, and parade the town with it and read it at every street-corner.

Peter Stockmann. You are surely not such an errant fool as that!

Dr. Stockmann. Yes, I am.

Aslaksen. You won't find a single man in the whole town to go with you.

Billing. No, I'm damned if you will.

Mrs. Stockmann. Don't give in, Thomas. I will tell the boys to go with you.

Dr. Stockmann. That is a splendid idea!

Mrs. Stockmann. Morten will be delighted; and Ejlif will do whatever he does.

Dr. Stockmann. Yes, and Petra!—And you too, Katherine!

Mrs. Stockmann. No, I won't do that; but I will stand at the window and watch you, that's what I will do.

Dr. Stockmann (*puts his arms round her and kisses her*). Thank you, my dear! Now you and I are going to try a fall, my fine gentlemen! I am going to see whether a pack of cowards can succeed in gagging a patriot who wants to purify society! (*He and his wife go out by the street door.*)

Peter Stockmann (*shaking his head seriously*). Now he has sent her out of her senses, too.

ACT IV

SCENE.—A big old-fashioned room in Captain Horster's house. At the back folding-doors, which are standing open, lead to an ante-room. Three windows in the left-hand wall. In the middle of the opposite wall a platform has been erected. On this is a small table with two candles, a water-bottle and glass, and a bell. The room is lit by lamps placed between the windows. In the foreground on the left there is a table with candles and a chair. To the right is a door and some chairs standing near it. The room is nearly filled with a crowd of townspeople of all sorts, a few women and schoolboys being amongst them. People are still streaming in from the back, and the room is soon filled.

1st Citizen (*meeting another*). Hullo, Lamstad! You here too?

2nd Citizen. I go to every public meeting, I do.

3rd Citizen. Brought your whistle too, I expect!

2nd Citizen. I should think so. Haven't you?

3rd Citizen. Rather! And old Evensen said he was going to bring a cow-horn, he did.

2nd Citizen. Good old Evensen! (*Laughter among the crowd.*)

4th Citizen (*coming up to them*). I say, tell me what is going on here tonight?

2nd Citizen. Dr. Stockmann is going to deliver an address attacking the Mayor.

4th Citizen. But the Mayor is his brother.

1st Citizen. That doesn't matter; Dr. Stockmann's not the chap to be afraid.

3rd Citizen. But he is in the wrong; it said so in the "People's Messenger."

2nd Citizen. Yes, I expect he must be in the wrong this time, because neither the Householder's Association nor the Citizen's Club would lend him their hall for his meeting.

1st Citizen. He couldn't even get the loan of the hall at the Baths.

2nd Citizen. No, I should think not.

A man in another part of the crowd. I say—who are we to back up in this?

Another Man (*beside him*). Watch Aslaksen, and do as he does.

Billing (*pushing his way through the crowd, with a writing-case under his arm*). Excuse me, gentleman—do you mind letting me through? I am reporting for the "People's Messenger." Thank you very much! (*He sits down at the table on the left.*)

A Workman. Who was that?

2nd Workman. Don't you know him? It's Billing, who writes for Aslaksen's paper.

(*Captain Horster brings in Mrs. Stickmann and Petra through the door on the right. Ejlif and Morten follow them in*)

Horster. I thought you might all sit here; you can slip out easily from here, if things get too lively.

Mrs. Stickmann. Do you think there will be a disturbance?

Horster. One can never tell—with such a crowd. But sit down, and don't be uneasy.

Mrs. Stickmann (*sitting down.*) It was extremely kind of you to offer my husband the room.

Horster. Well, if nobody else would—

Petra (*who has set down beside her mother*). And it was a plucky thing to do, Captain Horster.

Horster. Oh, it is not such a great matter as all that.

(*Hovstad and Aslaksen make their way through the crowd.*)

Aslaksen (*going up to Horster*). Has the Doctor not come yet?

Horster. He is waiting in the next room. (*Movement in the crowd by the door at the back.*)

Hovstad. Look—here comes the Mayor!

Billing. Yes, I'm damned if he hasn't come after all!

(*Peter Stockman makes his way gradually through the crowd, bows courteously, and takes up a position by the wall on the left. Shortly afterwards Dr. Stockmann comes in by the right-hand door. He is dressed in a black frockcoat, with a white tie. There is a little feeble applause, which is hushed down. Silence is obtained.*)

Dr. Stockmann (*in an undertone*). How do you feel, Katherine?

Mrs. Stockmann. All right, thank you. (*Lowering her voice.*) Be sure not to lose your temper, Thomas.

Dr. Stockmann. Oh, I know how to control myself. (*Looks at his watch, steps on to the platform, and bows.*) It is a quarter past—so I will begin. (*Takes his MS. Out of his pocket.*)

Aslaksen. I think we ought to elect a chairman first.

Dr. Stockmann. No, it is quite unnecessary.

Some of the Crowd. Yes—yes!

Peter Stockmann. Dr. Stockmann's lecture may possibly lead to a considerable conflict of opinion.

Voices in the Crowd. A chairman! A chairman!

Hovstad. The general wish of the meeting seems to be that a chairman should be elected.

Dr. Stockmann (*restraining himself*). Very well—let the meeting have its way.

Aslaksen. Will the Mayor be good enough to undertake the task?

Three Man (*clapping their hands*). Bravo! Bravo!

Peter Stockmann. For various reasons, which you will easily understand, I must beg to be excused. But fortunately we have amongst us a man who I think will be acceptable to you all. I refer to the President of the Householders' Association, Mr. Aslaksen.

Several voices. Yes—Aslaksen! Bravo Aslaksen!

(*Dr. Stockmann takes up his MS. and walks up and down the platform.*)

Aslaksen. Since my fellow-citizens choose to entrust me with this duty, I cannot refuse.

(*Loud applause. Aslaksen mounts the platform.*)

Billing (*writing*), "Mr. Aslaksen was elected with enthusiasm."

Aslaksen. And now, as I am in this position, I should like to say a few brief words. I am a quiet and peaceable man, who believes in discreet moderation, and—and—in moderate discretion. All my friends can bear witness to that.

Several Voices. That's right! That's right, Aslaksen!

Aslaksen. I have learned in the school of life and experience that moderation is the most valuable virtue a citizen can possess—

Peter Stockmann. Hear, hear!

Aslaksen.—And moreover, that discretion and moderation are what enable a man to be of most service to the community. I would therefore suggest to our esteemed fellow-citizen, who has called this meeting, that he should strive to keep strictly within the bounds of moderation.

A Man by the door. Three cheers for the Moderation Society!

A Voice. Shame!

Several Voices. Sh!—Sh!

Aslaksen. No interruptions, gentlemen, please! Does anyone wish to make any remarks?

Peter Stockmann. Mr. Chairman.

Aslaksen. The Mayor will address the meeting.

Peter Stockmann. In consideration of the close relationship in which, as you all know, I stand to the present Medical Officer of the Baths, I should have preferred not to speak this evening. But my official position with regard to the Baths and my solicitude for the vital interests of the town compel me to bring forward a motion. I venture to presume that there is not a single one of our citizens present who considers it desirable that unreliable and exaggerated accounts of the sanitary condition of the Baths and the town should be spread abroad.

Several Voices. No, no! Certainly not! We protest against it!

Peter Stockmann. Therefore, I should like to propose that the meeting should not permit the Medical Officer either to read or to comment on his proposed lecture.

Dr. Stockmann (*impatiently*). Not permit—! What the devil—!

Mrs. Stockmann (*coughing*). Ahem!—Ahem!

Dr. Stockmann (*collecting himself*). Very well, Go ahead!

Peter Stockmann. In my communication to the "People's Messenger," I have put the essential facts before the public in such a way that every fair-minded citizen can easily form his own opinion. From it you will see that the main result of the Medical Officer's proposals—apart from their constituting a vote of censure on the leading men of the town—would be to saddle the ratepayers with an unnecessary expenditure of at least some thousands of pounds.

(*Sounds of disapproval among the audience, and some cat-calls.*)

Aslaksen (*ringing his bell*). Silence, please, gentlemen! I beg to support the Mayor's motion. I quite agree with him that there is something behind this agitation started by the Doctor. He talks about the Baths; but it is a revolution he is aiming at—he wants to get the administration of the town put into new hands. No one doubts the honesty of the Doctor's intentions—no one will suggest that there can be any two opinions as to that, I myself am a believer in self-government for the people, provided it does not fall too heavily on the ratepayers. But that would be the case here; and that is why I will see Dr. Stockmann damned— I beg your pardon—before I go with him in the matter. You can pay too dearly for a thing sometimes; that is my opinion.

(*Loud applause on all sides.*)

Hovstad. I, too, feel called upon to explain my position. Dr. Stockmann's agitation appeared to be gaining a certain amount of sympathy at first, so I supported it as impartially as I could. But presently we had reason to suspect that we had allowed ourselves to be misled by misrepresentation of the state of affairs—

Dr. Stockmann. Misrepresentation—!

Hovstad. Well, let us say a not entirely trustworthy representation. The Mayor's statement has proved that. I hope no one here has any doubt as to my liberal principles; the attitude of the "People's Messenger" towards important political questions is well known to everyone. But the advice of experienced and thoughtful men has convinced me that in purely local matters a newspaper ought to proceed with a certain caution.

Aslaksen. I entirely agree with the speaker.

Hovstad. And, in the matter before us, it is now an undoubted fact that Dr. Stockmann has public opinion against him. Now, what is an editor's first and most obvious duty, gentlemen? Is it not to work in harmony with his readers? Has he not received a sort of tacit mandate to work persistently and assiduously for the welfare of those whose opinions he represents? Or is it possible I am mistaken in that?

Voices from the crowd. No, no! You are quite right!

Hovstad. It has cost me a severe struggle to break with a man in whose house I have been lately a frequent guest—a man who till today has been able to pride himself on the undivided goodwill of his fellow-citizens—a man whose only, or at all events whose essential, failing is that he is swayed by his heart rather than his head.

A few scattered voices. That is true! Bravo, Stockmann!

Hovstad. But my duty to the community obliged me to break with him. And there is another consideration that impels me to oppose him, and, as far as possible, to arrest him on the perilous course he has adopted; that is, consideration for his family—

Dr. Stockmann. Please stick to the water-supply and drainage!

Hovstad.—Consideration, I repeat, for his wife and his

children for whom he has made no provision.

Morten. Is that us, mother?

Mrs. Stockmann. Hush!

Aslaksen. I will now put the Mayor's proposition to the vote.

Dr. Stockmann. There is no necessity! Tonight I have no intention of dealing with all that filth down at the Baths. No; I have something quite different to say to you.

Peter Stockmann (*aside*). What is coming now?

A Drunken Man (*by the entrance door*). I am a ratepayer! And therefore, I have a right to speak too! And my entire—firm—inconceivable opinion is—

A number of voices. Be quiet, at the back there!

Others. He is drunk! Turn him out! (*They turn him out.*)

Dr. Stockmann. Am I allowed to speak?

Aslaksen (*ringing his bell*). Dr. Stockmann will address the meeting.

Dr. Stockmann. I should like to have seen anyone, a few days ago, dare to attempt to silence me as has been done tonight! I would have defended my sacred rights as a man, like a lion! But now it is all one to me; I have something of even weightier importance to say to you. (*The crowd presses nearer to him, Morten Kiil conspicuous among them.*)

Dr. Stockmann (*continuing*). I have thought and pondered a great deal, these last few days—pondered over such a variety of things that in the end my head seemed too full to hold them—

Peter Stockmann (*with a cough*). Ahem!

Dr. Stockmann.—But I got them clear in my mind at last, and then I saw the whole situation lucidly. And that is why I am standing here to-night. I have a great revelation to make to you, my fellow-citizens! I will impart to you a discovery of a far wider scope than the trifling matter that our water supply is poisoned and our medicinal Baths are standing on pestiferous soil.

A number of voices (*shouting*). Don't talk about the Baths! We won't hear you! None of that!

Dr. Stockmann. I have already told you that what I want to speak about is the great discovery I have made lately— the discovery that all the sources of our moral life are poisoned and that the whole fabric of our civic community is founded on the pestiferous soil of falsehood.

Voices of disconcerted Citizens. What is that he says?

Peter Stockmann. Such an insinuation—!

Aslaksen (*with his hand on his bell*). I call upon the speaker to moderate his language.

Dr. Stockmann. I have always loved my native town as a man only can love the home of his youthful days. I was not old when I went away from here; and exile, longing and memories cast as it were an additional halo over both the town and its inhabitants. (*Some clapping and applause.*) And there I stayed, for many years, in a horrible hole far away up north. When I came into contact with some of the people that lived scattered about among the rocks, I often thought it would of been more service to the poor half-starved creatures if a veterinary doctor had been sent up there, instead of a man like me. (*Murmurs among the crowd.*)

Billing (*laying down his pen*). I'm damned if I have ever heard—!

Hovstad. It is an insult to a respectable population!

Dr. Stockmann. Wait a bit! I do not think anyone will charge me with having forgotten my native town up there. I was like one of the eider-ducks brooding on its nest, and what I hatched was the plans for these Baths. (*Applause and protests.*) And then when fate at last decreed for me the great happiness of coming home again—I assure you, gentlemen, I thought I had nothing more in the world to wish for. Or rather, there was one thing I wished for—eagerly, untiringly, ardently—and that was to be able to be of service to my native town and the good of the community.

Peter Stockmann (*looking at the ceiling*). You chose a strange way of doing it—ahem!

Dr. Stockmann. And so, with my eyes blinded to the real facts, I revelled in happiness. But yesterday morning—no, to be precise, it was yesterday afternoon—the eyes of my mind were opened wide, and the first thing I realised was the colossal stupidity of the authorities—. (*Uproar, shouts and laughter, Mrs. Stockmann coughs persistently.*)

Peter Stockmann. Mr. Chairman!

Aslaksen (*ringing his bell*). By virtue of my authority—!

Dr. Stockmann. It is a petty thing to catch me up on a word, Mr. Aslaksen. What I mean is only that I got scent of the unbelievable piggishness our leading men had been responsible for down at the Baths. I can't stand leading men at any price!—I have had enough of such people in my time. They are like billy-goats on a young plantation; they do mischief everywhere. They stand in a free man's way, whichever way he turns, and what I should like best would be to see them exterminated like any other vermin—. (*Uproar.*)

Peter Stockmann. Mr. Chairman, can we allow such expressions to pass?

Aslaksen (*with his hand on his bell*). Doctor—!

Dr. Stockmann. I cannot understand how it is that I have only now acquired a clear conception of what these gentry are, when I had almost daily before my eyes in this town such an excellent specimen of them—my brother Peter—slow-witted and hide-bound in prejudice—. (*Laughter, uproar and hisses. Mrs. Stockmann Sits coughing assiduously. Aslaksen rings his bell violently.*)

The Drunken Man (*who has got in again*). Is it me he is talking about? My name's Petersen, all right—but devil take me if I—

Angry Voices. Turn out that drunken man! Turn him out. (*He is turned out again.*)

Peter Stockmann. Who was that person?

1st Citizen. I don't know who he is, Mr. Mayor.

2nd Citizen. He doesn't belong here.

3rd Citizen. I expect he is a navvy from over at— (*the rest is inaudible*).

Aslaksen. He had obviously had too much beer. Proceed, Doctor; but please strive to be moderate in your language.

Dr. Stockmann. Very well, gentlemen, I will say no more about our leading men. And if anyone imagines, from what I have just said, that my object is to attack these people this evening, he is wrong—absolutely wide of the mark. For I cherish the comforting conviction that these parasites—all these venerable relics of a dying school of thought—are most admirably paving the way for their own extinction; they need no doctor's help to hasten their end. Nor is it folk of that kind who constitute the most pressing danger to the community. It is not they who are most instrumental in poisoning the sources of our moral life and infecting the ground on which we stand. It is not they who are the most dangerous enemies of truth and freedom amongst us.

Shouts from all sides. Who then? Who is it? Name! Name!

Dr. Stockmann. You may depend upon it—I shall name them! That is precisely the great discovery I made yesterday. (*Raises his voice.*) The most dangerous enemy of truth and freedom amongst us is the compact majority—yes, the damned compact Liberal majority—that is it! Now you know!

(*Tremendous uproar. Most of the crowd are shouting, stamping and hissing. Some of the older men among them exchange stolen glances and seem to be enjoying themselves. Mrs. Stockmann gets up, looking anxious. Ejlif and Morten advance threateningly upon some schoolboys who are playing pranks. Aslaksen rings his bell and begs for silence. Hovstad and Billing both talk at once, but are inaudible. At last quiet is restored.*)

Aslaksen. As Chairman, I call upon the speaker to withdraw the ill-considered expressions he has just used.

Dr. Stockmann. Never, Mr. Aslaksen! It is the majority in our community that denies me my freedom and seeks to prevent my speaking the truth.

Hovstad. The majority always has right on its side.

Billing. And truth too, by God!

Dr. Stockmann. The majority never has right on its side. Never, I say! That is one of these social lies against which an independent, intelligent man must wage war. Who is it that constitute the majority of the population in a country? Is it the clever folk, or the stupid? I don't imagine you will dispute the fact that at present the stupid people are in an absolutely overwhelming majority all the world over. But, good Lord!—You can never pretend that it is right that the stupid folk should govern the clever ones! (*Uproar and cries.*) Oh, yes—you can shout me down, I know! But you cannot answer me. The majority has might on its side—unfortunately; but right it has not. I am in the right—I and a few other scattered individuals. The minority is always in the right. (*Renewed uproar.*)

Hovstad. Aha!—So Dr. Stockmann has become an aristocrat since the day before yesterday!

Dr. Stockmann. I have already said that I don't intend to waste a word on the puny, narrow-chested, short-winded crew whom we are leaving astern. Pulsating life no longer concerns itself with them. I am thinking of the few, the scattered few amongst us, who have absorbed new and vigorous truths. Such men stand, as it were, at the outposts, so far ahead that the compact majority has not yet been able to come up with them; and there they are fighting for truths that are too newly-born into the world of consciousness to have any considerable number of people on their side as yet.

Hovstad. So the Doctor is a revolutionary now!

Dr. Stockmann. Good heavens—of course I am, Mr. Hovstad! I propose to raise a revolution against the lie that the majority has the monopoly of the truth. What sort of truths are they that the majority usually supports? They are truths that are of such advanced age that they are beginning to break up. And if a truth is as old as that, it is also in a fair way to become a lie, gentlemen. (*Laughter and mocking cries.*) Yes, believe me or not, as you like; but truths are by no means as long-lived at Methuselah—as some folk imagine. A normally constituted truth lives, let us say, as a rule seventeen or eighteen, or at most twenty years—

seldom longer. But truths as aged as that are always worn frightfully thin, and nevertheless it is only then that the majority recognises them and recommends them to the community as wholesome moral nourishment. There is no great nutritive value in that sort of fare, I can assure you; and, as a doctor, I ought to know. These "majority truths" are like last year's cured meat—like rancid, tainted ham; and they are the origin of the moral scurvy that is rampant in our communities.

Aslaksen. It appears to me that the speaker is wandering a long way from his subject.

Peter Stockmann. I quite agree with the Chairman.

Dr. Stockmann. Have you gone clean out of your senses, Peter? I am sticking as closely to my subject as I can; for my subject is precisely this, that it is the masses, the majority—this infernal compact majority—that poisons the sources of our moral life and infects the ground we stand on.

Hovstad. And all this because the great, broadminded majority of the people is prudent enough to show deference only to well-ascertained and well-approved truths?

Dr. Stockmann. Ah, my good Mr. Hovstad, don't talk nonsense about well-ascertained truths! The truths of which the masses now approve are the very truths that the fighters at the outposts held to in the days of our grandfathers. We fighters at the outposts nowadays no longer approve of them; and I do not believe there is any other well-ascertained truth except this, that no community can live a healthy life if it is nourished only on such old marrowless truths.

Hovstad. But, instead of standing there using vague generalities, it would be interesting if you would tell us what these old marrowless truths are, that we are nourished on.

(*Applause from many quarters.*)

Dr. Stockmann. Oh, I could give you a whole string of such abominations; but to begin with I will confine myself to one well-approved truth, which at bottom is a foul lie, but upon which nevertheless Mr. Hovstad and the "People's Messenger" and all the "Messenger's" supporters are nourished.

Hovstad. And that is—?

Dr. Stockmann. That is, the doctrine you have inherited from your forefathers and proclaim thoughtlessly far and wide—the doctrine that the public, the crowd, the masses, are the essential part of the population—that they constitute the People—that the common folk, the ignorant and incomplete element in the community, have the same right to pronounce judgment and to approve, to direct and to govern, as the isolated, intellectually superior personalities in it.

Billing. Well, damn me if ever I—

Hovstad (*at the same time, shouting out*). Fellow-citizens, take good note of that!

A number of voices (*angrily*). Oho!—We are not the People! Only the superior folk are to govern, are they!

A Workman. Turn the fellow out for talking such rubbish!

Another. Out with him!

Another (*calling out*). Blow your horn, Evensen!

(*A horn is blown loudly, amidst hisses and an angry uproar.*)

Dr. Stockmann (*when the noise has somewhat abated*). Be reasonable! Can't you stand hearing the voice of truth for once? I don't in the least expect you to agree with me all at once; but I must say I did expect Mr. Hovstad to admit I was right, when he had recovered his composure a little. He claims to be a freethinker—

Voices (*in murmurs of astonishment*). Freethinker, did he say? Is Hovstad a freethinker?

Hovstad (*shouting*). Prove it, Dr. Stockmann! When have I said so in print?

Dr. Stockmann (*reflecting*). No, confound it, you are right!— You have never had the courage to. Well, I won't put you in a hole, Mr. Hovstad. Let us say it is I that am the freethinker, then. I am going to prove to you, scientifically, that the "People's Messenger" leads you by the nose in a shameful manner when it tells you that you—that the common people, the crowd, the masses, are the real essence of the People. That is only a newspaper lie, I tell you! The common people are nothing more than the raw material of which a People is made. (*Groans, laughter and uproar.*) Well, isn't that the case? Isn't there an enormous difference between a well-bred and an ill-bred strain of animals? Take, for instance, a common barn-door hen. What sort of eating do you get from a shrivelled up old scrag of a fowl like that? Not much, do you! And what sort of eggs does it lay? A fairly good crow or a raven can lay pretty nearly as good an egg. But take a well-bred Spanish or Japanese hen, or a good pheasant or a turkey—then you will see the difference. Or take the case of dogs, with whom we humans are on such intimate terms. Think first of an ordinary common cur—I mean one of the horrible, coarse-haired, low-bred curs that do nothing but run about the streets and befoul the walls of the houses. Compare one of these curs with a poodle whose sires for many generations have been bred in a gentleman's house, where they have had the best of food and had the opportunity of hearing soft voices and music. Do you not think that the poodle's brain is developed to quite a different degree from that of the cur? Of course it is. It is puppies of well-bred poodles like that, that showmen train to do incredibly clever tricks—things that a common cur could never learn to do even if it stood on its head.

(*Uproar and mocking cries.*)

A Citizen (*calls out*). Are you going to make out we are dogs, now?

Another Citizen. We are not animals, Doctor!

Dr. Stockmann. Yes but, bless my soul, we are, my friend! It is true we are the finest animals anyone could wish for; but, even among us, exceptionally fine animals are rare. There is a tremendous difference between the thoroughbreds and the mongrels. And the amusing part of it is, that Mr. Hovstad quite agrees with me as long as it is a question of four-footed animals—

Hovstad. Yes, it is true enough as far as they are concerned.

Dr. Stockmann. Very well. But as soon as I extend the principle and apply it to two-legged animals, Mr. Hovstad stops short. He no longer dares to think independently, or to pursue his ideas to their logical conclusion; so, he turns the whole theory upside down and proclaims in the "People's Messenger" that it is the barn-door hens and street curs that are the finest specimens in the menagerie. But that is always the way, as long as a man retains the traces of common origin and has not worked his way up to intellectual distinction.

Hovstad. I lay no claim to any sort of distinction, I am the son of humble country-folk, and I am proud that the stock I come from is rooted deep among the common people he insults.

Voices. Bravo, Hovstad! Bravo! Bravo!

Dr. Stockmann. The kind of common people I mean are not only to be found low down in the social scale; they crawl and swarm all around us—even in the highest social positions. You have only to look at your own fine, distinguished Mayor! My brother Peter is every bit as plebeian as anyone that walks in two shoes— (*laughter and hisses*)

Peter Stockmann. I protest against personal allusions of this kind.

Dr. Stockmann (*imperturbably*).—And that, not because he is like myself, descended from some old rascal of a pirate from Pomerania or thereabouts—because that is who we are descended from—

Peter Stockmann. An absurd legend. I deny it!

Dr. Stockmann.—But because he thinks what his superiors think, and holds the same opinions as they, People who do that are, intellectually speaking, common people; and, that is why my magnificent brother Peter is in reality so very far from any distinction—and consequently also so far from being liberal-minded.

Peter Stockmann. Mr. Chairman—!

Hovstad. So it is only the distinguished men that are liberal-minded in this country? We are learning something quite new! (*Laughter.*)

Dr. Stockmann. Yes, that is part of my new discovery too. And another part of it is that broad-mindedness is almost precisely the same thing as morality. That is why I maintain that it is absolutely inexcusable in the "People's Messenger" to proclaim, day in and day out, the false doctrine that it is the masses, the crowd, the compact majority, that have the monopoly of broad-mindedness and morality—and that vice and corruption and every kind of intellectual depravity are the result of culture, just as all the filth that is draining into our Baths is the result of the tanneries up at Mölledal! (*Uproar and interruptions. Dr. Stockmann is undisturbed, and goes on, carried away by his ardour, with a smile.*) And yet this same "People's Messenger" can go on preaching that the masses ought to be elevated to higher conditions of life! But, bless my soul, if the "Messenger's" teaching is to be depended upon, this very raising up the masses would mean nothing more or less than setting them straightway upon the paths of depravity! Happily the theory that culture demoralises is only an old falsehood that our forefathers believed in and we have inherited. No, it is ignorance, poverty, ugly conditions of life, that do the devil's work! In a house which does not get aired and swept every day—my wife Katherine maintains that the floor ought to be scrubbed as well, but that is a debatable question—in such a house, let me tell you, people will lose within two or three years the power of thinking or acting in a moral manner. Lack of oxygen weakens the conscience. And there must be a plentiful lack of oxygen in very many houses in this town, I should think, judging from the fact that the whole compact majority can be unconscientious enough to wish to build the town's prosperity on a quagmire of falsehood and deceit.

Aslaksen. We cannot allow such a grave accusation to be flung at a citizen community.

A Citizen. I move that the Chairman direct the speaker to sit down.

Voices (*angrily*). Hear, hear! Quite right! Make him sit down!

Dr. Stockmann (*losing his self-control*). Then I will go and shout the truth at every street corner! I will write it in other towns' newspapers! The whole country shall know what is going on here!

Hovstad. It almost seems as if Dr. Stockmann's intention were to ruin the town.

Dr. Stockmann. Yes, my native town is so dear to me that I would rather ruin it than see it flourishing upon a lie.

Aslaksen. This is really serious.

(*Uproar and cat-calls Mrs. Stockmann coughs, but to no purpose; her husband does not listen to her any longer.*)

Hovstad (*shouting above the din*). A man must be a public enemy to wish to ruin a whole community!

Dr. Stockmann (*with growing fervor*). What does the destruction of a community matter, if it lives on lies? It ought to be razed to the ground. I tell you—all who live by lies ought to be exterminated like vermin! You will end by infecting the whole country; you will bring about such a state of things that the whole country will deserve to be ruined. And if things come to that pass, I shall say from the bottom of my heart: Let the whole country perish, let all these people be exterminated!

Voices from the crowd. That is talking like an out-and-out enemy of the people!

Billing. There sounded the voice of the people, by all that's holy!

The whole crowd (*shouting*). Yes, yes! He is an enemy of the people! He hates his country! He hates his own people!

Aslaksen. Both as a citizen and as an individual, I am profoundly disturbed by what we have had to listen to. Dr. Stockmann has shown himself in a light I should never have dreamed of. I am unhappily obliged to subscribe to the opinion which I have just heard my estimable fellow-citizens utter; and I propose that we should give expression to that opinion in a resolution. I propose a resolution as follows: "This meeting declares that it considers Dr. Thomas Stockmann, Medical Officer of the Baths, to be an enemy of the people."

(*A storm of cheers and applause. A number of men surround the Doctor and hiss him. Mrs. Stockmann and Petra have got up from their seats. Morten and Ejlif are fighting the other schoolboys for hissing; some of their elders separate them.*)

Dr. Stockmann (*to the men who are hissing him*). Oh, you fools! I tell you that—

Aslaksen (*ringing his bell*). We cannot hear you now, Doctor. A formal vote is about to be taken; but, out of regard for personal feelings, it shall be by ballot and not verbal. Have you any clean paper, Mr. Billing?

Billing. I have both blue and white here.

Aslaksen (*going to him*). That will do nicely; we shall get on more quickly that way. Cut it up into small strips—yes, that's it. (*To the meeting.*) Blue means no; white means yes. I will come round myself and collect votes.

(*Peter Stockmann leaves the hall. Aslaksen and one or two others go round the room with the slips of paper in their hats.*)

1st Citizen (*to Hovstad*). I say, what has come to the Doctor? What are we to think of it?

Hovstad. Oh, you know how headstrong he is.

2nd Citizen (*to Billing*). Billing, you go to their house—have you ever noticed if the fellow drinks?

Billing. Well I'm hanged if I know what to say. There are always spirits on the table when you go.

3rd Citizen. I rather think he goes quite off his head sometimes.

1st Citizen. I wonder if there is any madness in his family?

Billing. I shouldn't wonder if there were.

4th Citizen. No, it is nothing more than sheer malice; he wants to get even with somebody for something or other.

Billing. Well certainly he suggested a rise in his salary on one occasion lately, and did not get it.

The Citizens (*together*). Ah!—Then it is easy to understand how it is!

The Drunken Man (*who has got among the audience again*). I want a blue one, I do! And I want a white one too!

Voices. It's that drunken chap again! Turn him out!

Morten Kiil. (*going up to Dr. Stockmann*). Well, Stockmann, do you see what these monkey tricks of yours lead to?

Dr. Stockmann. I have done my duty.

Morten Kiil. What was that you said about the tanneries at Mölledal?

Dr. Stockmann. You heard well enough. I said they were the source of all the filth.

Morten Kiil. My tannery too?

Dr. Stockmann. Unfortunately your tannery is by far the worst.

Morten Kiil. Are you going to put that in the papers?

Dr. Stockmann. I shall conceal nothing.

Morten Kiil. That may cost you dearly, Stockmann. (*Goes out.*)

A Stout Man (*going up to Captain Horster, without taking any notice of the ladies*). Well, Captain, so you lend your house to enemies of the people?

Horster. I imagine I can do what I like with my own possessions, Mr. Vik.

The Stout Man. Then you can have no objection to my doing the same with mine.

Horster. What do you mean, sir?

The Stout Man. You shall hear from me in the morning. (*Turns his back on him and moves off.*)

Petra. Was that not your owner, Captain Horster?

Horster. Yes, that was Mr. Vik the ship-owner.

Aslaksen (*with the voting-papers in his hands, gets up on to the platform and rings his bell*). Gentlemen, allow me to announce the result. By the votes of everyone here except one person—

A Young Man. That is the drunk chap!

Aslaksen. By the votes of everyone here except a tipsy man, this meeting of citizens declares Dr. Thomas Stockmann to be an enemy of the people. (*Shouts and applause.*) Three cheers for our ancient and honourable citizen community! (*Renewed applause.*) Three cheers for our able and energetic Mayor, who has so loyally suppressed the promptings of family feeling! (*Cheers.*) The meeting is dissolved. (*Gets down.*)

Billing. Three cheers for the Chairman!

The whole crowd. Three cheers for Aslaksen! Hurrah!

Dr. Stockmann. My hat and coat, Petra! Captain, have you room on your ship for passengers to the New World?

Horster. For you and yours we will make room, Doctor.

Dr. Stockmann (*as Petra helps him into his coat*), Good. Come, Katherine! Come, boys!

Mrs. Stockmann (*in an undertone*). Thomas, dear, let us go out by the back way.

Dr. Stockmann. No back ways for me, Katherine, (*Raising his voice.*) You will hear more of this enemy of the people, before he shakes the dust off his shoes upon you! I am not so forgiving as a certain Person; I do not say: "I forgive you, for ye know not what ye do."

Aslaksen (*shouting*). That is a blasphemous comparison, Dr. Stockmann!

Billing. It is, by God! It's dreadful for an earnest man to listen to.

A Coarse Voice. Threatens us now, does he!

Other Voices (*excitedly*). Let's go and break his windows! Duck him in the fjord!

Another Voice. Blow your horn, Evensen! Pip, pip!

(*Horn-blowing, hisses, and wild cries. Dr. Stockmann goes out through the hall with his family, Horster elbowing a way for them.*)

The Whole Crowd (*howling after them as they go*). Enemy of the People! Enemy of the People!

Billing (*as he puts his papers together*). Well, I'm damned if I go and drink toddy with the Stockmanns tonight!

(*The crowd press towards the exit. The uproar continues outside; shouts of "Enemy of the People!" are heard from without.*)

ACT V

SCENE.—Dr. Stockmann's study. Bookcases and cabinets containing specimens, line the walls. At the back is a door leading to the hall; in the foreground on the left, a door leading to the sitting-room. In the righthand wall are two windows, of which all the panes are broken. The Doctor's desk, littered with books and papers, stands in the middle of the room, which is in disorder. It is morning. Dr. Stockmann in dressing-gown, slippers and a smoking-cap, is bending down and raking with an umbrella under one of the cabinets. After a little while he rakes out a stone.

Dr. Stockmann (*calling through the open sitting-room door*). Katherine, I have found another one.

Mrs. Stockmann (*from the sitting-room*). Oh, you will find a lot more yet, I expect.

Dr. Stockmann (*adding the stone to a heap of others on the table*). I shall treasure these stones as relies. Ejlif and Morten shall look at them every day, and when they are grown up they shall inherit them as heirlooms. (Rakes about under a bookcase.) Hasn't—what the deuce is her name?—the girl, you know—hasn't she been to fetch the glazier yet?

Mrs. Stockmann (*coming in*). Yes, but he said he didn't know if he would be able to come today.

Dr. Stockmann. You will see he won't dare to come.

Mrs. Stockmann. Well, that is just what Randine thought—that he didn't dare to, on account of the neighbours. (*Calls into the sitting-room.*) What is it you want, Randine? Give it to me. (*Goes in, and comes out again directly.*) Here is a letter for you, Thomas.

Dr. Stockmann. Let me see it. (*Opens and reads it.*) Ah!—Of course.

Mrs. Stockmann. Who is it from?

Dr. Stockmann. From the landlord. Notice to quit.

Mrs. Stockmann. Is it possible? Such a nice man—

Dr. Stockmann (*looking at the letter*). Does not dare do otherwise, he says. Doesn't like doing it, but dare not do otherwise—on account of his fellow-citizens—out of regard for public opinion. Is in a dependent position—dares not offend certain influential men.

Mrs. Stockmann. There, you see, Thomas!

Dr. Stockmann. Yes, yes, I see well enough; the whole lot of them in the town are cowards; not a man among them dares do anything for fear of the others. (*Throws the letter on to the table.*) But it doesn't matter to us, Katherine. We are going to sail away to the New World, and—

Mrs. Stockmann. But, Thomas, are you sure we are well advised to take this step?

Dr. Stockmann. Are you suggesting that I should stay here, where they have pilloried me as an enemy of the people—branded me—broken my windows! And just look here, Katherine—they have torn a great rent in my black trousers too!

Mrs. Stockmann. Oh, dear!—And they are the best pair you have got!

Dr. Stockmann. You should never wear your best trousers when you go out to fight for freedom and truth. It is not that I care so much about the trousers, you know; you can always sew them up again for me. But that the common herd should dare to make this attack on me, as if they were my equals—that is what I cannot, for the life of me, swallow!

Mrs. Stockmann. There is no doubt they have behaved very ill toward you, Thomas; but is that sufficient reason for our leaving our native country for good and all?

Dr. Stockmann. If we went to another town, do you suppose we should not find the common people just as insolent as they are here? Depend upon it, there is not much to choose between them. Oh, well, let the curs snap—that is not the worst part of it. The worst is that, from one end of this country to the other, every man is the slave of his

Party. Although, as far as that goes, I daresay it is not much better in the free West either; the compact majority, and liberal public opinion, and all that infernal old bag of tricks are probably rampant there too. But there things are done on a larger scale, you see. They may kill you, but they won't put you to death by slow torture. They don't squeeze a free man's soul in a vice, as they do here. And, if need be, one can live in solitude. (*Walks up and down.*) If only I knew where there was a virgin forest or a small South Sea island for sale, cheap—

Mrs. Stockmann. But think of the boys, Thomas!

Dr. Stockmann (*standing still*). What a strange woman you are, Katherine! Would you prefer to have the boys grow up in a society like this? You saw for yourself last night that half the population are out of their minds; and if the other half have not lost their senses, it is because they are mere brutes, with no sense to lose.

Mrs. Stockmann. But, Thomas dear, the imprudent things you said had something to do with it, you know.

Dr. Stockmann. Well, isn't what I said perfectly true? Don't they turn every idea topsy-turvy? Don't they make a regular hotchpotch of right and wrong? Don't they say that the things I know are true, are lies? The craziest part of it all is the fact of these "liberals," men of full age, going about in crowds imagining that they are the broad-minded party! Did you ever hear anything like it, Katherine!

Mrs. Stockmann. Yes, yes, it's mad enough of them, certainly; but— (*Petra comes in from the sitting-room*). Back from school already?

Petra. Yes. I have been given notice of dismissal.

Mrs. Stockmann. Dismissal?

Dr. Stockmann. You too?

Petra. Mrs. Busk gave me my notice; so I thought it was best to go at once.

Dr. Stockmann. You were perfectly right, too!

Mrs. Stockmann. Who would have thought Mrs. Busk was a woman like that!

Petra. Mrs. Busk isn't a bit like that, mother; I saw quite plainly how it hurt her to do it. But she didn't dare do otherwise, she said; and so I got my notice.

Dr. Stockmann (*laughing and rubbing his hands*). She didn't dare do otherwise, either! It's delicious!

Mrs. Stockmann. Well, after the dreadful scenes last night—

Petra. It was not only that. Just listen to this, father!

Dr. Stockmann. Well?

Petra. Mrs. Busk showed me no less than three letters she received this morning—

Dr. Stockmann. Anonymous, I suppose?

Petra. Yes.

Dr. Stockmann. Yes, because they didn't dare to risk signing their names, Katherine!

Petra. And two of them were to the effect that a man, who has been our guest here, was declaring last night at the Club that my views on various subjects are extremely emancipated—

Dr. Stockmann. You did not deny that, I hope?

Petra. No, you know I wouldn't. Mrs. Busk's own views are tolerably emancipated, when we are alone together; but now that this report about me is being spread, she dare not keep me on any longer.

Mrs. Stockmann. And someone who had been a guest of ours! That shows you the return you get for your hospitality, Thomas!

Dr. Stockmann. We won't live in such a disgusting hole any longer. Pack up as quickly as you can, Katherine; the sooner we can get away, the better.

Mrs. Stockmann. Be quiet—I think I hear someone in the hall. See who it is, Petra.

Petra (*opening the door*). Oh, it's you, Captain Horster! Do come in.

Horster (*coming in*). Good morning. I thought I would just come in and see how you were.

Dr. Stockmann (*shaking his hand*). Thanks—that is really kind of you.

Mrs. Stockmann. And thank you, too, for helping us through the crowd, Captain Horster.

Petra. How did you manage to get home again?

Horster. Oh, somehow or other. I am fairly strong, and there is more sound than fury about these folk.

Dr. Stockmann. Yes, isn't their swinish cowardice astonishing? Look here, I will show you something! There are all the stones they have thrown through my windows. Just look at them! I'm hanged if there are more than two decently large bits of hard stone in the whole heap; the rest are nothing but gravel—wretched little things. And yet they stood out there bawling and swearing that they would do me some violence; but as for doing anything—you don't see much of that in this town.

Horster. Just as well for you this time, doctor!

Dr. Stockmann. True enough. But it makes one angry all the same; because if some day it should be a question of a national fight in real earnest, you will see that public opinion will be in favour of taking to one's heels, and the compact majority will turn tail like a flock of sheep, Captain Horster. That is what is so mournful to think of; it gives me so much concern, that——. No, devil take it, it is ridiculous to care about it! They have called me an enemy of the people, so an enemy of the people let me be!

Mrs. Stockmann. You will never be that, Thomas.

Dr. Stockmann. Don't swear to that, Katherine. To be called an ugly name may have the same effect as a pin-scratch in the lung. And that hateful name—I can't get quit of it. It is sticking here in the pit of my stomach, eating into me like a corrosive acid. And no magnesia will remove it.

Petra. Bah!—You should only laugh at them, father.

Horster. They will change their minds some day, Doctor.

Mrs. Stockmann. Yes, Thomas, as sure as you are standing here.

Dr. Stockmann. Perhaps, when it is too late. Much good may it do them! They may wallow in their filth then and rue the day when they drove a patriot into exile. When do you sail, Captain Horster?

Horster. Hm!—That was just what I had come to speak about—

Dr. Stockmann. Why, has anything gone wrong with the ship?

Horster. No; but what has happened is that I am not to sail in it.

Petra. Do you mean that you have been dismissed from your command?

Horster (*smiling*). Yes, that's just it.

Petra. You too.

Mrs. Stockmann. There, you see, Thomas!

Dr. Stockmann. And that for the truth's sake! Oh, if I had thought such a thing possible—

Horster. You mustn't take it to heart; I shall be sure to find a job with some ship-owner or other, elsewhere.

Dr. Stockmann. And that is this man Vik—a wealthy man, independent of everyone and everything—! Shame on him!

Horster. He is quite an excellent fellow otherwise; he told me himself he would willingly have kept me on, if only he had dared—

Dr. Stockmann. But he didn't dare? No, of course not.

Horster. It is not such an easy matter, he said, for a party man—

Dr. Stockmann. The worthy man spoke the truth. A party is like a sausage machine; it mashes up all sorts of heads together into the same mincemeat—fatheads and blockheads, all in one mash!

Mrs. Stockmann. Come, come, Thomas dear!

Petra (*to Horster*). If only you had not come home with us, things might not have come to this pass.

Horster. I do not regret it.

Petra (*holding out her hand to him*). Thank you for that!

Horster (*to Dr. Stockmann*). And so what I came to say was that if you are determined to go away, I have thought of another plan—

Dr. Stockmann. That's splendid!—If only we can get away at once.

Mrs. Stockmann. Hush!—Wasn't that someone knocking?

Petra. That is uncle, surely.

Dr. Stockmann. Aha! (*Calls out.*) Come in!

Mrs. Stockmann. Dear Thomas, promise me definitely—.

(*Peter Stockmann comes in from the hall.*)

Peter Stockmann. Oh, you are engaged. In that case, I will—

Dr. Stockmann. No, no, come in.

Peter Stockmann. But I wanted to speak to you alone.

Mrs. Stockmann. We will go into the sitting-room in the meanwhile.

Horster. And I will look in again later.

Dr. Stockmann. No, go in there with them, Captain Horster; I want to hear more about—.

Horster. Very well, I will wait, then. (*He follows Mrs. Stockmann and Petra into the sitting-room.*)

Dr. Stockmann. I daresay you find it rather draughty here today. Put your hat on.

Peter Stockmann. Thank you, if I may. (*Does so.*) I think I caught cold last night; I stood and shivered—

Dr. Stockmann. Really? I found it warm enough.

Peter Stockmann. I regret that it was not in my power to prevent those excesses last night.

Dr. Stockmann. Have you anything in particular to say to me besides that?

Peter Stockmann (*taking a big letter from his pocket*). I have this document for you, from the Baths Committee.

Dr. Stockmann. My dismissal?

Peter Stockmann. Yes, dating from today. (*Lays the letter on the table.*) It gives us pain to do it; but, to speak frankly, we dared not do otherwise on account of public opinion.

Dr. Stockmann (*smiling*). Dared not? I seem to have heard that word before, today.

Peter Stockmann. I must beg you to understand your position clearly. For the future you must not count on any practice whatever in the town.

Dr. Stockmann. Devil take the practice! But why are you so sure of that?

Peter Stockmann. The Householders' Association is circulating a list from house to house. All right-minded citizens are being called upon to give up employing you; and I can assure you that not a single head of a family will risk refusing his signature. They simply dare not.

Dr. Stockmann. No, no; I don't doubt it. But what then?

Peter Stockmann. If I might advise you, it would be best to leave the place for a little while—

Dr. Stockmann. Yes, the propriety of leaving the place has occurred to me.

Peter Stockmann. Good. And then, when you have had six months to think things over, if, after mature consideration, you can persuade yourself to write a few words of regret, acknowledging your error—

Dr. Stockmann. I might have my appointment restored to me, do you mean?

Peter Stockmann. Perhaps. It is not at all impossible.

Dr. Stockmann. But what about public opinion, then? Surely you would not dare to do it on account of public feeling—

Peter Stockmann. Public opinion is an extremely mutable thing. And, to be quite candid with you, it is a matter of great importance to us to have some admission of that sort from you in writing.

Dr. Stockmann. Oh, that's what you are after, is it! I will just trouble you to remember what I said to you lately about foxy tricks of that sort!

Peter Stockmann. Your position was quite different then. At that time you had reason to suppose you had the whole town at your back—

Dr. Stockmann. Yes, and now I feel I have the whole town on my back— (*flaring up*). I would not do it if I had the devil and his dam on my back—! Never—never, I tell you!

Peter Stockmann. A man with a family has no right to behave as you do. You have no right to do it, Thomas.

Dr. Stockmann. I have no right! There is only one single thing in the world a free man has no right to do. Do you know what that is?

Peter Stockmann. No.

Dr. Stockmann. Of course you don't, but I will tell you. A free man has no right to soil himself with filth; he has no right to behave in a way that would justify his spitting in his own face.

Peter Stockmann. This sort of thing sounds extremely plausible, of course; and if there were no other explanation for your obstinacy— but as it happens that there is.

Dr. Stockmann. What do you mean?

Peter Stockmann. You understand, very well what I mean. But, as your brother and as a man of discretion, I advise you not to build too much upon expectations and prospects that may so very easily fail you.

Dr. Stockmann. What in the world is all this about?

Peter Stockmann. Do you really ask me to believe that you are ignorant of the terms of Mr. Kiil's will?

Dr. Stockmann. I know that the small amount he possesses is to go to an institution for indigent old workpeople. How does that concern me?

Peter Stockmann. In the first place, it is by no means a small amount that is in question. Mr. Kiil is a fairly wealthy man.

Dr. Stockmann. I had no notion of that!

Peter Stockmann. Hm!—Hadn't you really? Then I suppose you had no notion, either, that a considerable portion of his wealth will come to your children, you and your wife having a life-rent of the capital. Has he never told you so?

Dr. Stockmann. Never, on my honour! Quite the reverse; he has consistently done nothing but fume at being so unconscionably heavily taxed. But are you perfectly certain of this, Peter?

Peter Stockmann. I have it from an absolutely reliable source.

Dr. Stockmann. Then, thank God, Katherine is provided for—and the children too! I must tell her this at once— (*calls out*) Katherine, Katherine!

Peter Stockmann (*restraining him*). Hush, don't say a word yet!

Mrs. Stockmann (*opening the door*). What is the matter?

Dr. Stockmann. Oh, nothing, nothing; you can go back.

(*She shuts the door. Dr. Stockmann walks up and down in his excitement.*) Provided for!—Just think of it, we are all provided for! And for life! What a blessed feeling it is to know one is provided for!

Peter Stockmann. Yes, but that is just exactly what you are not. Mr. Kiil can alter his will any day he likes.

Dr. Stockmann. But he won't do that, my dear Peter. The "Badger" is much too delighted at my attack on you and your wise friends.

Peter Stockmann (*starts and looks intently at him*). Aha, that throws a light on various things.

Dr. Stockmann. What things?

Peter Stockmann. I see that the whole thing was a combined manoeuvre on your part and his. These violent, reckless attacks that you have made against the leading men of the town, under the pretence that it was in the name of truth—

Dr. Stockmann. What about them?

Peter Stockmann. I see that they were nothing else than the stipulated price for that vindictive old man's will.

Dr. Stockmann (*almost speechless*). Peter—you are the most disgusting plebeian I have ever met in all my life.

Peter Stockmann. All is over between us. Your dismissal is irrevocable—we have a weapon against you now. (*Goes out.*)

Dr. Stockmann. For shame! For shame! (*Calls out.*) Katherine, you must have the floor scrubbed after him! Let—what's her name—devil take it, the girl who has always got soot on her nose—

Mrs. Stockmann. (*in the sitting-room*). Hush, Thomas, be quiet!

Petra (*coming to the door*). Father, grandfather is here, asking if he may speak to you alone.

Dr. Stockmann. Certainly he may. (*Going to the door.*) Come in, Mr. Kiil. (*Morten kiil comes in. Dr. Stockmann shuts the door after him.*) What can I do for you? Won't you sit down?

Morten Kiil. I won't sit. (*Looks around.*) You look very comfortable here today, Thomas.

Dr. Stockmann. Yes, don't we!

Morten Kiil. Very comfortable—plenty of fresh air. I should think you have got enough today of that oxygen you were talking about yesterday. Your conscience must be in splendid order today, I should think.

Dr. Stockmann. It is.

Morten Kiil. So I should think. (*Taps his chest.*) Do you know what I have got here?

Dr. Stockmann. A good conscience, too, I hope.

Morten Kiil. Bah!—No, it is something better than that. (*He takes a thick pocket-book from his breast-pocket, opens it, and displays a packet of papers.*)

Dr. Stockmann (*looking at him in astonishment*). Shares in the Baths?

Morten Kiil. They were not difficult to get today.

Dr. Stockmann. And you have been buying—?

Morten Kiil. As many as I could pay for.

Dr. Stockmann. But, my dear Mr. Kiil—consider the state of the Baths' affairs!

Morten Kiil. If you behave like a reasonable man, you can soon set the Baths on their feet again.

Dr. Stockmann. Well, you can see for yourself that I have done all I can, but——. They are all mad in this town!

Morten Kiil. You said yesterday that the worst of this pollution came from my tannery. If that is true, then my grandfather and my father before me, and I myself, for many years past, have been poisoning the town like three destroying angels. Do you think I am going to sit quiet under that reproach?

Dr. Stockmann. Unfortunately I am afraid you will have to.

Morten Kiil. No, thank you. I am jealous of my name and reputation. They call me "the Badger," I am told. A badger is a kind of pig, I believe; but I am not going to give them the right to call me that. I mean to live and die a clean man.

Dr. Stockmann. And how are you going to set about it?

Morten Kiil. You shall cleanse me, Thomas.

Dr. Stockmann. I!

Morten Kiil. Do you know what money I have bought these shares with? No, of course you can't know—but I will tell you. It is the money that Katherine and Petra and the boys will have when I am gone. Because I have been able to save a little bit after all, you know.

Dr. Stockmann (*flaring up*). And you have gone and taken

Katherine's money for this!

Morten Kiil. Yes, the whole of the money is invested in the Baths now. And now I just want to see whether you are quite stark, staring mad, Thomas! If you still make out that these animals and other nasty things of that sort come from my tannery, it will be exactly as if you were to flay broad strips of skin from Katherine's body, and Petra's, and the boys'; and no decent man would do that—unless he were mad.

Dr. Stockmann (*walking up and down*). Yes, but I am mad; I am mad!

Morten Kiil. You cannot be so absurdly mad as all that, when it is a question of your wife and children.

Dr. Stockmann (*standing still in front of him*). Why couldn't you consult me about it, before you went and bought all that trash?

Morten Kiil. What is done cannot be undone.

Dr. Stockmann (*walks about uneasily*). If only I were not so certain about it—! But I am absolutely convinced that I am right.

Morten Kiil (*weighing the pocket-book in his hand*). If you stick to your mad idea, this won't be worth much, you know. (*Puts the pocket-book in his pocket.*)

Dr. Stockmann. But, hang it all! It might be possible for science to discover some prophylactic, I should think—or some antidote of some kind—

Morten Kiil. To kill these animals, do you mean?

Dr. Stockmann. Yes, or to make them innocuous.

Morten Kiil. Couldn't you try some rat's-bane?

Dr. Stockmann. Don't talk nonsense! They all say it is only imagination, you know. Well, let it go at that! Let them have their own way about it! Haven't the ignorant, narrow-minded curs reviled me as an enemy of the people?—And haven't they been ready to tear the clothes off my back too?

Morten Kiil. And broken all your windows to pieces!

Dr. Stockmann. And then there is my duty to my family. I must talk it over with Katherine; she is great on those things.

Morten Kiil. That is right; be guided by a reasonable woman's advice.

Dr. Stockmann (*advancing towards him*). To think you could do such a preposterous thing! Risking Katherine's money in this way, and putting me in such a horribly painful dilemma! When I look at you, I think I see the devil himself—.

Morten Kiil. Then I had better go. But I must have an answer from you before two o'clock—yes or no. If it is no, the shares go to a charity, and that this very day.

Dr. Stockmann. And what does Katherine get?

Morten Kiil. Not a halfpenny. (*The door leading to the hall opens, and Hovstad and Aslaksen make their appearance.*) Look at those two!

Dr. Stockmann (*staring at them*). What the devil!—have YOU actually the face to come into my house?

Hovstad. Certainly.

Aslaksen. We have something to say to you, you see.

Morten Kiil (*in a whisper*). Yes or no—before two o'clock.

Aslaksen (*glancing at Hovstad*). Aha!

(*Morten Kiil goes out.*)

Dr. Stockmann. Well, what do you want with me? Be brief.

Hovstad. I can quite understand that you are annoyed with us for our attitude at the meeting yesterday—

Dr. Stockmann. Attitude, do you call it? Yes, it was a charming attitude! I call it weak, womanish—damnably shameful!

Hovstad. Call it what you like, we could not do otherwise.

Dr. Stockmann. You DARED not do otherwise—isn't that it?

Hovstad. Well, if you like to put it that way.

Aslaksen. But why did you not let us have word of it beforehand?—Just a hint to Mr. Hovstad or to me?

Dr. Stockmann. A hint? Of what?

Aslaksen. Of what was behind it all.

Dr. Stockmann. I don't understand you in the least—

Aslaksen (*with a confidential nod*). Oh yes, you do, Dr. Stockmann.

Hovstad. It is no good making a mystery of it any longer.

Dr. Stockmann (*looking first at one of them and then at the other*). What the devil do you both mean?

Aslaksen. May I ask if your father-in-law is not going round the town buying up all the shares in the Baths?

Dr. Stockmann. Yes, he has been buying Baths shares today; but—

Aslaksen. It would have been more prudent to get someone else to do it—someone less nearly related to you.

Hovstad. And you should not have let your name appear in the affair. There was no need for anyone to know that the attack on the Baths came from you. You ought to have consulted me, Dr. Stockmann.

Dr. Stockmann (*looks in front of him; then a light seems to dawn on him and he says in amazement.*) Are such things conceivable? Are such things possible?

Aslaksen (*with a smile*). Evidently they are. But it is better to use a little finesse, you know.

Hovstad. And it is much better to have several persons in a thing of that sort; because the responsibility of each individual is lessened, when there are others with him.

Dr. Stockmann (*composedly*). Come to the point, gentlemen. What do you want?

Aslaksen. Perhaps Mr. Hovstad had better—

Hovstad. No, you tell him, Aslaksen.

Aslaksen. Well, the fact is that, now we know the bearings of the whole affair, we think we might venture to put the "People's Messenger" at your disposal.

Dr. Stockmann. Do you dare do that now? What about public opinion? Are you not afraid of a storm breaking upon our heads?

Hovstad. We will try to weather it.

Aslaksen. And you must be ready to go off quickly on a

new tack, Doctor. As soon as your invective has done its work—

Dr. Stockmann. Do you mean, as soon as my father-in-law and I have got hold of the shares at a low figure?

Hovstad. Your reasons for wishing to get the control of the Baths are mainly scientific, I take it.

Dr. Stockmann. Of course; it was for scientific reasons that I persuaded the old "Badger" to stand in with me in the matter. So we will tinker at the conduit-pipes a little, and dig up a little bit of the shore, and it shan't cost the town a sixpence. That will be all right—eh?

Hovstad. I think so—if you have the "People's Messenger" behind you.

Aslaksen. The Press is a power in a free community, Doctor.

Dr. Stockmann. Quite so. And so is public opinion. And you, Mr. Aslaksen—I suppose you will be answerable for the Householders' Association?

Aslaksen. Yes, and for the Temperance Society. You may rely on that.

Dr. Stockmann. But, gentlemen—I really am ashamed to ask the question—but, what return do you—?

Hovstad. We should prefer to help you without any return whatever, believe me. But the "People's Messenger" is in rather a shaky condition; it doesn't go really well; and I should be very unwilling to suspend the paper now, when there is so much work to do here in the political way.

Dr. Stockmann. Quite so; that would be a great trial to such a friend of the people as you are. (*Flares up.*) But I am an enemy of the people, remember! (*Walks about the room.*) Where have I put my stick? Where the devil is my stick?

Hovstad. What's that?

Aslaksen. Surely you never mean—

Dr. Stockmann (*standing still*). And suppose I don't give you a single penny of all I get out of it? Money is not very easy to get out of us rich folk, please to remember!

Hovstad. And you please to remember that this affair of the shares can be represented in two ways!

Dr. Stockmann. Yes, and you are just the man to do it. If I don't come to the rescue of the "People's Messenger," you will certainly take an evil view of the affair; you will hunt me down, I can well imagine—pursue me—try to throttle me as a dog does a hare.

Hovstad. It is a natural law; every animal must fight for its own livelihood.

Aslaksen. And get its food where it can, you know.

Dr. Stockmann (*walking about the room*). Then you go and look for yours in the gutter; because I am going to show you which is the strongest animal of us three! (*Finds an umbrella and brandishes it above his head.*) Ah, now—!

Hovstad. You are surely not going to use violence!

Aslaksen. Take care what you are doing with that umbrella.

Dr. Stockmann. Out of the window with you, Mr. Hovstad!

Hovstad (*edging to the door*). Are you quite mad!

Dr. Stockmann. Out of the window, Mr. Aslaksen! Jump, I tell you! You will have to do it, sooner or later.

Aslaksen (*running round the writing-table*). Moderation, Doctor—I am a delicate man—I can stand so little— (*calls out*) help, help!

(*Mrs. Stockmann, Petra and Horster come in from the sitting-room.*)

Mrs. Stockmann. Good gracious, Thomas! What is happening?

Dr. Stockmann (*brandishing the umbrella*). Jump out, I tell you! Out into the gutter!

Hovstad. An assault on an unoffending man! I call you to witness, Captain Horster. (*Hurries out through the hall.*)

Aslaksen (*irresolutely*). If only I knew the way about here——. (*Steals out through the sitting-room.*)

Mrs. Stockmann (*holding her husband back*). Control yourself, Thomas!

Dr. Stockmann (*throwing down the umbrella*). Upon my soul, they have escaped after all.

Mrs. Stockmann. What did they want you to do?

Dr. Stockmann. I will tell you later on; I have something else to think about now. (*Goes to the table and writes something on a calling-card.*) Look there, Katherine; what is written there?

Mrs. Stockmann. Three big Noes; what does that mean?

Dr. Stockmann. I will tell you that too, later on. (*Holds out the card to Petra.*) There, Petra; tell sooty-face to run over to the "Badger's" with that, as quick as she can. Hurry up! (*Petra* *takes the card and goes out to the hall.*)

Dr. Stockmann. Well, I think I have had a visit from every one of the devil's messengers today! But now I am going to sharpen my pen till they can feel its point; I shall dip it in venom and gall; I shall hurl my inkpot at their heads!

Mrs. Stockmann. Yes, but we are going away, you know, Thomas.

(*Petra comes back.*)

Dr. Stockmann. Well?

Petra. She has gone with it.

Dr. Stockmann. Good.—Going away, did you say? No, I'll be hanged if we are going away! We are going to stay where we are, Katherine!

Petra. Stay here?

Mrs. Stockmann. Here, in the town?

Dr. Stockmann. Yes, here. This is the field of battle—this is where the fight will be. This is where I shall triumph! As soon as I have had my trousers sewn up I shall go out and look for another house. We must have a roof over our heads for the winter.

Horster. That you shall have in my house.

Dr. Stockmann. Can I?

Horsier. Yes, quite well. I have plenty of room, and I am almost never at home.

Mrs. Stockmann. How good of you, Captain Horster!

Petra. Thank you!

Dr. Stockmann (*grasping his hand*). Thank you, thank you! That is one trouble over! Now I can set to work in earnest at once. There is an endless amount of things to look through here, Katherine! Luckily I shall have all my time at my disposal; because I have been dismissed from the Baths, you know.

Mrs. Stockmann (*with a sigh*). Oh yes, I expected that.

Dr. Stockmann. And they want to take my practice away from me too. Let them! I have got the poor people to fall back upon, anyway—those that don't pay anything; and, after all, they need me most, too. But, by Jove, they will have to listen to me; I shall preach to them in season and out of season, as it says somewhere.

Mrs. Stockmann. But, dear Thomas, I should have thought events had showed you what use it is to preach.

Dr. Stockmann. You are really ridiculous, Katherine. Do you want me to let myself be beaten off the field by public opinion and the compact majority and all that devilry? No, thank you! And what I want to do is so simple and clear and straightforward. I only want to drum into the heads of these curs the fact that the liberals are the most insidious enemies of freedom—that party programmes strangle every young and vigorous truth—that considerations of expediency turn morality and justice upside down—and that they will end by making life here unbearable. Don't you think, Captain Horster, that I ought to be able to make people understand that?

Horster. Very likely; I don't know much about such things myself.

Dr. Stockmann. Well, look here—I will explain! It is the party leaders that must be exterminated. A party leader is like a wolf, you see—like a voracious wolf. He requires a certain number of smaller victims to prey upon every year, if he is to live. Just look at Hovstad and Aslaksen! How many smaller victims have they not put an end to—or at any rate maimed and mangled until they are fit for nothing except to be householders or subscribers to the "People's Messenger"! (*Sits down on the edge of the table.*) Come here, Katherine—look how beautifully the sun shines today! And this lovely spring air I am drinking in!

Mrs. Stockmann. Yes, if only we could live on sunshine and spring air, Thomas.

Dr. Stockmann. Oh, you will have to pinch and save a bit—then we shall get along. That gives me very little concern. What is much worse is, that I know of no one who is liberal-minded and high-minded enough to venture to take up my work after me.

Petra. Don't think about that, father; you have plenty of time before you. —Hello, here are the boys already!

(*Ejlif and Morten come in from the sitting-room.*)

Mrs. Stockmann. Have you got a holiday?

Morten. No; but we were fighting with the other boys between lessons—

Ejlif. That isn't true; it was the other boys were fighting with us.

Morten. Well, and then Mr. Rorlund said we had better stay at home for a day or two.

Dr. Stockmann (*snapping his fingers and getting up from the table*). I have it! I have it, by Jove! You shall never set foot in the school again!

The Boys. No more school!

Mrs. Stockmann. But, Thomas—

Dr. Stockmann. Never, I say. I will educate you myself; that is to say, you shan't learn a blessed thing—

Morten. Hooray!

Dr. Stockmann. —but I will make liberal-minded and high-minded men of you. You must help me with that, Petra.

Petra. Yes, father, you may be sure I will.

Dr. Stockmann. And my school shall be in the room where they insulted me and called me an enemy of the people. But we are too few as we are; I must have at least twelve boys to begin with.

Mrs. Stockmann. You will certainly never get them in this town.

Dr. Stockmann. We shall. (*To the boys.*) Don't you know any street urchins—regular ragamuffins—?

Morten. Yes, father, I know lots!

Dr. Stockmann. That's capital! Bring me some specimens of them. I am going to experiment with curs, just for once;

there may be some exceptional heads among them.

Morten. And what are we going to do, when you have made liberal-minded and high-minded men of us?

Dr. Stockmann. Then you shall drive all the wolves out of the country, my boys!

(*Ejlif looks rather doubtful about it; Morten jumps about crying "Hurrah!"*)

Mrs. Stockmann. Let us hope it won't be the wolves that will drive you out of the country, Thomas.

Dr. Stockmann. Are you out of your mind, Katherine? Drive me out! Now—when I am the strongest man in the town!

Mrs. Stockmann. The strongest—now?

Dr. Stockmann. Yes, and I will go so far as to say that now I am the strongest man in the whole world.

Morten. I say!

Dr. Stockmann (*lowering his voice*). Hush! You mustn't say anything about it yet; but I have made a great discovery.

Mrs. Stockmann. Another one?

Dr. Stockmann. Yes. (*Gathers them round him, and says confidentially:*) It is this, let me tell you—that the strongest man in the world is he who stands most alone.

Mrs. Stockmann (*smiling and shaking her head*). Oh, Thomas, Thomas!

Petra (*encouragingly, as she grasps her father's hands*). Father!

The End

GHOSTS

The Characters

Mrs. Helen Alving, widow of Captain Alving,
late Chamberlain to the King

Oswald Alving, her son, a painter

Pastor Manders

Jacob Engstrand, a carpenter

Regina Engstrand, Mrs. Alving's maid

(*The action takes place at Mrs. Alving's country house, beside one of the large fjords in Western Norway.*)

ACT I

A spacious garden-room, with one door to the left, and two doors to the right. In the middle of the room a round table, with chairs about it. On the table lie books, periodicals, and newspapers. In the foreground to the left a window, and by it a small sofa, with a worktable in front of it. In the background, the room is continued into a somewhat narrower conservatory, the walls of which are formed by large panes of glass. In the right-hand wall of the conservatory is a door leading down into the garden. Through the glass wall a gloomy fjord landscape is faintly visible, veiled by steady rain.

Engstrand, the carpenter, stands by the garden door. His left leg is somewhat bent; he has a clump of wood under the sole of his boot. Regina, with an empty garden syringe in her hand, hinders him from advancing.

Regina. (*In a low voice.*) What do you want? Stop where you are. You're positively dripping.

Engstrand. It's the Lord's own rain, my girl.

Regina. It's the devil's rain, *I* say.

Engstrand. Lord, how you talk, Regina. (*Limps a step or two forward into the room.*) It's just this as I wanted to say—

Regina. Don't clatter so with that foot of yours, I tell you! The young master's asleep upstairs.

Engstrand. Asleep? In the middle of the day?

Regina. It's no business of yours.

Engstrand. I was out on the loose last night—

Regina. I can quite believe that.

Engstrand. Yes, we're weak vessels, we poor mortals, my girl—

Regina. So it seems.

Engstrand.—And temptations are manifold in this world, you see. But all the same, I was hard at work, God knows, at half-past five this morning.

Regina. Very well; only be off now. I won't stop here and have rendez-vous (*Note: This and other French words by Regina are in that language in the original*) with you.

Engstrand. What do you say you won't have?

Regina. I won't have anyone find you here; so just you go about your business.

Engstrand. (*Advances a step or two.*) Blest if I go before I've had a talk with you. This afternoon I shall have finished my work at the school house, and then I shall take to-night's boat and be off home to the town.

Regina. (*Mutters.*) Pleasant journey to you!

Engstrand. Thank you, my child. To-morrow the Orphanage is to be opened, and then there'll be fine doings, no doubt, and plenty of intoxicating drink going, you know. And nobody shall say of Jacob Engstrand that he can't keep out of temptation's way.

Regina. Oh!

Engstrand. You see, there's to be heaps of grand folks here tomorrow. Pastor Manders is expected from town, too.

Regina. He's coming today.

Engstrand. There, you see! And I should be cursedly sorry if he found out anything against me, don't you understand?

Regina. Oho! Is that your game?

Engstrand. Is what my game?

Regina. (*Looking hard at him.*) What are you going to fool Pastor Manders into doing, this time?

Engstrand. Sh! Sh! Are you crazy? Do *I* want to fool Pastor Manders? Oh no! Pastor Manders has been far too good a friend to me for that. But I just wanted to say, you know— that I mean to be off home again to-night.

Regina. The sooner the better, say I.

Engstrand. Yes, but I want you with me, Regina.

Regina. (*Open-mouthed.*) You want me—? What are you talking about?

Engstrand. I want you to come home with me, I say.

Regina. (*Scornfully.*) Never in this world shall you get me home with you.

Engstrand. Oh, we'll see about that.

Regina. Yes, you may be sure we'll see about it! Me, that have been brought up by a lady like Mrs. Alving! Me, that am treated almost as a daughter here! Is it me you want to go home with you?—to a house like yours? For shame!

Engstrand. What the devil do you mean? Do you set yourself up against your father, you hussy?

Regina. (*Mutters without looking at him.*) You've said often enough I was no concern of yours.

Engstrand. Pooh! Why should you bother about that—

Regina. Haven't you many a time sworn at me and called me a—? *Fi donc!*

Engstrand. Curse me, now, if ever I used such an ugly word.

Regina. Oh, I remember very well what word you used.

Engstrand. Well, but that was only when I was a bit on, don't you know? Temptations are manifold in this world, Regina.

Regina. Ugh!

Engstrand. And besides, it was when your mother was that aggravating—I had to find something to twit her with, my child. She was always setting up for a fine lady. (*Mimics.*) "Let me go, Engstrand; let me be. Remember I was three years in Chamberlain Alving's family at Rosenvold." (*Laughs.*) Mercy on us! She could never forget that the Captain was made a Chamberlain while she was in service here.

Regina. Poor mother! You very soon tormented her into her grave.

Engstrand. (*With a twist of his shoulders.*) Oh, of course! I'm to have the blame for everything.

Regina. (*Turns away; half aloud.*) Ugh—! And that leg too!

Engstrand. What do you say, my child?

Regina. Pied de mouton.

Engstrand. Is that English, eh?

Regina. Yes.

Engstrand. Ay, ay; you've picked up some learning out here; and that may come in useful now, Regina.

Regina. (*After a short silence.*) What do you want with me in town?

Engstrand. Can you ask what a father wants with his only child? A'n't I a lonely, forlorn widower?

Regina. Oh, don't try on any nonsense like that with me! Why do you want me?

Engstrand. Well, let me tell you, I've been thinking of setting up in a new line of business.

Regina. (*Contemptuously.*) You've tried that often enough, and much good you've done with it.

Engstrand. Yes, but this time you shall see, Regina! Devil take me—

Regina. (*Stamps.*) Stop your swearing!

Engstrand. Hush, hush; you're right enough there, my girl. What I wanted to say was just this—I've laid by a very tidy pile from this Orphanage job.

Regina. Have you? That's a good thing for you.

Engstrand. What can a man spend his ha'pence on here in this country hole?

Regina. Well, what then?

Engstrand. Why, you see, I thought of putting the money into some paying speculation. I thought of a sort of a sailor's tavern—

Regina. Pah!

Engstrand. A regular high-class affair, of course; not any sort of pigsty for common sailors. No! damn it! It would be for captains and mates, and—and—regular swells, you know.

Regina. And I was to—?

Engstrand. You were to help, to be sure. Only for the look of the thing, you understand. Devil a bit of hard work shall you have, my girl. You shall do exactly what you like.

Regina. Oh, indeed!

Engstrand. But there must be a petticoat in the house; that's as clear as daylight. For I want to have it a bit lively like in the evenings, with singing and dancing, and so on. You must remember they're weary wanderers on the ocean of life. (*Nearer.*) Now don't be a fool and stand in your own light, Regina. What's to become of you out here? Your mistress has given you a lot of learning; but what good is that to you? You're to look after the children at the new Orphanage, I hear. Is that the sort of thing for you, eh? Are you so dead set on wearing your life out for a pack of dirty brats?

Regina. No; if things go as I want them to—Well there's no saying—there's no saying.

Engstrand. What do you mean by "there's no saying"?

Regina. Never you mind.—How much money have you saved?

Engstrand. What with one thing and another, a matter of seven or eight hundred crowns.[①]

Regina. That's not so bad.

Engstrand. It's enough to make a start with, my girl.

Regina. Aren't you thinking of giving me any?

Engstrand. No, I'm blest if I am!

Regina. Not even of sending me a scrap of stuff for a new dress?

Engstrand. Come to town with me, my lass, and you'll soon get dresses enough.

Regina. Pooh! I can do that on my own account, if I want to.

Engstrand. No, a father's guiding hand is what you want, Regina. Now, I've got my eye on a capital house in Little Harbour Street. They don't want much ready-money; and it could be a sort of a Sailors' Home, you know.

Regina. But I will not live with you! I have nothing whatever to do with you. Be off!

Engstrand. You wouldn't stop long with me, my girl. No such luck! If you knew how to play your cards, such a fine figure of a girl as you've grown in the last year or two—

Regina. Well?

Engstrand. You'd soon get hold of some mate—or maybe even

---

① A "krone" is equal to one shilling and three-halfpence.

a captain—

Regina. I won't marry anyone of that sort. Sailors have no *savoir-vivre*.

Engstrand. What's that they haven't got?

Regina. I know what sailors are, I tell you. They're not the sort of people to marry.

Engstrand. Then never mind about marrying them. You can make it pay all the same. (*More confidentially.*) He—the Englishman—the man with the yacht—he came down with three hundred dollars, he did; and she wasn't a bit handsomer than you.

Regina. (*Making for him.*) Out you go!

Engstrand. (*Falling back.*) Come, come! You're not going to hit me, I hope.

Regina. Yes, if you begin talking about mother I shall hit you. Get away with you, I say! (*Drives him back towards the garden door.*) And don't slam the doors. Young Mr. Alving—

Engstrand. He's asleep; I know. You're mightily taken up about young Mr. Alving—(*More softly.*) Oho! you don't mean to say it's him as—?

Regina. Be off this minute! You're crazy, I tell you! No, not that way. There comes Pastor Manders. Down the kitchen stairs with you.

Engstrand. (*Towards the right.*) Yes, yes, I'm going. But just you talk to him as is coming there. He's the man to tell you what a child owes its father. For I am your father all the same, you know. I can prove it from the church register.

(*He goes out through the second door to the right, which Regina has opened, and closes again after him. Regina glances hastily at herself in the mirror, dusts herself with her pocket handkerchief, and settles her necktie; then she busies herself with the flowers.*)

(*Pastor Manders, wearing an overcoat, carrying an umbrella, and with a small travelling-bag on a strap over his shoulder, comes through the garden door into the conservatory.*)

Manders. Good-morning, Miss Engstrand.

Regina. (*Turning round, surprised and pleased.*) No, really! Good morning, Pastor Manders. Is the steamer in already?

Manders. It is just in. (*Enters the sitting-room.*) Terrible weather we have been having lately.

Regina. (*Follows him.*) It's such blessed weather for the country, sir.

Manders. No doubt; you are quite right. We townspeople give too little thought to that. (*He begins to take off his overcoat.*)

Regina. Oh, mayn't I help you?—There! Why, how wet it is? I'll just hang it up in the hall. And your umbrella, too—I'll open it and let it dry.

(*She goes out with the things through the second door on the right. Pastor Manders takes off his travelling bag and lays it and his hat on a chair. Meanwhile Regina comes in again.*)

Manders. Ah, it's a comfort to get safe under cover. I hope everything is going on well here?

Regina. Yes, thank you, sir.

Manders. You have your hands full, I suppose, in preparation for to-morrow?

Regina. Yes, there's plenty to do, of course.

Manders. And Mrs. Alving is at home, I trust?

Regina. Oh dear, yes. She's just upstairs, looking after the young master's chocolate.

Manders. Yes, by-the-bye—I heard down at the pier that Oswald had arrived.

Regina. Yes, he came the day before yesterday. We didn't expect him before today.

Manders. Quite strong and well, I hope?

Regina. Yes, thank you, quite; but dreadfully tired with the journey. He has made one rush right through from Paris—the whole way in one train, I believe. He's sleeping a little now, I think; so perhaps we'd better talk a little quietly.

Manders. Sh!—As quietly as you please.

Regina. (*Arranging an armchair beside the table.*) Now, do sit down, Pastor Manders, and make yourself comfortable. (*He sits down; she places a footstool under his feet.*) There! Are you comfortable now, sir?

Manders. Thanks, thanks, extremely so. (*Looks at her.*) Do you know, Miss Engstrand, I positively believe you have grown since I last saw you.

Regina. Do you think so, Sir? Mrs. Alving says I've filled out too.

Manders. Filled out? Well, perhaps a little; just enough.

(*Short pause.*)

Regina. Shall I tell Mrs. Alving you are here?

Manders. Thanks, thanks, there is no hurry, my dear child.—By-the-bye, Regina, my good girl, tell me, how is your father getting on out here?

Regina. Oh, thank you, sir, he's getting on well enough.

Manders. He called upon me last time he was in town.

Regina. Did he, indeed? He's always so glad of a chance of talking to you, sir.

Manders. And you often look in upon him at his work, I daresay?

Regina. I? Oh, of course, when I have time, I—

Manders. Your father is not a man of strong character, Miss Engstrand. He stands terribly in need of a guiding hand.

Regina. Oh, yes; I daresay he does.

Manders. He requires someone near him whom he cares for, and whose judgment he respects. He frankly admitted as much when he last came to see me.

Regina. Yes, he mentioned something of the sort to me. But I don't know whether Mrs. Alving can spare me; especially now that we've got the new Orphanage to attend to. And then I should be so sorry to leave Mrs. Alving; she has always been so kind to me.

Manders. But a daughter's duty, my good girl—Of course, we should first have to get your mistress's consent.

Regina. But I don't know whether it would be quite proper for me, at my age, to keep house for a single man.

Manders. What! My dear Miss Engstrand! When the man is your own father!

Regina. Yes, that may be; but all the same—Now, if it were in a thoroughly nice house, and with a real gentleman—

Manders. Why, my dear Regina—

Regina. —One I could love and respect, and be a daughter to—

Manders. Yes, but my dear, good child—

Regina. Then I should be glad to go to town. It's very lonely out here; you know yourself, sir, what it is to be alone in the world. And I can assure you I'm both quick and willing. Don't you know of any such place for me, sir?

Manders. I? No, certainly not.

Regina. But, dear, dear Sir, do remember me if—

Manders. (*Rising.*) Yes, yes, certainly, Miss Engstrand.

Regina. For if I—

Manders. Will you be so good as to tell your mistress I am here?

Regina. I will, at once, sir. (*She goes out to the left.*)

Manders. (*Paces the room two or three times, stands a moment in the background with his hands behind his back, and looks out over the garden. Then he returns to the table, takes up a book, and looks at the title-page; starts, and looks at several books.*) Ha—indeed!

(*Mrs. Alving enters by the door on the left; she is followed by Regina, who immediately goes out by the first door on the right.*)

Mrs. Alving. (*Holds out her hand.*) Welcome, my dear Pastor.

Manders. How do you do, Mrs. Alving? Here I am as I promised.

Mrs. Alving. Always punctual to the minute.

Manders. You may believe it was not so easy for me to get away. With all the Boards and Committees I belong to—

Mrs. Alving. That makes it all the kinder of you to come so early. Now we can get through our business before dinner. But where is your portmanteau?

Manders. (*Quickly.*) I left it down at the inn. I shall sleep there to-night.

Mrs. Alving. (*Suppressing a smile.*) Are you really not to be persuaded, even now, to pass the night under my roof?

Manders. No, no, Mrs. Alving; many thanks. I shall stay at the inn, as usual. It is so conveniently near the landing-stage.

Mrs. Alving. Well, you must have your own way. But I really should have thought we two old people—

Manders. Now you are making fun of me. Ah, you're naturally in great spirits today—what with to-morrow's festival and Oswald's return.

Mrs. Alving. Yes, you can think what a delight it is to me! It's more than two years since he was home last. And now he has promised to stay with me all the winter.

Manders. Has he really? That is very nice and dutiful of him. For I can well believe that life in Rome and Paris has very different attractions from any we can offer here.

Mrs. Alving. Ah, but here he has his mother, you see. My own darling boy—he hasn't forgotten his old mother!

Manders. It would be grievous indeed, if absence and absorption in art and that sort of thing were to blunt his natural feelings.

Mrs. Alving. Yes, you may well say so. But there's nothing of that sort to fear with him. I'm quite curious to see whether you know him again. He'll be down presently; he's upstairs just now, resting a little on the sofa. But do sit down, my dear Pastor.

Manders. Thank you. Are you quite at liberty—?

Mrs. Alving. Certainly. (*She sits by the table.*)

Manders. Very well. Then let me show you—(*He goes to the chair where his travelling-bag lies, takes out a packet of papers, sits down on the opposite side of the table, and tries to find a clear space for the papers.*) Now, to begin with, here is—(*Breaking off.*) Tell me, Mrs. Alving, how do these books come to be here?

Mrs. Alving. These books? They are books I am reading.

Manders. Do you read this sort of literature?

Mrs. Alving. Certainly I do.

Manders. Do you feel better or happier for such reading?

Mrs. Alving. I feel, so to speak, more secure.

Manders. That is strange. How do you mean?

Mrs. Alving. Well, I seem to find explanation and confirmation of all sorts of things I myself have been thinking. For that is the wonderful part of it, Pastor Manders—there is really nothing new in these books, nothing but what most people think and believe. Only most people either don't formulate it to themselves, or else keep quiet about it.

Manders. Great heavens! Do you really believe that most people—?

Mrs. Alving. I do, indeed.

Manders. But surely not in this country? Not here among us?

Mrs. Alving. Yes, certainly; here as elsewhere.

Manders. Well, I really must say—!

Mrs. Alving. For the rest, what do you object to in these books?

Manders. Object to in them? You surely do not suppose that I have nothing better to do than to study such publications as these?

Mrs. Alving. That is to say, you know nothing of what you are condemning?

Manders. I have read enough about these writings to disapprove of them.

Mrs. Alving. Yes; but your own judgment—

Manders. My dear Mrs. Alving, there are many occasions in life when one must rely upon others. Things are so ordered in this world; and it is well that they are. Otherwise, what would become of society?

Mrs. Alving. Well, well, I daresay you're right there.

Manders. Besides, I of course do not deny that there may be much that is attractive in such books. Nor can I blame you for wishing to keep up with the intellectual movements that are said to be going on in the great world—where you have let your son pass so much of his life. But—

Mrs. Alving. But?

Manders. (*Lowering his voice.*) But one should not talk about it, Mrs. Alving. One is certainly not bound to account to everybody for what one reads and thinks within one's own four walls.

Mrs. Alving. Of course not; I quite agree with you.

Manders. Only think, now, how you are bound to consider the interests of this Orphanage, which you decided on founding at a time when—if I understand you rightly—you thought very differently on spiritual matters.

Mrs. Alving. Oh, yes; I quite admit that. But it was about the Orphanage—

Manders. It was about the Orphanage we were to speak; yes. All I say is: prudence, my dear lady! And now let us get to business. (*Opens the packet, and takes out a number of papers.*) Do you see these?

Mrs. Alving. The documents?

Manders. All—and in perfect order. I can tell you it was hard work to get them in time. I had to put on strong pressure. The authorities are almost morbidly scrupulous when there is any decisive step to be taken. But here they are at last. (*Looks through the bundle.*) See! Here is the formal deed of gift of the parcel of ground known as Solvik in the Manor of Rosenvold, with all the newly constructed buildings, schoolrooms, master's house, and chapel. And here is the legal fiat for the endowment and for the Bye-laws of the Institution. Will you look at them? (*Reads.*) "Bye-laws for the Children's Home to be known as 'Captain Alving's Foundation.'"

Mrs. Alving. (*Looks long at the paper.*) So there it is.

Manders. I have chosen the designation "Captain" rather than "Chamberlain." "Captain" looks less pretentious.

Mrs. Alving. Oh, yes; just as you think best.

Manders. And here you have the Bank Account of the capital lying at interest to cover the current expenses of the Orphanage.

Mrs. Alving. Thank you; but please keep it—it will be more convenient.

Manders. With pleasure. I think we will leave the money in the Bank for the present. The interest is certainly not what we could wish—four percent and six months' notice of withdrawal. If a good mortgage could be found later on—of course it must be a first mortgage and an unimpeachable security—then we could consider the matter.

Mrs. Alving. Certainly, my dear Pastor Manders. You are the best judge in these things.

Manders. I will keep my eyes open at any rate.—But now there is one thing more which I have several times been intending to ask you.

Mrs. Alving. And what is that?

Manders. Shall the Orphanage buildings be insured or not?

Mrs. Alving. Of course they must be insured.

Manders. Well, wait a moment, Mrs. Alving. Let us look into the matter a little more closely.

Mrs. Alving. I have everything insured; buildings and movables and stock and crops.

Manders. Of course you have—on your own estate. And so have I—of course. But here, you see, it is quite another matter. The Orphanage is to be consecrated, as it were, to a higher purpose.

Mrs. Alving. Yes, but that's no reason—

Manders. For my own part, I should certainly not see the smallest impropriety in guarding against all contingencies—

Mrs. Alving. No, I should think not.

Manders. But what is the general feeling in the neighbourhood? You, of course, know better than I.

Mrs. Alving. Well—the general feeling—

Manders. Is there any considerable number of people—really responsible people—who might be scandalised?

Mrs. Alving. What do you mean by "really responsible people"?

Manders. Well, I mean people in such independent and influential positions that one cannot help attaching some weight to their opinions.

Mrs. Alving. There are several people of that sort here, who would very likely be shocked if—

Manders. There, you see! In town we have many such people. Think of all my colleague's adherents! People would be only too ready to interpret our action as a sign that neither you nor I had the right faith in a Higher Providence.

Mrs. Alving. But for your own part, my dear Pastor, you can at least tell yourself that—

Manders. Yes, I know—I know; my conscience would be quite easy, that is true enough. But nevertheless we should not escape grave misinterpretation; and that might very likely react unfavourably upon the Orphanage.

Mrs. Alving. Well, in that case—

Manders. Nor can I entirely lose sight of the difficult—I may even say painful—position in which I might perhaps be placed. In the leading circles of the town, people take a lively interest in this Orphanage. It is, of course, founded partly for the benefit of the town, as well; and it is to be hoped it will, to a considerable extent, result in lightening our Poor Rates. Now, as I have been your adviser, and have had the business arrangements in my hands, I cannot but fear that I may have to bear the brunt of fanaticism—

Mrs. Alving. Oh, you mustn't run the risk of that.

Manders. To say nothing of the attacks that would assuredly be made upon me in certain papers and periodicals, which—

Mrs. Alving. Enough, my dear Pastor Manders. That consideration is quite decisive.

Manders. Then you do not wish the Orphanage to be insured?

Mrs. Alving. No. We will let it alone.

Manders. (*Leaning back in his chair.*) But if, now, a disaster were to happen? One can never tell—should you be able to make good the damage?

Mrs. Alving. No; I tell you plainly I should do nothing of the kind.

Manders. Then I must tell you, Mrs. Alving—we are taking no small responsibility upon ourselves.

Mrs. Alving. Do you think we can do otherwise?

Manders. No, that is just the point; we really cannot do otherwise. We ought not to expose ourselves to misinterpretation; and we have no right whatever to give offence to the weaker brethren.

Mrs. Alving. You, as a clergyman, certainly should not.

Manders. I really think, too, we may trust that such an institution has fortune on its side; in fact, that it stands under a special providence.

Mrs. Alving. Let us hope so, Pastor Manders.

Manders. Then we will let it take its chance?

Mrs. Alving. Yes, certainly.

Manders. Very well. So be it. (*Makes a note.*) Then—no insurance.

Mrs. Alving. It's odd that you should just happen to mention the matter today—

Manders. I have often thought of asking you about it—

Mrs. Alving.—For we very nearly had a fire down there yesterday.

Manders. You don't say so!

Mrs. Alving. Oh, it was a trifling matter. A heap of shavings had caught fire in the carpenter's workshop.

Manders. Where Engstrand works?

Mrs. Alving. Yes. They say he's often very careless with matches.

Manders. He has so much on his mind, that man—so many things to fight against. Thank God, he is now striving to lead a decent life, I hear.

Mrs. Alving. Indeed! Who says so?

Manders. He himself assures me of it. And he is certainly a capital workman.

Mrs. Alving. Oh, yes; so long as he's sober—

Manders. Ah, that melancholy weakness! But, he is often driven to it by his injured leg, he says. Last time he was in town I was really touched by him. He came and thanked me so warmly for having got him work here, so that he might be near Regina.

Mrs. Alving. He doesn't see much of her.

Manders. Oh, yes; he has a talk with her every day. He told me so himself.

Mrs. Alving. Well, it may be so.

Manders. He feels so acutely that he needs someone to keep a firm hold on him when temptation comes. That is what I cannot help liking about Jacob Engstrand: he comes to you so helplessly, accusing himself and confessing his own weakness. The last time he was talking to me—Believe me, Mrs. Alving, supposing it were a real necessity for him to have Regina home again—

Mrs. Alving. (*Rising hastily.*) Regina!

Manders.—You must not set yourself against it.

Mrs. Alving. Indeed I shall set myself against it. And besides—Regina is to have a position in the Orphanage.

Manders. But, after all, remember he is her father—

Mrs. Alving. Oh, I know very well what sort of a father he has been to her. No! She shall never go to him with my goodwill.

Manders. (*Rising.*) My dear lady, don't take the matter so warmly. You sadly misjudge poor Engstrand. You seem to be quite terrified—

Mrs. Alving. (*More quietly.*) It makes no difference. I have taken Regina into my house, and there she shall stay. (*Listens.*) Hush, my dear Mr. Manders; say no more about it. (*Her face lights up with gladness.*) Listen! There is Oswald coming downstairs. Now we'll think of no one but him.

(*Oswald Alving, in a light overcoat, hat in hand, and smoking a large meerschaum, enters by the door on the left; he stops in the doorway.*)

Oswald. Oh, I beg your pardon; I thought you were in the study. (*Comes forward.*) Good-morning, Pastor Manders.

Manders. (*Staring.*) Ah—! How strange—!

Mrs. Alving. Well now, what do you think of him, Mr. Manders?

Manders. I—I—can it really be—?

Oswald. Yes, it's really the Prodigal Son, sir.

Manders. (*Protesting.*) My dear young friend—

Oswald. Well, then, the Lost Sheep Found.

Mrs. Alving. Oswald is thinking of the time when you were so much opposed to his becoming a painter.

Manders. To our human eyes many a step seems dubious, which afterwards proves—(*Wrings his hand.*) But first of all, welcome, welcome home! Do not think, my dear Oswald—I suppose I may call you by your Christian name?

Oswald. What else should you call me?

Manders. Very good. What I wanted to say was this, my dear Oswald, you must not think that I utterly condemn the artist's calling. I have no doubt there are many who can keep their inner self unharmed in that profession, as in any other.

Oswald. Let us hope so.

Mrs. Alving. (*Beaming with delight.*) I know one who has kept both his inner and his outer self unharmed. Just look at him, Mr. Manders.

Oswald. (*Moves restlessly about the room.*) Yes, yes, my dear mother; let's say no more about it.

Manders. Why, certainly—that is undeniable. And you have begun to make a name for yourself already. The newspapers have often spoken of you, most favourably. Just lately, by-the-bye, I fancy I haven't seen your name quite so often.

Oswald. (*Up in the conservatory.*) I haven't been able to paint so much lately.

Mrs. Alving. Even a painter needs a little rest now and then.

Manders. No doubt, no doubt. And meanwhile he can be preparing himself and mustering his forces for some great work.

Oswald. Yes.—Mother, will dinner soon be ready?

Mrs. Alving. In less than half an hour. He has a capital appetite, thank God.

Manders. And a taste for tobacco, too.

Oswald. I found my father's pipe in my room—

Manders. Aha—then that accounts for it!

Mrs. Alving. For what?

Manders. When Oswald appeared there, in the doorway, with the pipe in his mouth, I could have sworn I saw his father, large as life.

Oswald. No, really?

Mrs. Alving. Oh, how can you say so? Oswald takes after me.

Manders. Yes, but there is an expression about the corners of the mouth—something about the lips—that reminds one exactly of Alving: at any rate, now that he is smoking.

Mrs. Alving. Not in the least. Oswald has rather a clerical curve about his mouth, I think.

Manders. Yes, yes; some of my colleagues have much the same expression.

Mrs. Alving. But put your pipe away, my dear boy; I won't have smoking in here.

Oswald. (*Does so.*) By all means. I only wanted to try it; for I once smoked it when I was a child.

Mrs. Alving. You?

Oswald. Yes. I was quite small at the time. I recollect I came up to father's room one evening when he was in great spirits.

Mrs. Alving. Oh, you can't recollect anything of those times.

Oswald. Yes, I recollect it distinctly. He took me on his knee, and gave me the pipe. "Smoke, boy," he said; "smoke away, boy!" And I smoked as hard as I could, until I felt I was growing quite pale, and the perspiration stood in great drops on my forehead. Then he burst out laughing heartily—

Manders. That was most extraordinary.

Mrs. Alving. My dear friend, it's only something Oswald has dreamt.

Oswald. No, mother, I assure you I didn't dream it. For—don't you remember this?—you came and carried me out into the nursery. Then I was sick, and I saw that you were crying. Did father often play such practical jokes?

Manders. In his youth he overflowed with the joy of life—

Oswald. And yet he managed to do so much in the world; so much that was good and useful; although he died so early.

Manders. Yes, you have inherited the name of an energetic and admirable man, my dear Oswald Alving. No doubt it will be an incentive to you—

Oswald. It ought to, indeed.

Manders. It was good of you to come home for the ceremony in his honour.

Oswald. I could do no less for my father.

Mrs. Alving. And I am to keep him so long! That is the best of all.

Manders. You are going to pass the winter at home, I hear.

Oswald. My stay is indefinite, sir. But, ah! It is good to be at home!

Mrs. Alving. (*Beaming.*) Yes, isn't it, dear?

Manders. (*Looking sympathetically at him.*) You went out into the world early, my dear Oswald.

Oswald. I did. I sometimes wonder whether it wasn't too early.

Mrs. Alving. Oh, not at all. A healthy lad is all the better for it, especially when he's an only child. He oughtn't to hang on at home with his mother and father, and get spoilt.

Manders. That is a very disputable point, Mrs. Alving. A child's proper place is, and must be, the home of his fathers.

Oswald. There I quite agree with you, Pastor Manders.

Manders. Only look at your own son—there is no reason why we should not say it in his presence—what has the consequence been for him? He is six or seven and twenty, and has never had the opportunity of learning what a well-ordered home really is.

Oswald. I beg your pardon, Pastor; there you're quite mistaken.

Manders. Indeed? I thought you had lived almost exclusively in artistic circles.

Oswald. So I have.

Manders. And chiefly among the younger artists?

Oswald. Yes, certainly.

Manders. But I thought few of those young fellows could afford to set up house and support a family.

Oswald. There are many who cannot afford to marry, sir.

Manders. Yes, that is just what I say.

Oswald. But they may have a home for all that. And several of them have, as a matter of fact; and very pleasant, well-ordered homes they are, too.

(*Mrs. Alving follows with breathless interest; nods, but says nothing.*)

Manders. But I'm not talking of bachelors' quarters. By a "home" I understand the home of a family, where a man lives with his wife and children.

Oswald. Yes; or with his children and his children's mother.

Manders. (*Starts; clasps his hands.*) But, good heavens—

Oswald. Well?

Manders. Lives with—his children's mother!

Oswald. Yes. Would you have him turn his children's mother out of doors?

Manders. Then it is illicit relations you are talking of! Irregular marriages, as people call them!

Oswald. I have never noticed anything particularly irregular about the life these people lead.

Manders. But how is it possible that a—a young man or young woman with any decency of feeling can endure to live in that way?—in the eyes of all the world!

Oswald. What are they to do? A poor young artist—a poor girl—marriage costs a great deal. What are they to do?

Manders. What are they to do? Let me tell you, Mr. Alving, what they ought to do. They ought to exercise self-restraint from the first; that is what they ought to do.

Oswald. That doctrine will scarcely go down with warm-blooded young people who love each other.

Mrs. Alving. No, scarcely!

Manders. (*Continuing.*) How can the authorities tolerate such things! Allow them to go on in the light of day! (*Confronting Mrs. Alving.*) Had I not cause to be deeply concerned about your son? In circles where open immorality prevails, and has even a sort of recognised position—!

Oswald. Let me tell you, sir, that I have been in the habit of spending nearly all my Sundays in one or two such irregular homes—

Manders. Sunday of all days!

Oswald. Isn't that the day to enjoy one's self? Well, never have I heard an offensive word, and still less have I witnessed anything that could be called immoral. No; do you know when and where I have come across immorality in artistic circles?

Manders. No, thank heaven, I don't!

Oswald. Well, then, allow me to inform you. I have met with it when one or other of our pattern husbands and fathers has come to Paris to have a look round on his own account, and has done the artists the honour of visiting their humble haunts. They knew what was what. These gentlemen could tell us all about places and things we had never dreamt of.

Manders. What! Do you mean to say that respectable men from home here would—?

Oswald. Have you never heard these respectable men, when they got home again, talking about the way in which immorality runs rampant abroad?

Manders. Yes, no doubt—

Mrs. Alving. I have too.

Oswald. Well, you may take their word for it. They know what they are talking about! (*Presses his hands to his head.*) Oh! That great, free, glorious life out there should be defiled in such a way!

Mrs. Alving. You mustn't get excited, Oswald. It's not good for you.

Oswald. Yes, you're quite right, mother. It's bad for me, I know. You see, I'm wretchedly worn out. I shall go for a little turn before dinner. Excuse me, Pastor, I know you can't take my point of view; but I couldn't help speaking out. (*He goes out by the second door to the right.*)

Mrs. Alving. My poor boy!

Manders. You may well say so. Then this is what he has come to!

(*Mrs. Alving looks at him silently.*)

Manders. (*Walking up and down.*) He called himself the Prodigal Son. Alas! Alas!

(*Mrs. Alving continues looking at him.*)

Manders. And what do you say to all this?

Mrs. Alving. I say that Oswald was right in every word.

Manders. (*Stands still.*) Right? Right! In such principles?

Mrs. Alving. Here, in my loneliness, I have come to the same way of thinking, Pastor Manders. But I have never dared to say anything. Well! Now my boy shall speak for me.

Manders. You are greatly to be pitied, Mrs. Alving. But now I must speak seriously to you. And now it is no longer your business manager and adviser, your own and your husband's early friend, who stands before you. It is the priest—the priest who stood before you in the moment of your life when you had gone farthest astray.

Mrs. Alving. And what has the priest to say to me?

Manders. I will first stir up your memory a little. The moment is well chosen. To-morrow will be the tenth anniversary of your husband's death. To-morrow the memorial in his honour will be unveiled. To-morrow I shall have to speak to the whole assembled multitude. But today I will speak to you alone.

Mrs. Alving. Very well, Pastor Manders. Speak.

Manders. Do you remember that after less than a year of married life you stood on the verge of an abyss? That you forsook your house and home? That you fled from your husband? Yes, Mrs. Alving—fled, fled, and refused to return to him, however much he begged and prayed you?

Mrs. Alving. Have you forgotten how infinitely miserable I was in that first year?

Manders. It is the very mark of the spirit of rebellion to crave for happiness in this life. What right have we human beings to happiness? We have simply to do our duty, Mrs. Alving! And your duty was to hold firmly to the man you had once chosen, and to whom you were bound by the holiest ties.

Mrs. Alving. You know very well what sort of life Alving was leading—what excesses he was guilty of.

Manders. I know very well what rumours there were about him; and I am the last to approve the life he led in his young days, if report did not wrong him. But a wife is not appointed to be her husband's judge. It was your duty to bear with humility the cross which a Higher Power had, in its wisdom, laid upon you. But instead of that you rebelliously throw away the cross, desert the backslider whom you should have supported, go and risk your good name and reputation, and—nearly succeed in ruining other people's reputation into the bargain.

Mrs. Alving. Other people's? One other person's, you mean.

Manders. It was incredibly reckless of you to seek refuge with me.

Mrs. Alving. With our clergyman? With our intimate friend?

Manders. Just on that account. Yes, you may thank God that I possessed the necessary firmness; that I succeeded in dissuading you from your wild designs; and that it was vouchsafed me to lead you back to the path of duty, and home to your lawful husband.

Mrs. Alving. Yes, Pastor Manders, that was certainly your work.

Manders. I was but a poor instrument in a Higher Hand. And what a blessing has it not proved to you, all the days of your life, that I induced you to resume the yoke of duty and obedience! Did not everything happen as I foretold? Did not Alving turn his back on his errors, as a man should? Did he not live with you from that time, lovingly and blamelessly, all his days? Did he not become a benefactor to the whole district? And did he not help you to rise to his own level, so that you, little by little, became his assistant in all his undertakings? And a capital assistant, too—oh, I know, Mrs. Alving, that praise is due to you. —But now I come to the next great error in your life.

Mrs. Alving. What do you mean?

Manders. Just as you once disowned a wife's duty, so you have since disowned a mother's.

Mrs. Alving. Ah—!

Manders. You have been all your life under the dominion of a pestilent spirit of self-will. The whole bias of your mind has been towards insubordination and lawlessness. You have never known how to endure any bond. Everything that has weighed upon you in life you have cast away without care or conscience, like a burden you were free to throw off at will. It did not please you to be a wife any longer, and you left your husband. You found it troublesome to be a mother, and you sent your child forth among strangers.

Mrs. Alving. Yes, that is true. I did so.

Manders. And thus you have become a stranger to him.

Mrs. Alving. No! no! I am not.

Manders. Yes, you are; you must be. And in what state of mind has he returned to you? Bethink yourself well, Mrs. Alving. You sinned greatly against your husband;—that you recognise by raising yonder memorial to him. Recognise now, also, how you have sinned against your son—there may yet be time to lead him back from the paths of error. Turn back yourself, and save what may yet be saved in him. For verily, Mrs. Alving, (*With uplifted forefinger*) you are a guilt-laden mother! This I have thought it my duty to say to you.

(*Silence.*)

Mrs. Alving. (*Slowly and with self-control.*) You have now spoken out, Pastor Manders; and to-morrow you are to speak publicly in memory of my husband. I shall not speak to-morrow. But now I will speak frankly to you, as you have spoken to me.

Manders. To be sure; you will plead excuses for your conduct—

Mrs. Alving. No. I will only tell you a story.

Manders. Well—?

Mrs. Alving. All that you have just said about my husband and me, and our life after you had brought me back to the path of duty—as you called it—about all that you know nothing from personal observation. From that moment you, who had been our intimate friend, never set foot in our house again.

Manders. You and your husband left the town immediately after.

Mrs. Alving. Yes, and in my husband's lifetime you never came to see us. It was business that forced you to visit me when you undertook the affairs of the Orphanage.

Manders. (*Softly and hesitatingly.*) Helen—if that is meant as a reproach, I would beg you to bear in mind—

Mrs. Alving. The regard you owed to your position, yes; and that I was a runaway wife. One can never be too cautious with such unprincipled creatures.

Manders. My dear—Mrs. Alving, you know that is an absurd exaggeration—

Mrs. Alving. Well well, suppose it is. My point is that your judgment as to my married life is founded upon nothing but common knowledge and report.

Manders. I admit that. What then?

Mrs. Alving. Well, then, Pastor Manders—I will tell you the truth. I have sworn to myself that one day you should know it—you alone!

Manders. What is the truth, then?

Mrs. Alving. The truth is that my husband died just as dissolute as he had lived all his days.

Manders. (*Feeling after a chair.*) What do you say?

Mrs. Alving. After nineteen years of marriage, as dissolute—in his desires at any rate—as he was before you married us.

Manders. And those—those wild oats—those irregularities—those excesses, if you like—you call "a dissolute life"?

Mrs. Alving. Our doctor used the expression.

Manders. I do not understand you.

Mrs. Alving. You need not.

Manders. It almost makes me dizzy. Your whole married life, the seeming union of all these years, was nothing more than a hidden abyss!

Mrs. Alving. Neither more nor less. Now you know it.

Manders. This is—this is inconceivable to me. I cannot grasp it! I cannot realise it! But how was it possible to—? How could such a state of things be kept secret?

Mrs. Alving. That has been my ceaseless struggle, day after day. After Oswald's birth, I thought Alving seemed to be a little better. But it did not last long. And then I had to struggle twice as hard, fighting as though for life or death, so that nobody should know what sort of man my child's father was. And you know what power Alving had of winning people's hearts. Nobody seemed able to believe anything but good of him. He was one of those people whose life does not bite upon their reputation. But at last, Mr. Manders—for you must know the whole story—the most repulsive thing of all happened.

Manders. More repulsive than what you have told me?

Mrs. Alving. I had gone on bearing with him, although I knew very well the secrets of his life out of doors. But when he brought the scandal within our own walls—

Manders. Impossible! Here!

Mrs. Alving. Yes, here in our own home. It was there (*Pointing towards the first door on the right*), in the dining-room, that I first came to know of it. I was busy with something in there, and the door was standing ajar. I heard our housemaid come up from the garden, with water for those flowers.

Manders. Well—?

Mrs. Alving. Soon after, I heard Alving come in too. I heard him say something softly to her. And then I heard—(*With a short laugh*)—oh! it still sounds in my ears, so hateful and yet so ludicrous—I heard my own servant-maid whisper, "Let me go, Mr. Alving! Let me be!"

Manders. What unseemly levity on his part! But it cannot have been more than levity, Mrs. Alving; believe me, it cannot.

Mrs. Alving. I soon knew what to believe. Mr. Alving had his way with the girl, and that connection had consequences, Mr. Manders.

Manders. (*As though petrified.*) Such things in this house—in this house!

Mrs. Alving. I had borne a great deal in this house. To keep him at home in the evenings, and at night, I had to make myself his boon companion in his secret orgies up in his room. There I have had to sit alone with him, to clink glasses and drink with him, and to listen to his ribald, silly talk. I have had to fight with him to get him dragged to bed—

Manders. (*Moved.*) And you were able to bear all this!

Mrs. Alving. I had to bear it for my little boy's sake. But when the last insult was added; when my own servant-maid—; then I swore to myself: This shall come to an end! And so I took the reins into my own hand—the whole control—over him and everything else. For now I had a weapon against him, you see; he dared not oppose me. It was then I sent Oswald away from home. He was nearly seven years old, and was beginning to observe and ask questions, as children do. That I could not bear. It seemed to me the child must be poisoned by merely breathing the air of this polluted home. That was why I sent him away. And now you can see, too, why he was never allowed to set foot inside his home so long as his father lived. No one knows what that cost me.

Manders. You have indeed had a life of trial.

Mrs. Alving. I could never have borne it if I had not had my work. For I may truly say that I have worked! All the additions to the estate—all the improvements—all the labour-saving appliances, that Alving was so much praised for having introduced—do you suppose he had energy for anything of the sort? He, who lay all day on the sofa, reading an old Court Guide! No; but I may tell you this too: when he had his better intervals, it was I who urged him on; it was I who had to drag the whole load when he relapsed into his evil ways, or sank into querulous wretchedness.

Manders. And it is to this man that you raise a memorial?

Mrs. Alving. There you see the power of an evil conscience.

Manders. Evil——? What do you mean?

Mrs. Alving. It always seemed to me impossible but that the truth must come out and be believed. So the Orphanage was to deaden all rumours and set every doubt at rest.

Manders. In that you have certainly not missed your aim, Mrs. Alving.

Mrs. Alving. And besides, I had one other reason. I was determined that Oswald, my own boy, should inherit nothing whatever from his father.

Manders. Then it is Alving's fortune that——?

Mrs. Alving. Yes. The sums I have spent upon the Orphanage, year by year, make up the amount——I have reckoned it up precisely——the amount which made Lieutenant Alving "a good match" in his day.

Manders. I don't understand——

Mrs. Alving. It was my purchase-money. I do not choose that that money should pass into Oswald's hands. My son shall have everything from me——everything.

(*Oswald Alving enters through the second door to the right; he has taken of his hat and overcoat in the hall.*)

Mrs. Alving. (*Going towards him.*) Are you back again already? My dear, dear boy!

Oswald. Yes. What can a fellow do out of doors in this eternal rain? But I hear dinner is ready. That's capital!

Regina. (*With a parcel, from the dining-room.*) A parcel has come for you, Mrs. Alving. (*Hands it to her.*)

Mrs. Alving. (*With a glance at Mr. Manders.*) No doubt copies of the ode for to-morrow's ceremony.

Manders. H'm—

Regina. And dinner is ready.

Mrs. Alving. Very well. We will come directly. I will just—(*Begins to open the parcel.*)

Regina. (*To Oswald.*) Would Mr. Alving like red or white wine?

Oswald. Both, if you please.

Regina. Bien. Very well, sir. (*She goes into the dining-room.*)

Oswald. I may as well help to uncork it. (*He also goes into the dining-room, the door of which swings half open behind him.*)

Mrs. Alving. (*Who has opened the parcel.*) Yes, I thought so. Here is the Ceremonial Ode, Pastor Manders.

Manders. (*With folded hands.*) With what countenance I am to deliver my discourse to-morrow—!

Mrs. Alving. Oh, you will get through it somehow.

Manders. (*Softly, so as not to be heard in the dining-room.*) Yes, it would not do to provoke scandal.

Mrs. Alving. (*Under her breath, but firmly.*) No. But then this long, hateful comedy will be ended. From the day after tomorrow, I shall act in every way as though he who is dead had never lived in this house. There shall be no one here but my boy and his mother.

(*From the dining-room comes the noise of a chair overturned, and at the same moment is heard:*)

Regina. (*Sharply, but in a whisper.*) Oswald! Take care! Are you mad? Let me go!

Mrs. Alving. (*Starts in terror.*) Ah—!

(*She stares wildly towards the half-open door. Oswald is heard laughing and humming. A bottle is uncorked.*)

Manders. (*Agitated.*) What can be the matter? What is it, Mrs. Alving?

Mrs. Alving. (*Hoarsely.*) Ghosts! The couple from the conservatory—risen again!

Manders. Is it possible! Regina—? Is she—?

Mrs. Alving. Yes. Come. Not a word—!

(*She seizes Pastor Manders by the arm, and walks unsteadily towards the dining-room.*)

ACT II

The same room. The mist still lies heavy over the landscape. Manders and Mrs. Alving enter from the dining-room.

Mrs. Alving. (*Still in the doorway.*) Velbekomme ①, Mr. Manders. (*Turns back towards the dining-room.*) Aren't you coming too, Oswald?

Oswald. (*From within.*) No, thank you. I think I shall go out a little.

Mrs. Alving. Yes, do. The weather seems a little brighter now. (*She shuts the dining-room door, goes to the hall door, and calls:*) Regina!

Regina. (*Outside.*) Yes, Mrs. Alving?

Mrs. Alving. Go down to the laundry, and help with the garlands.

---

① A phrase equivalent to the German Prosit die Mahlzeit—May good digestion wait on appetite.

Regina. Yes, Mrs. Alving.

(*Mrs. Alving assures herself that Regina goes, then shuts the door.*)

Manders. I suppose he cannot overhear us in there?

Mrs. Alving. Not when the door is shut. Besides, he's just going out.

Manders. I am still quite upset. I don't know how I could swallow a morsel of dinner.

Mrs. Alving. (*Controlling her nervousness, walks up and down.*) Nor I. But what is to be done now?

Manders. Yes, what is to be done? I am really quite at a loss. I am so utterly without experience in matters of this sort.

Mrs. Alving. I feel sure that, so far, no mischief has been done.

Manders. No, heaven forbid! But it is an unseemly state of things, nevertheless.

Mrs. Alving. It is only an idle fancy on Oswald's part; you may be sure of that.

Manders. Well, as I say, I am not accustomed to affairs of the kind. But I should certainly think—

Mrs. Alving. Out of the house she must go, and that immediately. That is as clear as daylight—

Manders. Yes, of course she must.

Mrs. Alving. But where to? It would not be right to—

Manders. Where to? Home to her father, of course.

Mrs. Alving. To whom did you say?

Manders. To her—But then, Engstrand is not—? Good God, Mrs. Alving, it's impossible! You must be mistaken after all.

Mrs. Alving. Unfortunately there is no possibility of mistake. Johanna confessed everything to me; and Alving could not deny it. So there was nothing to be done but to get the matter hushed up.

Manders. No, you could do nothing else.

Mrs. Alving. The girl left our service at once, and got a good sum of money to hold her tongue for the time. The rest she managed for herself when she got to town. She renewed her old acquaintance with Engstrand, no doubt let him see that she had money in her purse, and told him some tale about a foreigner who put in here with a yacht that summer. So she and Engstrand got married in hot haste. Why, you married them yourself.

Manders. But then how to account for——? I recollect distinctly Engstrand coming to give notice of the marriage. He was quite overwhelmed with contrition, and bitterly reproached himself for the misbehaviour he and his sweetheart had been guilty of.

Mrs. Alving. Yes; of course he had to take the blame upon himself.

Manders. But such a piece of duplicity on his part! And towards me too! I never could have believed it of Jacob Engstrand. I shall not fail to take him seriously to task; he may be sure of that.—And then the immorality of such a connection! For money—! How much did the girl receive?

Mrs. Alving. Three hundred dollars.

Manders. Just think of it—for a miserable three hundred dollars, to go and marry a fallen woman!

Mrs. Alving. Then what have you to say of me? I went and married a fallen man.

Manders. Why—good heavens!—What are you talking about! A fallen man!

Mrs. Alving. Do you think Alving was any purer when I went with him to the altar than Johanna was when Engstrand married her?

Manders. Well, but there is a world of difference between the two cases—

Mrs. Alving. Not so much difference after all—except in the price:—a miserable three hundred dollars and a whole fortune.

Manders. How can you compare such absolutely dissimilar cases? You had taken counsel with your own heart and with your natural advisers.

Mrs. Alving. (*Without looking at him.*) I thought you understood where what you call my heart had strayed to at the time.

Manders. (*Distantly.*) Had I understood anything of the kind, I should not have been a daily guest in your husband's house.

Mrs. Alving. At any rate, the fact remains that with myself I took no counsel whatever.

Manders. Well then, with your nearest relatives—as your duty bade you—with your mother and your two aunts.

Mrs. Alving. Yes, that is true. Those three cast up the account for me. Oh, it's marvellous how clearly they made out that it would be downright madness to refuse such an offer. If mother could only see me now, and know what all that grandeur has come to!

Manders. Nobody can be held responsible for the result. This, at least, remains clear: your marriage was in full accordance with law and order.

Mrs. Alving. (*At the window.*) Oh, that perpetual law and order! I often think that is what does all the mischief in this world of ours.

Manders. Mrs. Alving, that is a sinful way of talking.

Mrs. Alving. Well, I can't help it; I must have done with all this constraint and insincerity. I can endure it no longer. I must work my way out to freedom.

Manders. What do you mean by that?

Mrs. Alving. (*Drumming on the window frame.*) I ought never to have concealed the facts of Alving's life. But at that time I dared not do anything else—I was afraid, partly on my own account. I was such a coward.

Manders. A coward?

Mrs. Alving. If people had come to know anything, they would have said—"Poor man! with a runaway wife, no wonder he kicks over the traces."

Manders. Such remarks might have been made with a certain show of right.

Mrs. Alving. (*Looking steadily at him.*) If I were what I ought to be, I should go to Oswald and say, "Listen, my boy: your father led a vicious life—"

Manders. Merciful heavens—!

Mrs. Alving.—And then I should tell him all I have told you—every word of it.

Manders. You shock me unspeakably, Mrs. Alving.

Mrs. Alving. Yes, I know that. I know that very well. I myself am shocked at the idea. (*Goes away from the window.*) I am such a coward.

Manders. You call it "cowardice" to do your plain duty? Have you forgotten that a son ought to love and honour his father and mother?

Mrs. Alving. Do not let us talk in such general terms. Let us ask: Ought Oswald to love and honour Chamberlain Alving?

Manders. Is there no voice in your mother's heart that forbids you to destroy your son's ideals?

Mrs. Alving. But what about the truth?

Manders. But what about the ideals?

Mrs. Alving. Oh—ideals, ideals! If only I were not such a coward!

Manders. Do not despise ideals, Mrs. Alving; they will avenge themselves cruelly. Take Oswald's case: he, unfortunately, seems to have few enough ideals as it is; but I can see that his father stands before him as an ideal.

Mrs. Alving. Yes, that is true.

Manders. And this habit of mind you have yourself implanted and fostered by your letters.

Mrs. Alving. Yes; in my superstitious awe for duty and the proprieties, I lied to my boy, year after year. Oh, what a coward—what a coward I have been!

Manders. You have established a happy illusion in your son's heart, Mrs. Alving; and assuredly you ought not to undervalue it.

Mrs. Alving. H'm; who knows whether it is so happy after all—? But, at any rate, I will not have any tampering with Regina. He shall not go and wreck the poor girl's life.

Manders. No, good God—that would be terrible!

Mrs. Alving. If I knew he was in earnest, and that it would be for his happiness—

Manders. What? What then?

Mrs. Alving. But it couldn't be; for unfortunately Regina is not the right sort of woman.

Manders. Well, what then? What do you mean?

Mrs. Alving. If I weren't such a pitiful coward, I should say to him, "Marry her, or make what arrangement you please, only let us have nothing underhand about it."

Manders. Merciful heavens, would you let them marry! Anything so dreadful—! so unheard of—

Mrs. Alving. Do you really mean "unheard of"? Frankly, Pastor Manders, do you suppose that throughout the country there are not plenty of married couples as closely akin as they?

Manders. I don't in the least understand you.

Mrs. Alving. Oh yes, indeed you do.

Manders. Ah, you are thinking of the possibility that—Alas! yes, family life is certainly not always so pure as it ought to be. But in such a case as you point to, one can never know—at least with any certainty. Here, on the other hand—that you, a mother, can think of letting your son—

Mrs. Alving. But I cannot—I wouldn't for anything in the world; that is precisely what I am saying.

Manders. No, because you are a "coward," as you put it. But if you were not a "coward," then—? Good God! a connection so shocking!

Mrs. Alving. So far as that goes, they say we are all sprung from connections of that sort. And who is it that arranged the world so, Pastor Manders?

Manders. Questions of that kind I must decline to discuss with you, Mrs. Alving; you are far from being in the right frame of mind for them. But that you dare to call your scruples "cowardly"—!

Mrs. Alving. Let me tell you what I mean. I am timid and faint-hearted because of the ghosts that hang about me, and that I can never quite shake off.

Manders. What do you say hangs about you?

Mrs. Alving. Ghosts! When I heard Regina and Oswald in there, it was as though ghosts rose up before me. But I almost think we are all of us ghosts, Pastor Manders. It is not only what we have inherited from our father and mother that "walks" in us. It is all sorts of dead ideas, and lifeless old beliefs, and so forth. They have no vitality, but they cling to us all the same, and we cannot shake them off. Whenever I take up a newspaper, I seem to see ghosts gliding between the lines. There must be ghosts all the country over, as thick as the sands of the sea. And then we are, one and all, so pitifully afraid of the light.

Manders. Aha—here we have the fruits of your reading. And pretty fruits they are, upon my word! Oh, those horrible, revolutionary, free-thinking books!

Mrs. Alving. You are mistaken, my dear Pastor. It was you yourself who set me thinking; and I thank you for it with all my heart.

Manders. I!

Mrs. Alving. Yes—when you forced me under the yoke of what you called duty and obligation; when you lauded as right and proper what my whole soul rebelled against as something loathsome. It was then that I began to look into the seams of your doctrines. I wanted only to pick at a single knot; but when I had got that undone, the whole thing ravelled out. And then I understood that it was all machine-sewn.

Manders. (*Softly, with emotion.*) And was that the upshot of my life's hardest battle?

Mrs. Alving. Call it rather your most pitiful defeat.

Manders. It was my greatest victory, Helen—the victory over myself.

Mrs. Alving. It was a crime against us both.

Manders. When you went astray, and came to me crying, "Here I am; take me!" I commanded you, saying, "Woman, go home to your lawful husband." Was that a crime?

Mrs. Alving. Yes, I think so.

Manders. We two do not understand each other.

Mrs. Alving. Not now, at any rate.

Manders. Never—never in my most secret thoughts have I regarded you otherwise than as another's wife.

Mrs. Alving. Oh—indeed?

Manders. Helen—!

Mrs. Alving. People so easily forget their past selves.

Manders. I do not. I am what I always was.

Mrs. Alving. (*Changing the subject.*) Well well well; don't let us talk of old times any longer. You are now over head and ears in Boards and Committees, and I am fighting my battle with ghosts, both within me and without.

Manders. Those without I shall help you to lay. After all the terrible things I have heard from you today, I cannot in conscience permit an unprotected girl to remain in your house.

Mrs. Alving. Don't you think the best plan would be to get her provided for?—I mean, by a good marriage.

Manders. No doubt. I think it would be desirable for her in every respect. Regina is now at the age when—Of course I don't know much about these things, but—

Mrs. Alving. Regina matured very early.

Manders. Yes, I thought so. I have an impression that she was remarkably well developed, physically, when I prepared her for confirmation. But in the meantime, she ought to be at home, under her father's eye—Ah! But Engstrand is not—that he—that he—could so hide the truth from me!

(*A knock at the door into the hall.*)

Mrs. Alving. Who can this be? Come in!

Engstrand. (*In his Sunday clothes, in the doorway.*) I humbly beg your pardon, but—

Manders. Aha! H'm—

Mrs. Alving. Is that you, Engstrand?

Engstrand.—There was none of the servants about, so I took the great liberty of just knocking.

Mrs. Alving. Oh, very well. Come in. Do you want to speak to me?

Engstrand. (*Comes in.*) No, I'm obliged to you, ma'am; it was with his Reverence I wanted to have a word or two.

Manders. (*Walking up and down the room.*) Ah—indeed! You want to speak to me, do you?

Engstrand. Yes, I'd like so terrible much to—

Manders. (*Stops in front of him.*) Well, may I ask what you want?

Engstrand. Well, it was just this, your Reverence: we've been paid off down yonder—my grateful thanks to you, ma'am,—and now everything's finished, I've been thinking it would be but right and proper if we, that have been working so honestly together all this time—well, I was thinking we ought to end up with a little prayer-meeting to-night.

Manders. A prayer-meeting? Down at the Orphanage?

Engstrand. Oh, if your Reverence doesn't think it proper—

Manders. Oh yes, I do; but—h'm—

Engstrand. I've been in the habit of offering up a little prayer in the evenings, myself—

Mrs. Alving. Have you?

Engstrand. Yes, every now and then just a little edification, in a manner of speaking. But I'm a poor, common man, and have little enough gift, God help me!—And so I thought, as the Reverend Mr. Manders happened to be here, I'd—

Manders. Well, you see, Engstrand, I have a question to put to you first. Are you in the right frame of mind for such a meeting! Do you feel your conscience clear and at ease?

Engstrand. Oh, God help us, your Reverence! we'd better not talk about conscience.

Manders. Yes, that is just what we must talk about. What have you to answer?

Engstrand. Why—a man's conscience—it can be bad enough now and then.

Manders. Ah, you admit that. Then perhaps you will make a clean breast of it, and tell me—the real truth about Regina?

Mrs. Alving. (*Quickly.*) Mr. Manders!

Manders. (*Reassuringly.*) Please allow me—

Engstrand. About Regina! Lord, what a turn you gave me! (*Looks at Mrs. Alving.*) There's nothing wrong about Regina, is there?

Manders. We will hope not. But I mean, what is the truth about you and Regina? You pass for her father, eh!

Engstrand. (*Uncertain.*) Well—h'm—your Reverence knows all about me and poor Johanna.

Manders. Come now, no more prevarication! Your wife told Mrs. Alving the whole story before quitting her service.

Engstrand. Well, then, may—! Now, did she really?

Manders. You see we know you now, Engstrand.

Engstrand. And she swore and took her Bible oath—

Manders. Did she take her Bible oath?

Engstrand. No, she only swore; but she did it that solemn-like.

Manders. And you have hidden the truth from me all these years? Hidden it from me, who have trusted you without reserve, in everything.

Engstrand. Well, I can't deny it.

Manders. Have I deserved this of you, Engstrand? Have I not always been ready to help you in word and deed, so far as it lay in my power? Answer me. Have I not?

Engstrand. It would have been a poor look-out for me many a time but for the Reverend Mr. Manders.

Manders. And this is how you reward me! You cause me to

enter falsehoods in the Church Register, and you withhold from me, year after year, the explanations you owed alike to me and to the truth. Your conduct has been wholly inexcusable, Engstrand; and from this time forward I have done with you!

Engstrand. (*With a sigh.*) Yes! I suppose there's no help for it.

Manders. How can you possibly justify yourself?

Engstrand. Who could ever have thought she'd have gone and made bad worse by talking about it? Will your Reverence just fancy yourself in the same trouble as poor Johanna—

Manders. I!

Engstrand. Lord bless you, I don't mean just exactly the same. But I mean, if your Reverence had anything to be ashamed of in the eyes of the world, as the saying goes. We menfolk oughtn't to judge a poor woman too hardly, your Reverence.

Manders. I am not doing so. It is you I am reproaching.

Engstrand. Might I make so bold as to ask your Reverence a bit of a question?

Manders. Yes, if you want to.

Engstrand. Isn't it right and proper for a man to raise up the fallen?

Manders. Most certainly it is.

Engstrand. And isn't a man bound to keep his sacred word?

Manders. Why, of course he is; but—

Engstrand. When Johanna had got into trouble through that Englishman—or it might have been an American or a

Russian, as they call them—well, you see, she came down into the town. Poor thing, she'd sent me about my business once or twice before: for she couldn't bear the sight of anything as wasn't handsome; and I'd got this damaged leg of mine. Your Reverence recollects how I ventured up into a dancing saloon, where seafaring men was carrying on with drink and devilry, as the saying goes. And then, when I was for giving them a bit of an admonition to lead a new life—

Mrs. Alving. (*At the window.*) H'm—

Manders. I know all about that, Engstrand; the ruffians threw you downstairs. You have told me of the affair already. Your infirmity is an honour to you.

Engstrand. I'm not puffed up about it, your Reverence. But what I wanted to say was, that when she came and confessed all to me, with weeping and gnashing of teeth, I can tell your Reverence I was sore at heart to hear it.

Manders. Were you indeed, Engstrand? Well, go on.

Engstrand. So I says to her, "The American, he's sailing about on the boundless sea. And as for you, Johanna," says I, "you've committed a grievous sin, and you're a fallen creature. But Jacob Engstrand," says I, "he's got two good legs to stand upon, he has—" You see, your Reverence, I was speaking figurative-like.

Manders. I understand quite well. Go on.

Engstrand. Well, that was how I raised her up and made an honest woman of her, so as folks shouldn't get to know how as she'd gone astray with foreigners.

Manders. In all that you acted very well. Only I cannot approve of your stooping to take money—

Engstrand. Money? I? Not a farthing!

Manders. (*Inquiringly to Mrs. Alving.*) But—

Engstrand. Oh, wait a minute!—now I recollect. Johanna did have a trifle of money. But I would have nothing to do with that. "No," says I, "that's mammon; that's the wages of sin. This dirty gold—or notes, or whatever it was—we'll just flint, that back in the American's face," says I. But he was off and away, over the stormy sea, your Reverence.

Manders. Was he really, my good fellow?

Engstrand. He was indeed, sir. So Johanna and I, we agreed that the money should go to the child's education; and so it did, and I can account for every blessed farthing of it.

Manders. Why, this alters the case considerably.

Engstrand. That's just how it stands, your Reverence. And I make so bold as to say as I've been an honest father to Regina, so far as my poor strength went; for I'm but a weak vessel, worse luck!

Manders. Well, well, my good fellow—

Engstrand. All the same, I bear myself witness as I've brought up the child, and lived kindly with poor Johanna, and ruled over my own house, as the Scripture has it. But it couldn't never enter my head to go to your Reverence and puff myself up and boast because even the likes of me had done some good in the world. No, sir; when anything of that sort happens to Jacob Engstrand, he holds his tongue about it. It don't happen so terrible often, I daresay. And when I do come to see your Reverence, I find a mortal deal that's wicked and weak to talk about. For I said it before, and I says it again—a man's conscience isn't always as clean as it might be.

Manders. Give me your hand, Jacob Engstrand.

Engstrand. Oh, Lord! your Reverence—

Manders. Come, no nonsense (*wrings his hand*). There we are!

Engstrand. And if I might humbly beg your Reverence's pardon—

Manders. You? On the contrary, it is I who ought to beg your pardon—

Engstrand. Lord, no, Sir!

Manders. Yes, assuredly. And I do it with all my heart. Forgive me for misunderstanding you. I only wish I could give you some proof of my hearty regret, and of my good-will towards you—

Engstrand. Would your Reverence do it?

Manders. With the greatest pleasure.

Engstrand. Well then, here's the very chance. With the bit of money I've saved here, I was thinking I might set up a Sailors' Home down in the town.

Mrs. Alving. You?

Engstrand. Yes; it might be a sort of Orphanage, too, in a manner of speaking. There's such a many temptations for seafaring folk ashore. But in this Home of mine, a man might feel like as he was under a father's eye, I was thinking.

Manders. What do you say to this, Mrs. Alving?

Engstrand. It isn't much as I've got to start with, Lord help me! But if I could only find a helping hand, why—

Manders. Yes, yes; we will look into the matter more closely. I entirely approve of your plan. But now, go before me and make everything ready, and get the candles lighted, so as to give the place an air of festivity. And then we will pass an edifying hour together, my good fellow; for now I quite believe you are in the right frame of mind.

Engstrand. Yes, I trust I am. And so I'll say good-bye, ma'am, and thank you kindly; and take good care of Regina for me—(*Wipes a tear from his eye*)—poor Johanna's child. Well, it's a queer thing, now; but it's just like as if she'd growd into the very apple of my eye. It is, indeed. (*He bows and goes out through the hall.*)

Manders. Well, what do you say of that man now, Mrs. Alving? That was a very different account of matters, was it not?

Mrs. Alving. Yes, it certainly was.

Manders. It only shows how excessively careful one ought to be in judging one's fellow creatures. But what a heartfelt joy it is to ascertain that one has been mistaken! Don't you think so?

Mrs. Alving. I think you are, and will always be, a great baby, Manders.

Manders. I?

Mrs. Alving. (*Laying her two hands upon his shoulders.*) And I say that I have half a mind to put my arms round your neck, and kiss you.

Manders. (*Stepping hastily back.*) No, no! God bless me! What an idea!

Mrs. Alving. (*With a smile.*) Oh, you needn't be afraid of me.

Manders. (*By the table.*) You have sometimes such an exaggerated way of expressing yourself. Now, let me just collect all the documents, and put them in my bag. (*He does so.*) There, that's all right. And now, good-bye for the present. Keep your eyes open when Oswald comes back. I shall look in again later. (*He takes his hat and goes out through the hall door.*)

Mrs. Alving. (*Sighs, looks for a moment out of the window, sets the room in order a little, and is about to go into the dining-room, but stops at the door with a half-suppressed cry.*) Oswald, are you still at table?

Oswald. (*In the dining-room.*) I'm only finishing my cigar.

Mrs. Alving. I thought you had gone for a little walk.

Oswald. In such weather as this?

(*A glass clinks. Mrs. Alving leaves the door open, and sits down with her knitting on the sofa by the window.*)

Oswald. Wasn't that Pastor Manders that went out just now?

Mrs. Alving. Yes; he went down to the Orphanage.

Oswald. H'm. (*The glass and decanter clink again.*)

Mrs. Alving. (*With a troubled glance.*) Dear Oswald, you should take care of that liqueur. It is strong.

Oswald. It keeps out the damp.

Mrs. Alving. Wouldn't you rather come in here, to me?

Oswald. I mayn't smoke in there.

Mrs. Alving. You know quite well you may smoke cigars.

Oswald. Oh, all right then; I'll come in. Just a tiny drop more first. There! (*He comes into the room with his cigar, and shuts the door after him. A short silence.*) Where has the pastor gone to?

Mrs. Alving. I have just told you; he went down to the Orphanage.

Oswald. Oh, yes; so you did.

Mrs. Alving. You shouldn't sit so long at table, Oswald.

Oswald. (*Holding his cigar behind him.*) But I find it so pleasant, mother. (Strokes and caresses her.) Just think what it is for me to come home and sit at mother's own table, in mother's room, and eat mother's delicious dishes.

Mrs. Alving. My dear, dear boy!

Oswald. (*Somewhat impatiently, walks about and smokes.*) And what else can I do with myself here? I can't set to work at anything.

Mrs. Alving. Why can't you?

Oswald. In such weather as this? Without a single ray of sunshine the whole day? (*Walks up the room.*) Oh, not to be able to work—!

Mrs. Alving. Perhaps it was not quite wise of you to come home?

Oswald. Oh, yes, mother; I had to.

Mrs. Alving. You know I would ten times rather forgo the joy of having you here, than let you——

Oswald. (*Stops beside the table.*) Now just tell me, mother: does it really make you so very happy to have me home again?

Mrs. Alving. Does it make me happy!

Oswald. (*Crumpling up a newspaper.*) I should have thought it must be pretty much the same to you whether I was in existence or not.

Mrs. Alving. Have you the heart to say that to your mother, Oswald?

Oswald. But you've got on very well without me all this time.

Mrs. Alving. Yes; I have got on without you. That is true.

(*A silence. Twilight slowly begins to fall. Oswald paces to and fro across the room. He has laid his cigar down.*)

Oswald. (*Stops beside Mrs. Alving.*) Mother, may I sit on the sofa beside you?

Mrs. Alving. (*Makes room for him.*) Yes, do, my dear boy.

Oswald. (*Sits down.*) There is something I must tell you, mother.

Mrs. Alving. (*Anxiously.*) Well?

Oswald. (*Looks fixedly before him.*) For I can't go on hiding it any longer.

Mrs. Alving. Hiding what? What is it?

Oswald. (*As before.*) I could never bring myself to write to you about it; and since I've come home—

Mrs. Alving. (*Seizes him by the arm.*) Oswald, what is the matter?

Oswald. Both yesterday and today I have tried to put the thoughts away from me—to cast them off; but it's no use.

Mrs. Alving. (*Rising.*) Now you must tell me everything, Oswald!

Oswald. (*Draws her down to the sofa again.*) Sit still; and then I will try to tell you. —I complained of fatigue after my journey—

Mrs. Alving. Well? What then?

Oswald. But it isn't that that is the matter with me; not any ordinary fatigue—

Mrs. Alving. (*Tries to jump up.*) You are not ill, Oswald?

Oswald. (*Draws her down again.*) Sit still, mother. Do take it quietly. I'm not downright ill, either; not what is commonly called "ill." (*Clasps his hands above his head.*) Mother, my mind is broken down—ruined—I shall never be able to work again! (*With his hands before his face, he buries his head in her lap, and breaks into bitter sobbing.*)

Mrs. Alving. (*White and trembling.*) Oswald! Look at me! No, no; it's not true.

Oswald. (*Looks up with despair in his eyes.*) Never to be able to work again! Never!—Never! A living death! Mother, can you imagine anything so horrible?

Mrs. Alving. My poor boy! How has this horrible thing come upon you?

Oswald. (*Sitting upright again.*) That's just what I cannot possibly grasp or understand. I have never led a dissipated life—never, in any respect. You mustn't believe that of me, mother! I've never done that.

Mrs. Alving. I am sure you haven't, Oswald.

Oswald. And yet this has come upon me just the same—this awful misfortune!

Mrs. Alving. Oh, but it will pass over, my dear, blessed boy. It's nothing but overwork. Trust me, I am right.

Oswald. (*Sadly.*) I thought so too, at first; but it isn't so.

Mrs. Alving. Tell me everything, from beginning to end.

Oswald. Yes, I will.

Mrs. Alving. When did you first notice it?

Oswald. It was directly after I had been home last time, and had got back to Paris again. I began to feel the most violent pains in my head—chiefly in the back of my head, they seemed to come. It was as though a tight iron ring was being screwed round my neck and upwards.

Mrs. Alving. Well, and then?

Oswald. At first I thought it was nothing but the ordinary headache I had been so plagued with while I was growing up—

Mrs. Alving. Yes, yes—

Oswald. But it wasn't that. I soon found that out. I couldn't work anymore. I wanted to begin upon a big new picture, but my powers seemed to fail me; all my strength was crippled;

I could form no definite images; everything swam before me—whirling round and round. Oh, it was an awful state! At last I sent for a doctor—and from him I learned the truth.

Mrs. Alving. How do you mean?

Oswald. He was one of the first doctors in Paris. I told him my symptoms; and then he set to work asking me a string of questions which I thought had nothing to do with the matter. I couldn't imagine what the man was after—

Mrs. Alving. Well?

Oswald. At last he said: "There has been something worm-eaten in you from your birth." He used that very word—vermoulu.

Mrs. Alving. (*Breathlessly.*) What did he mean by that?

Oswald. I didn't understand either, and begged him to explain himself more clearly. And then the old cynic said— (*Clenching his fist*) Oh—!

Mrs. Alving. What did he say?

Oswald. He said, "The sins of the fathers are visited upon the children."

Mrs. Alving. (*Rising slowly.*) The sins of the fathers—!

Oswald. I very nearly struck him in the face—

Mrs. Alving. (*Walks away across the room.*) The sins of the fathers—

Oswald. (*Smiles sadly.*) Yes; what do you think of that? Of course I assured him that such a thing was out of the question.

But do you think he gave in? No, he stuck to it; and it was only when I produced your letters and translated the passages relating to father—

Mrs. Alving. But then—?

Oswald. Then of course he had to admit that he was on the wrong track; and so I learned the truth—the incomprehensible truth! I ought not to have taken part with my comrades in that lighthearted, glorious life of theirs. It had been too much for my strength. So I had brought it upon myself!

Mrs. Alving. Oswald! No, no; do not believe it!

Oswald. No other explanation was possible, he said. That's the awful part of it. Incurably ruined for life—by my own heedlessness! All that I meant to have done in the world—I never dare think of it again—I'm not able to think of it. Oh! if I could only live over again, and undo all I have done!

(*He buries his face in the sofa. Mrs. Alving wrings her hands and walks, in silent struggle, backwards and forwards.*)

Oswald. (*After a while, looks up and remains resting upon his elbow.*) If it had only been something inherited—something one wasn't responsible for! But this! To have thrown away so shamefully, thoughtlessly, recklessly, one's own happiness, one's own health, everything in the world—one's future, one's very life—!

Mrs. Alving. No, no, my dear, darling boy; this is impossible!

(*Bends over him.*) Things are not so desperate as you think.

Oswald. Oh, you don't know—(*Springs up.*) And then, mother, to cause you all this sorrow! Many a time I have almost wished and hoped that at bottom you didn't care so very much about me.

Mrs. Alving. I, Oswald? My only boy! You are all I have in the world! The only thing I care about!

Oswald. (*Seizes both her hands and kisses them.*) Yes, yes, I see it. When I'm at home, I see it, of course; and that's almost the hardest part for me.—But now you know the whole story and now we won't talk anymore about it today. I daren't think of it for long together. (*Goes up the room.*) Get me something to drink, mother.

Mrs. Alving. To drink? What do you want to drink now?

Oswald. Oh, anything you like. You have some cold punch in the house.

Mrs. Alving. Yes, but my dear Oswald—

Oswald. Don't refuse me, mother. Do be kind, now! I must have something to wash down all these gnawing thoughts. (*Goes into the conservatory.*) And then—it's so dark here! (*Mrs. Alving pulls a bell-rope on the right.*) And this ceaseless rain! It may go on week after week, for months together. Never to get a glimpse of the sun! I can't recollect ever having seen the sunshine all the times I've been at home.

Mrs. Alving. Oswald—you are thinking of going away from me.

Oswald. H'm—(*Drawing a heavy breath.*)—I'm not thinking of anything. I cannot think of anything! (*In a low voice.*) I let thinking alone.

Regina. (*From the dining-room.*) Did you ring, ma'am?

Mrs. Alving. Yes; let us have the lamp in.

Regina. Yes, ma'am. It's ready lighted. (*Goes out.*)

Mrs. Alving. (*Goes across to Oswald.*) Oswald, be frank with me.

Oswald. Well, so I am, mother. (*Goes to the table.*) I think I have told you enough.

(*Regina brings the lamp and sets it upon the table.*)

Mrs. Alving. Regina, you may bring us a small bottle of champagne.

Regina. Very well, ma'am. (*Goes out.*)

Oswald. (*Puts his arm round Mrs. Alving's neck.*) That's just what I wanted. I knew mother wouldn't let her boy go thirsty.

Mrs. Alving. My own, poor, darling Oswald; how could I deny you anything now?

Oswald. (*Eagerly.*) Is that true, mother? Do you mean it?

Mrs. Alving. How? What?

Oswald. That you couldn't deny me anything.

Mrs. Alving. My dear Oswald—

Oswald. Hush!

Regina. (*Brings a tray with a half-bottle of champagne and two glasses, which she sets on the table.*) Shall I open it?

Oswald. No, thanks. I will do it myself.

(*Regina goes out again.*)

Mrs. Alving. (*Sits down by the table.*) What was it you meant—that I mustn't deny you?

Oswald. (*Busy opening the bottle.*) First let us have a glass—or two.

(*The cork pops; he pours wine into one glass, and is about to pour it into the other.*)

Mrs. Alving. (*Holding her hand over it.*) Thanks, not for me.

Oswald. Oh! Won't you? Then I will!

(*He empties the glass, fills, and empties it again; then he sits down by the table.*)

Mrs. Alving. (In expectancy.) Well?

Oswald. (*Without looking at her.*) Tell me—I thought you and Pastor Manders seemed so odd—so quiet—at dinner today.

Mrs. Alving. Did you notice it?

Oswald. Yes. H'm—(*After a short silence.*) Tell me: what do you think of Regina?

Mrs. Alving. What do I think?

Oswald. Yes; isn't she splendid?

Mrs. Alving. My dear Oswald, you don't know her as I do—

Oswald. Well?

Mrs. Alving. Regina, unfortunately, was allowed to stay at home too long. I ought to have taken her earlier into my house.

Oswald. Yes, but isn't she splendid to look at, mother? (*He fills his glass.*)

Mrs. Alving. Regina has many serious faults—

Oswald. Oh, what does that matter? (*He drinks again.*)

Mrs. Alving. But I am fond of her, nevertheless, and I am responsible for her. I wouldn't for all the world have any harm happen to her.

Oswald. (*Springs up.*) Mother, Regina is my only salvation!

Mrs. Alving. (*Rising.*) What do you mean by that?

Oswald. I cannot go on bearing all this anguish of soul alone.

Mrs. Alving. Have you not your mother to share it with you?

Oswald. Yes, that's what I thought; and so I came home to you. But that will not do. I see it won't do. I cannot endure my life here.

Mrs. Alving. Oswald!

Oswald. I must live differently, mother. That is why I must leave you. I will not have you looking on at it.

Mrs. Alving. My unhappy boy! But, Oswald, while you are so ill as this—

Oswald. If it were only the illness, I should stay with you, mother, you may be sure; for you are the best friend I have in the world.

Mrs. Alving. Yes, indeed I am, Oswald; am I not?

Oswald. (*Wanders restlessly about.*) But it's all the torment, the gnawing remorse—and then, the great, killing dread. Oh—that awful dread!

Mrs. Alving. (*Walking after him.*) Dread? What dread? What do you mean?

Oswald. Oh, you mustn't ask me anymore. I don't know. I can't describe it.

Mrs. Alving. (*Goes over to the right and pulls the bell.*)

Oswald. What is it you want?

Mrs. Alving. I want my boy to be happy—that is what I want. He sha'n't go on brooding over things. (*To Regina, who appears at the door:*) More champagne—a large bottle. (*Regina goes.*)

Oswald. Mother!

Mrs. Alving. Do you think we don't know how to live here at home?

Oswald. Isn't she splendid to look at? How beautifully she's built! And so thoroughly healthy!

Mrs. Alving. (*Sits by the table.*) Sit down, Oswald; let us talk quietly together.

Oswald. (*Sits.*) I daresay you don't know, mother, that I owe Regina some reparation.

Mrs. Alving. You!

Oswald. For a bit of thoughtlessness, or whatever you like to call it—very innocent, at any rate. When I was home last time—

Mrs. Alving. Well?

Oswald. She used often to ask me about Paris, and I used to tell her one thing and another. Then I recollect I happened to say to her one day, "Shouldn't you like to go there yourself?"

Mrs. Alving. Well?

Oswald. I saw her face flush, and then she said, "Yes, I should like it of all things." "Ah, well," I replied, "it might perhaps be managed"—or something like that.

Mrs. Alving. And then?

Oswald. Of course I had forgotten all about it; but the day before yesterday I happened to ask her whether she was glad I was to stay at home so long—

Mrs. Alving. Yes?

Oswald. And then she gave me such a strange look, and asked, "But what's to become of my trip to Paris?"

Mrs. Alving. Her trip!

Oswald. And so it came out that she had taken the thing seriously; that she had been thinking of me the whole time, and had set to work to learn French—

Mrs. Alving. So that was why—!

Oswald. Mother—when I saw that fresh, lovely, splendid girl standing there before me—till then I had hardly noticed her—but when she stood there as though with open arms ready to receive me—

Mrs. Alving. Oswald!

Oswald.—Then it flashed upon me that in her lay my salvation; for I saw that she was full of the joy of life.

Mrs. Alving. (*Starts.*) The joy of life? Can there be salvation in that?

Regina. (*From the dining-room, with a bottle of champagne.*) I'm sorry to have been so long, but I had to go to the cellar. (*Places the bottle on the table.*)

Oswald. And now bring another glass.

Regina. (*Looks at him in surprise.*) There is Mrs. Alving's glass, Mr. Alving.

Oswald. Yes, but bring one for yourself, Regina. (*Regina starts and gives a lightning-like side glance at Mrs. Alving.*) Why do you wait?

Regina. (*Softly and hesitatingly.*) Is it Mrs. Alving's wish?

Mrs. Alving. Bring the glass, Regina.

(*Regina goes out into the dining-room.*)

Oswald. (*Follows her with his eyes.*) Have you noticed how she walks?—So firmly and lightly!

Mrs. Alving. This can never be, Oswald!

Oswald. It's a settled thing. Can't you see that? It's no use saying anything against it.

(*Regina enters with an empty glass, which she keeps in her hand.*)

Oswald. Sit down, Regina.

(*Regina looks inquiringly at Mrs. Alving.*)

Mrs. Alving. Sit down. (*Regina sits on a chair by the dining-room door, still holding the empty glass in her hand.*) Oswald—what were you saying about the joy of life?

Oswald. Ah, the joy of life, mother—that's a thing you don't know much about in these parts. I have never felt it here.

Mrs. Alving. Not when you are with me?

Oswald. Not when I'm at home. But you don't understand that.

Mrs. Alving. Yes, yes; I think I almost understand it—now.

Oswald. And then, too, the joy of work! At bottom, it's the same thing. But that, too, you know nothing about.

Mrs. Alving. Perhaps you are right. Tell me more about it, Oswald.

Oswald. I only mean that here people are brought up to believe that work is a curse and a punishment for sin, and that life is something miserable, something it would be best to have done with, the sooner the better.

Mrs. Alving. "A vale of tears," yes; and we certainly do our best to make it one.

Oswald. But in the great world people won't hear of such things. There, nobody really believes such doctrines any longer. There, you feel it a positive bliss and ecstasy merely to draw the breath of life. Mother, have you noticed that everything I have painted has turned upon the joy of life?—Always, always upon the joy of life?—Light and sunshine and glorious air and faces radiant with happiness. That is why I'm afraid of remaining at home with you.

Mrs. Alving. Afraid? What are you afraid of here, with me?

Oswald. I'm afraid lest all my instincts should be warped into ugliness.

Mrs. Alving. (*Looks steadily at him.*) Do you think that is what would happen?

Oswald. I know it. You may live the same life here as there, and yet it won't be the same life.

Mrs. Alving. (*Who has been listening eagerly, rises, her eyes big with thought, and says:*) Now I see the sequence of things.

Oswald. What is it you see?

Mrs. Alving. I see it now for the first time. And now I can speak.

Oswald. (*Rising.*) Mother, I don't understand you.

Regina. (*Who has also risen.*) Perhaps I ought to go?

Mrs. Alving. No. Stay here. Now I can speak. Now, my boy, you shall know the whole truth. And then you can choose. Oswald! Regina!

Oswald. Hush! The Pastor—

Manders. (*Enters by the hall door.*) There! We have had a most edifying time down there.

Oswald. So have we.

Manders. We must stand by Engstrand and his Sailors' Home. Regina must go to him and help him—

Regina. No thank you, sir.

Manders. (*Noticing her for the first time.*) What—? You here? And with a glass in your hand!

Regina. (*Hastily putting the glass down.*) Pardon!

Oswald. Regina is going with me, Mr. Manders.

Manders. Going! With you!

Oswald. Yes, as my wife—if she wishes it.

Manders. But, merciful God—!

Regina. I can't help it, sir.

Oswald. Or she'll stay here, if I stay.

Regina. (*Involuntarily.*) Here!

Manders. I am thunderstruck at your conduct, Mrs. Alving.

Mrs. Alving. They will do neither one thing nor the other; for now I can speak out plainly.

Manders. You surely will not do that! No, no, no!

Mrs. Alving. Yes, I can speak and I will. And no ideals shall suffer after all.

Oswald. Mother—what is it you are hiding from me?

Regina. (*Listening.*) Oh, ma'am, listen! Don't you hear shouts outside. (*She goes into the conservatory and looks out.*)

Oswald. (*At the window on the left.*) What's going on? Where does that light come from?

Regina. (*Cries out.*) The Orphanage is on fire!

Mrs. Alving. (*Rushing to the window.*) On fire!

Manders. On fire! Impossible! I've just come from there.

Oswald. Where's my hat? Oh, never mind it—Father's Orphanage—! (*He rushes out through the garden door.*)

Mrs. Alving. My shawl, Regina! The whole place is in a blaze!

Manders. Terrible! Mrs. Alving, it is a judgment upon this abode of lawlessness.

Mrs. Alving. Yes, of course. Come, Regina. (*She and Regina hasten out through the hall.*)

Manders. (*Clasps his hands together.*) And we left it uninsured! (*He goes out the same way.*)

ACT III

Scene.—The room as before. All the doors stand open. The lamp is still burning on the table. It is dark out of doors; there is only a faint glow from the conflagration in the background to the left. Mrs. Alving, with a shawl over her head, stands in the conservatory, looking out. Regina, also with a shawl on, stands a little behind her.

Mrs. Alving. The whole thing burnt!—Burnt to the ground!

Regina. The basement is still burning.

Mrs. Alving. How is it Oswald doesn't come home? There's nothing to be saved.

Regina. Should you like me to take down his hat to him?

Mrs. Alving. Has he not even got his hat on?

Regina. (*Pointing to the hall.*) No, there it hangs.

Mrs. Alving. Let it be. He must come up now. I shall go and look for him myself. (She goes out through the garden door.)

Manders. (*Comes in from the hall.*) Is not Mrs. Alving here?

Regina. She has just gone down the garden.

Manders. This is the most terrible night I ever went through.

Regina. Yes, isn't it a dreadful misfortune, sir?

Manders. Oh, don't talk about it! I can hardly bear to think of it.

Regina. How can it have happened——?

Manders. Don't ask me, Miss Engstrand! How should I know? Do you, too——? Is it not enough that your father——?

Regina. What about him?

Manders. Oh, he has driven me distracted——

Engstrand. (*Enters through the hall.*) Your Reverence——

Manders. (*Turns round in terror.*) Are you after me here, too?

Engstrand. Yes, strike me dead, but I must——! Oh, Lord! what am I saying? But this is a terrible ugly business, your Reverence.

Manders. (*Walks to and fro.*) Alas! alas!

Regina. What's the matter?

Engstrand. Why, it all came of this here prayer-meeting, you see. (*Softly.*) *The bird's limed, my girl.* (*Aloud.*) And to think it should be my doing that such a thing should be his Reverence's doing!

Manders. But I assure you, Engstrand——

Engstrand. There wasn't another soul except your Reverence as ever laid a finger on the candles down there.

Manders. (*Stops.*) So you declare. But I certainly cannot recollect that I ever had a candle in my hand.

Engstrand. And I saw as clear as daylight how your Reverence took the candle and snuffed it with your fingers, and threw away the snuff among the shavings.

Manders. And you stood and looked on?

Engstrand. Yes; I saw it as plain as a pikestaff, I did.

Manders. It's quite beyond my comprehension. Besides, it has never been my habit to snuff candles with my fingers.

Engstrand. And terrible risky it looked, too, that it did! But is there such a deal of harm done after all, your Reverence?

Manders. (*Walks restlessly to and fro.*) Oh, don't ask me!

Engstrand. (*Walks with him.*) And your Reverence hadn't insured it, neither?

Manders. (*Continuing to walk up and down.*) No, no, no; I have told you so.

Engstrand. (*Following him.*) Not insured! And then to go straight away down and set light to the whole thing! Lord, Lord, what a misfortune!

Manders. (*Wipes the sweat from his forehead.*) Ay, you may well say that, Engstrand.

Engstrand. And to think that such a thing should happen to a benevolent institution, that was to have been a blessing both to town and country, as the saying goes! The newspapers won't be for handling your Reverence very gently, I expect.

Manders. No, that is just what I am thinking of. That is almost the worst of the whole matter. All the malignant attacks and imputations——! Oh, it makes me shudder to think of it!

Mrs. Alving. (*Comes in from the garden.*) He is not to be persuaded to leave the fire.

Manders. Ah, there you are, Mrs. Alving.

Mrs. Alving. So you have escaped your Inaugural Address, Pastor Manders.

Manders. Oh, I should so gladly—

Mrs. Alving. (*In an undertone.*) It is all for the best. That Orphanage would have done no one any good.

Manders. Do you think not?

Mrs. Alving. Do you think it would?

Manders. It is a terrible misfortune, all the same.

Mrs. Alving. Let us speak of it plainly, as a matter of business.—Are you waiting for Mr. Manders, Engstrand?

Engstrand. (*At the hall door.*) That's just what I'm a-doing of, ma'am.

Mrs. Alving. Then sit down meanwhile.

Engstrand. Thank you, ma'am; I'd as soon stand.

Mrs. Alving. (*To Manders.*) I suppose you are going by the steamer?

Manders. Yes, it starts in an hour.

Mrs. Alving. Then be so good as to take all the papers with you. I won't hear another word about this affair. I have other things to think of—

Manders. Mrs. Alving—

Mrs. Alving. Later on I shall send you a Power of Attorney to settle everything as you please.

Manders. That I will very readily undertake. The original destination of the endowment must now be completely changed, alas!

Mrs. Alving. Of course it must.

Manders. I think, first of all, I shall arrange that the Solvik property shall pass to the parish. The land is by no means without value. It can always be turned to account for some purpose or other. And the interest of the money in the Bank I could, perhaps, best apply for the benefit of some undertaking of acknowledged value to the town.

Mrs. Alving. Do just as you please. The whole matter is now completely indifferent to me.

Engstrand. Give a thought to my Sailors' Home, your Reverence.

Manders. Upon my word, that is not a bad suggestion. That must be considered.

Engstrand. Oh, devil take considering—Lord forgive me!

Manders. (*With a sigh.*) And unfortunately I cannot tell how long I shall be able to retain control of these things—whether public opinion may not compel me to retire. It entirely depends upon the result of the official inquiry into the fire—

Mrs. Alving. What are you talking about?

Manders. And the result can by no means be foretold.

Engstrand. (*Comes close to him.*) Ay, but it can though. For here stands old Jacob Engstrand.

Manders. Well well, but——?

Engstrand. (*More softy.*) And Jacob Engstrand isn't the man to desert a noble benefactor in the hour of need, as the saying goes.

Manders. Yes, but my good fellow——how——?

Engstrand. Jacob Engstrand may be likened to a sort of a guardian angel, he may, your Reverence.

Manders. No, no, I really cannot accept that.

Engstrand. Oh, that'll be the way of it, all the same. I know a man as has taken others' sins upon himself before now, I do.

Manders. Jacob! (*Wrings his hand.*) Yours is a rare nature. Well, you shall be helped with your Sailors' Home. That you may rely upon. (*Engstrand tries to thank him, but cannot for emotion.*)

Manders. (*Hangs his travelling-bag over his shoulder.*) And now let us set out. We two will go together.

Engstrand. (*At the dining-room door, softly to Regina.*) You come along too, my lass. You shall live as snug as the yolk in an egg.

Regina. (*Tosses her head.*) Merci! (*She goes out into the hall and fetches Manders' overcoat.*)

Manders. Good-bye, Mrs. Alving! And may the spirit of Law and Order descend upon this house, and that quickly.

Mrs. Alving. Good-bye, Pastor Manders. (*She goes up towards the conservatory, as she sees Oswald coming in through the garden door.*)

Engstrand. (*While he and Regina help Manders to get his coat on.*) Good-bye, my child. And if any trouble should come to you, you know where Jacob Engstrand is to be found. (*Softly.*) *Little Harbour Street, h'm*—! (*To Mrs. Alving and Oswald.*) And the refuge for wandering mariners shall be called "Chamberlain Alving's Home," that it shall! And if so be as I'm spared to carry on that house in my own way, I make so bold as to promise that it shall be worthy of the Chamberlain's memory.

Manders. (*In the doorway.*) H'm—h'm!—Come along, my dear Engstrand. Good-bye! Good-bye! (*He and Engstrand go out through the hall.*)

Oswald. (Goes towards the table.) What house was he talking about?

Mrs. Alving. Oh, a kind of Home that he and Pastor Manders want to set up.

Oswald. It will burn down like the other.

Mrs. Alving. What makes you think so?

Oswald. Everything will burn. All that recalls father's memory is doomed. Here am I, too, burning down. (*Regina starts and looks at him.*)

Mrs. Alving. Oswald! You oughtn't to have remained so long down there, my poor boy.

Oswald. (*Sits down by the table.*) I almost think you are right.

Mrs. Alving. Let me dry your face, Oswald; you are quite wet. (*She dries his face with her pocket-handkerchief.*)

Oswald. (*Stares indifferently in front of him.*) Thanks, mother.

Mrs. Alving. Are you not tired, Oswald? Should you like to sleep?

Oswald. (*Nervously.*) No, no—not to sleep! I never sleep. I only pretend to. (*Sadly.*) That will come soon enough.

Mrs. Alving. (*Looking sorrowfully at him.*) Yes, you really are ill, my blessed boy.

Regina. (*Eagerly.*) Is Mr. Alving ill?

Oswald. (*Impatiently.*) Oh, do shut all the doors! This killing dread—

Mrs. Alving. Close the doors, Regina.

(*Regina shuts them and remains standing by the hall door. Mrs. Alving takes her shawl off; Regina does the same. Mrs. Alving draws a chair across to Oswald's, and sits by him.*)

Mrs. Alving. There now! I am going to sit beside you—

Oswald. Yes, do. And Regina shall stay here too. Regina shall be with me always. You will come to the rescue, Regina, won't you?

Regina. I don't understand—

Mrs. Alving. To the rescue?

Oswald. Yes—when the need comes.

Mrs. Alving. Oswald, have you not your mother to come to the rescue?

Oswald. You? (*Smiles.*) No, mother; that rescue you will never bring me. (*Laughs sadly.*) You! ha ha! (*Looks earnestly at her.*) Though, after all, who ought to do it if not you?

(*Impetuously.*) Why can't you say "thou" to me, Regina? Why don't you call me "Oswald"?

Regina. (*Softly.*) I don't think Mrs. Alving would like it.

Mrs. Alving. You shall have leave to, presently. And meanwhile sit over here beside us.

(*Regina seats herself demurely and hesitatingly at the other side of the table.*)

Mrs. Alving. And now, my poor suffering boy, I am going to take the burden off your mind—

Oswald. You, mother?

Mrs. Alving.—All the gnawing remorse and self-reproach you speak of.

Oswald. And you think you can do that?

Mrs. Alving. Yes, now I can, Oswald. A little while ago you spoke of the joy of life; and at that word a new light burst for me over my life and everything connected with it.

Oswald. (*Shakes his head.*) I don't understand you.

Mrs. Alving. You ought to have known your father when he was a young lieutenant. He was brimming over with the joy of life!

Oswald. Yes, I know he was.

Mrs. Alving. It was like a breezy day only to look at him. And what exuberant strength and vitality there was in him!

Oswald. Well—?

Mrs. Alving. Well then, child of joy as he was—for he was like a child in those days—he had to live at home here in a half-grown town, which had no joys to offer him—only dissipations. He had no object in life—only an official position. He had no work into which he could throw himself heart and soul; he had only business. He had not a single comrade that could realise what the joy of life meant—only loungers and boon-companions—

Oswald. Mother—!

Mrs. Alving. So the inevitable happened.

Oswald. The inevitable?

Mrs. Alving. You told me yourself, this evening, what would become of you if you stayed at home.

Oswald. Do you mean to say that father—?

Mrs. Alving. Your poor father found no outlet for the overpowering joy of life that was in him. And I brought no brightness into his home.

Oswald. Not even you?

Mrs. Alving. They had taught me a great deal about duties and so forth, which I went on obstinately believing in. Everything was marked out into duties—into my duties, and his duties, and—I am afraid I made his home intolerable for your poor father, Oswald.

Oswald. Why have you never spoken of this in writing to me?

Mrs. Alving. I have never before seen it in such a light that I could speak of it to you, his son.

Oswald. In what light did you see it, then?

Mrs. Alving. (*Slowly.*) I saw only this one thing: that your father was a broken-down man before you were born.

Oswald. (*Softly.*) Ah—! (*He rises and walks away to the window.*)

Mrs. Alving. And then, day after day, I dwelt on the one thought that by rights Regina should be at home in this house—just like my own boy.

Oswald. (*Turning round quickly.*) Regina—!

Regina. (*Springs up and asks, with bated breath.*) I—?

Mrs. Alving. Yes, now you know it, both of you.

Oswald. Regina!

Regina. (*To herself.*) So mother was that kind of woman.

Mrs. Alving. Your mother had many good qualities, Regina.

Regina. Yes, but she was one of that sort, all the same. Oh, I've often suspected it; but—And now, if you please, ma'am, may I be allowed to go away at once?

Mrs. Alving. Do you really wish it, Regina?

Regina. Yes, indeed I do.

Mrs. Alving. Of course you can do as you like; but—

Oswald. (*Goes towards Regina.*) Go away now? Your place is here.

Regina. *Merci*, Mr. Alving!—Or now, I suppose, I may say Oswald. But I can tell you this wasn't at all what I expected.

Mrs. Alving. Regina, I have not been frank with you—

Regina. No, that you haven't indeed. If I'd known that Oswald was an invalid, why—And now, too, that it can never come to anything serious between us—I really can't stop out here in the country and wear myself out nursing sick people.

Oswald. Not even one who is so near to you?

Regina. No, that I can't. A poor girl must make the best of her young days, or she'll be left out in the cold before she knows where she is. And I, too, have the joy of life in me, Mrs. Alving!

Mrs. Alving. Unfortunately, you leave. But don't throw yourself away, Regina.

Regina. Oh, what must be, must be. If Oswald takes after his father, I take after my mother, I daresay.—May I ask, ma'am, if Pastor Manders knows all this about me?

Mrs. Alving. Pastor Manders knows all about it.

Regina. (*Busied in putting on her shawl.*) Well then, I'd better make haste and get away by this steamer. The Pastor is such a nice man to deal with; and I certainly think I've as much right to a little of that money as he has—that brute of a carpenter.

Mrs. Alving. You are heartily welcome to it, Regina.

Regina. (*Looks hard at her.*) I think you might have brought me up as a gentleman's daughter, ma'am; it would have suited me better. (*Tosses her head.*) But pooh—what does it matter! (*With a bitter side glance at the corked bottle.*) I may come to drink champagne with gentlefolks yet.

Mrs. Alving. And if you ever need a home, Regina, come to me.

Regina. No, thank you, ma'am. Pastor Manders will look after me, I know. And if the worst comes to the worst, I know of one house where I've every right to a place.

Mrs. Alving. Where is that?

Regina. "Chamberlain Alving's Home."

Mrs. Alving. Regina—now I see it—you are going to your ruin.

Regina. Oh, stuff! Good-bye. (*She nods and goes out through the hall.*)

Oswald. (*Stands at the window and looks out.*) Is she gone?

Mrs. Alving. Yes.

Oswald. (*Murmuring aside to himself.*) I think it was a mistake, this.

Mrs. Alving. (*Goes up behind him and lays her hands on his shoulders.*) Oswald, my dear boy—has it shaken you very much?

Oswald. (*Turns his face towards her.*) All that about father, do you mean?

Mrs. Alving. Yes, about your unhappy father. I am so afraid it may have been too much for you.

Oswald. Why should you fancy that? Of course it came upon me as a great surprise; but it can make no real difference to me.

Mrs. Alving. (*Draws her hands away.*) No difference! That your father was so infinitely unhappy!

Oswald. Of course I can pity him, as I would anybody else, but—

Mrs. Alving. Nothing more! Your own father!

Oswald. (*Impatiently.*) Oh, "father,"—"father"! I never knew anything of father. I remember nothing about him, except that he once made me sick.

Mrs. Alving. This is terrible to think of! Ought not a son to love his father, whatever happens?

Oswald. When a son has nothing to thank his father for? Has never known him? Do you really cling to that old superstition?—You who are so enlightened in other ways?

Mrs. Alving. Can it be only a superstition—?

Oswald. Yes, surely you can see that, mother. It's one of those notions that are current in the world, and so—

Mrs. Alving. (*Deeply moved.*) Ghosts!

Oswald. (*Crossing the room.*) Yes, you may call them ghosts.

Mrs. Alving. (*Wildly.*) Oswald—then you don't love me, either!

Oswald. You I know, at any rate—

Mrs. Alving. Yes, you know me; but is that all!

Oswald. And, of course, I know how fond you are of me, and I can't but be grateful to you. And then you can be so useful to me, now that I am ill.

Mrs. Alving. Yes, cannot I, Oswald? Oh, I could almost bless the illness that has driven you home to me. For I see very plainly that you are not mine; I have to win you.

Oswald. (*Impatiently.*) Yes, yes, yes; all these are just so many phrases. You must remember that I am a sick man, mother. I can't be much taken up with other people; I have enough to do thinking about myself.

Mrs. Alving. (*In a low voice.*) I shall be patient and easily satisfied.

Oswald. And cheerful too, mother!

Mrs. Alving. Yes, my dear boy, you are quite right. (*Goes towards him.*) Have I relieved you of all remorse and self-reproach now?

Oswald. Yes, you have. But now who will relieve me of the dread?

Mrs. Alving. The dread?

Oswald. (*Walks across the room.*) Regina could have been got to do it.

Mrs. Alving. I don't understand you. What is this about dread— and Regina?

Oswald. Is it very late, mother?

Mrs. Alving. It is early morning. (*She looks out through the conservatory.*) The day is dawning over the mountains. And the weather is clearing, Oswald. In a little while you shall see the sun.

Oswald. I'm glad of that. Oh, I may still have much to rejoice in and live for—

Mrs. Alving. I should think so, indeed!

Oswald. Even if I can't work—

Mrs. Alving. Oh, you'll soon be able to work again, my dear boy—now that you haven't got all those gnawing and depressing thoughts to brood over any longer.

Oswald. Yes, I'm glad you were able to rid me of all those fancies. And when I've got over this one thing more—(*Sits on the sofa.*) Now we will have a little talk, mother—

Mrs. Alving. Yes, let us. (*She pushes an armchair towards the sofa, and sits down close to him.*)

Oswald. And meantime the sun will be rising. And then you will know all. And then I shall not feel this dread any longer.

Mrs. Alving. What is it that I am to know?

Oswald. (*Not listening to her.*) Mother, did you not say a little while ago, that there was nothing in the world you would not do for me, if I asked you?

Mrs. Alving. Yes, indeed I said so!

Oswald. And you'll stick to it, mother?

Mrs. Alving. You may rely on that, my dear and only boy! I have nothing in the world to live for but you alone.

Oswald. Very well, then; now you shall hear—Mother, you have a strong, steadfast mind, I know. Now you're to sit quite still when you hear it.

Mrs. Alving. What dreadful thing can it be—?

Oswald. You're not to scream out. Do you hear? Do you promise me that? We will sit and talk about it quietly. Do you promise me, mother?

Mrs. Alving. Yes, yes, I promise. Only speak!

Oswald. Well, you must know that all this fatigue—and my inability to think of work—all that is not the illness itself—

Mrs. Alving. Then what is the illness itself?

Oswald. The disease I have as my birthright—(*He points to his forehead and adds very softly*)—is seated here.

Mrs. Alving. (*Almost voiceless.*) Oswald! No—no!

Oswald. Don't scream. I can't bear it. Yes, mother, it is seated here waiting. And it may break out any day—at any moment.

Mrs. Alving. Oh, what horror—!

Oswald. Now, quiet, quiet. That is how it stands with me—

Mrs. Alving. (*Springs up.*) It's not true, Oswald! It's impossible! It cannot be so!

Oswald. I have had one attack down there already. It was soon over. But when I came to know the state I had been in, then the dread descended upon me, raging and ravening; and so I set off home to you as fast as I could.

Mrs. Alving. Then this is the dread—!

Oswald. Yes—it's so indescribably loathsome, you know. Oh, if it had only been an ordinary mortal disease—! For I'm not so afraid of death—though I should like to live as long as I can.

Mrs. Alving. Yes, yes, Oswald, you must!

Oswald. But this is so unutterably loathsome. To become a little baby again! To have to be fed! To have to—Oh, it's not to be spoken of!

Mrs. Alving. The child has his mother to nurse him.

Oswald. (*Springs up.*) No, never that! That is just what I will not have. I can't endure to think that perhaps I should lie in that state for many years—and get old and grey. And in the meantime you might die and leave me. (*Sits in Mrs. Alving's chair.*) For the doctor said it wouldn't necessarily prove fatal at once. He called it a sort of softening of the brain—or something like that. (*Smiles sadly.*) I think that expression sounds so nice. It always sets me thinking of cherry-coloured velvet—something soft and delicate to stroke.

Mrs. Alving. (*Shrieks.*) Oswald!

Oswald. (*Springs up and paces the room.*) And now you have taken Regina from me. If I could only have had her! She would have come to the rescue, I know.

Mrs. Alving. (*Goes to him.*) What do you mean by that, my darling boy? Is there any help in the world that I would not give you?

Oswald. When I got over my attack in Paris, the doctor told me that when it comes again—and it will come—there will be no more hope.

Mrs. Alving. He was heartless enough to—

Oswald. I demanded it of him. I told him I had preparations to make—(*He smiles cunningly.*) And so I had. (*He takes a little box from his inner breast pocket and opens it.*) Mother, do you see this?

Mrs. Alving. What is it?

Oswald. Morphia.

Mrs. Alving. (*Looks at him horror-struck.*) Oswald—my boy!

Oswald. I've scraped together twelve pilules—

Mrs. Alving. (*Snatches at it.*) Give me the box, Oswald.

Oswald. Not yet, mother. (*He hides the box again in his pocket.*)

Mrs. Alving. I shall never survive this!

Oswald. It must be survived. Now if I'd had Regina here, I should have told her how things stood with me—and begged her to come to the rescue at the last. She would have done it. I know she would.

Mrs. Alving. Never!

Oswald. When the horror had come upon me, and she saw me lying there helpless, like a little new-born baby, impotent, lost, hopeless—past all saving—

Mrs. Alving. Never in all the world would Regina have done this!

Oswald. Regina would have done it. Regina was so splendidly light-hearted. And she would soon have wearied of nursing an invalid like me.

Mrs. Alving. Then heaven be praised that Regina is not here.

Oswald. Well then, it is you that must come to the rescue, mother.

Mrs. Alving. (*Shrieks aloud.*) I!

Oswald. Who should do it if not you?

Mrs. Alving. I! your mother!

Oswald. For that very reason.

Mrs. Alving. I, who gave you life!

Oswald. I never asked you for life. And what sort of a life have you given me? I will not have it! You shall take it back again!

Mrs. Alving. Help! Help! (*She runs out into the hall.*)

Oswald. (*Going after her.*) Do not leave me! Where are you going?

Mrs. Alving. (*In the hall.*) To fetch the doctor, Oswald! Let me pass!

Oswald. (*Also outside.*) You shall not go out. And no one shall come in. (*The locking of a door is heard.*)

Mrs. Alving. (*Comes in again.*) Oswald! Oswald—my child!

Oswald. (*Follows her.*) Have you a mother's heart for me—and yet can see me suffer from this unutterable dread?

Mrs. Alving. (*After a moment's silence, commands herself, and says:*) Here is my hand upon it.

Oswald. Will you——?

Mrs. Alving. If it should ever be necessary. But it will never be necessary. No, no, it is impossible.

Oswald. Well, let us hope so. And let us live together as long as we can. Thank you, mother.

(*He seats himself in the armchair which Mrs. Alving has moved to the sofa. Day is breaking. The lamp is still burning on the table.*)

Mrs. Alving. (*Drawing near cautiously.*) Do you feel calm now?

Oswald. Yes.

Mrs. Alving. (*Bending over him.*) It has been a dreadful fancy of yours, Oswald—nothing but a fancy. All this excitement has been too much for you. But now you shall have a long rest; at home with your mother, my own blessed boy. Everything you point to you shall have, just as when you were a little child.—There now. The crisis is over. You see how easily it passed! Oh, I was sure it would.—And do you see, Oswald, what a lovely day we are going to have? Brilliant sunshine! Now you can really see your home.

(*She goes to the table and puts out the lamp. Sunrise. The glacier and the snow peaks in the background glow in the morning light.*)

Oswald. (*Sits in the armchair with his back towards the landscape, without moving. Suddenly he says:*) Mother, give me the sun.

Mrs. Alving. (*By the table, starts and looks at him.*) What do you say?

Oswald. (*Repeats, in a dull, toneless voice.*) The sun. The sun.

Mrs. Alving. (*Goes to him.*) Oswald, what is the matter with you?

Oswald seems to shrink together to the chair; all his muscles relax; his face is expressionless, his eyes have a glassy stare.)

Mrs. Alving. (*Quivering with terror.*) What is this? (*Shrieks.*) Oswald! what is the matter with you? (*Falls on her knees beside him and shakes him.*) Oswald! Oswald! Look at me! Don't you know me?

Oswald. (*Tonelessly as before.*) The sun.—The sun.

Mrs. Alving. (*Springs up in despair, entwines her hands in her hair and shrieks.*) I cannot bear it! (*Whispers, as though petrified*); I cannot bear it! Never! (*Suddenly.*) Where has he got them? (*Fumbles hastily in his breast.*) Here! (*Shrinks back a few steps and screams:*) No! No, no!—Yes!—No; no! (*She stands a few steps away from him with her hands twisted in her hair, and stares at him in speechless horror.*)

Oswald. (*Sits motionless as before and says.*) The sun.—The sun.

The End